Domestic Violence
in Postcommunist States

Domestic Violence in Postcommunist States

Local Activism, National Policies, and Global Forces

EDITED BY **KATALIN FÁBIÁN**

Indiana University Press
Bloomington and Indianapolis

This book is a publication of

Indiana University Press
601 North Morton Street
Bloomington, Indiana 47404-3797 USA

www.iupress.indiana.edu

Telephone orders	800-842-6796
Fax orders	812-855-7931
Orders by e-mail	iuporder@indiana.edu

♾ The paper used in this publication meets the minimum requirements of the
American National Standard for Information Sciences—Permanence of Paper
for Printed Library Materials, ANSI Z39.48-1992.

Manufactured in the United States of America

Library of Congress Cataloging-in-Publication Data

Domestic violence in postcommunist states : local activism, national policies, and
  global forces / edited by Katalin Fábián.
       p.   cm.
    Includes bibliographical references and index.
    ISBN 978-0-253-35504-1 (cloth : alk. paper) — ISBN 978-0-253-22218-3
  (pbk. : alk. paper) 1. Family violence—Europe. 2. Family violence—Asia.
  3. Post-communism—Europe. 4. Post-communism—Asia. I. Fábián, Katalin.
    HV6626.23.E85D64   2010
    362.82'92091717—dc22
                                                                    2009052663

1 2   3   4   5   15   14   13   12   11   10

Dedicated to Éva Nagy and Anna Nagy,
and all our mothers, aunts, and sisters

CONTENTS

ACKNOWLEDGMENTS

This volume is the culmination of more than five years of work that began when Laura Brunell, Alexandra Hrycak, Janet Elise Johnson, Magdi Vanya, and I presented together on a conference panel of the American Association for the Advancement for Slavic Studies. From the seeds of our discussions blossomed further cooperation and the plans for this volume. I am grateful for the fruitful cooperation with all the contributors to this project. Lafayette College, Reed College, and the John Jay College of the City University of New York generously supported the publication of this book.

The manuscript has been greatly improved by the generosity of the many individuals who read and commented on portions of it. Special thanks are due to Lesley Cameron for her insightful and careful suggestions on the text and to Mercedes Benitez Sharpless for her always precise, reliable, and kind assistance. I also thank my research assistants Raquel Aledo, Blagovest Baychev, and Eva Neykova, who were supported by Lafayette College grants.

My most sincere gratitude goes to Andrew Kortyna. His encouragement and daily support were essential during the many rounds of editing, correspondence, formatting, and what seemed like never-ending revisions.

KATALIN FÁBIÁN

Domestic Violence
in Postcommunist States

CHAPTER 1

Introduction: The Politics of Domestic Violence in Postcommunist Europe and Eurasia

KATALIN FÁBIÁN

The issue of violence relates directly to the wider and more complex issue of the nature of power. Since the 1989 postcommunist transitions, the nature of power has changed dramatically, albeit to various degrees, in the large and diverse territory of Central and Eastern Europe and Eurasia. Nearly every aspect of these societies has undergone some degree of transformation, with the role and methods of patriarchy being no exception. At this point in history we cannot fully assess how strong patriarchy became after the regime change, but its historical continuity has certainly not faltered, and many political, economic, and cultural facets of the different postcommunist societies indicate a more self-assured symbolic and actual male dominance. A rare countertrend to this is a slowly emerging postcommunist feminist movement and related movements against domestic violence.

Traditionally, partner violence against women has been accepted, occasionally even glorified, and seen as a private matter. Power structures within patriarchal societies normalize and legitimate male violence against women, and the discipline and appeal of violence as a means of claiming and defending privilege can be so great that women and children may slip into complicity without realizing it. The women's movement, acting from moral and political arguments such as fairness and equal rights, has, since its inception in the early nineteenth century, focused on various forms of discrimination against women. However, only relatively recently have activists turned their attention to domestic violence and managed to develop successful campaigns against the bodily harm and emotional abuse that women often suffer within intimate settings (Jefferson 2003; Renzetti et al. 2001).

To expose partner violence against women, activists most often formed nongovernmental organizations (NGOs) to more effectively engage with their own governments, other states' embassies, local and international police and law professionals, a wide variety of international organizations, and fellow social movements. The chapters in this volume offer evidence that the composition of and the interaction between these local, national, and international actors have been subject to different kinds of political, economic, and cultural pressures. The case studies in this book show that the internal and external pressures produced reactions in postcommunist Europe and Eurasia, most notably in the form of an increasing recognition of domestic violence, and consequently a trend of laws and services emerged to help victims.

However, it is important to emphasize that the interaction between the various actors is diverse and dynamic in both process and outcome. The changing international (political and economic) environment maintains, and occasionally continues to enhance, the regional differentiations between the vast territories that we now call Central Europe, Eastern Europe, the Balkans, Russia, and Central Asia. At the same time, old and new tensions also abound.

The power differentials between what we used to call "East" (communist) and "West" (capitalist/democratic) continue to create new tensions around what the term "domestic violence" means, and how to help its victims and punish the perpetrators. There are also new, often surprising developments, such as the unexpectedly strong impact of the United Nations (UN) and the European Union (EU) on laws introduced against domestic violence in the postcommunist countries (see chapters by Avdeyeva, Hrycak, Fábián, and Montoya in the present volume). However, the European Union has no enforceable rules or explicit expectations of member states in the field of domestic violence. Instead, the EU uses implicit value expectations ("good practices" and recommendations, the so-called "soft" law) to steer member states and especially to cajole candidates to consider domestic violence as a crime and adopt laws against it. While the European Union's licenses as a supranational entity imply that it could use levers and impose conditions on its member states, membership candidates, numerous affiliates, and trading partners so that they introduce laws against domestic violence to promote human rights and enhance democracy, it has generally refrained from doing so. In contrast, the UN's Committee on the Elimination of Discrimination against Women (CEDAW), which lacks such supranational licenses, has been particularly active in encouraging states to acknowledge violence against women and, by extension, domestic violence. The definition, legal approaches, and especially the implementation are highly debated among the various and internationally connected actors. Domestic violence is not a simple issue (Thomas 2008). This collection of essays may not provide all the answers, but it will pose many thought-provoking questions.

This book focuses on domestic violence as a significant public policy issue of transnational character and mobilization that demonstrates how global forces have interacted with various postcommunist European and Eurasian governments, diverse women's groups, and human rights activists. Why did we decide to discuss the emergence of the term "domestic violence" and the global and local organizations that have made this an issue for public debate in postcommunist European and Eurasian countries? Domestic violence is one of the most contested and suppressed topics in the contemporary postcommunist region. At the same time, activism related to the elimination (or at least the meaningful reduction) of domestic violence has been in many ways one of the most successful encounters between local activists and international organizations and movements. The regime transitions have opened up a space where gender analysis, social movement activism, and domestic and international economic and political changes collide.

The Interactive Effects of Global Forces and Local Activism on Postcommunist Gender Relations

Local and global events are becoming increasingly intertwined. The political and economic changes that followed the fall of communism introduced global flows and exchanges to the region with breathtaking speed (Åslund 2007a). Despite the potentially homogenizing effects of the incoming global forces, with their ideals of capitalism and liberal democracy, the postcommunist region developed highly divergent patterns in its politics and economic development. But among the differences, one common feature emerged: the changing nature of patriarchy, brought on by international (mostly neoliberal) forces and the elimination of the Marxist-inspired and state-sponsored, albeit rhetorical, support for equality of the sexes (Watson 1993).

After two decades of postcommunist development, there is now enough data to reflect on the considerable diversity in political and economic performances that occurred both among the countries and during the twenty years since the regime transitions began. Some countries introduced economic reforms quickly, while others moved slowly or inconsistently (Åslund and Olcott 1999; Svejnar 2002). Although all previously communist countries suffered an often dramatic drop in GDP and experienced increased unemployment, inflation, and income inequality as they opened up their markets to global markets, the Baltics (Estonia, Latvia, and Lithuania), Slovenia, and the Central European countries of Poland, the Czech Republic, Slovakia, and Hungary recovered within a decade and managed to join the European Union in 2004.

Romania and Bulgaria followed them in 2007, but other countries, such as Albania, Montenegro, and Ukraine, are only now becoming successful market economies. Russia joined the regional economic recovery thanks to the global oil boom, but its democratic development plateaued around 2000. Vladimir Putin, first as the post-Soviet era's second president and then as prime minister, increasingly restricted, and even tried to eliminate, independent media, political opposition, and what little was left of the autonomy of regional governments (EBRD 2005; McFaul and Stoner-Weiss 2008). In countries such as Serbia, Bosnia-Herzegovina, Georgia, Armenia, Azerbaijan, and Tajikistan, where ethnic and religious conflicts broke out after the collapse of the regimented order of the communist system, the respective political systems and economic orders became so compromised that radical nationalist ideologies, authoritarian rule, and endemic corruption wreaked further havoc. Although the communist party dictatorships have been replaced by elected governments, functioning democracies have emerged in only a handful of the twenty-seven postcommunist European and Eurasian countries (Berg-Schlosser 2007; Rose et al. 1998).[1] With international trends increasingly affecting the postcommunist region, the internal changes became deeply interwoven with events and fluctuations in the global markets, politics, and culture, and thus they influenced gender relations as well.

The pressure of international exposure has strongly contributed to two apparently divergent effects on gender relations that this region is still sorting through. The newly revitalized capitalist economy maintained and in many cases added to traditional gender segregation and made it more difficult for women to find and keep full-time jobs, especially during their reproductive years (Bukodi 2005; Frey 1999; Lyon 2007; Nagy 2001). They became increasingly defined in terms of their roles as mothers and as sexual symbols. However, international norms, including democratization, human rights, and various global social movements, such as environmentalism, anarchism, and especially feminism, contributed to at least a superficial relaxing of the traditional social barriers between the sexes. Following mostly Western European and North American patterns, postcommunist gender studies also began to flourish at this time (Kamp 2009; Pető 2006; Zimmermann 2007).

Analyses of how the regime transition affected women came from a variety of disciplines, bringing different sensitivities, vocabularies, and, maybe most importantly, methodologies to measure gender inequality. The three main waves of writings on women's experiences in the postcommunist environment have produced an increasingly solid framework and more reliable data on domestic violence. The reflections on gender and gender inequality have most recently arrived at the difficult intersection of highly contentious, previously taboo or unrecognized policy issues, such as domestic violence, that have explicitly political, economic, cultural, and psychological aspects. In addition to the idiosyncratic constellation of political and social conditions in each postcommunist country, the rather narrow international consensus on what domestic violence is and how to assist its victims significantly limits the toolbox that activists, politicians, and state bureaucrats can use and rely on. However, the various tensions between approaches, ideologies, actors, and so on, not only constrain, but also provide new opportunities to reconsider best practices regarding domestic violence according to regional needs.[2]

The first wave of writing on women's issues in the postcommunist context was dominated by Western Europeans and North Americans such as Buckley (1992, 1997), Clements et al. (1991), Deacon et al. (1992), Einhorn (1993), and the frequently cited Funk and Mueller (1993). In a wave of what can be described as a "surprise syndrome,"[3] these studies of Eastern Europe presented a broad portrayal of incipient responses to the dramatic changes, often bemoaning the lack of feminist responses to the withdrawal of broad welfare services and reproductive freedoms. Although many of the authors were longtime observers of the region, even the most attuned found it difficult to avoid some undertones of the then exceedingly popular Western triumphalism. The trend of describing the knowledge and money transfer as going from an unproblematic West to an problematic East has been endemic ever since, despite being followed by more nuanced interpretations as well (see Funk 2006).

Western European and North American authors and publishers also dominated the second generation of writing, but their focus shifted to history and political sociology to highlight the differences in communist-era and postcommunist gender socialization and women's organizing (Aivazova 1994; Bucur and Wingfield 2006; Sperling 1999; True 2003). Supported by the data gathered during the first wave of postcommunist scholarship and the additional women-specific historiography, the theory-building phase also commenced (Gal and Kligman 2000a, 2000b).

The recent third wave of books by authors including Hemment (2007), Johnson (2009), Johnson and Robinson (2007), and Weiner (2007) on the gender politics of the postcommunist region covers a broad array of studies that converge to untangle the complicated East-West relations, often showing some ambiguous or outright contradictory outcomes of Western aid (Evans et al. 2005; Henderson 2003). As a result of international, and especially Western, engagements, new themes in gender relations have started to emerge, particularly the politics of the gendered body both as an actual physical object and as a symbolic representation of power relations in advertisements and the media.

Many activists and scholars from the postcommunist region have been, and continue to be, preoccupied by the question of how to make their voices heard. At least three main types of response have developed among gender scholars that reflect both the increasing global integration and the parallel process of separation/differentiation (Fodor and Varsa 2009). One less frequently publicly expressed but nonetheless popular solution was to counter the hegemony of Western academic thought and emphasize the unique experience of the postcommunist region. The alienation generated by the position of petitioner tends to render explanations of East Europeanness and its gender relations as profoundly different and unintelligible when seen through a "Western" lens (Tóth 1993). Other researchers have tended to emphasize the need for a "constant interchange between East and West" (Pető and Szapor 2007) and the need for "redistributive politics" to alleviate inequalities between center (i.e., the West) and periphery (i.e., the postcommunist world in this context; Tímár 2007). Cerwonka, a US gender scholar residing in Hungary, offers a third approach by questioning whether the concept of "hegemony" is useful to describe the relationship between Western feminist theory and postcommunist gender research (2008). Cerwonka claims theories are "transculturated"—that is, adapted, modified, and rethought for each specific context—and when Western feminist theories travel to Eastern Europe, they too change and become more sophisticated and refined.

These three main approaches to global interactions and, in particular, Western dominance in conceptualization, terminology, and crucially, funding (in this case relating to gender, human rights, and women's rights, and domestic violence) have repeatedly and strongly reappeared and shaped the agenda of scholars and activists alike. The obvious tensions arising among these approaches also generate urgent calls for meaningful dialogue and opportunities to share the desire that "self-reflective East-West dialogue must continue if there is to be a constructive, just transnational women's movement" (Funk 2007: 204).

Western, especially North American, scholarship and teaching on gender has started to gain a foothold among a number of mostly female academics. Gender studies in several postcommunist countries has received significant foreign funding because "gender studies [played] the role of a 'symbolic marker' of Westernization and the compliant incorporation of the Central and Eastern European/former Soviet region into the Western-dominated global system" (Zimmermann 2007: 9). As Robnik notes in this book, it was mostly these female academics who introduced the notion of "domestic violence" through their writings and often their activism. They embodied the transforming personal effects of global exchanges, encountering, translating, and applying the concepts and (human rights) norms that led to internationally engaged political activism and, eventually, transposed policy instruments, such as distancing ordinance, domestic violence courts, and shelters.

International networking on domestic violence among women's groups was not palpably evident until the beginning of the twenty-first century when NGOs to help victims of rape and domestic violence started to emerge in postcommunist Europe and Eurasia. The NGOs appeared partly in response to domestic needs and partly because Western feminist concepts were now seen as applicable, and funding from Western governments and international governmental organizations (IGOs) unarguably appealing.[4] The chapters of this volume demonstrate that there are quite a few variants in the postcommunist environment on how external support emerged and influenced the appearance of internal actors who were willing to acknowledge the problem and cooperate transnationally. "Domestic violence" was gradually moving into the public arena, but it often remains difficult to convince people to recognize it as a problem.

What Is Domestic Violence?

Domestic violence is a global problem, but its staggering political, social, and psychological costs are only now beginning to emerge as subjects of national as well as international concern (Heise 1994; Walby 2004b). The extent, validity, and reliability of the data indicating the prevalence of domestic violence are critical in determining the magnitude of the problem and the necessary policies that address it. However, domestic violence is notoriously difficult to measure, and the available data lack both comprehensiveness and international and temporal comparability. Most data record only explicit and often extreme physical abuse, partially because respondents may be in danger if they reveal their problems and partially because they may not recognize that they face abuse. In 1993, the World Bank calculated that domestic violence and rape accounted for one in five disability adjusted life years lost in women aged 15–44 worldwide (UNICEF 2000).[5] The costs range from direct expenses, such as goods and social services used to treat and prevent domestic violence (estimated at CDN$10 billion in Canada and US$5–10 billion in the US [Clark et al. 2002; Day 1995; Laurence and Spalter-Roth 1996]), to economic and social multiplier effects in labor markets, intergenerational transmission of violence, and unmeasured pain and suffering (Buvinić et al. 1999; Yodanis et al. 2000).

Gender inequality and the socially constructed division between the public and private spheres have long shielded domestic violence. Although communist societies ordered (male) privilege and the division of public and private differently from other political systems, they did not collapse these traditional hierarchies. On the contrary, as the chapters of this volume attest, the patriarchal heritage of the communist period not only survived but was often transformed and strengthened due to increased interactions with the contemporary international environment.

Since the early 1980s, domestic violence has been a prime subject in international human rights discourse (Coomaraswamy 2000; Merry 2006), and transnational activist networks of the feminist movement successfully used the universal claims of the human rights framework to explicitly include women's rights (Keck and Sikkink 1998). In an effort to avoid the diverse cultural interpretations of women's rights, activists in the 1980s focused on one relatively common platform: the sanctity of bodily integrity. Violence against women has since emerged as one of the most powerful examples of the untenable division between public and private spheres—where the private sphere served essentially defended crimes that would otherwise be considered torture, assault, harassment, intimidation, theft, rape, and even homicide. Domestic violence was an important part of the tragically broad concept of violence against women in the eyes of the feminist groups that first called attention to this issue. Using decades of data and libraries of research, Parrot and Cummings (2006) created a comprehensive account of violence against women, including the killing of female infants and fetuses, female genital cutting, sexual violence, sexual slavery, trafficking of women, intimate partner violence, and honor killing. The varied types of brutalization many women experience during their lifetime illuminate the diverse ideologies and cultural conditions that condone and perpetuate global violence against women. Domestic violence is only one of many types of violence overwhelmingly perpetrated against women (UNICEF 1999; WHO 1996).

As liberal democracy spread, feminist movements struggled to gain a greater voice in politics. Slowly, and still only partially, they managed to convince some governments and international organizations to produce more gender-sensitive laws and policies that included protective orders, domestic violence courts, and shelters, as well as trained jurors, police, health professionals, and social workers to recognize and sensitively assist victims. These policy recommendations became part of an emerging international norm on how to address domestic violence that includes state intervention and support for victims (Burton 2008; McCue 2008; Verrity 2007).

The international women's movement developed the argument stating that violence in the home is not an individual or cultural problem, but a violation of human rights against which individual states and the broader community of nations, such as the UN and the European Union, should provide protection. If the state fails to do so, it should be held responsible. Activists contend that victims of domestic violence come from all economic classes, religions, and nationalities, and the obstacles they face in reaching out for help may differ considerably according to circumstance.

Campaigns against domestic violence and the roots of the shelter movement originated in the UK, where, in 1971, Erin Pizzey established what is considered to be the first battered women's shelter.[6] Similar shelters were established in the United States by the mid-1970s and the concept was soon transplanted back to Western Europe, where many movements emerged to provide protection and services for victims and aimed to change societal perceptions and eventually laws about domestic violence (Dobash and Dobash 1992; Tierney 1982). The international women's movement has since established a complex (and still contentious) definition of domestic violence as a subcategory of violence against women that analytically separates it from other forms of violence, such as child or elder abuse (see, for example, Buzawa and Buzawa 2002; Marcus 1994; Weldon 2002). The Minnesota Advocates for Human Rights (MAHR), for example, which has been increasingly involved with promoting legal change regarding domestic violence crimes in Eastern Europe and Eurasia, uses Anne Ganley and Susan Schechter's (1995: 17–18) definition:

> Domestic violence is a pattern of abusive and threatening behaviors that may include physical, emotional, economic and sexual violence as well as intimidation, isolation and coercion. The purpose

of domestic violence is to establish and exert power and control over another; men most often use it against their intimate partners, such as current or former spouses, girlfriends, or dating partners. While other forms of violence within the family are also serious, this site will address the unique characteristics of violence against women in their intimate relationships. (Minnesota Advocates for Human Rights 2006)

Despite the stark clarity of these terms, how to distinguish normal behavior from abuse remains a subject of constant debate (Gelles 1997). This may be particularly true for the abused, who are often reluctant to see themselves as victims because they know their abusers, and because the recurring, different types of violence reinforce silence, self-doubt, and self-blame. Women tend to develop coping mechanisms that others consider maladaptive: pleasing the abuser or numbing themselves with alcohol, for example. Meanwhile, social and economic isolation frequently restrict victims' opportunities to leave their abusive environments (see examples in Bumiller 2008).

The term "domestic violence" has been debated since its early 1970s introduction into the women's movement agenda and then its acceptance as part of the human rights movement. Moving away from a unitary and often simplistic conceptualization of the genders and the power dynamics between them, scholars and activists have started to reflect on the pluralistic nature of masculinities and femininities (Brod and Kaufman 1994; Holter 2005). This more nuanced understanding of patriarchy incorporates a "prismatic effect" of violence, in which the permanence of direct/physical violence is understood in relation with the coexistence of structural, cultural, and symbolic violence (Thapar-Björkert et al. 2006).

Re-theorizing patriarchy and violence within this broader framework allows us to recognize that physical violence is not always a prerequisite for the exercise of power. Disciplinary power, which is less overt, tends to be an internalized and less visible form of violence (Foucault 1977). Exercising discipline through internal and small-community surveillance (such as family, friends, or kinship/*avlod* as Sharipova and Fábián describe in the chapter on Tajikistan) produces a much more effective (and oppressively silent) capacity to oversee and control.

Gendered identities can easily become unstable through consent, complicity, and misrecognition (Bourdieu 1999). Gender-solidarity and even self-interest can be rendered uncertain and confused by the established patriarchal order's discipline and its incentives. The gendered analysis of violence reveals the influence of symbolic power on direct violence, which is supported by structural violence. However, addressing, and especially changing, structural conditions is a mighty affair. Recognizing the enormous difficulties involved in changing cultural traditions and political and economic institutions, activists within the domestic violence movement have for long disagreed about whether the problem should be addressed by helping individual victims or by putting their energies into changing the pervasive social attitudes and reluctant institutions (see Tifft 1993).[7] As Johnson and Zaynullina as well as Robnik astutely describe in this volume, the arrival of activists from postcommunist Europe and Eurasia has strengthened the previously more latent international attention to economic (structural) interventions to decrease and eliminate domestic violence.

Responses from Postcommunist Countries to the Frame of Domestic Violence

After the fall of the communist system, a broad human rights framework and policy recommendations—most notably the Austrian framework of criminalizing domestic violence, emulating the Duluth model from Minnesota, United States—migrated to Central and Eastern Europe and the newly independent former Soviet republics (Minnesota Advocates for Human Rights 2008). Transnational norms and international actors pressured the region, usually only indirectly but occasionally directly, to deal with the newly named but long-standing problem of domestic violence. Central and Eastern European and Eurasian women's groups routinely implied in their appeals to the various local authorities that the degree to which postcommunist countries were willing to respond to domestic violence could be used as a measure of these countries' desire to honor their integration into the community of democratic nations. That domestic violence even became a publicly discussed topic in Central and Eastern Europe and Eurasia testifies to the skill of the activists and the strength of the international women's movement that wants to address abuse and exploitation.

Unlike scholarly research on women's experience in the world of work and politics, writings and activism on domestic violence have no roots in, tradition of, or history during communism. This omission is not unique to communism: activists all over the world have had to face often enormous resistance and continue to struggle to convince their broader environments to consider domestic violence seriously.

The unique characteristic of communist practice was its proclamation that it had solved the "women's question," that is, achieved equality between the sexes (see, for example, Rule and Noonan 1996). While sexual equality remained an item at least in the rhetoric and propaganda of communist states, negation and/or embarrassment surrounded issues of the body, sexuality, and sexual violence. Neither academic discourse nor legislation raised or dealt with these issues. The authors and activists in postcommunist countries who decided to address domestic violence had to literally and conceptually translate the terms "violence against women" and "domestic violence." This process of translation (in its broadest sense) is still ongoing, as the chapters of this volume demonstrate.

The recent emergence of domestic violence as a subject of social movement activism and policy demands in postcommunist Europe and Eurasia has not only highlighted problems of conceptualization but also raised concerns of foreign agenda-setting for local human rights and feminist activists. With the implications and meanings of masculinity/ femininity contingent on culture, context, and time, gender images in Eastern Europe and Eurasia have also been changed by these countries' opening toward contemporary Western cultures.

The concept of domestic violence in Eastern Europe and Eurasia came from Western feminist literature and activism, which offered new intellectual and practical opportunities for many postcommunist women activists to address gender inequality and oppression. While domestic violence as a focus of activism was novel to Eastern Europe and Eurasia, activists quickly recognized that it could earn the politically, practically, and symbolically important support of Western funding agencies.

However, the imported framework was neither easily translatable nor immediately resonant in activists' respective national environments. To reduce the gap between their home environments and the Western agencies' novel, but service-oriented, interpretation of domestic violence and to make it more applicable to their clients and meaningful to themselves, postcommunist European and Eurasian activists added economic (that is, structural) inequalities of the sexes. NGOs in Russia and Slovenia, influenced by their many decades of communist experience (see Johnson and Zaynullina, and Robnik, in this volume), have started to include "economic violence" as part of their definition of domestic violence. The postcommunist European and Eurasian definition of domestic violence has stretched the earlier liberal feminist concept by adding a economic/structural consideration of gender inequality.

Stretching the earlier feminist interpretation of domestic violence demonstrated a feedback mechanism from postcommunist Europe and Eurasia that could enhance the otherwise limited range of successful political opportunities for activism. This postcommunist emphasis on economic/structural aspects of domestic violence exemplifies a new iteration of the debates in the 1970s and 1980s when the feminist movement employed the perlocutionary force of words. This means that words were transformed from a "medium of communication to an instrument of force" (Das 1998: 117) by connecting their agenda to the framework of universal human rights. However, the willingness of the liberal democratic framework to incorporate this structural enhancement of the domestic violence frame both in and outside of postcommunist Europe and Eurasia is still an issue for debate.

Activists against Domestic Violence: Women's Movements East and West

A major achievement of the feminist movement is that both gender inequality and the division between the public and private spheres emerged as main topics and both have been critiqued in many of their permutations (Peterson and Runyan 1999; Sassoon 1987). Feminist scholarship showed how liberalism carried and naturalized the division between the sexes and the separation of public and private. Scholars analyzed how liberalism continued to relegate women to the private realm and excluded them from full personhood and political participation (Pateman 1988; Phillips 1991). While several feminists argue that women cannot rely fully on liberal politics (Brown 1995; Elshtain 1995; MacKinnon 1989), activists have used liberal ideology extensively, especially its descendant human rights framework, to address some aspects of male domination, to show how patriarchy causes inequality and exploitation, and to demand equal rights and opportunities for women (Mahoney 1994; Marcus 1994).

Liberalism provided a philosophical basis for the claim that a woman was not property and had rights of her own, such as being educated and employed, owning property, and voting in democracies. Although the first suffragist wave of international feminist activism could strengthen its arguments and appeal by referring to the basic claim of equality in a liberal democracy, the movement confronted many legal and social obstacles during the late nineteenth and early twentieth centuries. A century later, many of its aims are still unrealized. Even in democracies, without addressing the many and interlinked economic and cultural conditions that keep women in an inferior position, women's electoral choices remain only superficially equal to those of men. In the turbulent 1960s and 1970s in Western Europe and North America, the second wave of the women's movement started to address the many deep and interconnected economic and cultural foundations of gender inequality that go beyond superficially equal voting rights. As with the first wave of the international women's movement, many of the aims of the second wave remain only partially fulfilled, especially in a global comparison (for a particularly convincing set of data, see the UNDP's many gender-specific regional or country reports, e.g., 1995, 2000, 2005, 2007).

Until the end of World War I, Eastern European women's groups had played an active part in the first wave of the international women's movement (Acsády 2004; Rupp 1997). However, as the paths of Eastern and Western Europe started to diverge in 1922 with the establishment of the Soviet Union, the women's movements also started to separate from one another during the interwar years. After a short but intense period of reconnecting during 1945–1948, the divergence between East and West and their respective women's movements became even more pronounced. The communist regimes claimed to have solved "the women's question," with women's quotas to the communist legislative bodies and women's full-time and purportedly nearly universal entry to employment. However, they had only one Communist Party–affiliated women's organization symbolically in charge of women's issues in each Eastern Bloc country (Buckley 1992). After seventy years in the former Soviet Union territories and forty years in the Eastern European satellite countries, these political, economic, and cultural arrangements left a heavy mark on gender relations and contemporary women's movements.

While the communist regimes created many women-friendly policies in employment and welfare, these policies first and foremost served the regimes' immediate economic needs, and women needed to adjust accordingly (Fodor 2003). The orthodox Marxist interpretation of needs and the respective Communist Parties' monopoly of political life cut off Eastern Europe and Eurasia nearly entirely from meaningful information, and especially from participation in the 1960s and 1970s movements that were shaking and would eventually transform the contemporaneous liberal democracies.

Information about the 1960s and 1970s student, civil rights, peace, and women's movements was presented as proof of the superiority of the communist system—the masses in the West were revolting against the oppressive capitalist regimes—and proof of the capitalist system's inherent rottenness that allowed for such impermissible access and liberties as bra-burning, "women's lib," gay and lesbian rights, and sexual liberation. All these individual-focused and rights-centered Western social movements were fundamentally threatening to the hierarchically ordered and dictatorially ruled communist regimes, but in a projection of unshakable self-confidence, the propaganda machine painted these new social movements as unpopular and despised. By indirectly proving that the order of gender relations is a prerogative of any political rule and its discipline, the feminist movement has especially incurred the ire of those in power (Goven 1993).

Communist-era official anti-feminism found an unlikely and more successful successor. Wanting to undermine the communist state, the Eastern European resistance movements made feminism seem even more nonsensical by pointing out how men and women were in solidarity together against the evil oppressive communist system. In the politics of "anti-politics" (to use Konrád's [1984] oft-used term of the dissident movement), the home and the private sphere appeared as a haven against the intrusive state apparatus (Penn 2005).[8] In other situations where individual lives have been entrenched in violence, fear, and suffering, gender has also often taken a backstage role (Farmer 2003).

The Soviet satellite countries in Eastern Europe staged periodic revolts and revolutions against the communist system and basked in the occasional glow of Western approval during political "thaws." Even these temporary softenings of the grip of the regime ensured that their populations and official women's movements had only very limited and officially controlled contacts with feminist movements elsewhere.[9] With the exception of Tito's socialist Yugoslavia, Eastern Europe remained isolated from both the concerns and the language of the various Western and postcolonial women's movements until the late 1980s. In theory there could have been ideological bridges between the postcolonial and the Eastern European and Eurasian women's agendas, but the information and contact between them were and remain extremely scarce (see Chari and Verdery 2007).

However, Eastern Europe was missing out on more than information on both the 1960s sexual revolution and the 1970s second-wave feminist movements worldwide. Other fundamental political rights were also conspicuous by their absence. Conversely, during the seventy (in the Soviet Union)/forty (in the Central and Eastern European satellites) years of communist rule, the otherwise oppressive state apparatus also established laws that promoted at least some numerical gender equality in the public sphere, and it provided low-quality but exceptionally broad welfare services that supported women's "double burden" of full-time employment and a nearly exclusive responsibility for family care.[10] Similarly broad economic support for working mothers is still largely nonexistent in most capitalist countries, despite their occasionally strong feminist movements (Guichon et al. 2006; Haussman and Sauer 2007; Lovenduski 2005).

With these different political trajectories in their respective gender relations, the experience of postcommunist Europe and Eurasia raises some pertinent issues for those interested in enhancing gender equality: a) the role of the state in promoting gender equality; b) the influence of NGOs and social movements on decisionmakers; and c) the democratic (ideally open and transparent) nature of exchange between the state and its citizens. The remnants of the extensive communist-era welfare system, a sense of solidarity between the sexes, and the belief that feminism is a Western import make the general public and many decisionmakers in the postcommunist region highly dubious of NGOs' claims that there are many female victims of domestic violence and that they need new, specific, and extensive services.

NGOs and social movements have emerged since democracy's superficial victory in the Eastern Block. Whether and to what degree the state should or could promote gender equality has been a persistent and contentious question all over the world, but it is an especially provocative and useful question to pose in the postcommunist region, given the state's earlier prominent role in promoting its now ideologically suspect version. This debate on the desired and effective role of the state and its disciplinary forces—such as the police, judges, the media, and schools—fundamentally affects if, how, and when domestic violence is taken seriously enough to act against it (Kantola 2006a).

With this historical background, the postcommunist women's movements that managed to form after the regime transitions carried a very different set of emotional affinities and political affiliations than the Western feminist movements. The 1990s political and economic transitions fundamentally rearranged women's employment opportunities and their socially supported roles away from paid labor and back to the household. Women in the postcommunist environment confronted a dramatically different political, economic, and cultural reality, with higher rates of unemployment, decreasing rates of female employment, the feminization of poverty, and a large gender wage gap despite women's higher educational achievements. At the same time, they were being told that everything is possible and individuals are in charge of their fate. The transition years have been very confusing for women in postcommunist countries because the previous generations' knowledge and experience were not applicable to contemporary problems (see Neményi and Kende 1999) and the language to demand support for broad welfare services or more employment opportunities was ideologically incompatible with the dominant neoliberal expectations. The recognition of domestic violence and the need for shelters for its victims—concepts that entered only via Western feminism, from the 1990s—could only happen if the terminology to describe them existed. However, not only did the terminology not exist but the mindset focusing on the female individual, her individual rights, and the network of civil society capable of addressing such a complex and large issue as domestic violence were distant and, for a long time, nearly unimaginable.

Because the cultural and individual-centered advances of the second-wave feminist movement did not reach Eastern Europe and Eurasia in the 1960s and 1970s, the trajectories of the respective movements only met in the late 1980s. By that time, the international women's movement had produced a focus on women's rights as human rights, and domestic violence was part of the globally resonant agenda of eliminating violence against women.

Conceptualizations of Domestic Violence in Postcommunist Europe and Eurasia

Since the late 1980s and early 1990s, various actors from the postcommunist European and Eurasian countries have entered the international debates on the meanings of domestic violence and the policies that could potentially curb this problem. The rather abrupt entry of new Eastern European and Eurasian feminist and human rights movements, as well as the postcommunist governments, into the global debates on domestic violence has highlighted the profound and long-standing effects of their previous political, economic, and social arrangements on gender.

Globalization and domestic violence are deeply contentious topics everywhere in the world, and they are especially and acutely controversial in contemporary postcommunist Europe and Eurasia. Globalization has profoundly contributed to the establishment of an environment conducive to an open discussion about domestic violence, and the attitudes of Eastern European and Eurasian activists, governments, and general publics toward domestic violence simultaneously reveal these actors' complex and contradictory relationship to globalization.

The debates and solutions regarding domestic violence in Eastern Europe and Eurasia are evidence of an international exchange, although the interactions also reveal that the parties have been rather unequal in their influence over one another. Many of the chapters in this volume attest that one option is to submit to the hegemonic Euro-American linguistic and theoretical toolkit of scholarly writing and legal practice. However, this approach may attract only a handful of supporters in the respective postcommunist countries, or for that matter, anywhere in the world. Previously very little, if any, adaptation or accommodation was detectable on the part of most Western scholars, especially those at the helm of influential academic or economic institutions (for a detailed discussion, see Cerwonka 2008; Gal 1997; Tímár 2007).

In addition to full co-optation, three other, distinct approaches emerged from postcommunist social movements' engagement with earlier conceptualizations of domestic violence. Many, in fact probably most, of the newly established postcommunist NGOs may first have seen an intellectual and practical opportunity in importing the Western terminology and applying the rather stable feminist framework when naming and calling for action to deal with domestic violence. In the second stage, as Snajdr discusses in this volume, many East European and Eurasian activists realized that they needed to adjust the imported terminology, the services their NGOs offered, and even their policy recommendations to the governments if they wanted to be heard and to work more effectively. Consequently, many NGOs hybridized Western feminist terminology with more nationalist, maternity-focused, and community-oriented concepts, as Hrycak points out in her discussion on Ukraine. The third, and probably most challenging, approach is to reinterpret and broaden the Western, individual-centered definitions and policy frameworks. Within the stream of reinterpreting the originally Western conceptualization, Eastern European and Eurasian activists have increasingly developed an emphasis on economic domestic violence. Johnson and Zaynullina as well as Robnik note how the Russian and Slovenian NGOs managed to influence fellow activists and their respective governments to consider economic violence as part of domestic violence. Additionally, the chapters by Snajdr as well as Sharipova and Fábián emphasize that domestic violence is a deeply embedded social problem. Until we address every fundamental and powerful political, economic, social, historical, and religious force that contributes to the toleration of domestic violence in postcommunist societies, any reduction in its occurrence and severity will be merely partial and temporary at best. But the entry of domestic violence into the vocabulary of the general public and decisionmakers alike is itself a major accomplishment and testimony to the work of many dedicated activists.

Only the most doctrinaire would have denied that domestic violence existed in the communist countries. However, it was clearly systematically ignored and suppressed in an ideological context where the state could easily apply pressure to an individual and, if the local political leadership so chose, intervene in family problems (see Haney 2002; Johnson 2009). Under communism, the state's supervision of private matters was so pervasive that it was less likely to tolerate individual transgressions (although the political leadership was most often exempt). As Sharipova and Fábián describe, with fear permeating every cell of Soviet-era communist societies, the self-disciplining of the population may have also contributed to an environment that condoned, but did not encourage, intimate violence. Also, the relative accessibility of public housing and a wide network of welfare institutions made it comparatively easier then for a victim to find shelter if forced to leave the family home. However, the comparison between the prevalence of and the possible solutions to domestic violence in contemporary times and the communist period is speculative at best. It is important to note that we have no reliable evidence of the occurrence of violence between intimate partners during the communist regime (Haney 2002).

Closer to the beginning of the twenty-first century, with the agendas of the international human rights and women's movements deeply and successfully engaging with one another, and the communist states' omnipresent monopoly on violence dissipating, one might have expected a favorable gender regime system change for decreasing the occurrence of domestic violence as well. However, the direction of political and economic changes ushered in a mixed, and in many respects more unfavorable, gender regime for women. The ideal of the autonomous family was strengthened in the postcommunist period both rhetorically and economically, as well as specifically through changes in welfare provisions. The previous possibility of direct state intervention in family affairs was regarded as an encroachment on privacy and a threat to private property (Glass and Fodor 2007). The increasing dominance of the private would be difficult to miss in postcommunist countries, especially against the backdrop of the Europe-wide erosion of social democratic regimes that are moving toward more market-oriented modes of operation.

To further complicate matters, although the concept of domestic violence stretches across countries and continents, it remains vague. Opponents of feminist groups have intensively scrutinized this conceptual vagueness in postcommunist Europe and Eurasia. The many critics of feminist groups objected to both the portrayal of the family as a dangerous place and the focus on men as the perpetrators of domestic violence, when the family and intimate relationships were the main bastions of protection against both the criminal over-reach of the communist regime and the many difficulties of the emerging market relations. How, under difficult political and economic conditions, did NGOs in postcommunist Europe and Eurasia start to address this previously anonymous—and officially nonexistent—issue?

How did the recognition of domestic violence begin? Essentially, the process of recognition and actions all began with finding an acceptable name. Each activist and group had to first understand the term and then attempt to translate it into their own language. This task was neither inconsequential nor self-evident. The problem (and its solution) could not formally exist without a name, and so long as it had no name, even an operational name, individual and state responsibilities could not be separated in a domestic violence policy that law enforcement could then implement. However, in the process of naming the issue, the enmeshed condition of culture/traditions, of "how we do things," collided with the new international norms.

Each language and its related culture labeled the problem differently. Direct translations of nearly all the terms used in Western, especially English-language, discourse were tried, from "wife beating" and "wife abuse," to "spousal violence" and "partner abuse," but these focused too narrowly on violence within only sexual relationships. Eventually, broader terms such as "domestic violence" (*domácího násilí* in Czech, *domáce násilie* in Slovak, *domashnee nasilie* in Russian, and *domashno nasilie* in Bulgarian) and "violence in the family" (*családon belüli erőszak* in Hungarian, *przemoc w rodzinie* in Polish, and *nasilie v sem'e* in Russian) emerged as most frequently used in each country (see Chivens, and Brunell and Johnson, in this volume; Vanya 2001). Debates raged in each country about the implied meaning of violence among intimate partners. Tracing the course of these terminological debates about domestic violence carries a more complex and important message than a simple description could about the trends in word choice or a chronology of who suggested what and when. Analysis of why the naming of domestic violence caused heated debates also highlights the underlying causes of the (predominantly male) lawmakers' objections and popular resistance to altering the previous arrangement of power and authority.

Naming "domestic violence" in an inclusive but unconfrontational manner was a crucial but difficult task, hampered by numerous challenges. First, identifying the hurt party became problematic because each term that was borrowed from Western European and US definitions placed different emphases on who the vulnerable parties are. If the general term becomes "violence against women" (which has been the usage in feminist-inspired international discourse), this implies that only women can be the victims. This terminology was quite unpalatable to Eastern European and Eurasian decisionmakers, and therefore many social movement activists decided to shift the language to gender-neutral territory in order to effectively engage them. Most politicians and scholars in the Eastern European and Eurasian region habitually note that if a policy framework accepts the term as violence against women, then abuse against the elderly, children, and men would be omitted from the notion of violence in the home (see Chivens' and Fábián's essays in the present volume). Feminists wished to retort that these are distinct legal issues and policy categories, and to claim that much of the violence against children, the elderly, and even young men springs from women's oppression, because intimate partners often try to exert power over women by hurting other family members. Unfortunately, these responses rarely reach mainstream media, and usually a lone feminist legal scholar (such as Krisztina Morvai used to be in Hungary) or activist (such as Ursula Nowakowska in Poland) becomes the often-ostracized spokesperson for this theme. The debate continues to evolve: can anyone, regardless of sex, age, or marital status, become a victim of violence in the family, or is there a need to emphasize that gender-based violence is a manifestation of the prevailing patriarchic order and should be separated from the other types of crimes?

Second, specifying location in the term "violence in the home/family" turned out to be similarly challenging, because both "the home" and "the family" are vague. The image of violence in the family offended and politically distanced many social conservatives, who wished to envision the family and their domicile as a homogeneous and harmonious entity.

Third, should only violence in marital relations be subject to the scrutiny of public view, as the term "wife abuse" suggests? With cohabiting and divorce rates in Central and Eastern Europe reaching record highs (Bradatan and Kulcsár 2008; Kulcsár 2007), the traditional approach of limiting domestic violence to married partners living at the same address was not tenable. The obvious alternative to "wife abuse" would have been "partner violence," but this can also imply homosexual relationships, and legitimating homosexual partnerships even in such an opaque way would be an unacceptable risk for most politicians in increasingly homophobic Eastern Europe and Eurasia.[11]

The current solution to the terminological quandary is "domestic violence" and "violence in the family." Violence was conditionally and partially extricated from male power, but "violence against women" or "wife abuse" were used extremely rarely in the various postcommunist contexts. Using "domestic violence" or "violence in the family" omits gender connotations about probable victimhood and perpetrator and, by ignoring women's higher likelihood of suffering from domestic violence, demonstrates the continued influence of patriarchic cultural arrangements.[12] Despite the profound social changes that affected gender roles during and after communism, this aspect of the power imbalance between men and women had escaped the scrutiny of the state and the general public until now.

Even the toned-down, minimally confrontational term "domestic violence" presents many problems, as some anti-feminist scholars and policymakers are eager to point out. Fundamental features of democratic procedures such as equality before the law, the usual methods of evidence-gathering at a crime scene, and the ideal of balancing gender equality and difference are all questioned in the case of violence in the family. For example, the type of admissible evidence of violence between intimate partners presented a challenge for the new, rule of law-based judicial systems. The neophyte advocacy of clearly transparent and corroborated evidence was eager to reject any semblance to the hearsay testimonials of communism's show trials. How could evidence be sought in cases of emotional abuse? Should only physical violence be criminalized? What kind of witness evidence would be permissible? Although the effects of beating can be more easily and unambiguously demonstrated, physical violence is frequently the consequence of the escalating progression of often long-term emotional and psychological maltreatment (Gilligan 1996: 223–225). However, psychological/emotional abuses do not fit neatly into existing legal categories, and proving such abuses is especially difficult in postcommunist environments where the fear of framing innocent victims, a hangover from their most recent pasts, endures.

Similarities and Differences in Interpreting Domestic Violence between East and West

Some Eastern European and Eurasian politicians and activists claim that the communist experience also distinguished the postcommunist region from the West in its approach to domestic violence. First, both male and female public figures in Central and Eastern Europe, if they are willing to consider this issue at all, feel the need to be "balanced"; that is, to include both genders equally in all types of public policies on domestic violence, including its definition and policies related to curbing it in all its forms. In an obligatory dismissive remark toward communism, populist politicians assert that "here, women beat men" (author interviews, Hungarian Parliament, July 2003, and Slovenian Parliament, October 2004). Second, as seen in worldwide debates (Burton 2008; Penn and Nardos 2003; Stychin 2003; Warrior 1976: 20–21), the effectiveness of legal (criminal) approaches to eliminate domestic violence has often been questioned in postcommunist Eastern Europe and Eurasia, because criminalization in that region evokes the now resented omnipotence of the state and its intrusion in private life.

Avdeyeva's essay in this volume convincingly shows that in contrast to the universal human rights–based claim to act persuasively and effectively against domestic violence stands the overwhelming number of Eastern European and Eurasian cases of official intransigence in establishing and especially implementing separate domestic violence laws. As the cases of Hungary and Slovakia testify, even international warnings from CEDAW and the Council of Europe to numerous postcommunist states seem to go unheeded (A. T. v Hungary 2003; European Roma Rights Center 2006). This resistance alone is not unusual in the international environment, because in every social context it was exceedingly difficult to change legislation and pursue its meaningful implementation to recognize and support victims of domestic violence. What is unusual and perplexing about the postcommunist countries' behavior is that they tend to sign international treaties on gender equality (such as CEDAW and its Optional Protocol) in the name of democratization and human rights, but they rarely implement them.

However, if the primary political value of a democratic system is indeed equality, no one can persistently ignore women's rights without consequences. As many cases, such as the interwar Czechoslovak democracy, show (Feinberg 2006), fears of implementing equal rights for women initially lead not only to disregarding laws, but in the long run, they seriously contribute to the weakening of democracy itself. Despite opening up (rapidly in Central and Eastern Europe and only partially in Eurasia) toward the international arena, the gendered aspects of democratic political participation and international human rights norms have not reached more than a narrow set of politically engaged actors. Even this relatively restricted set of actors, though, has been rather successful in using references to the international arena and the human rights framework to engage their governments and often the general public to name domestic violence and at least consider it as a problem.

Although many of the problems in postcommunist Europe and Eurasia are familiar from the international literature, the conceptual vagueness of domestic violence has not undermined the hard-won capacity to deal with this problem in Western democracies, given the presence of a strong constituency supporting feminist and shelter movements (see Deanham and Gillespie 1999; Moghadam 2005; Weldon 2002). Brunell and Johnson also point out in this volume that the higher the density of transnational feminist actors, the higher the likelihood that legislative actors and services will develop in support of victims of domestic violence in postcommunist countries as well. While acknowledging the considerable differences, there are many similarities between both the obstacles and the solutions (even if partial) for dealing with domestic violence in postcommunist Europe/Eurasia and Western Europe. For example, debates in the 1970s in the UK revealed that conservative male members of parliament were "particularly worried about the role of the police in transgressing the public/private distinction and intervening in 'domestic disputes'" (Kantola 2006b: 158). A second (and related) set of parallels emerges between the postcommunist world and Western Europe with the persistent conflict between feminist conceptualizations of domestic violence and the family dynamics approach (see table 1.1).

In this dichotomy, the family dynamics approach appears as more moderate and prudent than the feminist interpretation that focuses on violence against women and points to patriarchy as the root cause of violence. While the tension between these two important concerns have repeatedly slowed down the development of a coherent and efficient approach toward domestic violence, Brunell and Johnson demonstrate in this volume the importance of the contact between women's and human rights NGOs in Central and Eastern Europe and Eurasia and their international counterparts. The postcommunist NGOs could use not only the implied Western leverage but also many of the policy lessons and recommendations that the earlier examples provided in pushing for change in public perceptions of violence in the private sphere.

Both the muffled/subterranean and the more open debates on what domestic violence is and how it plays out in different political and economic settings are eerily reminiscent of the Cold War–era East-West confrontations about the definition of human rights. Then, the Communist Bloc stressed economic rights as basic and denied the importance of political rights, while the West emphasized exactly the reverse (Jhabvala 1984; Myers 1993). We can detect a similar internal fragmentation between individualist and communitarian traditions in contemporary feminist arguments. "Particularly women from non-Western, or in general from originally more collectivist, cultures are left to defend their traditions against liberal feminists who base their battle for women's rights on the individualist approach" (Hellsten 2006: 54). These conflicts

Table 1.1. Differences in Refuge Ideologies

	FAMILY DYNAMICS APPROACH	FEMINIST APPROACH
Concept	Family violence	Battered women
Relationship to feminism	Negative	Highly positive
Cause of family violence	Relationship problems	Patriarchal society
Nature of family violence	Social sickness	Crime
Victim	Both women and men	Only women
Children	Very important	Less important
Openness of the activities	Very open	Very closed
Accepting men	Accepted as personnel and visitors	Not accepted at all
Form of action	Private conversations	Groups
Target of action	Family	Women's self-confidence
Personnel	Professional	Non-professional
Relationship to the state	Cooperation	Independent
Participation in politics	Weak	Strong

Source: Kantola (2006b: 159), quoting Peltoniemi

tend to come to the fore in the global context, which can dramatically amplify or negate certain claims. Celeste Montoya shows in her chapter that in the case of the European Union, international organizations selectively exert pressure on governments to consider the demands of women's groups to pass and implement legislation criminalizing domestic violence. A culturally flexible but still conceptually coherent approach could promote women's rights across the politically and economically integrating Europe and provide a dialogue-based process of deliberation as a pattern to follow in other parts of the world. Facing these differences instead of hiding or suppressing them would be a beneficial step, similar to earlier conflicts between Northern and Southern feminists that "also helped Western feminist discourse to reorient itself to recognize difference and marginalization, not merely between the sexes, but within gender discourse and in action aimed at realizing social and gender justice in a global context" (Hellsten 2006: 54).

Women's activism adroitly exploited the global wave of democratization and human rights by recognizing that their most immediate past made contemporary postcommunist Europe and Eurasia at least potentially sensitive to human rights violations. With the Central European postcommunist countries integrating this knowledge into current diplomacy, the political leadership recently chose to be in the forefront of international organizations pursuing a human rights agenda (McMahon 2005). In this pursuit, these countries may have rhetorically trapped themselves on the side of universality. In Russia and the Central Asian post-Soviet republics, where the appeal of democratization and the leverage of international organizations were weaker than in postcommunist Central Europe, NGOs faced the even more challenging task of balancing (and hybridizing) local demands and the expectations of international funders. By trying to harmonize universal claims with regional, cultural, and historical specificity regarding domestic violence policies, the postcommunist countries continue their long history of negotiation between forces of various Eastern and Western legal and cultural traditions.

Challenges of Postcommunism: In Lieu of Conclusion

In postcommunist Europe and Eurasia, the process of acknowledging domestic violence has been, and continues to be, particularly complex and challenging. The difficulties lie partly in the region's very recent and partial integration into many global trends, such as democratization and respect for human rights. During the communist regime, any discussion of domestic violence was taboo. Effectively nameless, the issue went unrecognized and unacknowledged. However, this situation has changed dramatically. In every postcommunist country the issue of domestic violence has been raised, and in most, NGOs have pursued and often succeeded in achieving legal changes to assist victims of domestic violence. Despite the changes effected by acknowledging and at least partially addressing domestic violence, many problems have emerged, and they continue to block the effective naming of and dealing with violence among intimate partners.

What is so challenging about naming and dealing with violence among intimate partners? Considering domestic violence as a crime challenges the legitimacy of established power relations, both within intimate relationships and also in the context of the state and its law-enforcement methods. In recognizing domestic violence as a crime and in calling for collective resistance to unjust authority, we question basic social patterns of behavior, such as traditional gender roles, perception of appropriate behavior, individuals' rights, and the state's responsibility. In the postcommunist societies where social dislocations and transformations have been especially rapid, the last vestiges of what feels like stability in intimate relations may be especially difficult to deal with. NGOs' raising the issue of violence in intimate settings, along with the stories of women seeking shelter from abuse, have dramatically revealed the gap between the presumption and the reality of security and welfare.

How then did domestic violence become a central topic of debate among Eastern European and Eurasian general publics, governments, international organizations, and NGOs from the early 1990s onward? The authors in this volume posit that globalization and its increasing leverage to disperse—albeit in a rather inconsistent manner—the norms of democratization and human rights have allowed for the discussion on domestic violence to come into the public arena. As the case studies in this book exemplify, these norms would not appear in their full (ideal) form, but would become muddled in an international and domestic give-and-take and settle uncomfortably into a compromise between the specific needs of local environments and international trends.

The public debate on domestic violence in postcommunist Europe and Eurasia demonstrates the extent of the transformation from communism to democracy, but this book also addresses one of gender studies' most problematic and hotly debated topics: gender equality and its application to public policies (Charlton et al. 1989; Inglehart and Norris 2003; Sainsbury 1999). The gender-specific nature of domestic violence became a major point of contention during discussions on the nature of domestic violence in postcommunist Europe and Eurasia. Are women mostly, or nearly exclusively, the victims of domestic violence, as most feminist scholarship shows (Hanmer and Itzin 2000; Penn and Nardos 2003; Schechter 1982), or is intimate violence more complex than this monolithic, legal approach, as both revisionist feminist (Miller 2005; Mills 2003) and conservative thinkers and politicians attest? In response to the many pressures to act from both outside and inside their boundaries, the postcommunist European and Eurasian governments are increasingly adopting a middle ground in terms of policies between what feminists consider to be international standards and taking no action at all.

The authors of this volume examine how domestic violence emerged as a new term in the postcommunist European and Eurasian context. They investigate how the actions of NGOs and international organizations have often dramatically altered life for women suffering violence in intimate settings. The various chapters draw upon different combinations of social science research to 1) theorize how, when, and why postcommunist states choose to consider domestic violence as a problem in need of intervention; 2) assess what role domestic and international politics play in these decisions; 3) consider the changes in attitudes and policy related to domestic violence; and 4) reflect on the feedback that the interventions of postcommunist societies have had on transnational feminist advocacy and on international organizations, such as the European Union and the UN.

Two analytical approaches form the two parts of this volume that aspire to provide 20/20 vision with both close (national) and distant (global) foci. The first part offers six case studies on how global forces have affected internal processes in national settings. The second part evaluates the interactions of various actors on the international scene that affect domestic violence activism and policies in the postcommunist countries. The first four case studies examine the development of domestic violence policies in the Soviet successor states, while the last two offer lessons on the development of Central European domestic violence policies. The book's second part uses the emerging literature of globalization and various international organizations to gauge these forces' effects on the emergence and development of domestic violence policies in the postcommunist Eastern European and Eurasian contexts.

This volume interweaves the more traditional area-studies perspectives with a less conventional focus on global interactions and their effects on the local environments. The topic of domestic violence is examined from interdisciplinary perspectives. The essays connect history, economics, politics, sociology, and cultural anthropology with public policy and gender analysis. The applied methodologies range from statistics (as in Avdeyeva's, Brunell and Johnson's, and Robnik's chapters), to network analysis (in Montoya's contribution), qualitative interview analysis (Hrycak's, Chivens's, and Sharipova and Fábián's chapters), and participant observations (Snajdr's and Fábián's writings). Participant observations range in time and detail—all the authors have extensive scholarly experience writing about communist and postcommunist Europe and Eurasia, and many of them hail from and live in the region that they study.

The disciplinary diversity may explain the different angles from which the issue of domestic violence is approached. While all the authors discuss how local movements are tied to the global institutions and the often unholy alliances activists make, they focus variously on outcome (Avdeyeva, Hrycak, Robnik, Sharipova), the discursive aspects with an emphasis on national actors (Snajdr, Chivens, Johnson and Zaynullina), the relationship between national and global activisms and norms (Brunell and Johnson, Fábián), or the effect of any one of the major actors, such as the European Union (Montoya).

Each chapter reveals in its own way the complexity of the East-West relationship. They also demonstrate that the movement against domestic violence cannot be understood in isolation as either the sole product of Western intervention or its local dependence on funding, because the state, the international system, norms, the most recent communist past, and the international human rights and women's movements all play a significant role, with some actors more dominant than others. The essays discuss the power differentials between the actors of interpreting domestic violence and portray how the global positions become more negotiable in local environments. The process that the chapters describe reveals an exchange that takes place between the actors, sometimes clearly and straightforwardly, either in a friendly/cooperative manner or in a more confrontational manner, and sometimes in a more muffled and subterranean manner.

With this diversity and complexity of actors and exchanges, the authors of this volume also show different trajectories of the movements they describe. For example, Snajdr confirms Keck and Sikkink's (1998) boomerang model of global/local relations in the case of *Podrugi*, the Kazakh NGO working with victims of domestic violence, from its appearance to the international women's movement strengthening it, while Hrycak and Sharipova with Fábián describe the Ukrainian and Tajik movements that emerged as a result of activities of international organizations, especially the UN (for Tajikistan) and the European Union (in the case of Ukraine). Assessments of the local movements are also quite different. Snajdr notes significant milestones reached in Kazakhstan, even though there is still no law against domestic violence there, whereas Avdeyeva, Hyrcak, and Chivens remain quite pessimistic in their discussions of countries signing international treaties and creating laws against domestic violence.

Using domestic violence as it focal point, this volume demonstrates some of the rapid and extensive changes that happen, often surprisingly, alongside many continuities in the politics of gender in the postcommunist European and Eurasian countries. The contemporary tensions that these essays describe offer evidence that the gender socialization of the communist era is still the primary influence on Eastern European and Eurasian responses about something literally and figuratively as "close to home" as the issues of domestic violence. The postcommunist countries' continued lack of meaningful attention to domestic violence points to a historically and culturally different type of political and gender socialization in the region. At the same time, these resistances can also remind us of the limitations of universal applicability, whether regarding the assumption of women's victimhood, the criminalization of domestic violence, or the use of programs to rehabilitate perpetrators.

The essays in this volume draw conclusions that show the increasingly interconnected nature of globalization, local activism, and changes in domestic violence laws and attitudes in postcommunist Europe and Eurasia. The authors not only recognize the many new forces affecting the politics of gender, they also point to some unexpected lessons. First, domestic violence has remained a highly contentious concept that has often been the subject of direct political confrontation between more liberal and traditional forces. At the same time, traditional forces in postcommunist Europe and Eurasia have also embraced enhanced services for victims of domestic violence on occasion, if this served their immediate political interests. Second, the frequently superficial postcommunist acceptance of international obligations to assist victims of domestic violence has led to weak and most often gender-neutral policies. Third, activism related to domestic violence in the postcommunist European and Eurasian countries highlights the limitations of the original Western, liberal, and individual-centered approach. Postcommunist activism added economic violence as a structural consideration to a previously service-oriented understanding of domestic violence.

The actors described in these essays enhance the concept of violence itself, extending the previous definition that included physical and emotional violence to include the economic realm. It may appear paradoxical that a region that rebelled against and rejected communism would offer this Marxist-influenced structural addition to the Western feminist conceptualization of domestic violence. However, with both the early economic reality (in which the regime transitions produced major market imbalances and increased inequality, poverty, and unemployment) and the work of post-Soviet academia remaining implicitly based on Marxist-Leninist premises of social research (Ousmanova 2003), the addition of a structural critique to Western feminist definitions of domestic violence appears self-evident.

By turning the public eye toward violence against women in the intimate sphere, activists created a space beyond the public or private. Amid plenty of controversy and tensions, they also opened up national deliberations to include the global arena in which human rights and dignity, rather than local custom and laws, prevail. Global and local change have taken place simultaneously, and often in a mutually reinforcing manner. Women's groups and human rights activists have frequently acted as the linchpins that forced these originally distant spheres and their institutions closer together.

NOTES

1. Democracy and democratization have emerged as two of the most pertinent and popular themes in the social sciences, political science in particular. The increasing number of case studies and conceptualizations have produced not only various contending definitions of what constitutes a democracy and what can be called a consolidated democracy (Diamond 1999; Linz and Stephan 1996) but also many different ways of measuring the quality of democracy (Berg-Schlosser 2004; Munck and Verkuilen 2002). These measures of democracy range from ratings of "political rights" and "civil liberties" by Freedom House (1978) to the even more complex World Bank indices on the "rule of law" (Kaufman et al. 2008). Among the shortcomings of these increasingly complex measures is that their heavily institutional focus (such as political parties and electoral competition) limits the inclusion of human rights. Only gross human rights violations, such as genocide or mass political terror, are included in even the most recent measures of democracy. While new indices such as the UNDP's GEM (Gender Empowerment Measure) and the Gender Gap Index (GGI), compiled by the World Economic Forum (Hausmann, Tyson, and Zahidi 2007), have begun to focus on how women fare politically, economically, and in terms of leadership worldwide, violence against women and terror in the family (domestic violence) have been excluded from measures of meaningful democratization. It should be noted that, due to the nature of domestic violence, many pieces of empirical data that would normally be used to measure effects of human rights violations are unavailable on a reliable and country-by-country bases. With estimates of women suffering from domestic violence ranging from 20 percent to 50 percent (Khan 2000: 1), measuring the achievements and the continuing problems of assisting victims of domestic violence is in ongoing need of global attention and funding.

2. Considerable controversy has emerged among scholars about the relevance of domestic violence in the postcommunist region. The arguments on both sides evoke contemporary debates on colonialization. Nanette Funk (2006) even labeled one side as the "imperialist critique" of Western feminist influence. According to this stance, followed by a smaller number of activists, with support from a large proportion of the general population and a few scholars, domestic violence is a term imported from the West, a problem that is largely irrelevant to their often very difficult present-day realities, and a diversion away from more crucial, often gender-specific problems (see Ishkanian 2007). On the other side of the debate, most activists view raising the issue

of domestic violence as long overdue and they tend to welcome Western support for their projects, while interpreting the fierce debates on domestic violence paradigm(s) as a sign of resistance from a newly strengthened patriarchy. Although both sides assert that they take seriously the claims of women and activists in the postcommunist region, both encompass only a segment of a population, most of whom are befuddled by the newly generated attention to domestic violence, all adding to the complexity of the discussion and producing an often unbalanced power dynamic between "East" and "West," and all those traveling between them.

3. Thanks to Sarah D. Phillips for offering this fitting descriptor.

4. The one notable exception to this late-1990s emergence and 2000s internationalization was the Yugoslav case, where feminist connections produced a viable independent women's movement and a shelter network in the 1970s that managed to survive through, and often vocally protested against, the wars between the successor states (Hughes, Mladjenovic, and Mrsevic 1995).

5. Disability adjusted life years (DALY) is a measure of healthy years of life lost to premature death or disability. Note that this calculation only refers to women during their most reproductive years. However, girls younger than fifteen and women older than forty-four years old can also be targets of violence in family settings.

6. Erin Pizzey also stressed that women could be perpetrators of domestic violence, too. Her book *Prone to Violence* (1982) was hotly debated because of its explicitly non-gender-specific orientation. Pizzey argued that British feminists substituted the anti-capitalist Marxist critique with a similarly general attack on all men (Pizzey 2005).

7. Tifft refers to David Gil's suggestion that the US Constitution include the universal right to work, work sharing, and equal rights for women.

8. The idealization of the home as the one reliably safe place in life supposedly created more of an alliance between men and women as they faced the state as a tyrant intruder during times of oppression in communism. This resistance was termed the "politics of anti-politics" (Konrád 1984). The deepest moral shocks about the depth of the state's infiltration emerged in the former East Germany and Romania, where secret service documents showed that family members also spied, although often under duress, against one another (Childs and Popplewell 1996; Deletant 1995).

9. Reading feminist criticism before 1989 was taken as political opposition to the communist system. Enikő Bollobás, for example, tells the story of her returning to Hungary in the 1980s after a conference in the "West" and crossing the border with feminist literary analysis in her luggage. The border patrol stopped her and the books were confiscated as politically dangerous material (Bollobás 2006).

10. For an overview of the historical trajectory of changes in welfare, see Inglot (2008).

11. Homophobia has become rapidly politicized in Central and Eastern Europe, with increasing numbers of physical attacks against gays, lesbians, bisexuals, and transgendered people (see Amnesty International 2008; Hammarberg 2006; Kitlinski and Leszkowicz 2005; Takács, Mocsonaki, and P. Tóth 2007).

12. According to Thomas Chivens, one of the contributors to this volume, the translators (and some of the early sculptors) of the Polish law chose to translate it as a "domestic violence" law, most likely consciously implying domestic violence against women. A more literal translation would present it as a family violence law, with strong non-feminist connotations. The decision to use "domestic violence" in the

title is probably a smart strategic move, although whether or not this is a fair empirical description is debatable, particularly as the implementation has been harshly criticized by the measure's strongest supporters. In some ways, Poland can be seen as having no policy related to domestic violence against women—but saying this would undercut the work of many activists and politicians, as well as the ultimate hope of the law, which is amendable. Likewise, this criticism could be levied against most (if not all) states, given the increasing requirement to apply gender-neutral language.

WORKS CITED

A. T. v Hungary, CEDAW Communication No. 2/2003, U.N. Doc.CEDAW/C/32/D/2/ 2003. CEDAW meeting on January 26, 2005. University of Minnesota Human Rights Library. www1.umn.edu/humanrts/cedaw/decisions/2-2003.html (accessed November 7, 2009).

Acsády, Judit. 2004. *Emancipáció és identitás* (Emancipation and identity). Ph.D. diss. Budapest, Hungary: Eötvös Loránd Tudományegyetem (ELTE) Sociology Department.

Aivazova, Svetlana, 1994. "Feminism in Russia, Debates from the Past." In *Women in Russia, A New Era in Russian Feminism,* ed. Anastasia Posadskaya, 154–164. London: Verso.

Amnesty International. 2008. Overview of Lesbian and Gay Rights in Eastern Europe. May 17. http://amnesty.org.uk/news_details.asp?NewsID=17757 (accessed November 7, 2009).

Åslund, Anders. 2007a. *How Capitalism Was Built: The Transformation of Central and Eastern Europe, Russia, and Central Asia.* New York: Cambridge University Press.

———. 2007b. *Russia's Capitalist Revolution: Why Market Reform Succeeded and Democracy Failed.* Washington, D.C.: Peterson Institute for International Economics.

Åslund, Anders, and Martha Brill Olcott, eds. 1999. *Russia After Communism.* Washington, D.C.: Carnegie Endowment for International Peace.

Berg-Schlosser, Dirk, 2004. "Concepts, Measurements, and Subtypes in Democratization Research." In *Democratization,* ed. Dirk Berg-Schlosser, 52–64. Wiesbaden: VS Verlag.

———. 2007. "The Quality of Post-Communist Democracy." In *Developments in Central and East European Politics,* ed. Stephen White, Judy Batt, and Paul Lewis, 264–275. Durham, N.C.: Duke University Press.

Bollobás, Enikő. 2006. "A társadalmi nem az amerikai kultúra és irodalom oktatásában: Az elmúlt 25 év tapasztalatainak összegzése" (Teaching gender in American culture and literature: Summary of the lessons from past twenty-five years). In *A társadalmi nemek oktatása Magyarországon* (Teaching gender studies in Hungary), ed. Andrea Pető, 22–29. Budapest: Ifjúsági, Családügyi, Szociális és Esélyegyenlőségi Minisztérium (ICSSZEM) (Ministry of Youth, Family, Welfare, and Equal Opportunity).

Bourdieu, Pierre. 1999. *Language and Symbolic Power.* Cambridge, Mass.: Harvard University Press.

Bradatan, Cristina, and László Kulcsár. 2008. "Choosing between Marriage and Cohabitation: Women First Union Patterns in Hungary." *Journal of Comparative Family Studies* 39: 491–507.

Brod, Harry, and Michael Kaufman, eds. 1994. *Theorizing Masculinities.* Thousand Oaks, Calif.: Sage.

Brown, Wendy. 1995. *States of Injury: Power and Freedom in Late Modernity.* Princeton, N.J.: Princeton University Press.

Buckley, Mary, ed. 1992. *Perestroika and Soviet Women.* Cambridge: Cambridge University Press.

———. 1997. *Post-Soviet Women: From the Baltic to Central Asia.* Cambridge: Cambridge University Press.

Bucur, Maria, and Nancy Wingfield, eds. 2006. *Gender and War in Twentieth-Century Eastern Europe.* Bloomington: Indiana University Press.

Bukodi, Erzsébet. 2005. "Női munkavállalás és munkaidő-felhasználás (Women in the labor market and time Uue)." In *Szerepváltozások 2005: Jelentés a nők és férfiak helyzetéről* (2005 Report on the changing roles of women and men in Hungary), ed. Ildikó Nagy, Tiborné Pongrácz, and István György Tóth. Budapest: TÁRKI.

Bumiller, Kristin. 2008. *In an Abusive State: How Neoliberalism Appropriated the Feminist Movement Against Sexual Violence.* Durham, N.C.: Duke University Press.

Burton, Mandy. 2008. *Legal Responses to Domestic Violence.* London: Routledge-Cavendish.

Buvinić, Mayra, Andrew Morrison, and Michael Shifter. 1999. "Violence in the Americas: A Framework for Action." In *Too Close to Home: Domestic Violence in the Americas,* ed. Andrew Morrison and María Loreto Biehl, 3–34. Washington, D.C.: Inter-American Development Bank.

Buzawa, Eve, and Carl Buzawa. 2002. *Domestic Violence: The Criminal Justice Response.* Thousand Oaks, Calif.: Sage.

Cerwonka, Allaine. 2008. "Traveling Feminist Thought: 'Difference' and Transculturation in Central and Eastern European Feminism." *Signs: Journal of Women in Culture and Society* 33(4): 809–832.

Chari, Sharad, and Katherine Verdery. 2007. Thinking Between the Posts: Postcolonialism, Postsocialism, and Ethnography After the Cold War. http://webtools.uiuc.edu/calendar/Calendar?ACTION=VIEW_EVENT&calId=596&skinId=544&DATE=1/26/2007&eventId=52639 (accessed November 7, 2009).

Charlton, Sue, Jana Everett, and Kathleen Staudt, eds. 1989. *Women, the State, and Development.* Albany: State University of New York Press.

Childs, David, and Richard Popplewell. 1996. *The Stasi: The East German Intelligence and Security.* New York: New York University Press.

Clark, Kathryn Andersen, Andrea Biddle, and Sandra Martin. 2002. "A Cost-benefit Analysis of the Violence against Women Act of 1994." *Violence Against Women* 8(4): 417–428.

Clements, Barbara, Barbara Engel, and Christine Worobec, eds. 1991. *Russia's Women: Accommodation, Resistance, Transformation*. Berkeley: University of California Press.

Coomaraswamy, Radhika. 2000. "Combating Domestic Violence: Obligations of the State." *Innocenti Digest* 6: 10–11. www.unicef-icdc.org/publications/pdf/digest6e.pdf (accessed November 7, 2009).

Das, Veena. 1998. "Language and Body: Transactions in the Era of Globalisation." *Anthropology and Humanism* 22(1): 115–118.

Day, Tannis. 1995. *Health-Related Costs of Violence against Women in Canada: The Tip of the Iceberg*. London, Ontario: Centre for Research on Violence against Women.

Deacon, Bob, Mita Castle-Kanerova, and Nick Manning, eds. 1992. *The New Eastern Europe: Social Policy Past, Present, and Future*. London: Sage.

Deanham, Dinna, and Joan Gillespie. 1999. *Two Steps Forward . . . One Step Back*. Health Canada: Family Violence Prevention Unit.

Deletant, Dennis. 1995. *Ceausescu and the Securitate: Coercion and Dissent in Romania, 1965–1989*. Armonk, N.Y.: M.E. Sharpe.

Diamond, Larry, ed. 1999. *Developing Democracy: Toward Consolidation*. Baltimore, Md.: Johns Hopkins University Press.

Dobash, Emerson, and Russell Dobash. 1992. *Women, Violence and Social Change*. New York: Routledge.

Einhorn, Barbara. 1993. *Cinderella Goes to Market: Citizenship, Gender, and Women's Movements in East Central Europe*. New York: Verso.

Elshtain, Jean. 1995. *Democracy on Trial*. New York: Basic Book.

European Bank for Reconstruction and Development (EBRD). 2005. *Transition Report 2005: Business in Transition*. London: EBRD.

European Roma Rights Center (ERRC). 2006. Coercive Sterilization of Romani Women in Central Europe: Slovakia, 15 August report submitted to US Congressional record, 2006. www.errc.org/db/03/81/m00000381.pdf (accessed November 7, 2009).

Evans, Alfred, Laura Henry, and Lisa McIntosh Sundstrom, eds. 2005. *Russian Civil Society: A Critical Assessment*. M.E. Sharpe.

Farmer, Paul. 2003. *Pathologies of Power: Health, Human Rights, and the New War on the Poor*. Berkeley: University of California.

Feinberg, Melissa. 2006. *Elusive Equality: Gender, Citizenship, and the Limits of Democracy in Czechoslovakia, 1918–1950*. Pittsburgh, Pa.: University of Pittsburgh Press.

Fodor, Éva. 2003. *Working Difference: Women's Working Lives in Hungary and Austria 1945–1995*. Durham, N.C.: Duke University.

Fodor, Éva, and Eszter Varsa. 2009. "At the Crossroads of 'East' and 'West': Gender Studies in Hungary." In *Global Gender Research: Transnational Perspectives*, ed. Christine Bose and Minjeong Kim. London: Routledge.

Foucault, Michel. 1977. *Discipline and Punish: the Birth of the Prison*, trans. Alan Sheridan. 1st American edition. New York: Pantheon Books.

Frey, Mária. 1999. "Nők a munkaerőpiacon" (Women in the labor force). In *Szerepváltozások: Jelentés a nők és férfiak helyzetéről* (1999 Report on the changing roles of women and men in Hungary), ed. Tiborné Pongrácz and István György Tóth, 84–96. Budapest, Hungary: TÁRKI.

Funk, Nanette. 2006. "Women's NGOs in Central and Eastern Europe and the Former Soviet Union: The Imperialist Criticism." In *Women and Citizenship in Central and Eastern Europe*, ed. Jasmina Lukić, Joanna Regulska, and Darja Zavirsek, 265–286. Burlington, Vt.: Ashgate Publishing.

————. 2007. "Fifteen Years of the East-West Women's Dialogue." In *Living Gender After Communism*, ed. Janet Elise Johnson and Jean Robinson, 203–226. Bloomington: Indiana University Press.

Funk, Nanette, and Magda Mueller, eds. 1993. *Gender Politics and Post-Communism: Reflections from Eastern Europe and the Former Soviet Union*. London and New York: Routledge.

Gal, Susan. 1997. "Feminism and Civil Society." In *Transitions, Recognition Struggles, and Social Movements: Contested Identities, Power, and Agency*, ed. Joan Scott, Cora Kaplan, and Debra Keats, 93–120. New York: Cambridge University Press.

Gal, Susan, and Gail Kligman, eds. 2000a. *Reproducing Gender: Politics, Publics and Everyday Life After Socialism*. Princeton, N.J.: Princeton University Press.

————. 2000b. *The Politics of Gender after Socialism: A Comparative-Historical Essay*. Princeton, N.J.: Princeton University Press.

Ganley, Anne, and Susan Schechter. 1995. *Domestic Violence: A National Curriculum for Family Preservation Practitioners*, 17–18. Family Violence Prevention Fund.

Gelles, Richard. 1997. *Intimate Violence in Families*. 3rd ed. Thousand Oaks, Calif.: Sage.

Gilligan, James. 1996. *Violence: Our Deadly Epidemic and Its Causes*. New York: G.P. Putnam.

Glass, Christy, and Éva Fodor. 2007. "From Public to Private Maternalism? Gender and Welfare in Poland and Hungary after 1989." *Social Politics: International Studies in Gender, State, and Society* 14(3): 323–350.

Goven, Joanna. 1993. "Gender Politics in Hungary: Autonomy and Antifeminism." In *Gender Politics and Post-communism: Reflections from Eastern Europe and the Former Soviet Union*, ed. Nanette Funk and Magda Mueller, 224–241. New York: Routledge.

Guichon, Audrey, Christien van den Anker, and Irina Novikova, eds. 2006. *Women's Social Rights and Entitlements*. New York: Palgrave Macmillan.

Hammarberg, Thomas. 2006. Protect the Right to Gay Pride. 27 July. *TOL: Transitions On-Line*. www.tol.cz/look/TOL/article.tpl?IdLanguage=1&IdPublication=4&NrIssue=177&NrSection=2&NrArticle=17409&search=search&SearchKeywords=gay+parade&SearchMode=on&SearchLevel=0 (accessed November 7, 2009).

Haney, Lynne. 2002. *Inventing the Needy: Gender and the Politics of Welfare in Hungary*. Berkeley: University of California Press.

Hanmer, Jalna, and Catherine Itzin, eds. 2000. *Home Truths about Domestic Violence: Feminist Influences on Policy and Practice.* New York: Routledge.

Haussman, Melissa, and Birgit Sauer, eds. 2007. *Gendering the State in the Age of Globalization: Women's Movements and State Feminism in Post-Industrial Democracies.* Lanham, Md.: Rowman and Littlefield.

Hausmann, Ricardo, Laura Tyson, and Saadia Zahidi. 2007. *Global Gender Gap Report.* Geneva: World Economic Forum.

Heise, Lori, Jacqueline Pitanguy, and Adrienne Germain. 1994. *Violence against Women: The Hidden Health Burden.* World Bank Discussion Paper No. 255. Washington, D.C.: World Bank.

Hellsten, Sirkku, Anne Holli, and Krassimira Daskalova, eds. 2006. *Women's Citizenship and Political Rights.* New York: Palgrave-Macmillan.

Hemment, Julie. 2007. *Empowering Women in Russia: Activism, Aid, and NGO.* Bloomington: Indiana University Press.

Henderson, Sarah. 2003. *Building Democracy in Contemporary Russia: Western Support for Grassroots Organizations.* Ithaca, N.Y.: Cornell University Press.

Holter, Øystein. 2005. "Social Theories for Researching Men and Masculinities: Direct Gender Hierarchy and Structural Inequality." *Handbook of Studies on Men and Masculinities,* ed. Robert Connell, Jeff Hearn, and Michael Kimmel, 15–34. Thousand Oaks: Sage.

Hughes, Donna, Lepa Mladjenovic, and Zorica Mrsevic. 1995. "Feminist Resistance in Serbia." *European Journal of Women's Studies.* 2(4): 509–532.

Inglehart, Ronald, and Pippa Norris. 2003. *Rising Tide: Gender Equality and Cultural Change Around the World.* Cambridge: Cambridge University Press.

Inglot, Tomasz. 2008. *Welfare States in East Central Europe, 1919–2004.* New York: Cambridge University Press.

Ishkanian, Armine. 2007. "En-Gendering Civil Society and Democracy Building: The Anti-Domestic Violence Campaign in Armenia." *Social Politics: International Studies in Gender, State & Society* 14(4): 488–525.

Jefferson, LeShawn. 2003. "Refusing to Go Away: Strategies of the Women's Rights Movement." *Human Rights Dialogue* 2(10) (Fall): 33–34.

Jhabvala, Farrokh. 1984. "The Practice of the Covenant's Human Rights Committee 1976–82: Review of State Party Reports." *Human Rights Quarterly* 6(1): 81–106.

Johnson, Janet. 2009. *Gender Violence in Russia: The Politics of Feminist Intervention.* Bloomington: Indiana University Press.

Johnson, Janet, and Jean Robinson, eds. 2007. *Living Gender after Communism.* Bloomington: Indiana University Press.

Kamp, Marianne. 2009. "Women's Studies and Gender Studies in Central Asia: Are We Talking to One Another." *Central Eurasian Studies Review* (CESR) 8(1): 4–14.

Kantola, Johanna. 2006a. *Feminists Theorize the State.* New York: Palgrave-Macmillan.

———. 2006b. "Transnational and National Gender Equality Politics: The European Union's Impact on Domestic Violence in Britain and Finland." In *Women's*

Citizenship and Political Rights, ed. Sirkku Hellsten, Anne Holli, and Krassimira Daskalova, 154–176. New York: Palgrave-Macmillan.

Kaufman, Daniel, Aart Kraay, and Massimo Mastruzzi. 2008. *Governance Matters VII: Aggregate and Individual Governance Indicators, 1996–2007*. World Bank Policy Research Working Paper No. 4654. http://papers.ssrn.com/sol3/papers .cfm?abstract_id=1148386 (accessed November 7, 2009).

Keck, Margaret, and Kathryn Sikkink. 1998. *Activists Beyond Borders: Transnational Activist Networks in International Politics*. Ithaca, N.Y.: Cornell University Press.

Khan, Mehr. 2000. "Editorial: Domestic Violence Against Women and Girls." *Innocenti Digest* 6: 11. www.unicef-icdc.org/publications/pdf/digest6e.pdf (accessed November 7, 2009).

Kitlinski, Tomek, and Pawel Leszkowicz. 2005. "God and Gay Rights in Poland." *Gay and Lesbian Review* (May/June): 26–28.

Konrád, György. 1984. *Anti-Politics*. New York: Holt.

Kulcsár, László. 2007. "Something Old, Something New: The Hungarian Marriage Patterns in Historical Perspective." *Journal of Family History* 32: 323–338.

Laurence, Louise, and Roberta Spalter-Roth. 1996. *Measuring the Costs of Domestic Violence Against Women*. Washington, D.C.: Center for Women Policy Studies.

Linz, Juan, and Alfred Stepan. 1996. *Problems of Democratic Transition and Consolidation: Southern Europe, South America, and Post-communist Europe*. Baltimore, Md.: Johns Hopkins University Press.

Lovenduski, Joni, ed. 2005. *State Feminism and Political Representation*. New York: Cambridge University Press.

Lyon, Tania Rands. 2007. "Housewife Fantasies, Family Realities in the New Russia." In *Living Gender after Communism*, ed. Janet Elise Johnson and Jean Robinson, 25–39. Bloomington: Indiana University Press.

MacKinnon, Catherine. 1989. *Toward a Feminist Theory of the State*. Cambridge, Mass.: Harvard University Press.

Mahoney, Martha. 1994. "Victimization of Oppression? Women's Lives, Violence, and Agency." In *The Public Nature of Private Violence*, ed. Martha Fineman and Roxanne Mykitiuk, 59–92. New York: Routledge.

Marcus, Isabel. 1994. "Reframing 'Domestic Violence': Terrorism in the Home." In *The Public Nature of Private Violence*, ed. Martha Fineman and Roxanne Mykitiuk, 11–35. New York: Routledge.

McCue, Margi. 2008. *Domestic Violence: A reference handbook*. Santa Barbara, Calif.: ABC-CLIO.

McFaul, Michael, and Kathryn Stoner-Weiss. 2008. "The Myth of the Authoritarian Model: How Putin's Crackdown Holds Russia Back." *Foreign Affairs* 87(1) (Jan.–Feb.). http://www.foreignaffairs.org/20080101faessay87105/michael-mcfaul-kathryn-stoner-weiss/the-myth-of-the-authoritarian-model.html (accessed November 7, 2009).

McMahon, Robert. 2005. "Peripheral Visions: Central and Eastern European States are Bringing New Energy to the Human Rights Debate at the UN." *Transitions*

On-Line (TOL). January 25. http://www.tol.cz/look/TOL/article.tpl?IdLanguage= 1&IdPublication=4&NrIssue=100&NrSection=3&NrArticle=13383&search= search&SearchKeywords=Peripheral+Visions&SearchMode=on&SearchLevel=0 (accessed November 7, 2009).

Merry, Sally Engle. 2006. *Human Rights and Gender Violence: Translating International Law into Local Justice.* Chicago: University of Chicago Press.

Miller, Susan. 2005. *Victims as Offenders: The Paradox of Women's Violence in Relationships.* New Brunswick, N.J.: Rutgers University Press.

Mills, Linda. 2003. *Insult to Injury: Rethinking our Responses to Intimate Abuse.* Princeton, N.J.: Princeton University Press.

Minnesota Advocates for Human Rights (MAHR). 2006. What is Domestic Violence? www.stopvaw.org/What_Is_Domestic_Violence2.html (accessed November 7, 2009).

———. 2008. Regional Conference on Domestic Violence Legal Reform. www. stopvaw.org/Regional_Conference_on_Domestic_Violence_Legal_Reform.html (accessed November 7, 2009).

Moghadam, Valentine, and Lucie Senftova. 2005. "Measuring Women's Empowerment: Participation and Rights in Civil, Political, Social, Economic, and Cultural Domains." *International Social Science Journal* 57(184): 389–412.

Morvai, Krisztina. 2003. *Terror a családban* (Terror in the family). Budapest: Kossuth Kiadó.

Munck, Geraldo, and Jay Verkuilen. 2002. "Conceptualizing and Measuring Democracy—Evaluating Alternative Indices." *Comparative Political Studies* 35(1) (February): 5–34.

Myers, Robert. 1993. "Rethinking Human Rights." *Society* 30(1): 58–63.

Nagy, Beáta. 2001. *Női menedzserek. (Female managers).* Budapest: Aula Kiadó.

Neményi, Mária, and Anna Kende. 1999. "Anyák és lányok" (Mothers and daughters). *Replika* 35: 117–141.

Ousmanova, Almira. 2003. "On the Ruins of Orthodox Marxism: Gender and Cultural Studies in Eastern Europe." *Studies in East European Thought* 55(1): 37–50.

Parrot, Andrea, and Nina Cummings. 2006. *Forsaken Females: The Global Brutalization of Women.* Lanham, Md.: Rowman and Littlefield.

Pateman, Carole. 1988. *The Sexual Contract.* Stanford, Calif.: Stanford University Press.

Penn, Michael, and Rahel Nardos. 2003. *Overcoming Violence against Women and Girls: The International Campaign to Eradicate a Worldwide Problem.* Lanham, Md.: Rowman and Littlefield.

Penn, Shena. 2005. *Solidarity's Secret: The Women who Defeated Communism in Poland.* Ann Arbor: University of Michigan Press.

Peterson, Spike, and Anne Runyan. 1999. *Global Gender Issues.* Boulder, Colo.: Westview Press.

Pető, Andrea, ed. 2006. *A társadalmi nemek oktatása Magyarországon* (Teaching Gender Studies in Hungary). Budapest: ICSSZEM.

Pető, Andrea, and Judit Szapor. 2007. "The State of Women's and Gender Studies in Eastern Europe—The Case of Hungary." In *Gendering Transnational Historiographies: Selection of Papers for the History Practice Section of the Journal of Women's History,* ed. Teresa Fernández-Acenes and Karen Hagemann, 19(1): 160–166.

Phillips, Anne. 1991. *Engendering Democracy.* University Park, Pa.: Penn State University Press.

Pizzey, Erin. 2005. Domestic Violence is not a Gender Issue. http://fathersforlife.org/pizzey/DV_is_not_a_gender_issue.htm (November 7, 2009).

———. 1982. *Prone to Violence.* London: Hamlyn. www.menweb.org/pronevio.htm (accessed November 9, 2009).

Renzetti, Claire, Jeffrey Edleson, and Raquel Kennedy Bergen, eds. 2001. *Sourcebook on Violence Against Women.* Thousand Oaks, Calif.: Sage.

Rose, Richard, William Mischler, and Christian Haepfer. 1998. *Democracy and its Alternatives: Understanding Post-communist Societies.* Baltimore, Md.: Johns Hopkins University Press.

Rule, Wilma, and Norma C. Noonan, eds. 1996. *Russian Women in Politics and Society.* Westport, Conn.: Greenwood Press.

Rupp, Leila. 1997. *Worlds of Women: The Making of an International Women's Movement.* Princeton, N.J.: Princeton University Press.

Sainsbury, Diane, ed. 1999. *Gender and Welfare State.* New York: Oxford University Press.

Sassoon, Anne, ed. 1987. *Women and the State: The Shifting Boundaries of Public and Private.* London: Hutchinson Education.

Schechter, Susan. 1982. *Women and Male Violence: The Visions and Struggles of the Battered Women's Movement.* Boston, Mass.: South End Press.

Sperling, Valerie. 1999. *Organizing Women in Contemporary Russia: Engendering Transition.* Cambridge: Cambridge University Press.

Stychin, Carl. 2003. *Governing Sexuality: The Changing Politics of Citizenship and Law Reform.* Oxford, UK: Hart.

Svejnar, Jan. 2002. "Transition Economies: Performance and Challenges." *Journal of Economic Perspectives* 16(1)(Winter): 3–28.

Takács, Judit, László Mocsonaki, and Tamás P. Tóth. 2007. *A leszbikus, meleg, biszexuális és transznemű (LMBT) emberek társadalmi kirekesztettsége Magyarországon* (Discrimination against GLBT in Hungary). Budapest: Labrisz Leszbikus Egyesület (Labrisz Lesbian Association), Háttér Társaság a Melegekért szervezet (Háttér Society for Gays and Lesbians in Hungary), MTA Szociológiai Kutatóintézet (Sociological Research Institute of the Hungarian Academy of Sciences), by request of the Szociális és Munkaügyi Minisztérium (Ministry of Social Affairs and Labor). http://www.labrisz.hu/node/296 (accessed November 7, 2009).

Thapar-Björkert, Suruchi, Karen Morgan, and Nira Yuval-Davis. 2006. "Framing Gendered Identities: Local Conflicts/Global Violence." *Women's Studies International Forum* 29(5): 433–440.

Thomas, Cheryl. 2008. "Legal Reform on Domestic Violence in Central and Eastern Europe and the Former Soviet Union." Expert Paper prepared for May 26–28, 2008 meeting of the United Nations Division for the Advancement of Women, Expert Group meeting on good practices in legislation on violence against women.

Tierney, Kathleen. 1982. "The Battered Women's Movement and the Creation of the Wife Beating Problem." *Social Problems* 29(3): 207–220.

Tifft, Larry. 1993. *Battering of Women: The Failure of Intervention and the Case for Prevention.* Boulder, Colo.: Westview Press.

Tímár, Judit. 2007. "Gender Studies in the Gender-Blind Post-Socialist Geographies of East Central Europe." *Belgeo* 3: 349–369.

Tóth, Olga. 1993. "No Envy, No Pity." In *Gender Politics and Post-communism: Reflections from Eastern Europe and the Former Soviet Union,* ed. Nanette Funk and Magda Mueller. New York: Routledge.

True, Jacqui. 2003. *Gender, Globalization, and Post-Socialism: The Czech Republic after Communism.* New York: Columbia University Press.

United Nations Development Program (UNDP). 1995. *Human Development Report: Gender and Human Development.* New York: UNDP. http://hdr.undp.org/en/reports/global/hdr1995 (accessed November 7, 2009).

———. 2000. *Human Development in South Asia: The Gender Question.* New York: UNDP. http://hdr.undp.org/xmlsearch/reportSearch?y=*&c=*&t=gender&k=&orderby=year/ (accessed November 7, 2009).

———. 2005. *Arab Human Development Report: Empowerment of Arab Women.* New York: UNDP. http://hdr.undp.org/en/reports/regionalreports/arabstates/name,3403,en.html (accessed November 7, 2009).

———. 2007. *Gender Attitudes in Azerbaijan: Trends and Challenges.* New York: UNDP. http://hdr.undp.org/en/reports/nationalreports/europethecis/azerbaijan/name,3325,en.html (November 7, 2009).

UNICEF. 1999. *Women in Transition: Regional Monitoring Report #6,* UNICEF: International Children Development Center. http://ideas.repec.org/p/ucf/remore/remore99-1.html (accessed November 7, 2009).

UNICEF. 2000. "Domestic Violence Against Women and Girls." *Innocenti Digest* 6.

Vanya. Magda. 2001. "Domáce Násilie v Predstavách Slovenských Žien" (What Slovak Women Perceive to Be Domestic Violence). *Sociológia* 33(3): 275–296.

Verrity, Patricia, ed. 2007. *Violence and Aggression around the Globe.* New York: Nova Science Publishers.

Walby, Sylvia. 2004a. "European Union and Gender Equality: Emergent Varieties of Gender Regime." *Social Politics* 11(1): 4–29.

———. 2004b. "The Cost of Domestic Violence." Research Summary. United Kingdom Home Office Research Study 217. The full report is available online at: www.womenandequalityunit.gov.uk (accessed November 7, 2009).

Warrior, Betsy. 1976. *Wife Beating*. Somerville, Mass.: New England Free Press.

Watson, Peggy. 1993. The Rise of Masculinism in Eastern Europe. *New Left Review* I/198 (March–April).

Weiner, Elaine. 2007. *Market Dreams: Gender, Class, and Capitalism in the Czech Republic*. Ann Arbor: University of Michigan Press.

Weldon, Laurel. 2002. *Protest, Policy, and the Problem of Violence Against Women: A Cross-national Comparison*. Pittsburgh, Pa.: University of Pittsburgh Press.

World Health Organization (WHO). 1996. *Violence Against Women* RH/WHD/97.8. WHO Consultation Geneva: WHO.

Yodanis, Carrie, Alberto Godenzi, and Elizabeth Stanko. 2000. "The Benefits of Studying Costs: A Review and Agenda for Studies on the Economic Costs of Violence Against Women." *Policy Studies* 21(3): 263–276. An earlier version is available online at: http://www.eurowrc.org/06.contributions/1.contrib_en/28 .contrib.en.htm (accessed November 8, 2009).

Zimmermann, Susan. 2007. "The Institutionalization of Women and Gender Studies in Higher Education in Central and Eastern Europe and the Former Soviet Union: Asymmetric Politics and the Regional-transnational Configuration." *East-Central Europe/L'Europe du Centre-Est: Eine wissenschaftliche Zeitschrift* 33: 1–2.

PART 1

The Development of Domestic Violence Policy in Postcommunist States

CHAPTER 2

Transnational Advocacy Campaigns and Domestic Violence Prevention in Ukraine

ALEXANDRA HRYCAK

Drawing on research conducted in Ukraine, this chapter examines why efforts to reform the state's handling of domestic violence have been successful in Ukraine. Ukraine stands out among post-Soviet states as a puzzling case: although the Ukrainian women's movement is highly factionalized and remains disconnected from transnational advocacy networks such as Women Against Violence Europe (WAVE), the country nonetheless exhibits what feminist scholars call "dual response," when the state both grants women access to policy formation and establishes policy decisions consistent with the agenda of the women's movement (McBride 2001).

Ukraine is one of the few post-Soviet states that is taking steps to establish a comprehensive system against domestic violence that conforms to the recommendations of the United Nations, the Council of Europe, and global campaigns.[1] While in most post-Soviet countries domestic violence remains unacknowledged by local law enforcement personnel, in Ukraine between 6,000 and 7,000 protective orders are issued annually to perpetrators of domestic violence (*nasyl'stvo v sim'i*) and more than 90,000 complaints of domestic violence are recorded and processed by local state authorities.[2] The state is committed by law to expanding services for women in crisis. As of 2008, state authorities operated eighteen crisis centers for women and twenty-four centers that provide psychological and medical assistance to women who are victims of violence. The number of shelters for victims of domestic abuse that municipalities fund has expanded from one to six. More are expected, as state programs and domestic violence legislation obligate every major city to establish at least one battered women's shelter.

These state efforts to address domestic violence were initiated by a lobbying campaign carried out by Ukrainian women's groups. Their activities swiftly resulted in legislative success. In 2001, Ukraine became the first postcommunist state to pass legislation that defined domestic violence as a specific offense, introduced temporary restraining orders, and mandated state support for nationwide networks of crisis centers, shelters, and other services to assist victims of abuse. Since then, domestic monitors of women's rights, parliamentary committees, and state agencies concerned with women's rights have applied considerable pressure upon the state to act on its commitments to fight against domestic violence (Ukrainian Helsinki Union 2007). The government has responded by issuing directives clarifying the procedures that should be used when law enforcement personnel respond to complaints of domestic violence. Parliamentary hearings assessing gender-based violence, held in 2006, have further expanded the influence of domestic women's organizations. Indeed, in 2008 their recommendations led lawmakers to pass amendments that bring domestic violence legislation into closer conformity with international treaties and global policy recommendations.[3]

Why have efforts to politicize women's rights abuses succeeded in pressuring the Ukrainian state to address the issue of domestic violence, when similar campaigns have largely failed in other post-Soviet states? Most post-Soviet states expressed commitments to Western-style democracy after the Soviet Union collapsed. Rather than following through, however, Ukraine and nearly all other post-Soviet states developed into what Levitsky and Way (2002) call "competitive authoritarian" regimes.[4] Elections were regularly held, but incumbents routinely denied their opponents adequate media coverage, harassed opposition candidates and their supporters, and in some cases manipulated electoral results, while spying on, threatening, arresting, and in some cases assaulting or murdering journalists and other government critics (Way 2005a; Way 2005b). International pressure on post-Soviet states to conform to Western norms met with "show organizations" and "show campaigns." Behind these institutional facades, however, powerholders continued to operate more or less as they had in the Soviet era (Allina-Pisano 2006).

In this chapter, I clarify how, in the context of deepening polarization between authoritarian regimes and postcommunist domestic elites who seek membership in the European Union, "Potemkin villages" can become the basis for shelters, crisis centers, and other institutions necessary to address domestic violence. I first sketch out my theoretical argument about the domestic determinants of successful campaigns against violence in relationship to a chief alternative explanation (Keck and Sikkink 1998). Next, I provide an overview of the structure of domestic political alliances and the issues women's organizations raised prior to the arrival of Western projects. Then I explore how three sets of domestic actors worked together on reforms inspired by the 1995 Beijing Platform for Action: non-feminist political insiders who were aligned with the country's ruling elite, women reformers who emerged from the country's national independence movement, and a handful of feminists who worked with Western foundations and aid projects.

Theorizing Campaigns against Abuses of Human Rights

The primary theory for understanding how human rights abuses are placed on the agendas of authoritarian states is offered by Keck and Sikkink (1998). In *Activists beyond Borders: Advocacy Networks in International Politics,* Keck and Sikkink examine how domestic groups employ transnational advocacy networks to exert international pressure upon governments that violate human rights. Using historical and contemporary case studies, they argue that a "boomerang pattern" helps to explain the impact of domestic campaigns to stem violations of human rights in authoritarian countries: they posit that domestic activists are most successful when they are able to forge "strong and dense linkages" to Western sympathizers, who then use their own state to place pressure externally on the target state that committed human rights violations.[5]

Keck and Sikkink contend that domestic political structures, alliances, and political culture cannot account for the variable impact of challenges against authoritarian states. Indeed, they argue that forging ties to transnational allies helps domestic groups succeed not only because it unleashes external pressure, but also because it facilitates the reframing of domestic concerns around global norms and international treaties. Specifically, they posit that domestic challengers tend to have the most impact upon the behavior of authoritarian states when they learn from Western allies how to reframe their aims around defense of rights and protection of the vulnerable from bodily harm.

Keck and Sikkink offer valuable insights into anti-violence policy-making in Ukraine and other post-Soviet countries. The case I analyze below illustrates that international contact does indeed facilitate a discursive shift and leads domestic policymakers to adopt a new understanding of women's issues that is grounded in principles of women's empowerment and protection from bodily harm. But, as I show below, the differing impact of transnational advocacy across post-Soviet cases cannot be explained using Keck and Sikkink's boomerang model. Domestic women's groups in Ukraine did not use Western sympathizers to launch a boomerang. Instead, Western sympathizers and states exerted influence mainly by providing the funds that facilitated attendance at international women's conferences. This exposed domestic actors to a new gender-based paradigm for framing women's rights and drew domestic interest to establishing local crisis centers and shelters.

What, then, explains the surprising success of women's activism in Ukraine? Below I argue that, just as has been found to be the case in Russia and other post-Soviet cases, the outcomes of the policy campaign that domestic activists launched in Ukraine cannot be explained by the density and strength of transnational ties or by international pressure. Turning Keck and Sikkink's argument on its head, the key explanation I offer for the differing impact of transnational advocacy campaigns across post-Soviet cases lies in the structure of domestic alliances and opportunities.

Success in policymaking requires domestic alliances to develop between non-feminist political insiders and the independent women's organizations that work closely with Western foundations and aid projects (Johnson and Brunell 2006, Richter 2002, Sperling 1999). However, as I demonstrate below, close relationships to powerholders are not enough to persuade authoritarian regimes to address abuses of human rights. Thus far, domestic violence legislation has passed only in those countries that experienced cycles of repression that resulted in "electoral revolutions."[6] In Ukraine and such countries as Georgia and Kyrgyzstan, sharp cleavages emerged between regimes that were increasingly authoritarian and a growing set of political challengers that sought closer ties with Western countries. In order to advance their bids for candidacy in the European Union, domestic political challengers have passed a number of laws and policies to secure equal opportunities for men and women in the workplace, protect women from gender discrimination, and promote equal involvement of men and women in the family. These steps have been taken because legislators and state officials know that the European Union requires prospective members to harmonize their legislation with the laws of the European Union, including gender equity directives. The gradual victory of Western-leaning political forces in a post-Soviet country consequently creates greater openings for advocates of policies to protect women's rights.

The Emergence of Rival Women's Organizations in Ukraine

Like other post-Soviet states, Ukraine initially ignored the issue of domestic violence. As a member of the United Nations since 1945, Ukraine is a party to international human rights and women's rights treaties that were intended to oblige signatories to protect women from violence, including domestic violence.[7] Nevertheless, violations of women's rights went unrecognized and unacknowledged as a political issue during the Soviet era, when powerholders paid lip service to human rights norms (Rudneva 2000). After Ukraine became independent in 1991, the state declared an intention to democratize. But at first it took no steps toward implementing international treaties and the state's human rights commitments were not widely discussed or publicized (interview, Humanitarian Initiative Feminist Alliance, Kharkiv, May 30, 2001). Consequently, women's rights remained a non-issue for women's organizations. Indeed, most representatives of women's organizations remained unaware that women as a group possessed rights (interview, former executive director, Kharkiv City Women's Fund, Kharkiv, May 22, 2001).

The women's movement that emerged in Ukraine after independence was divided between three opposed networks of women: "ex-Partocrats"—former Communist Party officials whom the Soviet establishment chose as its representatives on women's issues; their critics, activists in the Ukrainian independence movement whom the Soviet establishment labeled "nationalists" (in some cases quite inaccurately); and a small cohort of local scholars who were experimenting with feminist theory.[8]

After independence, these three networks rarely cooperated. The women's movement remained disunified and weak. The structure of domestic and transnational alliances reinforced cleavages within the movement. Each of these three networks remained linked more closely with its principal external allies and power bases than with other women activists. The ex-Partocrats allied with the former members of the former Communist Party nomenklatura who retained control over the government and the state after Ukraine's independence. The so-called nationalist wing of the women's movement remained affiliated with national democratic parties that occupied a small but growing niche in Ukraine's parliament (D'Anieri 2007; D'Anieri et al. 1999). Feminists forged linkages to Western foundations that, at least initially, operated mainly from offices based in Moscow and Western capitals.

Ideological conflicts were a further factor that prevented the women's movement from forming a coherent agenda. Each network understood women's issues and interests very differently (Bohachevsky-Chomiak 1997, 1998; Pavlychko 1992). The ex-Partocrats held on to a quasi-Soviet frame that generally understood balancing the demands of employment and childcare to be women's chief concern. Consequently, they focused mainly on encouraging the formation of small businesses that women could operate out of their home. The main issues national democratic women's groups raised in Ukraine were violence in the military, the impact of environmental problems on children's health, and the need to revive Ukrainian national identity and defend the country's independence.[9] These commitments led nationalist women's groups to be concerned mainly with policies to improve children's welfare and upbringing. Meanwhile, feminist scholars largely concerned themselves, at least initially, with exploring Western philosophy and literary criticism. They mainly sought to reform the curriculum of universities and challenge the treatment of gender issues within their fields of expertise. Most had little interest in addressing policy or politics. As a consequence of their diverse affiliations as well as their divergent agendas, during the initial years after Ukraine's independence, defense of "women's rights" was not a priority for the country's three main women's networks and remained a non-issue for powerholders.

Beijing and Beyond

Keck and Sikkink consider international conferences to play a vital role in establishing linkages between transnational advocacy networks and domestic women's groups in authoritarian states. Indeed, international events were responsible for exposing Ukrainian women advocates to new understandings of women's issues that allowed them to develop a common agenda they used to make new demands upon the state. But they did not become occasions for forging the kind of dense, strong transnational ties that Keck and Sikkink associated with successful transnational campaigns.

The Fourth World Conference on Women in 1995 was the primary catalyst in Ukraine that led local women's groups to pressure the state to address new issues like domestic violence and, more broadly, gender equality (Zhurzhenko 2004). In preparation for Beijing, the Ukrainian parliament and state officials held a parliamentary hearing in 1995 to examine Ukraine's progress toward meetings its obligations to implement the UN Declaration on the Elimination of All Forms of Discrimination against Women.[10] Male state officials treated the hearing dismissively, perhaps because they associated women's rights with the official campaigns of the Soviet era. However, for the heads of women's groups that were invited to participate, the hearing initiated a process of agenda-setting that would eventually lead to the passage of legislation to address domestic violence and, later, gender equality. Furthermore, the hearing helped initiate a realignment of domestic alliances among a new faction of women activists who embraced global women's rights discourse.

The hearing was the first event that raised awareness of Ukraine's treaty obligations regarding women's rights not only within the state, but also among women's organizations (Rudneva 2000). The hearing was also important because it revealed to those present the extent of domestic violence and, more broadly, gender inequality. The Soviet state denied that systematic violations of women's rights were possible under Communist Party rule. As a consequence, violence against women and gender inequality could not be discussed in public and had remained invisible in Soviet Ukraine. Furthermore, the hearing provided an opportunity for women representing the state and a broad range of women's organizations to participate in identifying concerns they had about the status of women. Finally, upon its conclusion, the hearing resulted in an important policy step when state officials issued a call for the state to address the specific problems women victims of violence face, first by establishing a network of shelters and crisis centers, and second by undertaking legal and institutional reforms in order to protect women from violence (*Laboratoriia zakonodavchykh initsiiatyv* 2004). These were the discursive and procedural commitments that, in time, would create leverage for actual policy shift.

Participation in the World Conference on Women not only spurred discursive realignment;[11] it also facilitated the consolidation of a new local advocacy network of reformers who urged the state to take action to protect women's rights. This new group consisted of several influential leaders who previously belonged to the opposing networks of ex-Partocrats, nationalists, and feminists (interview, former deputy director, Ministry of Family and Youth, Kyiv, July 27, 2001).[12] After Beijing, representatives from these three networks built a new alliance of reformers who together set to work on the women's rights issues raised by the Beijing Platform for Action (interview, president and founder, Ukrainian Women's Union, Kyiv, June 8, 2001).

It was also in response to Beijing that domestic violence first emerged as a hot-button issue within the women's movement as well as among state officials concerned with women's issues. The increasing importance of domestic violence to the women's movement in Ukraine became evident in May 1998 at the First Congress of Women in Ukraine, an event the state sponsored in order to receive input from women's organizations.[13] A distinct subunit of the Congress, the Section on Violence Against

Women, examined the problem of domestic violence within a broader analysis of violence against women. Arguing that violence is "a widespread phenomenon in our society that remains invisible because women are ashamed to talk about its occurrence," the section issued a call for the public and the government to take action against increases in the prevalence of violence in Ukraine. They argued that it was particularly urgent for the government to respond to a very dangerous new form of violence against women, human trafficking of Ukrainian women into forced prostitution abroad.[14] Building upon this agenda, the Congress as a whole issued a broader set of resolutions, including a statement calling on the government and the public to develop concrete solutions to fight violence against women and human trafficking. Among the steps the Congress recommended were, first, for Parliament to amend legislation and the Criminal Code of Ukraine to define three new categories of violence against women: domestic violence, forced prostitution, and trafficking in women. Second, echoing the recommendations of the parliamentary hearings and the Beijing Call for Action, they demanded that the state create "service networks, shelters, and centers of rehabilitation for women who have suffered from violence, including within the family" (*Rezoliutsii Vseukrains'koho Konhresu Zhinok* 1998). They also urged the government to support the crisis centers for women that had already come into existence in Ukraine through support from Western benefactors.

The State and Domestic Violence

In response to the Beijing Platform for Action as well as the encouragement of the women's movement, the issue of domestic violence first rose to the top of the agenda for several women who were ex-Partocrats. Before Ukraine became independent, these women had been employed in the Soviet era within Communist Party structures that dealt with women, families, and children.[15] After Ukraine became independent and the Communist Party system ceased to exist, these women lost their high-ranking positions (interview, School of Equal Opportunities; former deputy director, Ministry of Family and Youth, Kyiv, July 27, 2001).[16] But they retained their informal ties to President Leonid Kuchma and the other former members of the Soviet nomenklatura who took control of the government and state institutions after independence. Before they attended the Beijing World Conference, they pressured powerholders to take steps to honor the country's commitments to international treaties on women's rights by creating new state administrative units devoted to "women's problems" (*zhinochi problemy;* interview, National Council of Women, Kyiv, July 12, 2001; interview, president and founder, Ukrainian Women's Union, Kyiv, June 8, 2001). After attending Beijing, these ex-Party functionaries reframed their demand. Arguing that administrative structures focusing on *gender equality* existed throughout the world, they insisted that Ukraine also needed to adopt such an approach.[17]

Prior to Beijing, there were no state agencies in Ukraine that were responsible for implementing and monitoring Ukraine's international treaty commitments regarding women's rights and gender equality (Mel'nyk 1999; Rudneva 2000). In response to Beijing, various local women's organizations placed pressure on the state to create such mechanisms. But it was ex-Party officials who engineered the formation of new state agencies and were hired to work in them, and who thereby helped to establish new foundations for domestic violence prevention advocacy networks and crisis centers. In response to pressure by these ex-Partocrats, the government created a series of new state administrative units.[18] At the local level, a Department of Assistance to Women and Insecure Strata of the Population was created within the municipal administration of the city of Kyiv (interview, National Council of Women, Kyiv, July 12, 2001; interview, Center for Work with Women, Kyiv, July 4, 2001). In 1995, at the national level, the Committee on Women, Maternity and Childhood under the Authority of the President was formed to address the status of women, mothers, and children (interview, League of Women Voters 50/50, Kyiv, May 3, 2001). The following year this structure was expanded to create the Ministry of Family and Youth, whose purpose was implementation of policy on the family, women, youth, and children (Kulachek 2005; Mel'nyk 1999; Rudneva 2000).

The Ministry of Family and Youth developed a comprehensive state program that was based on the Beijing Platform and included projects for drafting legislation on domestic violence prevention and other measures to reform the state's handling of domestic violence.[19] The ministry program called for the development of "centers for work with women" throughout the country that would operate crisis centers and shelters for women who are victims of violence (*Derzhavnyi komitet molodizhnoi polityky* 2001; Kolos and Danyleiko 1999). State officials stressed that the main way that they planned to work on domestic violence would be through the establishment of a set of new domestic networks that would bring together state officials and (nongovernmental) women's organizations. These networks would be built by "encouraging close cooperation between state structures and organs of local administration with women's groups through coordinating councils on women's affairs, joint projects, and support for initiatives of civic organizations in the regions" (Kolos and Danyleiko 1999: 85). In short, the state agency promised not only to create crisis centers and shelters for victims of violence, it also pledged to create access points for domestic women's NGOs.

Keck and Sikkink suggest that activist groups that are autonomous of the state are the type of domestic actor most capable of bridging effectively between domestic and transnational frames. In the case of transnational women's rights activism, for instance, they consider autonomous women's groups that work closely with Western and international NGOs, but remain unconnected to the state, to be best suited to achieving success at using international pressure to initiate such normative changes in domestic policy regarding women. According to their argument, one might perhaps expect autonomous feminist groups to be best suited for working with the ministry to pressure it to address global women's rights issues. However, the ministry was placed under the management of Valentina Dovzhenko, an ex-Partocrat who disliked feminism and eschewed contact with feminist groups and their Western sponsors. Dovzhenko was a top Communist Party official in charge of women's affairs during the final years of Soviet rule. After Ukraine's independence, she became the deputy director of the Union of Women of Ukraine, a women's organization that purported to be an NGO but in reality was a quasi-governmental entity. More importantly, she also befriended Ludmila Kuchma, the wife of Leonid Kuchma, who was prime minister after Ukraine's independence and from 1994 until 2004 served two terms as president. From the start, as minister, Dovzhenko made clear her rejection of feminism (Zherebkina 2003). Instead of working with autonomous feminist groups, she indicated a clear preference for women who belonged to the ex-Partocrat network, although she eventually learned to tolerate the activities of a handful of women activists who split off from nationalist networks to work on domestic women's rights advocacy.

The Influence of Changing Priorities within the Domestic Political Context

The Ukrainian state's reaction to local advocacy around the Beijing Platform for Action led to the establishment of a new agenda. Several significant achievements resulted from the efforts of local advocates who accepted this new agenda: they built new state agencies and pledged to develop new approaches to address domestic violence and other violations of women's rights. Henceforth, state policy toward women was to be based on international human rights treaties the government had signed. In contrast to the Soviet era, state policy also provided for a significant role to be played by civic groups in shaping legislation and policy, assisting with monitoring and enforcement activities, and participating in the implementation of policies. Such partnerships between state officials and local women's NGOs led to the passage of the 2001 Law on Domestic Violence and several other laws and state programs that made international treaties the basis for Ukrainian policy on issues of violence.

However, the creation of these state administrative structures also had negative repercussions for the women's movement.[20] First and foremost, new state agencies were established during a period of rising authoritarianism and were used to expand the power of the former Soviet nomenklatura. Once women's issues became the subject of official state plans and reports, civic organizations concerned with women's rights and gender equality became considerably less active (interview, former deputy director, Ministry of Family and Youth, Kyiv, July 27, 2001). Instead of empowering women's groups, state policymakers in large part displaced them, preventing them from continuing their work on policies to support women's rights. Thus the women's movement lost the leverage it had developed over the state, and as a consequence it was initially not able to monitor or participate in the implementation of the state programs that resulted from collaboration with women's NGOs (Skoryk 2006).

Paradoxically, the ex-Partocrats who helped initiate reforms in the state's handling of domestic violence also suffered once powerholders shifted their priorities away from state women's rights projects. This is clearly illustrated by the subsequent fate of the ministry that the ex-Partocrats helped found after Beijing. In 1999, before its projects had been implemented fully, the ministry that was founded to implement international women's rights treaties began an organizational odyssey that led it to be bundled with a series of other state units that were concerned not only with children and youth but also sport and tourism. First, the ministry was dissolved and the administrative status of state policy on family and youth issues was downgraded. Initially, the new state structure that resulted from this reorganization was the State Committee on Family and Youth. In 2000 this committee was downgraded still further. It was renamed the State Department of Family and Youth and placed under the jurisdiction of a broader agency, the

State Committee of Ukraine on Youth Policy, Sport and Tourism. But in 2001, that state committee was dissolved and the State Committee on Family and Youth was reestablished (Skoryk 2006). In February 2004, after much lobbying, the State Committee on Family and Youth was upgraded, its ministerial status was restored, and the Ministry of Family, Children, and Youth was founded. In 2005, however, this unit merged with the Ministry of Youth and Sport, forming the Ministry of Family, Youth, and Sport.

Rather than employing state agencies dealing with women's issues to carry out state policy, however, powerholders began to use state agencies to commit fraud during elections and pressure women's organizations to participate in activities supporting the regime. Thus, for example, in 2002, Valentina Dovzhenko, who was then head of the State Committee of Family and Youth, illegally organized a new party, the Women for the Future Party, mainly by employing her staff and allied women's groups to distribute food and other gifts to needy citizens (Kuzio 2003) and hold grandiose rock concerts (Diuk and Gongadze 2002). Similarly in 2004, in the months prior to the Orange Revolution, the Ministry of Family, Children, and Youth placed illegal pressure on women's organizations to campaign on behalf of candidates closely connected to President Leonid Kuchma and his associates.[21]

As these examples illustrate, after Beijing, state agencies came into being ostensibly to show the state's commitment toward advancing women's equality. But, as is clear from their subsequent organizational fate, for the most part, they did not at first fulfill their initial mandate to empower women. Indeed, state mechanisms for implementing international women's rights treaties remained Potemkin villages, institutional facades. They concerned themselves with an amorphous set of assistance categories that typically included children and mothers, and they participated illegally in activities intended to solidify the regime's power. But they did relatively little toward their ostensible mission of advancing gender equality (Skoryk 2006).

State projects to protect women's rights also remained largely unimplemented because they were considered a low priority in subsequent state budgets.[22] For instance, in 2001, the state granted only enough funding to carry out a tenth of the activities called for by the National Plan of Action for the Advancement of Women's Status and Gender Equality for 2001–2005 (Kissyeliova 2004). From January 1, 2001, to January 1, 2005, the main state program on women received 47 percent of the funds it had been promised for implementing the National Plan of Action. Ukraine's official report on the first ten years of implementation of the Beijing Action Plan cited, as the two main obstacles to achieving gender equality in Ukraine, frequent reorganization of administrative structures responsible for implementing state policy on women and a lack of state funding (Government of Ukraine 2004). Similarly, within the current Ministry of Family, Youth, and Sport, women's issues are handled by of a unit that is small, has low status, is devoted mainly to the family, and is a low budget priority.[23] Overall, the budget of this ministry is devoted mainly to organized sports, in particular, participation in the Olympics and other international athletic competitions.[24] Hence, somewhat in keeping with tendencies inherited from the Soviet era, women's rights programs developed by state agencies in Ukraine remained, at first, mere facades behind which occurred systematic violations of state laws and basic human rights principles—for instance, when state officials placed pressure on women's organizations to campaign for candidates favored by powerholders and coerced state employees into organizing affiliated semi-official women's political groups to alter the results of elections (Diuk and Gongadze 2002).

"Transnational Partnerships" between Ukrainian State Agencies, the United Nations, and Local NGOs

After an initially progressive response to Beijing, the Ukrainian state failed to follow through on its promises. Yet several important *legislative* advances were nonetheless made during the period of rising authoritarianism and state closure that began in the late 1990s. Who picked up the baton, in the absence of the state officials who suddenly found themselves under-resourced and preoccupied by projects that took them away from women's rights? Keck and Sikkink note that foundations have been crucial funders of new women's NGOs that work on transnational campaigns to combat violence against women. Western benefactors did indeed fund crisis centers, shelters, and other domestic efforts to carry out the domestic advocacy networks agenda to fight domestic violence. However, projects sponsored by Western aid did not forge the kinds of dense, strong, and horizontal ties Keck and Sikkink consider to be crucial for the success of transnational advocacy campaigns. Indeed, many domestic women's groups considered Western grants to be a divisive force that further divided the women's movement by increasing competition among activists with similar commitments (Hrycak 2007a). Furthermore, the autonomous feminist groups that received the most Western support were, for the most part, uninterested in policy formation. In addition, Dovzhenko and her staff for the most part refused to work with them.

Who, then, helped to coordinate domestic efforts to draft legislation and pressure the state to respond to the demands of this nascent domestic women's rights advocacy network? Of central importance to further solidifying the domestic partnerships that were behind the domestic violence campaign was the Ukrainian staff of the United Nations Development Program (Mel'nyk 1999; Rudneva 2000). In 1997, as part of a broader UN initiative to provide assistance to postcommunist countries, the Gender in Development unit of the United Nations Development Program started a Project for Equal Opportunities in Ukraine. A unit referred to as the Gender Bureau directs the activities of this project, which aim to integrate the principles of gender parity into all spheres of life in Ukrainian society (Smolyar 1999, 2001; United Nations Development Program 2003). The Bureau was assigned the role of working directly with Ukrainian state agencies and government officials on implementing programs concerned with protecting women's rights. Following a seminar on domestic violence that the Gender Bureau organized in 1999 in cooperation with state officials concerned with family and youth, a working group of local NGOs was set up to develop the draft law on the prevention of violence against women. The Gender Bureau also worked on coordinating the development and implementation of other new policies and programs focused on the prevention of domestic violence. These local partners also monitored the progress and implementation of government programs for the advancement of women that emerge from Ukraine's obligations regarding international treaties, in particular the Convention on the Elimination of All Forms of Discrimination Against Women (CEDAW). The Gender Bureau also organized seminars and workshops on the elimination of violence against women and on achieving relationships based on partnership within the family. The new networks the Gender Bureau forged around the issue of domestic violence prevention were vital to the success of the campaign to establish new laws.

While the Gender Bureau and its allies drew upon global policy ideas, in practice they did not engage in applying boomerang-style pressure from transnational advocacy networks. Instead, their transnational activities mainly took the form of appealing for funding from abroad, and using resources from abroad to further work on the campaign against violence. Serendipitously, in 1997, the United States government decided to make prevention of human trafficking a priority in post-Soviet foreign aid (Johnson 2005). This led to a considerable increase in funding for activities aimed at preventing domestic violence in Ukraine and other post-Soviet countries, as the US government viewed violence as a root cause of trafficking, and other Western funders later followed suit.[25] The United States government, which soon became the single largest source of funding for women's organizations (Sydorenko 2001), thus enabled the women's movement to continue to work on its new agenda, in the absence of funding and support from the state.

Funding from US sources encouraged the formation and professionalization of dozens of new local women's organizations that modeled themselves on American women's NGOs. It also shifted their priorities to domestic violence prevention because this was a main target of US funding (interview, Women's Information Consultative Center, Kyiv, March 22, 2001). However, Conra Keck and Sikkink, the transnational relationships US projects facilitated, were mainly domestic. The Americans who coordinated US projects were hired to manage particular projects. They left Ukraine after relatively brief stints.

One key outcome of the UNDP's Gender Bureau's efforts to work with Ukrainian state agencies and policy actors was the Law on the Prevention of Domestic Violence. This law, drafted by local women's advocates who worked with state officials and the Gender Bureau, was introduced to Parliament in 1999, and passed in 2001. It became the first piece of legislation in post-Soviet countries to address domestic violence using a comprehensive approach based on Western models of domestic violence prevention. The Law on the Prevention of Domestic Violence calls for the state to provide funding to crisis centers, shelters, hot lines, and other facilities that provide medical and social rehabilitation to victims of domestic violence. It specifies conditions under which temporary restraining orders are to be issued. The law also requires perpetrators of domestic violence to attend training sessions on patterns of nonviolent behavior. The implementation of this law and its provisions were made a priority in a broad range of state programs and plans (Government of Ukraine 2004).

State officials initiated the development of the law against domestic violence. But it was the UNDP's Gender Bureau that coordinated the work that went into drafting and promoting the law, facilitated cooperation among the domestic women's and youth NGOs that worked on its content, lobbied legislators to vote for it, and then persuaded two prominent members of parliament, one of whom was deputy speaker, to act as its sponsors in parliament (interview, Kharkiv Women's Studies Center, Kharkiv, May 30, 2001). The main local NGO that coordinated the drafting of this law was the feminist *Kharkovskii tsentr zhenskikh issledovanii*—the Kharkiv Women's Studies Center.[26] This organization was also one of the main organizers of the lobbying campaign that built support for the passage of the 2001 Law on Domestic Violence by mobilizing the support of dozens of youth groups. Furthermore, efforts to develop and pass this law received the strong support of local and national state officials concerned with women, and also a variety of women's organizations that worked closely with Western programs (interview, Kharkiv Women's Studies Center, Kharkiv, May 30, 2001; former deputy director, Ministry of Family and Youth, Kyiv, July 27, 2001). The Kharkiv Women's Studies Center was one of the few feminist groups resembling the kind of domestic actor Keck and Sikkink consider crucial to successful transnational campaigns that participated in the domestic advocacy process.

The Slow Pace of Domestic Violence Prevention Reforms

The development of state programs and the passage of specific legislation to protect women against domestic violence were important steps forward. A North American observer might imagine (as I did myself when I read the 2001 Law on Domestic Violence) that victims of domestic violence in Ukraine have made significant strides in defending their rights. If you log on to state social service agency websites in Ukraine, you can find not only instructions explaining how to bring domestic violence complaints, but also a list of state services open to those who have suffered domestic abuse.[27] Yet, if you investigate further, what you will find is that state agency websites direct victims of domestic violence to avail themselves of crisis centers, shelters, hot lines, and other services that are mandated by state law and state programs but that are only now, many years later, coming into existence in most municipalities in Ukraine. As I will elaborate further below, Western donors have funded numerous projects to provide such services, but most of these activities ceased once the grants upon which they were based were over. In short, activities to address domestic violence in Ukraine were oriented in large part toward creating and maintaining institutional facades.

Somewhat similarly, one also might imagine that the domestic violence advocates who worked on the development and implementation of the Law on the Prevention of Domestic Violence and related state programs would have continued to make great strides in influencing the state and monitoring its approach to domestic violence. However, this was not the case initially. The feminists who worked on the Law on Domestic Violence were shocked to find that when it was still in draft form, the legislators who sponsored it had added a clause on "behaving like a victim" (*viktimnist'*). The activists suspected that this clause would create opportunities for law enforcement personnel to accuse the victim of having incited violence, shifting blame away from the perpetrator.[28] Turning a deaf ear to such concerns, the lawmakers who sponsored the law refused to meet with representatives of women's NGOs who sought to persuade them to leave this clause out of the final draft of the law (interview, Kharkiv Women's Studies Center, Kharkiv, May 30, 2001; personal communication, Nicole Edgar Morford, October 16, 2006). Women's advocates continued criticizing the state for failing to implement the law and related policy reforms and state programs that had been developed to eliminate violence. Their criticism was made clear at parliamentary hearings held in November 2006 on eliminating gender-based violence and achieving gender equality. Legislators and advocates who participated in the hearings all agreed, first, that this clause on victim behavior needed to be removed, and second, that the law remained largely unimplemented and the state needed to take action to respond to its mandates.[29] Parliament did not pass these amendments until 2008, however, more than seven years after such criticism was first leveled.

Just as the passage of the Law on Domestic Violence in 2001 at first did little to alter the situation for most victims of domestic violence, the pace of change has been slow since the Orange Revolution. Indeed, the frequent political realignments within the government that followed the Orange Revolution have further complicated the work of domestic violence prevention advocacy. Women's organizations have had to search for donors willing to support projects to train law enforcement personnel to apply the law as it was intended as well as to provide ongoing support for crisis centers and shelters that the Ukrainian state was obligated and committed to fund. Police officers have continued to resist enforcing this law both because they strongly believe that it concerns "family matters" in which the state should not intrude, and also because many law enforcement personnel "are more sympathetic to the male perpetrator than to the female victim" (Fedkovych 2005).

However, with the election of a government that seeks entry into the European Union, the state has slowly started to implement domestic violence legislation and initiate broader efforts to promote women's rights. Dovzhenko and the ex-Partocrats have been dismissed. In their place, the government has appointed women who support global women's rights campaigns and are working more actively with transnational as well as local women's groups. The outcome has been positive. The state has considerably expanded the network of shelters and crisis centers for battered women and their families. The state also started to seek out and address recommendations and demands women's groups have made. Although the state has more actively committed itself to implementing women's rights laws, the struggle over enforcement continues. According to a report monitoring the first three years of implementation of Ukraine's Law on Domestic Violence, there is a growing demand for the services and support that the legislation offers (Romanova et al. 2008). But so far, the state has done little to help *most* women suffering violence. According to monitoring carried out by a government think tank, at most 10 percent of women who experience domestic violence currently use the services that the state and NGOs provide to women in crisis. Indeed, independent monitoring of the state's handling of domestic violence indicates that there continue to be "cases where police officers have taken bribes from the perpetrator, closed the case" and failed to "provide any help or protection to the victim" (Sedova 2001). Furthermore, although the Law on Domestic Violence includes provisions for temporary protective orders, perpetrators who have committed violence are currently forbidden to repeat violent acts, but they are not evicted from the home (Fedkovych 2006). As a consequence, victims of severe abuse are usually the ones that must leave the home.

Sustaining Local Crisis Centers and Shelters: The Kyiv Center for Work with Women

Transnational advocacy around the issue of violence against women considers legal and procedural changes to be important steps to take. However, in order to adequately protect victims, states need to provide psychosocial support and other services to survivors of domestic violence (Webhofer 2008). The difficulties associated with implementing new policies to prevent domestic violence are clearly evident in local efforts to sustain crisis centers and shelters that international donors discontinue funding. In response to various state programs, including the Law on Domestic Violence, the Ukrainian state is obliged to create local centers throughout Ukraine that provide support, shelter, and other services to victims of violence.[30] Numerous projects to establish crisis center and shelters have been funded by Western grants. In 1999, Winrock International, a USAID (United States Agency for

International Development) contractor, received several million dollars in funding from the US government for two main projects that focused on domestic violence prevention, Community Responses to Domestic Violence and Trafficking and the Anti-Trafficking Program.[31] These two projects established a nationwide network of crisis centers, each operated by a designated local women's NGO. Local advocates hoped that the passage of the 2001 Law on Domestic Violence would help sustain these new projects by obliging the local government to provide them with funding and support after donor funding was discontinued (interview, Kharkiv Women's Studies Center, Kharkiv, May 30, 2001). However, after the conclusion of the USAID grants that funded these projects, most of these crisis centers were closed and their local NGO sponsor sharply curtailed its programs and services (interview, West Ukrainian Center Women's Perspectives, Lviv, July 7, 2005).

It is instructive to examine the case of one such Western-inspired crisis center for assisting domestic violence victims that later succeeded in securing municipal funding. The *Tsentr roboty z zhinkamy*, or Kyiv Center for Work with Women, was founded in late 1998. This project resulted from the cooperation of the mayor of Kyiv, a group of municipal officials (ex-Partocrats who were concerned with women's issues), foreign donors, and representatives of domestic feminist women's groups that worked closely with Western donors (interview, Center for Work With Women, Kyiv, July 4, 2001; interview, National Council of Women, Kyiv, July 12, 2001). Initially, the women's center received widespread media coverage. Its opening was attended by Nina Karpochova, Human Rights Ombudsman for the Ukrainian parliament and a close ally of President Kuchma, as well as by representatives from USAID and US foreign aid projects concerned with preventing domestic violence (NIS-US Women's Consortium, Fourth Quarterly Progress Report, Year 2: West NIS October 1997–December 1997). The Center, as well as the partnership upon which it was based, were held up in various contexts as a model of new state responsiveness to transnational and international advocacy in support of women's rights. For instance, even though it was funded by the US government, the center was mentioned prominently in the official state report on progress toward implementation of the National Plan on Improving Women's Status for 1997–2000 (*Derzhavnyi komitet molodizhnoi polityky* 2001).

The Center for Work with Women, which also operates a municipal shelter for battered woman, illustrates some of the complexities associated with transplanting foreign nonprofit organizations to the Ukrainian context. The Center initially offered several kinds of resources and services to survivors of violence. These included legal and psychological services, a program to provide computer training, a library providing information on women's activism, and women's leadership trainings. Each service was provided by a distinct local feminist women's NGO through a grant from USAID (NIS-US Women's Consortium, Fourth Quarterly Progress Report, Year 2: West NIS October 1997–December 1997). As an indicator of the Center's success, it was duly noted in a report to USAID that during August 1997, the first month of operation in its permanent location, hundred women used the services of the Women's Center for activities that included five trainings, three round-tables, and two meetings of women's organizations.

However, after one and a half years, the USAID grant that funded these activities ended (interview, Center for Work With Women, Kyiv, July 4, 2001). All but one of the NGOs that worked with the Center for Work with Women stopped participating. According to Cara Galbraith, the coordinator who was employed by Winrock International (the USAID contractor that carried out this project), the NGOs left the Center both to work on other projects and because of "the growing influence and pressure of the city administration over their activities" (Galbraith 2000). City funding and occasional Western grants allow the Center to remain in operation on a somewhat reduced scale even after the donors who originally took an interest in financing this project moved on. According to its own records, the Kyiv City Centre for Work with Women has provided free legal, psychological, information, and medical and social support to roughly 39,000 women and 3,500 men since its opening, and the Center's hotline handled 446 calls in 2007.

The Center continues to offer computer courses and counseling. It is also used as a meeting space for certain women's organizations (interview, president and founder, Ukrainian Women's Union, Kyiv, June 8, 2001; interview, president, *Soiuz Ukrainok*, Kyiv, March 2001). Other women's advocates have told the center's staff that it is impossible to tell whether the center is a state agency or a nonstate organization, presumably because it is run like an NGO and is modeled on the respectful, client-centered style of work that is the norm within women's organizations (interview, Center for Work With Women, Kyiv, July 4, 2001). Indeed, I found it remarkably friendly toward strangers, particularly when compared to the atmosphere of indifference that is the rule in state-run organizations in Ukraine.

The shelter affiliated with the Kyiv Center for Work with Women is no longer the only one in the country, but it is the most well established and provides an illustration of the influence and limitations of local efforts to respond to the Beijing Platform.[32] The Center's representatives claim that it is easy for a battered woman to access their shelter. For example, when interviewed by a reporter for the *Ukrainian Weekly* in 2001, the Center's staff indicated that

> all a battered woman needs to gain entry to the shelter for herself and her children is an internal passport and a medical card, both of which every Ukrainian adult is required to have. The woman then is able to receive psychological and legal counseling at the associated Center for Work with Women. She is supplied with food and clothing as well, and has access to a doctor's services twenty-four hours a day. (Sedova 2001:3)

However, the Center's representatives admitted that women who are victims of violence were initially reluctant to enter the shelter, and, after two full years in operation, only150 women and children had spent time in residence (Sedova 2001). Quite often, women who are experiencing domestic violence seek help from professionals in the crisis center or through the crisis hotline that is affiliated with the Center for Work with Women. According to the Center's staff, about 40 percent of the women who have contacted the Center's crisis hotline were experiencing domestic violence. Yet the staff of the facility reported that only a small portion of the women who contact them accept an offer to live at the shelter's sites.[33] Indeed, according to the deputy coordinator of the Women's Center, roughly one out of three women who initially decide to stay at the shelter change their mind at the last minute when they see the shelter's representative waiting for them. They turn around and leave without entering.

The number of clients using the shelter has increased slightly since its first years. Annually, around sixty women and twenty-five children who are suffering from domestic violence take refuge in the Kyiv municipal shelter (Ukrainian Helsinki Union 2007). This is only a small handful of the large number of women who are experiencing domestic violence in Kyiv, a city of around three million people. There are several reasons given by the staff for this reluctance on the part of victims of domestic violence to use the shelter. Larysa Varenyk, the deputy coordinator of the Women's Center, stressed that not only are women in Ukraine ashamed to discuss domestic abuse, but they are also not accustomed to talking to strangers about problems of a "deeply personal nature" (interview, Larysa Varenyk, Center for Work With Women, Kyiv, July 4, 2001). Second, Varenyk points out that shelters (*prytulky*) are themselves a new phenomenon that is associated mainly with homeless youth (indeed, she has considered renaming her shelter to make it sound more like a medical clinic or other local institution to which women in Ukraine are already accustomed to turn for help regarding their health). In addition, she believes that a third key reason the shelter may not be an attractive option is that it is designed as a temporary refuge. According to Varenyk, "Women can stay at the shelter for a maximum of thirty days. During this time, they are encouraged to come to a decision about whether or not to divorce or leave the abuser. But divorce proceedings here last a long time and so does the legal process of settling issues with residence."

Representatives of local women's NGOs, some of whom worked on the original NGO partnership, disagree with this explanation. Arguing that the shelter is underutilized because it places too many bureaucratic obstacles in the way of women suffering from abuse, some of these advocates are raising funds to open a nongovernmental shelter and crisis center (interview, Ukrainian Women's Fund, Kyiv, July 14, 2005). They note, for instance, that before being admitted to the Kyiv municipal shelter, a battered woman must present several documents, including a negative HIV test, a gynecological exam guaranteeing that she is free of sexually transmitted diseases, and a Kyiv mandatory residential registration permit or *propyska* (Iakshchovy Zaznaly 2010).[34] In the Soviet Union, access to public services such as housing, pensions, medical care, and schooling were all based on the *propyska* system, which was used by the state to control the population. Many long-term residents of Kyiv never received a residential registration permit and remained second-class citizens after independence, unable, for instance, to access medical services. Indeed, in 2001, the Constitutional Court ruled that the *propyska* registration system was unconstitutional, and a new "informational" residential registration mechanism was planned, but it still has not been fully implemented (US Department of State 2005, US Department of State 2006). By limiting services to women who have a Kyiv residential registration permit and who have documentation that they are free of STDs, the Kyiv shelter does indeed make it less likely that women who are in crisis will be able to qualify for its services.

Among the various organizations in Ukraine that provide services and shelter for survivors of violence, the Kyiv Women's Center is the most well established. It has operated continuously for a decade. Unlike other crisis center and shelter projects, it has managed to secure local funding after the conclusion of its Western seed grant. However, the staff continues to struggle to sustain the crisis center and shelter. In 2008, the crisis center nearly closed when Kyiv authorities refused to renew the center's lease and ordered the staff to vacate the premises in order to return the property to the city for sale or rent to another organization. The center's staff was for the time being able to stave off eviction by reaching out to local women's organizations for support and mobilizing a successful protest campaign. Yet its future remains uncertain. City authorities may attempt another eviction: similar eviction orders have been issued to other cultural and social service organizations in downtown Kyiv. Real estate prices and rents have skyrocketed in the downtown in recent years, placing in jeopardy municipal shelters and crisis centers that are located there.

The previous case study demonstrates that campaigns on domestic violence in postcommunist countries are in no simple way driven by a boomerang pattern (Keck and Sikkink 1998). Activists did not start to raise issues of violence at the local level and then turn to international allies to create leverage in their fight to compel their home state to respond to local advocacy on behalf of domestic violence victims. First, attendance at international conferences and exposure to foreign funding initiated local interest in the issue of domestic violence. Next, Western grants allowed local advocates to experiment with new techniques and models that were developed abroad within very different contexts. These activities at first achieved remarkable and swift success, which is particularly surprising given that, at the start of the advocacy cycle, there were no local advocates and the issue of domestic violence was unrecognized. Several key changes in policy occurred that followed the strategic objectives established by the Beijing Action Platform for eliminating violence against women, including the passage of the Law on Domestic Violence in 2001 and the development of several state projects that place priority on developing integrated measures to prevent and eliminate violence against women. However, these changes remain largely unimplemented. Yet, even though local advocates experienced a decline in influence after the law's passage and though, even today, they struggle to sustain valuable local projects, most Western donors declared success and moved on once they completed their local domestic violence prevention projects (Hrycak 2007c).

I argue here that the shifting structure of alliances and political opportunities helps explain Ukraine's surprising responsiveness to the demands of women reformers. The dynamics of the Ukrainian campaign against domestic violence bear little resemblance to the ideal model of transnational advocacy campaigns examined by Keck and Sikkink. The coalition of women who initiated the process of state-building and lobbying that brought about a gradual convergence upon global campaigns to stop violence against women were closely tied to government actors. Those who have recently renewed efforts to implement Ukraine's policies are closely tied to the "nationalist" political elites that emerged from Ukraine's independence movement and later became the basis for the Orange Revolution. What is more, key women officials for the most part considered autonomous domestic feminist groups, along with their transnational benefactors, to be naïve upstarts who were ignorant of the rules of the game. These elites kept both at arm's length, preferring to work with local women whose primary alliances were domestic.

Future work on other cases should further expand upon the political opportunity model offered here. The Ukrainian case suggests that within postcommunist countries, the success of efforts to adapt policy solutions inspired by international activism and supported by transnational feminist advocacy, remains largely dependent upon the agendas of local state actors. Local activists achieved results when domestic political elites exhibited openness to Western geopolitical alignment, but they experienced retrenchment when powerholders began to resort to increasingly authoritarian methods. International organizations such as the United Nations, and Western donors, particularly the United States (which has been by the far the largest donor in Ukraine but has largely discontinued funding women's initiatives there), also play an important role as gatekeepers to resources that allow activists to experiment with new approaches. But the international actors are unable to determine the subsequent course of the policies they provide. Finally, in Ukraine, political elites act as the primary gatekeepers within the women's movement and local government. They are able to obstruct or facilitate further work on domestic violence prevention. The response of these powerholders to incentives created abroad by such bodies as the European Union is crucial to the shape that advocacy will likely take in postcommunist countries, particularly after Western donors have turned their attention to their next set of projects.

NOTES

This chapter is based on nine months of ethnographic fieldwork and interviews conducted in Kyiv, Lviv, and Kharkiv in 2001, 2005, and 2008 with financial support from the International Research and Exchanges Board and Reed College. I thank

Katalin Fábián and reviewers for thoughtful comments that strengthened my argument. I am also grateful to the many people who generously helped me conduct my research. In particular, I wish to thank the women's rights advocates in Ukraine who agreed to be interviewed for this study.

1. Only the Kyrgyz Republic (in 2003), Georgia (in 2006), and Moldova (in 2007) have passed similar legislation.

2. For statistics on the incidence of domestic violence cases for the years 2005 through 2008, see Ukrainian Ministry of Family, Youth, and Sport, "Nasyl'stvo ruinuie sim'i, robyt' ditei syrotamy" [Violence ruins families and makes children orphans], press release, October 18, 2008, www.kmu.gov.ua/sport/control/uk/publish/article;jsessionid=4F0456D1DD1C8D5DC8E73FC5652989DB?art_id=98153 &cat_id=98931 (accessed January 22, 2010).

3. As I discuss further below, a controversial clause was deleted from domestic violence legislation that could lead women to be blamed for provoking violence, and thus permit perpetrators to avoid prosecution. Another clause was added that obligates the state to develop rehabilitative programs for perpetrators of domestic violence.

4. The main exceptions are the Baltic countries.

5. The boomerang pattern posits that, when domestic actors are blocked from domestic political processes and cannot communicate grievances to their own state (State A), they turn to international allies for support, activating a transnational advocacy network. The network, comprising primarily NGOs, then attempts to pressure either its own state (State B) or third party intergovernmental organizations (e.g., the United Nations) into coercing State A to address the demands of the domestic group.

6. Three of the post-Soviet countries that have passed laws against domestic violence experienced "colored revolutions" (Georgia in 2003, Ukraine in 2004, Kyrgyzstan in 2005). Meanwhile Moldova, the one exception, witnessed similar protests against alleged electoral fraud in 2009 in what some have called the Twitter Revolution.

7. These documents include the International Covenant on Civil and Political Rights (signed in 1968, ratified in 1973) and the Convention on the Elimination of All Forms of Discrimination Against Women (signed in 1980, ratified in 1981). The Government of Ukraine also signed and then ratified the Declaration on the Elimination of Violence Against Women (1993) and the Platform for Action of the UN Fourth World Conference on Women (1995).

8. I take the categories "Partocrat" and "nationalist" from the women's advocates I interviewed. For a discussion of the label "Partocrats," see Maria Orlyk, "Problemy dostupu zhinok do politychnoi vlady, intehratsii ikh v inshi vladni struktury," in *Zhinka v Ukraini*, ed. A. I. Komarova (Kyiv: Natsional'na Rada Zhinok Ukrainy, 2001), 115. For a discussion of "nationalist" women's activism and its relationship to Ukrainian feminism, see Tatiana Zhurzhenko, *Ukrainian Feminism(s): Between Nationalist Myth and Anti-Nationalist Critique* (Vienna: International World Bank Working Paper, 2001).

9. The Soiuz Ukrainok's initial activities focused on Ukrainian cultural revival, not on women's rights (author's interview, Common Action, Lviv, June 15, 2001; author's interview, Common Action, Lviv, June 18, 2001; author's interview, president, Soiuz Ukrainok, Kyiv, March 2001).

10. For the text of this hearing, see: www.rada.gov.ua/zakon/sk12/BUL23/ 120795_97.htm (accessed October 30, 2005).

11. Many of the women I interviewed agreed that Beijing contributed to a paradigm shift in how domestic advocates understood women's issues (interview, League of Women Voters 50/50, Kyiv, May 3, 2001; interview, National Council of Women, Kyiv, July 12, 2001; interview, president and founder, Ukrainian Women's Union, Kyiv, June 8, 2001; interview, Women's Information Consultative Center, Kyiv, March 22, 2001; interview, Ukrainian Women's Studies Center, Kyiv, June 27, 2005; interview, Kharkiv City Women's Fund, "Kharkiv Oblast Diia," Kharkiv, May 29, 2001).

12. These new coalitions were at first formal, and they did not bring together organizations but rather tended to link sets of individuals who typically were dissatisfied with the traditionalism of the main women's organizations and who formed their own new groups oriented toward Western women's rights agendas. For further analysis of such advocates, see Hrycak, "Seeing Orange: Women's Activism and Ukraine's Orange Revolution," *Women's Studies Quarterly* 35(3/4): 208–225.

13. For the full text of the Congress' resolutions, see Valentyna Dovzhenko, ed., *Zhinka na porozi XXI stolittia: Stanovyshche, problemy, shliakhy sotsial'noho rozvytku: Zbirnyk materialiv Vseukrains'koho Konhresu Zhinok, Kyiv, 21–23 travnia 1998 roku* (Kyiv: Ukrains'kyi instytut sotsial'nykh doslidzhen', 1998). For a statement by two Ukrainian state officials on their overall response to the Congress and corresponding state projects to eliminate violence, see L. Ie. Kolos and O. M. Danyleiko, "Uchast' derzhavnoho komitetu Ukrainy u sprauakh pravakh sim'i ta molodi v realizatsii polozhen' kompleksnoi prohramy po zapobihanniu nasyl'stvu v sim'i," in *Problemy nasyl'stva v sim'i: Pravovi ta sotsial'ni aspekty,* ed. Oleksandra Rudneva (Kharkiv: Pravo, 1999).

14. For the full text of the recommendations of the Section on Violence Against Women, see Kateryna Levchenko, "Informatsiia pro robotu Sektsii 6 'Nasyl'stvo shchodo zhinok,'" in *Zhinka na porozi XXI stolittia,* ed. Valentyna Dovzhenko.

15. In the Soviet era, women Communist Party members occupied positions at every level within state and party structures, but most were concentrated at the bottom of the system. A handful of women belonged to the nomenklatura and were typically in charge of the education of children and youth. Two kinds of positions were unofficially set aside for such women. One was the so-called third secretary within a regional party bureau. The other was the deputy director of a municipality. Both of these positions were concerned mainly with schools and youth organizations. They tended to be staffed by women who were educators and had risen through the ranks of the school system and the Communist Party. See Hrycak, "Gender and the Orange Revolution," *Journal of Communist Studies and Transition Politics* 23(1) (2007): 152–179.

16. Some of these women believe that they lost their positions because they were perceived to be "mere Partocrats" who possessed insufficient national consciousness. See Orlyk, "Problemy dostupu zhinok do politychnoi vlady intehratsii ikh v inshi vladni struktury." In *Zhinka v Ukraini,* ed. A. I. Komarova, 114–117. Kyiv: Natsional'na Rada Zhinok Ukrainy," 115.

17. In response to Beijing and other events that introduced them to international women's rights activism, several of these activists embraced new Western models of

women's rights advocacy that focused on achieving gender equality (interview, former deputy director, Ministry of Family and Youth, Kyiv, July 27, 2001).

18. For further details on state agencies concerned with women, see Olha Kulachek, *Rol' zhinky v derzhavnomu upravlinni: Stari obrazy, novi obrii* (Kyiv: Vydavnytstvo Solomiii Pavlychko "Osnovy," 2005), 239.

19. In most respects, state officials who worked with the Ministry of Family and Youth echoed the demands that activists had made in response to Beijing. For instance, during the congress, they too described Ukraine as being in the grip of a "silent crisis" of domestic violence. Furthermore, in keeping with the Beijing agenda, the ministry's officials promised state funding to create a "set of networks to link international organizations, foreign foundations, state officials, and local women's NGOs that are involved in advocacy against domestic violence, the reform of laws, and the provision of social services to victims." See L. Ie. Kolos and O. M. Danyleiko, "Uchast' derzhavnoho komitetu Ukrainy u spravakh sim'i ta molodi v realizatsii polozhen' kompleksnoi prohramy po zapobihanniu nasyl'stvu v sim'i." In *Problemy nasyl'stva v sim'i: Pravovi ta sotsial'ni aspekty,* ed. Oleksandra Rudneva, 83–86. Kharkiv: Pravo. In addition, they also promised to direct funding to civic organizations that were involved in domestic violence prevention (an unusual promise for the state to make at that time, since state officials frequently viewed civic organizations as adversaries, not partners). Furthermore, arguing that organizations in outlying regions needed to be a top funding priority because they could not otherwise participate in the programs of international organizations and foreign foundations or attend seminars and conferences abroad, the ministry's officials singled out organizations that worked outside the capital as particularly in need of the state's aid. They also unveiled a plan to start offering seminars on domestic violence for state officials employed in agencies concerned with women's issues. The goal of these seminars was to help state agencies' officials to get started on two specific projects aimed at speeding the institutionalization of new approaches to domestic violence that would later become the focus of state programs to protect women's rights. For the full text of the state's policy initiative on the prevention of violence, see Kolos and Danyleiko, "Uchast' derzhavnoho komitetu Ukrainy u spravakh sim'i ta molodi v realizatsii polozhen' kompleksnoi prohramy po zapobihanniu nasyl'stvu v sim'i."

20. For a discussion of increases in authoritarian tendencies within the Ukrainian state at this time, see Taras Kuzio, "Regime Type and Politics in Ukraine under Kuchma," *Communist and Postcommunist Studies* 38(2) (2005): 167–190.

21. Indeed, Dovzhenko's illegal participation in campaigning for Yanukovych reached the level of farce when the Orange Revolution broke out, and she ordered the protesters to go home so they wouldn't catch cold. For a discussion of the employment of state administrative resources during and after the Orange Revolution, see Hrycak, "Gender and the Orange Revolution."

22. The staff of these new agencies felt that women's issues were treated as a low priority by the government, particularly once the original Ministry of Family and Youth was dissolved (interview, National Council of Women, Kyiv, July 12, 2001).

23. Once again, with this reorganization, the status of family and youth issues was downgraded. Policy on the family was split apart from policy on youth. Each of these policy domains was placed under the jurisdiction of a distinct department of the

Ministry of Family, Youth, and Sport. The unit within this ministry that was given jurisdiction over family policy was called the Department of Family, Gender Policy, and Demographic Development. One of this department's four subunits is devoted to gender equality (the other three focus on recreation, population growth, and cooperation with civic associations).

24. According to the analysis of Ukrainian political scientist Olha Kulachek, it is "unfortunate that in February 2005 the issue of sport was added to the Ministry of Family, Children, and Youth, as sport has always been given priority over the social welfare of children and youth." See Kulachek, *Rol' zhinky v derzhavnomu upravlinni*, 240. For more detailed information on the Ministry of Family, Youth, and Sport, see www.kmu.gov.ua/sport/ (accessed January 22, 2010).

25. Western projects to halt illegal immigration tied together the issues of domestic violence and trafficking in women because they assumed that victims of domestic abuse could not remain in the country and fell into the hands of cross-border human trafficking rings. For a further discussion of how USAID applied this theory in Ukraine, see Kateryna Pishchikova, "Lost in Translation: USAID Assistance to Democracy Building in Postcommunist Ukraine" (Ph.D. dissertation, University of Amsterdam, 2006).

26. For further details on their activities and aims, see www.kcws.kharkov.ua/ (accessed November 18, 2009).

27. See, for instance, instructions provided by the Ministry of Family, Youth, and Sport, under the title "Iakshcho by zaznaly nasyl'stva v sim'i" [If you have experienced domestic violence]: www.kmu.gov.ua/sport/control/uk/publish/article?art_id=73689&cat_id=73687 (accessed September 11, 2009).

28. For a summary of local women's advocates' criticisms of the draft law, see Suzanna Banwell et al., *Domestic Violence in Ukraine* (Minneapolis, Minnesota: Minnesota Advocates for Human Rights, 2000). A further critique of the existing law is summarized in Ruth Rosenberg, *Domestic Violence in Europe and Eurasia* (Aguirre Division of JBS International, for the Social Transition Team, Office of Democracy, Governance and Social Transition of the United States Agency for International Development, USAID, 2006); available at http://www.usaid.gov/locations/europe_eurasia/dem_gov/docs/domestic_violence_study_final.pdf (accessed May 21, 2007).

29. On the 2004 parliamentary hearings, see Verkhovna Rada Ukrainy, *Rekomendatsii parlaments'kykh slukhan' "Stanovyshche zhinok"* (2004); available at http://gska2.rada.gov.ua:7777/pls/zweb/webproc34?id=&pf3511=18506&pf35401=5 4521 (accessed June 8, 2006). On the 2006 parliamentary hearings, see Informatsiine upravlinnia Verkhovnoi Rady Ukrainy, *Parlaments'ki slukhannia 21 lystopada 2006 roku na temu: "'1. Suchasnyi stan ta aktual'ni zavdannia u sferi poperedzhennia hendernoho nasyl'stva. 2. Rivni prava ta rivni mozhlyvosti v Ukraini: Realii ta perspektyvy* (Verkhovna Rada Ukrainy, 2006); available at http://portal.rada.gov.ua/control/uk/publish/article/news_left?art_id=80452&cat_id=46666 (accessed December 13, 2006).

30. For further details on the steps mandated by state law regarding domestic violence prevention, see V. Bondarovs'ka et al., *Zapobihannia nasyl'stvu v sim'i* (Kyiv: Shkola rivnykh mozhlyvostei, 2004).

31. In 1999 the US government awarded the project "Community Responses to Domestic Violence and Trafficking" the first of three grants that totaled over US$3 million. The project trained several local NGOs in Ukraine (as well as Moldova,

Armenia, and Uzbekistan) to conduct lobbying, advocacy, and public awareness campaigns. Women's NGOs formed local advisory boards composed of community representatives to strengthen the coordination of efforts for prevention of domestic violence and trafficking. These women's NGOs also conducted advocacy initiatives to increase the level of awareness of policymakers in local and national government about domestic violence and trafficking in humans, working through public hearings in city councils and national parliaments on human rights, gender-based violence, and government response to crimes against women. In addition, USAID awarded Winrock $4.3 million over 1998–2004 to operate a project called the Anti-Trafficking Program. This project created trafficking prevention centers in seven Ukrainian cities (L'viv, Dnipropetrovs'k, and Donetsk in 1998; Zhytomyr, Kherson, Chernivtsy, and Rivne in 2001). These centers provided services to assist women who were experiencing domestic violence and lacked economic alternatives, and who were therefore viewed as vulnerable to trafficking. Each of these centers was based in a partnership between Winrock and a local NGO. See Winrock International (www.winrock.org/).

32. There are six shelters for battered women that are funded by the state and another two are run by NGOs. See Halyna Fedkovych, *Violence against Women: Does the Government Care in Ukraine?* (2006); available at www.stopvaw.org/ (accessed May 20, 2007).

33. In 2000, Minnesota Advocates for Human Rights conducted an assessment of responses by the state and NGOs to domestic violence. They interviewed a representative of the Center for Work with Women, who told them there were only two women staying in the shelter, which had a capacity of fifteen beds at that time. The assessment noted that while many local activists argued that there was a need for shelters and other services to assist victims, the shelter in Kyiv "appeared underutilized" because the general public was not aware of its existence. See Banwell et al., *Domestic Violence in Ukraine*, 26. Another battered women's shelter I visited in 2001 also appeared to be underutilized.

34. For the rules and requirements of the Kyiv municipal shelter for women victims of domestic violence, see Bondarovs'ka et al., *Zapobihannia nasyl'stvu v sim'i*, 104–105.

WORKS CITED

Allina-Pisano, Jessica. 2006. "Klychkov i Pustota: Post-Soviet Bureaucrats and the Production of Institutional Facades." Paper presented at the Second Annual Danyliw Research Seminar, Chair of Ukrainian Studies, University of Ottawa, October 12–14.

Banwell, Suzanna, Erin Barclay, Elisabeth Duban, and Robin Philips. 2000. *Domestic Violence in Ukraine.* Minneapolis: Minnesota Advocates for Human Rights.

Bohachevsky-Chomiak, Martha. 1997. "Women's Organizations in Independent Ukraine: Prospects of Power." Eastern European Perceptions and Perspectives: The J. B. Rudnyckyj Distinguished Lecture Series, ed. Tatiana Nazarenko and Orest Cap. University of Manitoba, Winnipeg, Manitoba.

———. 1998. "Women in Ukraine: The Political Potential of Community Organizations." *Harvard Ukrainian Studies* 22: 29–47.

Bondarovs'ka, V., V. Bryzhyk, L. Kolos, O. Liaskovs'ka, O. Musienko, Iu. Onyshko, V. Petrovs'kyi, and K. Tarannikova. 2004. *Zapobihannia nasyl'stvu v sim'i*. Kyiv: Shkola rivnykh mozhlyvostei.

D'Anieri, Paul J. 2007. *Understanding Ukrainian Politics: Power, Politics, and Institutional Design*. Armonk, N.Y.: M.E. Sharpe.

D'Anieri, Paul J., Robert S. Kravchuk, and Taras Kuzio. 1999. *Politics and Society in Ukraine*. Boulder, Colo.: Westview Press.

Derzhavnyi komitet molodizhnoi polityky, sportu i turyzmu Ukrainy. 2001. "Natsional'nyi plan dii shchodo polipshennia stanovyshcha zhinok ta pidvyshchennia ikh rol' u suspil'stvi za 1997–2000 roky. Analitychnyi zvit." In *Zhinka v Ukraini*, ed. A. I. Komarova, 173–234. Kyiv: Natsional'na Rada zhinok Ukrainy, 2001.

Diuk, Nadia, and Myroslava Gongadze. 2002. "Post-Election Blues in Ukraine." *Journal of Democracy* 13(4): 157–167.

Dovzhenko, Valentyna, ed. 1998. *Zhinka na porozi XXI stolittia: Stanovyshche, problemy, shliakhy sotsial'noho rozvytku: Zbirnyk materialiv Vseukrains'koho Konhresu Zhinok, Kyiv, 21–23 travnia 1998 roku*. Kyiv: Ukrains'kyi instytut sotsial'nykh doslidzhen.'

Fedkovych, Halyna. 2005. "Domestic Violence Prevention Law—3 Years of Implementation in Ukraine." Minnesota Advocates for Human Rights. www.stopvaw.org/4Apr20055.html (accessed September 11, 2009).

———. 2006. Violence against Women: Does the Government Care in Ukraine? www.stopvaw.org/uploads/UKRAINE_VAW_FACT_SHEET_2006.pdf (accessed November 8, 2009).

Galbraith, Cara K. 2000. "The Ukrainian Women's Movement: Contextualizing Feminism." Master's thesis, University of Oregon.

Government of Ukraine. 2004. "Ukraine: Beijing +10 National Report on Implementation of the Beijing Platform for Action." Progress Report Prepared by the Government of Ukraine for the United Nations Beijing +10 Review in March 2005 http://www.unece.org/gender/documents/question/UKRAINE-English.pdf (accessed September 8, 2009).

Hrycak, Alexandra. 2007a. "From Global to Local Feminisms: Transnationalism, Foreign Aid and the Women's Movement in Ukraine." *Advances in Gender Research* 11: 75–94.

———. 2007b. "Gender and the Orange Revolution." *Journal of Communist Studies and Transition Politics* 23(1): 152–179.

———. 2007c. "Seeing Orange: Women's Activism and Ukraine's Orange Revolution." *Women's Studies Quarterly* 35(3/4): 208–225.

"Iakshcho vy zaznaly nasyl'stvo vy simi" (What to do if you have experienced domestic violence). 2010. Ministry of Family, Youth, and Sport, http://www.kmu.gov.ua/sport/control/uk/publish/article?art_id=73689&cat_id=73687 (accessed January 22, 2010).

Informatsiine upravlinnia Verkhovnoi Rady Ukrainy. 2006. Parlaments'ki slukhannia 21 lystopada 2006 roku na temu: 1. Suchasnyi stan ta aktual'ni zavdannia u sferi poperedzhennia hendernoho nasyl'stva. 2. Rivni prava ta rivni mozhlyvosti v Ukraini: Realii ta perspektyvy. Verkhovna Rada Ukrainy, http://portal.rada.gov.ua/control/uk/publish/article/news_left?art_id=80452&cat_id=46666 (accessed November 8, 2009).

Johnson, Janet Elise. 2005. "Public-Private Permutations: Domestic Violence Crisis Centers in Barnaul." In *Russian Civil Society: A Critical Assessment*, ed. Alfred B. Evans, Laura A. Henry, and Lisa McIntosh Sundstrom, 266–283. Armonk, N.Y.: M.E. Sharpe.

Johnson, Janet Elise, and Laura Brunell. 2006. "The Emergence of Contrasting Domestic Violence Regimes in Postcommunist Europe." *Policy and Politics* 34(4): 578–598.

Keck, Margaret E., and Kathryn Sikkink. 1998. *Activists Beyond Borders: Advocacy Networks in International Politics*. Ithaca, N.Y.: Cornell University Press.

Kissyeliova, Oksana. 2004. "Background Paper I: Women's Economic Empowerment and Access to Financing and Assets in CIS Countries: Issues, Good Practices and Policy Options." United Nations Economic Council for Europe, Regional Symposium on Mainstreaming Gender into Economic Policies, Geneva, 28–30 January 2004. www.unece.org/oes/gender/gensymp-doc.htm (accessed November 8, 2009).

Kolos, L. Ie., and O. M. Danyleiko. 1999. "Uchast' derzhavnoho komitetu Ukrainy u spravakh sim'i ta molodi v realizatsii polozhen' kompleksnoi prohramy po zapobihanniu nasyl'stvu v sim'i." In *Problemy nasyl'stva v sim'i: Pravovi ta sotsial'ni aspekty*, ed. Oleksandra Rudneva, 83–86. Kharkiv: Pravo.

Kulachek, Olha. 2005. *Rol' zhinky v derzhavnomu upravlinni: Stari obrazy, novi obrii*. Kyiv: Vydavnytstvo Solomiii Pavlychko "Osnovy."

Kuzio, Taras. 2005. "Regime Type and Politics in Ukraine under Kuchma." *Communist and Postcommunist Studies* 38(2): 167–190.

———. 2003. "The 2002 Parliamentary Elections in Ukraine: Democratization or Authoritarianism?" *Journal of Communist Studies and Transition Politics* 19(2): 24–54.

Laboratoriia zakonodavchykh initsiiatyv. 2004. Svitova praktyka ta Ukrains'kyi dosvid vykorystannia mekhanizmu parlamentskykh slukhan' ta slukhan' u komitetakh iak instrument kontrol'noi funktsii parlamentu. Chastyna 3. Laboratoriia zakonodavchykh initsiiatyv, Prohrama spryiannia parlamentu Ukrainy Universytetu Indiany SShA. Available at www.parlament.org.ua (accessed May 28, 2007).

Levchenko, Kateryna. 1998. Informatsiia pro robotu sektsii 6 "Nasyl'stvo shchodo zhinok." In *Zhinka na porozi XXI stolittia*, ed. Valentyna Dovzhenko, 154–155. Kyiv: Ukrains'kyi instytut sotsial'nykh doslidzhen.'

Levitsky, Steven, and Lucan A. Way. 2002. "The Rise of Competitive Authoritarianism." *Journal of Democracy* 13(2) (April): 51–65.

McBride, Dorothy E., ed. 2001. *Abortion Politics, Women's Movements, and the Democratic State: a Comparative Study of State Feminism, Gender and Politics.* Oxford and New York: Oxford University Press.

Mel'nyk, Tamara. 1999. *Henderna polityka v Ukraini.* Kyiv: Lohos.

NIS-US Women's Consortium. 1998. *Fourth Quarterly Progress Report, Year 2: West NIS October 1997–December 1997.* Arlington, Va.: Winrock International, NIS-US Women's Consortium.

Orlyk, Maria. 2001. "Problemy dostupu zhinok do politychnoi vlady, intehratsii ikh v inshi vladni struktury." In *Zhinka v Ukraini,* ed. A. I. Komarova, 114–117. Kyiv: Natsional'na Rada Zhinok Ukrainy.

Pavlychko, Solomea. 1992. "Between Feminism and Nationalism: New Women's Groups in the Ukraine." In *Perestroika and Soviet Women,* ed. Mary Buckley, 82–96. Cambridge: Cambridge University Press.

Pishchikova, Kateryna. 2006. "Lost in Translation: USAID Assistance to Democracy Building in Postcommunist Ukraine." Ph.D. diss., University of Amsterdam.

Rezoliutsii Vseukrains'koho Konhresu Zhinok. 1998. In *Zhinka na porozi XXI stolittia,* ed. Valentyna Dovzhenko, 168–174. Kyiv: Ukrains'kyi instytut sotsial'nykh doslidzhen.'

Richter, James. 2002. "Evaluating Western Assistance to Women's Organizations." In *The Power and Limits of NGOs: A Critical Look at Building Democracy in Eastern Europe and Eurasia,* ed. Sarah Elizabeth Mendelson and John K. Glenn, 54–90. New York: Columbia University Press.

Romanova, N., T. V. Semyhina, and V. Levchenko. 2008. "Vyvchennia vitchyznianoi praktyky nadannia posluh poterpilym vid nasyl'stva v sim'i." *Sotsial'na robota v Ukraini: Teoriia i praktyka,* 4, 70–84.

Rosenberg, Ruth. 2006. "Domestic Violence in Europe and Eurasia." Aguirre Division of JBS International, for the Social Transition Team, Office of Democracy, Governance and Social Transition of the United States Agency for International Development, USAID. http://pdf.usaid.gov/pdf_docs/PNADG302.pdf (accessed November 8, 2009).

Rudneva, Oleksandra. 2000. "Ukraine." In *The First CEDAW Impact Study: Final Report,* ed. Marilou McPhedran, 215–232. Toronto: York University Centre for Feminist Research.

Sedova, Yana. 2001. "One-of-a-Kind Shelter in Kyiv for Victims of Domestic Violence Reflects Societal Views." *The Ukrainian Weekly.* Sunday, October 28, No. 43 p.3 http://www.scribd.com/doc/12842876/The-Ukrainian-Weekly-200143 (accessed November 8, 2009).

Skoryk, Marfa. 2006. "Na shliakhu do hendernoi polityky." In *Rozvytok demokratii v Ukraini, 2001–2002,* ed. Zh. Bezpiatchuk, I. L. Bilan, and S. A. Horobchyshyn, 71–92. Kyiv: Ukrains'kyi nezalezhnyi politychnyi tsentr.

Smolyar, Liudmyla. 2001. "The Women's Movement as a Factor of Gender Equality and Democracy in Ukrainian Society." In *Zhinochi orhanizatsii Ukrainy. Ukrainian Women's Non-Profit Organizations,* ed. Oleksandr Sydorenko, 27–44. Kyiv: Innovation and Development Center.

————, ed. 1999. *Zhinochi studii v Ukraini: Zhinka v istorii ta s'ohodni*. Odessa: Astroprint.

Sperling, Valerie. 1999. *Organizing Women in Contemporary Russia: Engendering Transition*. Cambridge; New York: Cambridge University Press.

Sydorenko, Oleksandr. 2001. "Zhinochi orhanizatsii Ukrainy: Tendentsii stanovlennia." In *Zhinochi orhanizatsii Ukrainy: Dovidnyk*, ed. Oleksandr Sydorenko, 45–52. Kyiv: Tsentr innovatsii ta rozvytku.

Ukrainian Helsinki Union. 2007. Paralel'nyi zvit ukrains'koi hel'sins'koi spilky z prav liudyny ta mizhnarodnoho fondu "Vidrodzhennia" shchodo zabezpechennia Ukrainoiu ekonomichnykh, sotsial'nykh i kul'turnykh prav do komitetu OON z ekonomichnykh, sotsial'nykh ta kul'turnykh prav. Ukrainian Helsinki Union, www.helsinki.org.ua/index.php?print=1193993286 (accessed June 19, 2008).

Ukrainian Ministry of Family, Youth, and Sport. 2008. "Nasyl'stvo ruinuie sim'I, robyt' ditei syrotamy (Violence ruins families and makes children orphans)." www .km.gov.ua/sport/control/uk/publish/articly;jsessionid=4F0456D1DD1C8D5DC8E 73FC5652989DB?art_id=98153&cat_id=98931 (accessed January 22, 2010).

United Nations Development Program. 2003. *Gender Issues in Ukraine: Challenges and Opportunities*. Kyiv: UNDP.

United States Department of State. 2005. "Ukraine: Country Reports on Human Rights Practices—2004." February 2, Bureau of Democracy, Human Rights, and Labor of the US Department of State. www.state.gov/g/drl/rls/hrrpt/2004/41715. htm (accessed November 8, 2009).

————. 2006. "Ukraine: Country Reports on Human Rights Practices—2005." Bureau of Democracy, Human Rights, and Labor of the US Department of State. www.state.gov/g/drl/rls/hrrpt/2005/61682.htm (accessed November 19, 2006).

Verkhovna Rada Ukrainy. 2004. Rekomendatsii parlaments'kykh slukhan' stanovyshche zhinok. http://gska2.rada.gov.ua:7777/pls/zweb/webproc34?id=&pf3511=1 8506&pf35401=54521 (accessed June 8, 2006; no longer available).

Way, Lucan. 2005a. "Authoritarian State Building and the Sources of Regime Competitiveness in the Fourth Wave: The Cases of Belarus, Moldova, Russia, and Ukraine." *World Politics* 57(2): 231–261.

————. 2005b. "Rapacious Individualism and Political Competition in Ukraine, 1992–2004." *Communist and Postcommunist Studies* 38(2): 191–205.

Webhofer, Regina. 2008. *Wave Country Report 2008: A Reality Check on European Services for Women and Children Victims of Violence*. Vienna: WAVE Network.

Zherebkina, Irina. 2003. "On the Performativity of Gender: Gender Studies in Post-Soviet Higher Education." *Studies in East European Thought* 55(1): 63–79.

Zhurzhenko, Tatiana. 2001. *Ukrainian Feminism(s): Between Nationalist Myth and Anti-Nationalist Critique*. Vienna: International World Bank Working Paper.

————. 2004. "Strong Woman, Weak State: Family Politics and Nationbuilding in Post-Soviet Ukraine." In *Post-Soviet Women Encountering Transition: Nation Building, Economic Survival, and Civic Activism*, ed. Kathleen R. Kuehnast and Carol Nechemias, 23–43. Washington, D.C.: Woodrow Wilson Center Press and Johns Hopkins University Press.

CHAPTER 3

Global Feminism, Foreign Funding, and Russian Writing about Domestic Violence

JANET ELISE JOHNSON AND GULNARA ZAYNULLINA

Only a decade ago, if Russians were asked about "domestic violence," the overwhelming response would have been "what do you mean?" This confusion would have been at the most basic level, because there was hardly any language with which even to ask this question. The abuse of women by current or former intimate partners was so widely seen as acceptable behavior that even most academics, women's activists, and legislators concerned with women's issues would have been puzzled by the terminology. By 2006, the situation was remarkably different. There was an entirely new language for talking about the problem. Russian activists, journalists, scholars, and even some policymakers have published thousands of articles, using various new terms for domestic violence.[1] How these Russian authors write about domestic violence is the central focus of this chapter.

The transformation in these opinion leaders' awareness of the problem of domestic violence is part of the global circulation of ideas—in this case, the production and transnational circulation of new ideas linking women's rights to human rights (Merry 2006). After more than a decade of deep divisions between the global North and the global South, women's activists at the United Nations (UN) came together in the mid-1990s to create a collective concept of violence against women. These activists linked into one global movement various national campaigns against issues such as rape, domestic violence, female genital mutilation, torture of political prisoners, and dowry deaths, which, until the mid 1970s, had been treated separately from one another (Keck and Sikkink 1998: 171). This consolidation in turn allowed activists around the world, many of whom had been resistant to raising the issue of domestic violence because it had been broached in the United States and Great Britain, to begin to focus on domestic violence. This new global feminist consensus also included norms about the meaning of domestic violence, making a distinction between domestic violence (by current or former boyfriends, husbands, or partners of adult women), which the activists saw as a mechanism of gendered power, and other forms of violence within a family, such as child abuse, incest, or elder abuse.[2] Because lack of knowledge about domestic violence has been a significant obstacle, feminist activists appealed for a new society-wide commitment to documenting gender violence. For example, Article 4(k) of the Declaration on the Elimination of Violence Against Women, or DEVAW, called on states to "encourage research on the causes, nature, seriousness and consequences of violence against women" (United Nations General Assembly 1993). For scholars of domestic violence (Heise et al. 1994: 1174–1176), research is important in increasing "levels of awareness of the nature, context and response to the problem rather than to provide off-the-shelf technical solutions," helping formulate, implement, and assess policy, and establishing legitimacy of the issue.

As elsewhere in the formerly communist countries in Europe and Eurasia, Russian society has felt the influence of this new global feminist consensus. The international conferences where this consensus emerged, such as the 1993 UN Conference on Human Rights in Vienna and the nongovernmental forum at the 1995 UN Conference on Women in China, occurred simultaneously with the opening up of Russian borders. Many Russian activists—or soon-to-be-activists—got their first taste of the possibility of political engagement outside of the socialist state at these international gatherings. The new global feminist consensus also created the possibility of alliances between transnational feminists and international donors and human rights advocates just as they were beginning to direct attention to the region (Keck and Sikkink 1998: ch. 5; Moghadam 2005). These alliances with international development agencies and large charitable foundations generated financial support for transnational research on gender violence often conducted by women's nongovernmental organizations (NGOs) (Merry 2006; Moghadam 2005).

This chapter explores the results of this circulation of global feminist ideas on the evolution in Russian activist thinking on domestic violence. Such an exploration forms part of this volume's investigation into the impact of foreign actors and ideas on postcommunist European and Eurasian domestic violence politics. Similar to Edward Snajdr's analysis of Kazakhstani activists in chapter 4 in this volume, we address whether the new global feminist norms are proving helpful to Russian activists who wish to bring new attention to the issue, or whether such norms are brought by "parachute feminist" telling locals "how things are done." As Katalin Fábián (2006: 136) does in her similar study of Central Europe, we also look for feedback on global norms and international actors, exploring whether Russian writing has impacted the way outsiders write and think about domestic violence. Our rationale is that "transnational organizing is not a unidirectional process" but a global-local intersection where resources, ideas, and benefits can flow both "in" and "out" (Sperling, Ferree, and Risman 2001: 1155). As we are among those committed to addressing gender violence, our objective is to provide insights into how the global feminist consensus can be a useful tool for activists seeking to expand services for women experiencing violence as well as for transforming the oppressive structures of gender inequality that create the problem.

In brief, we find that, despite concerns about global feminist and donor interventions (see chapter 2 in this volume), Russian feminist scholars/activists, with their postcommunist European colleagues, have constructed a new way of thinking about the old problem of domestic violence informed by both global feminist norms and local concerns. Most interestingly, they have incorporated ideas about "economic violence," giving them innovative ways to critique not just domestic violence and gender inequality, but also the state's failure to provide social services. While it is early, we also find some evidence of the influence of these new conceptualizations of domestic violence on transnational feminism and human rights advocacy, suggesting that the new global feminist consensus is indeed more inclusive and responsive than earlier attempts to create global sisterhood. In the next section, as a background for our analysis, we provide information on domestic violence as an issue in the New Russia, including the role of a new women's crisis center movement. Then, we elaborate on our research approach. In the bulk of the chapter, we trace the shifts over time in the writing about domestic violence by Russians as well as by international observers.

Russian Skepticism and the Women's Crisis Center Movement

Global feminist norms about domestic violence were very different from the dominant beliefs about domestic violence in Russian society up through the 1990s. Under Soviet rule, the incidence of violence between current or former partners, especially in communal apartments, was a common theme for discussions in literature, in the press, and among women, but there was no critique of this violence as violating women's rights. Such violence was even sometimes addressed through criminal articles against "hooliganism," a catch-all crime for any violation of the public order, although police attention was never about empowering women but only about maintaining social control (Shelley 1987; Sperling 1990). The communist state's support for female workers, such as maternity leave, subsidized day care, full-day (8 AM– 5 PM) primary education, also created some exit options from abusive and dependent relationships about which many American women could only dream. However, the state's housing policies also forced women to stay living with their abusers even after divorce or to live with abusive men who were not current or former intimates.

The early post-Soviet response seemed even worse for women suffering from domestic violence. By the mid-1990s, police and prosecutors stopped even using the guise of hooliganism to regulate domestic violence (Human Rights Watch 1997). They refused to see any abuse in the family, while aggressively prosecuting similar violence inflicted by strangers. While Russian authorities freely employed coercion elsewhere (as in Chechnya or against people from the Caucuses on the streets of major Russian cities), liberalization of the regime appeared to delegitimate the earlier customary police response to domestic violence, even if women requested such assistance. The state's support for social services, which had been at least partially helpful, deflated until such services became meaningless to women. As the Soviet authority waned, the communist commitment to "woman's emancipation" also disappeared (Bridger, Pinnick, and Kay 1996).

In contrast to global feminist norms, which place responsibility for violence on the perpetrator, Russian belief systems have tended to hold women accountable for the violence used against them or to see such violence as a normal part of loving relationships. Even early Bolshevik ideology—with its feminist critiques of the economic injustice of the bourgeois family—raised little objection to other than exclusively economic kinds of unequal power within families. There had been no state-sponsored gendered critique of the structure of power, only some bureaucratic attempts to alleviate some of the problems women faced as either workers or mothers. By the late Soviet period, scholars tended to blame women and women's emancipation for "provoking" violence, arguing that domestic violence was caused by women's failure to perform their domestic duties "selflessly" and by their declining moral values (Attwood 1997: 107). The post-Soviet popularity of explaining a range of political and social phenomena by physiology only reinforced the idea that women are somehow to blame for the violence that others choose to use against them. None of these misogynist ways of thinking about domestic violence could accommodate the consideration that domestic violence might be a mechanism of gendered power or a violation of human rights.

Yet, simultaneous with this backsliding in the early 1990s, the breakdown of the Soviet one-party monopoly over society also allowed for new possibilities for collective action. As independent NGOs began to emerge in Russia, women's groups gathered momentum. Most notably, activists gathered in Dubna in 1991 for what came to be called the First Independent Women's Forum (Kay 2000; Noonan and Nechemias 2001; Sperling 1999). This gathering, widely considered a watershed in the development of a Russian women's movement, and the follow-up meeting the next year, generated a sister movement, a women's crisis center movement. The feminist movement, along with several large donors such as Ford Foundation, the US Agency for International Development, and the European Union, brought violence against women as their primary issue. More than other gender-related issues, the critique of domestic violence seemed to resonate with many Russian women activists (Sundstrom 2005).

The hallmark of this movement is crisis centers for women victims of violence (see Johnson 2009 for in-depth description of the movement). The first crisis centers were founded in Moscow and St. Petersburg in 1993 (Hemment 2004a; Johnson 2001; Zabelina 1996). By the mid-1990s additional crisis centers were founded in these two major Russian cities, and afterward the movement spread eastward. By 1998, Moscow-based researchers located 24 organizations that worked in the sphere of "prevention and elimination of violence against women" from Murmansk to Irkutsk (Abubikirova et al. 1998: 9). In 2004, there was an umbrella organization of some 47 crisis centers and a looser (somewhat overlapping) network created by the Moscow crisis center ANNA, which included 121 organizations engaged in addressing domestic violence in Russia. By the middle of the first decade of the next millennium, growth had slowed—with many organizations struggling to survive—as the foreign funding that had allowed the movement to proliferate dried up.[3]

As is the case for domestic violence-related activism around the world (Merry 2006), the primary—and defining—activity of these women's crisis centers is a hotline for victims of sexual and domestic violence. A hotline is a relatively inexpensive way to reach out to women to provide to others emotional support, empowerment, and medical and legal referrals. Many centers also provide in-person psychological and legal assistance. Some centers also have political goals, seeking to educate the public about the problem of violence against women and to change the behavior of the police, prosecutors, medical examiners, judges, social workers, and psychologists (Johnson 2001). Other centers, especially those founded later, were essentially state social services that turned their attention to domestic violence during the late 1990s, when there was a lot of international pressure, but were gradually becoming politicized by the autonomous feminist crisis centers (Johnson 2006).

Research and writing on domestic violence is part of the crisis centers' public education and policy reform work, but other scholars and feminist activists have also contributed. Together they have produced reflections, sociological surveys, and other scholarly analysis, sometimes working with feminists from other countries. The women's crisis center movement is the major force for appropriating and translating the global feminist human rights norms against domestic violence into the Russian vernacular.

Our Approach

To examine the circulation of global feminist norms through Russia, we chose a representative sample of significant Russian writing on domestic violence connected to the women's crisis movement (see table 3.1). The selection reflects the variety of studies—and funding sources—from 1995 to 2005. All nine texts are also substantial in length and scope covered—i.e., either books or major reports, not newspaper articles, magazine articles, or internet publications—and found in the resource rooms of women's NGOs across Russia. Most are anthologies, collecting various voices familiar with domestic violence in Russia. Reflecting the movement's growth from the Western metropolises of Moscow and St. Petersburg, the sample is biased toward authors from and writing about those cities. Although these writings are the texts that seem to have been the most influential to the movement, in selecting them we do not claim to speak for Russia's diversity: almost all of them came from areas dominated by scholars of Russian ethnicity. All the studies came from areas with majority Orthodox Christian cultural backgrounds. This reflects the nature of the movement, at least in the Russian language, although more recently there has been greater penetration of the movement into communities where ethnic minorities have more sway, such as Tatarstan, Buryatia, the Udmurt Republic, and the Republic of Komi (see Johnson 2009: ch. 3).

In this chapter, we analyze these Russian texts chronologically. We look at the changes in conceptualization of domestic violence over time, and we compare them to early global feminist documents about gender

TABLE 3.1. SAMPLE OF RUSSIAN WRITING ON DOMESTIC VIOLENCE, 1995-2005

TITLE OF TEXT	AUTHOR(S)	DATE PUBLISHED
Kak sozdat' krizisnyi tsentr [How to Create a Crisis Center]	E. V. Israelian, T. Iu. Zabelina	1995
Dostizheniia i nahodki: krizisnye tsentri Rossii [Achievements and Findings: of Crisis Centers of Russia]	T. Iu Zabelina, E. V. Israelian	1999
Nasilie i Sotsial'nye Izmeneniia [Violence and Social Change]	ANNA Crisis Center	2000
Sotsial'nomu Rabotniku o Probleme Domashnego Nasiliia [To the Social Worker on the Problem of Domestic Violence]	ANNA Crisis Center (with the Russian Min. of Labor and Social Development's Dept. on Children, Women, and Family)	2001
Sotsial'no-pravovaia zashchita zhenshchin. Predotvrashchenie nasiliia v otnoshenii zhenchin i detei. [Socio-Legal Protection of Women: Prevention of Violence against Women and Children]	D. E. Balibalova, P. P. Gluchenko, E. M. Tikhomirova	2001
Rossiia: Nasilie v sem'e—nasilie v obshchestve [Russia: Domestic Violence— Violence in Society]	T. Iu. Zabelina	2002

LOCATION OF ACTIVISTS OR RESEARCHERS	FINANCED BY	BRIEF DESCRIPTION
Moscow	Canadian Embassy in Moscow	Transnational anthology of practical recommendations of psychologists, sociologists, jurists, medical doctors, etc., on how to best help victims of gender violence
Moscow	Canadian Embassy in Moscow	Summary of Russian crisis centers' experience, their founding principles and main types of work
Moscow	TACIS (European Union), CARITAS (Austria)	Anthology of three Russian scholar-activists from ANNA
Moscow	Canadian Fund supporting Russian women	Practical instructions for social workers based on the work of crisis centers
St. Petersburg	St. Petersburg Humanitarian University of Unions	A manual for local administrations, NGOs, etc., on how to address the problem of violence against women and children
Moscow	UNIFEM, UNFPA	Results of public opinion research conducted in Russia within the frame of the UNIFEM Regional Public Awareness Campaign for Women's Rights to a Life Free of Violence

TABLE 3.1. SAMPLE OF RUSSIAN WRITING ON DOMESTIC VIOLENCE, 1995–2005

TITLE OF TEXT	AUTHOR(S)	DATE PUBLISHED
NCRB: A Network for Crisis Centres in the Barents Region (also published in Russian)	A. Saarinen, O. Liapounova I. Drachova	2003
Nasilie nad zhenami v sovremennykh rossiiskikh sem'iakh [Violence against Women in Contemporary Russian Families]	I. D. Gorshkova, I. I. Shurygina	2003
Razorvat' krug molchaniia [To Break the Circle of Silence]	N. M. Rimasheevskaia, ed.	2005

violence, such as the Declaration on the Elimination of Violence against Women (DEVAW) and the General Recommendations of the Convention on the Elimination of All Forms of Discrimination Against Women (CEDAW) Committee. We consider the effect of foreign funding on the process of appropriation and translation as well as its unintended consequences. To assess the influence of Russian writing on global feminist norms, we contrast these Russian studies on domestic violence with recent global feminist documents. These include Amnesty International's (2005) and the UN's Special Rapporteur Yakin Erturk's (2006) reports on violence against women in Russia, which, as they are about Russia, are most likely to reflect the Russian authors' rhetoric. Similarly, we look to the UNIFEM-supported Minnesota Advocates for Human Right's Stop Violence Against Women campaign (www.stopvaw.org), which, as we elaborate below, has focused on the postcommunist region, publishing in both English and Russian. To examine broader impact, we also analyze the rhetoric used by the UN's Secretary General and General Assembly.

LOCATION OF ACTIVISTS OR RESEARCHERS	FINANCED BY	BRIEF DESCRIPTION
Murmansk, Arkhangelsk, Severomorsk, Apatity, Karelia, St. Petersburg, Barnaul, and several Nordic cities	Ministry of Industry, Employment and Communication, Division for Gender Equality in Sweden	Report of a multiyear Nordic project with Russian crisis centers in the Barents region
Moscow	Ford Foundation (US-based)	Report on survey research on the scale and character of violence against women in Russian urban and rural locations
Moscow	Moscow Center of Gender Studies, Russian Academy of Sciences Institute of Socioeconomic Problems of Population	Anthology of academic analyses, interviews with state authorities, and reports by activists

Although global activism around gender violence does not constitute a singular "seamlessly coherent ideological or institutional whole" (Fábián 2006: 137), we see these UN and other human rights advocates' texts as indicative of the recent elaboration of the global feminist consensus.

This chapter draws upon the international relations theory of "norm diffusion" and the anthropological study of "appropriation" and "translation" of human rights norms (Merry 2006; see also Johnson 2009: chs.1 and 4, for elaboration). According to theorists of international relations, impact on national contexts occurs when norms diffuse across borders through dynamic networks of social relationships at the local, national, and global level. The growing acceptance of these norms among different actors and states leads to a "norms cascade" as the new norms become pervasive and internalized. Cultural and legal anthropologist Sally Merry describes this process as one of making norms into the vernacular, "adjusting the rhetoric and structure of these programs or interventions to local circumstances" (Merry 2006: 135). In this vein, we examine whether global feminist norms have been "localized" in Russia as Merry found had happened in other parts of the world. Like Merry (2006), we hold that the most effective norm diffusion/vernacularization processes are those that can carefully balance the need to challenge the existing social order with adaptation to the given cultural context.[4] If a norm has much resonance with local traditions and beliefs, it ceases to be a challenge in that particular setting; if it has no resonance, then the norm has no rhetorical power in that society.

This process of norm diffusion is facilitated by the intervention of individual policy entrepreneurs (in the language of international relations)—or "intermediaries" (in the language of anthropology) (Merry 2006)—such as national political elites, human rights or feminist activist leaders, service providers, legal professionals or academics, social movements, and broader networks of activists. Keck and Sikkink (1998) have characterized these participants as forming "transnational advocacy networks," but we, following Moghadam (2005), refer to them as "transnational feminist networks." These activist individuals and their groups may help the norm travel by taking responsibility to advance it transnationally and locally, but alternatively, they also may foster nationalist resistance to foreign intervention.

Our study is also informed by non-Western feminist critiques of earlier global feminism, most often labeled as postcolonial feminist scholarship (e.g., Mohanty 1991). This literature argued that feminism, although claiming universal applicability, derived only from the experiences of some middle-class white women living in the West, and that it erased the huge global inequalities fostered by the West's foreign and trade policies and stunk of missionary zeal.[5] Following the demise of the Soviet regime, scholars from Eastern and Central Europe raised similar objections toward Western feminism. For example, Croatian writer Slavenka Drakulić (1993) criticized Western feminists for collapsing differences between West and East, and within the East, into simple declarations about women in postcommunism. Other scholars—including some of the authors in this volume—have raised similar concerns about the new global feminist consensus (e.g., Hemment 2004a). The rhetoric of global feminism and human rights, often articulated and sometimes enforced by industrialized countries, runs the risk of reproducing old colonial relationships and related language about who gets to be considered civilized (Merry 2006). Yet global feminism itself is derived from a transnational and relatively consensual process of deliberation, making it the best collective wisdom we have for addressing what appears to be a globally entrenched problem, gender inequality (ibid. 227). Weldon's study (2006) of the global movement suggests that feminists have developed new "norms of inclusivity," innovative mechanisms and respect for autonomous organizing that under favorable conditions can balance centripetal and centrifugal forces. We have turned these concerns and debates into our central object of study in Russia.

This analysis comes out of a multi-year project researching the Russian women's crisis center movement. One of us (Johnson) has been doing fieldwork for more than a decade in the region as well as at transnational feminist venues (such as the 2005 Beijing +10 conference in New York City and a 2005 conference on gender violence in Sweden). The other (Zaynullina) grew up in Uzbekistan and then worked in the Europe and Central Asian Division at Human Rights Watch, contributing to a report on bride kidnapping and domestic violence in Kyrgyzstan (Human Rights Watch 2006). Since 2004, we have been working to analyze systematically the evolution of the women's crisis center movement and the changing attention to various issues of violence against women in postcommunist Russia (see Johnson 2009).

Global Feminist Impact on Russian Research

Appropriating North American Practices and Global Feminist Norms

The first significant publication on gender violence in Russia was *How to Start a Crisis Center,* a practical guide for a variety of NGO practitioners on how best to help victims of gender violence (Israelian and Zabelina 1995). Edited by two scholars who helped to establish the Moscow-based sexual violence crisis center *Syostri* (Sisters) in 1994, the book was loosely modeled on a US activist publication, the 1972 booklet *How to Start a Rape Crisis Center.* The US booklet summarized the founding of a Washington, D.C., women's crisis center and offered suggestions on practical problems of working with women and with the authorities. In addition to providing important information, this US pamphlet also became a model for other North American crisis centers wishing to reflect on and publicize their work. The Russian version includes some (literal) translations of Canadian and US experiences in creation of crisis centers, and it draws upon the work of Americans, such as the ideas of Santa Monica (California) rape crisis center founder Gail Abarbanel on individual psychotherapy.

At the same time that the Russian version drew upon North American models and theories, the authors also incorporated ideas from the new global feminist consensus. The Russian editors and the authors viewed violence against women as a violation of women's human rights, a claim that was not part of the original *How to Start a Rape Crisis Center*. One of the Russian editors described the 1993 DEVAW in detail, including the concept that violence against women was a manifestation of historically unequal power relations (13–18). Whereas the original pamphlet was targeted against sexual violence, the Russian version also drew upon the global feminist concept of "violence against women," linking sexual violence with "domestic violence." Domestic violence was a novel concept for Russia, and thus the authors applied a literal translation of the English term (*domashnee nasilie*). From this first publication in 1995, Russian writing and theorizing on domestic violence illustrates the appropriation of North American models and global feminist norms.

Adding "Economic Violence"

Most remarkably, this first publication on domestic violence suggests that, even at this early date, Russian activists were beginning to vernacularize the global/dominant norms to fit the Russian context by reinforcing the notion of economic violence. Early US feminists, as for example in the Duluth Power and Control Wheel, had included the idea of "economic abuse" (see also Fábián's definition of domestic violence in this volume). Similarly, for the Russian authors in our sample, domestic violence includes not just physical, sexual, and psychological violence as defined in DEVAW, but also "economic dependence—the prohibition against finding a job, the deprivation or threat of deprivation of financial resources, etc." (Israelian and Zabelina 1995: 15). Later Russian authors then labeled this phenomenon *ekonomicheskoe nasilie* (economic violence), perhaps a mistake in the literal translation, but one that suggests actual physical harm, not just intimidation (as implied by "abuse"). The terms "violence," "abuse," and "dependence" are often used interchangeably, without clarification as to their different meanings, but while Americans tend to use the latter terms, Russians have more recently relied on "economic violence." All of the texts in our sample—except for the Nordic-Russian collaboration (Saarinen, Liapounova, and Drachova 2003)—include this idea (although not all the authors in all the anthologies do). The Nordic editor explained that, although "economic violence" had come up in various discussions within the project that formed the basis for their book, they decided not to include it because, illustrating another notion of economic violence, they use the same term as a "critique of the state as the main violator of social justice," and not as a critique of gender violence.[6]

Economic dependence itself constituting violence is different from most Western and transnational conceptualizations, at least until recently. For early gender violence activists, economic injustice was seen as key in creating the conditions for domestic violence. Most activists still critique poverty and the lack of social services as huge obstacles for women leaving violent abusers and seeing economic deprivation by partners as part of the cycle of control that allows for domestic violence. Especially in Anglo-American contexts, however, these economic critiques had been de-radicalized by legal norms of violence that specify the use of physical violence and perceivable bodily harm. US activists have also been leery of raising the issue of economics because there is a sordid history of policymakers blaming poverty (and genetics) for all sorts of problems, including the tendency toward violence. Nordic activists, coming from states such as Norway, Sweden, and Finland, may also downplay this problem because their generous welfare states provide more options for women to leave violent relations.

Perhaps as a result of Western social history and legal culture, which are more rooted in the individual, the concept of economic violence was not part of the foundational global feminist documents. Economic violence was not included in CEDAW; the documents of the 1985 UN conference on women in Nairobi; General Recommendations 12 and 19 of the CEDAW Committee, which added violence against women to CEDAW; DEVAW; or the 1995 Beijing Platform for Action, which took a strong stand against gender violence. In 1996, the special rapporteur on violence against women to the UN's Commission on Human Rights defined domestic violence as follows:

> . . . from simple assaults to aggravated physical battery, kidnapping, threats, intimation, coercion, stalking, humiliating verbal abuse, forcible or unlawful entry, arson, destruction of property, sexual violence, marital rape, dowry or bride-price related violence, female genital mutilation, [and] violence related to exploitation through prostitution. (Coomaraswamy 1996: II.C.11)

These kinds of violence (or threats of violence) correspond to what North American activists and human rights advocates have long considered violence.

The Russian idea of economic violence appears to have come from the shared Marxist-influenced thinking and experience in the region.[7] The earliest reference to economic violence we could find was by a crisis center in the former Yugoslavia, the first postcommunist society to establish such organizations. The SOS Hotline Belgrade, in the mid-1990s, focused on economic violence (or "economic abuse"). They understood economic violence to indicate the "means by which women's property, income, and work are subjected to abuse" (Mrševic 2000: 384–386; also Mrševic and Hughes 1997). They assumed this economic violence "to be a basic feature of all cases of domestic violence." As the founder of the Belgrade hotline reflected in 2006, her fellow activists discovered that

> [h]ard-working women's salaries were regularly taken away by force for alcohol for their husbands, even food dedicated primarily to children were taken also. Women's typical answer was to work even more hard [sic] with intention to provide enough for both, greedy husbands and hungry children. Many of them after working hours in factories, tended to little gardens around houses for vegetables, or tailored clothes for friends, or cleaned others' houses, typewrote, etc., all for small sums, hoping that these would not be noticed by their violent husbands and thus not taken away. Generations of children were raised on that additional money their mother earned investing last remnants of their energy. In [sic] the same time men boasted as "bread winners"![8]

According to many East European women activists, the concept of economic violence is the abuse of family members for the abuser's economic gain (or for economic control), even if physically violent means are not employed. Ukrainian activists similarly used the term "economic violence" as they developed their domestic violence legislation in 1996–1999,[9] as does the 2008 Family Violence Prevention Act in Slovenia (see Robnik in this volume). Activists in these postcommunist societies, many of whom had been raised reading Marx, were more likely to see economic exploitation than Western, especially Anglo-American, activists.[10]

Also remarkable is that the circulation of this concept among postcommunist societies appears to have been fostered by the transnational feminist networks. None of the major donors to crisis centers in the region employed the idea of economic violence, but several transnational feminist networks active in the region did. For example, the Network of East-West Women (NEWW) was disseminating the idea of economic violence in 1996.[11] Women Against Violence Europe (see Brunell and Johnson chapter in this volume) also incorporated the idea (Kaselitz 2006) as did UNIFEM (which did provide some funding; Heyzer 1998). Further, organizing against neoliberalism and economic injustice has become a primary concern of transnational feminist networks (Moghadam 2005).

Translating Global Feminist Norms into Russian Cultural Context

The next three Russian publications in our sample appeared as a result of a new funding environment in which donors paid small amounts for research. These three documents are anthologies written between 1999 and 2001 by scholar-activists affiliated with the two Moscow-based crisis centers Syostri and ANNA. Zabelina and Israelian's 1999 *Achievements and Findings of the Crisis Centers of Russia* borrowed heavily from their 1995 publication, *How to Start a Crisis Center,* but the new book also provided more examples of the Russian crisis centers' experience.[12] The other two books are anthologies based on ANNA's experiences.[13] The first is another book designed to assist those who work or want to in women's crisis centers; it includes three analytical chapters about ANNA's work (ANNA Crisis Center 2000). The second volume consists of eight such chapters—including a revision of one of the chapters originally published in the first book. Directed toward state social workers, the 2001 book emerged from a project with the Ministry of Labor and Social Development following a high-level 1998 Russia–United States conference on domestic violence attended by Hillary Clinton (ANNA Crisis Center 2001).

The two ANNA books manage to further the work of situating the global feminist idea of domestic violence within postcommunist Russia. The first book, titled *Violence and Social Change,* is explicit that the concept of domestic violence is foreign, but it moves away from simply appropriating the language of DEVAW. The book contextualizes the problem of domestic violence within family relations in Soviet and post-Soviet times. The second volume, *To the Social Worker on the Problem of Domestic Violence,* experiments with other terms for the problem of domestic violence, such as "violence in the family" (*nasilie v sem'e*) and "family violence" (*semeinoe nasilie*) that regional crisis centers found to have more resonance with Russian society.

A chapter by Pisklakova and Sinel'nikov in the second volume by ANNA goes the furthest in linking global norms to the Russian local context, arguing that domestic violence is a manifestation of Russian patriarchal traditions but rooted in Soviet state control. For example, the authors point to Stalin's recriminalization of abortion in 1936. They argue that the German prescription for women—"*Kinder, Kirche, Küche*" (children, church, kitchen)—had been applied, and emphasize the importance of the Soviet addition of paid work outside the home, producing the formula "Children, Work, Kitchen." Soviet commendations also reinforced gendered norms: men received medals as soldiers, women for birthing five and more children. Pisklakova and Sinel'nikov argue that together these state-constructed and enforced gender norms helped reinforce women in submitting to violence. In their discussion of particular Soviet communist and postcommunist obstacles preventing abused women from freeing themselves of their abusers, the authors highlight the housing permit system (ANNA Crisis Center 2001: 39). This system—which was ruled unconstitutional but still operates in most places—protects a man's right to the apartment, or room in the apartment, even if he is abusive. Bringing global feminist ideas to Russia, Pisklakova and Sinel'nikov emerge as global feminist norm entrepreneurs—Russian activists with fluency in English and significant experience observing European and US activism who seek to bridge Russian, Western, and global feminist theory and praxis.

A Move toward Gender-Neutrality

By 2001, the concept of domestic violence resonated sufficiently with Russians that authors not directly related to the independent women's crisis center movement could also begin to write on domestic violence, some even publishing without Western support. One such text was *Socio-Legal Protection of Women: Preventing Violence against Women and Children* (Balibalova, Glushchenko, and Tikhomirova 2001), published with support from the St. Petersburg local government. As in previous Russian texts, the authors draw upon global feminist documents, such as CEDAW and DEVAW. Repeating a global feminist argument, the authors criticize the Russian government for not having a law that would prohibit domestic violence. They claim that "[t]he separation of the problem of violence in the family into an independent social problem . . . is the first step directed toward the solution" (ibid. 124). However, they translate domestic violence in Russian as "violence in the family," referring not only to intimate partner violence (against women), but also to violence against the elderly and children. Their localization of global feminist norms resonates so closely with already existing protectionist norms— about the need for women, children, and the elderly to be protected— that it threatens to minimize the violence that adult women face.

As is clear in many chapters in this volume, the tendency toward subsuming domestic violence against adult women within the larger category of violence in the family is typical across postcommunist

Europe and Eurasia (also, Johnson and Brunell 2006; Krizsán, Paantjens, and van Lamoen 2005). This reconceptualization makes the feminist concept of domestic violence gender-neutral by erasing the gendered critique of power. According to Katalin Fábián's (2006: 136) study of the impact of global networks on local activism in Poland, Slovakia, the Czech Republic, Slovenia, and Hungary, "NGOs in Central Europe found that by moving to a gender-neutral territory of interpretation they were more likely to be accepted in governmental-level deliberations about policy." In Russia, several crisis centers, especially those outside Moscow and St. Petersburg, similarly used this more traditional way of thinking about domestic violence (see Johnson 2001).

Other Russian activists, with more support for research than Balibalova, Glushchenko, and Tikhomirova (2001), kept the feminist way of seeing domestic violence. The first of two large-scale surveys on domestic violence in our sample—*Russia: Domestic Violence—Violence in Society* (Zabelina 2002)—was conducted by a Russian scholar-activist associated with two of the previous studies in our sample.[14] Borrowing heavily from her own earlier work, the introduction to the survey illustrated continued commitment to global feminism by referring to CEDAW and DEVAW, and the survey applied the concept of economic violence. The survey asked respondents whether they considered as a form of domestic violence the "deprivation of the money required for basic needs, such as food, clothing, shoes, personal hygiene products."

In contrast to Zabelina's book and survey, however, the second survey, conducted by researchers affiliated with Moscow State University, demonstrates a high degree of skepticism toward global feminist norms among the researchers. Although it too investigates the Russian concept of economic violence, this study, *Violence against Women in Modern Russian Families* (Gorshkova and Shurygina 2003), expresses a skepticism similar to that of the Soviet period, through the assumption that women provoke violence.[15] In the survey itself, questions suggested such a bias. For example, one question asked respondents to finish the following statement: "A husband has a right to beat his wife, if she . . ." (*Muzh imeet pravo pobit' zhenu, esli ona . . .*), suggesting that there were cases when such action is justified. Further, departing from the global feminist and Russian feminist claims that domestic violence happens in poor and rich families alike, the study's authors pointed to socioeconomic conditions as explanatory, arguing that the problem was typical only to poor and uneducated people living outside of metropolitan centers such as Moscow (38).[16] In contrast to the other authors in our sample, these researchers were neither activists nor self-identified feminist scholars.

A Fruitful Tension?

Another anthology published at approximately the same time—*NCRB: A Network for Crisis Centres for Women in the Barents Region* (Saarinen, Liapounova, and Drachova 2003)—documented and assessed a joint project by investigators in three Nordic countries and northwestern Russia that took place between 1999–2002. This Barents Region project linked women's crisis centers to share experiences and information in an effort to combat violence against women and children. Working with a multilingual Russian (the third editor), the Finnish and Russian coordinators of the project were also the book's editors. Although similar to the first book, *How to Start a Crisis Center*, in its transborder character, this anthology represented a transnational feminist collaboration. The editors cast themselves as working as part of an "ongoing process of activism and dialogue across the former East-West divide in the Barents Region in the northernmost parts of Northwest Russia, Finland, Sweden, and Norway" (ibid. 5). The Finnish editor, Aino Saarinen, was especially sensitive about the transborder relations. The Russian participants, according to their anonymous evaluations given to the project directors and included in this book, confirmed that the project was relatively participatory because the participating Russian crisis centers felt themselves to be "co-organizers" and not just recipients of Western intervention (ibid. 54).

Explicitly linking themselves to the second wave of the global women's movement, especially its expression at the UN women's world meetings, Saarinen, Liapounova, and Drachova's (2003) understanding of violence against women illustrated a melding of social-democratic and postcommunist approaches to gender violence. The editors defined gendered violence as "interwoven with . . . overall structural oppression, poverty and suppression under male power in all spheres of life," arguing that such a definition was required "because of the economic regression of the early 1990s in Russia [which] was deeply gendered and resulted in mass unemployment of women, drastic increase and feminization of poverty and collapse of the public safety networks" (ibid. 15). Eight chapters by Russian activists about their crisis centers or the movement as a whole reflected a variety of approaches to gender violence, influenced by global feminism, Nordic feminism, and Russian experience.

The last book from our sample, *To Break the Circle of Silence* (Rimashevskaia 2005), was published ten years after the creation of the first crisis center in Russia and appeared without foreign assistance. This domestically funded book well demonstrated the evolution of Russian intersections with global feminism. Modeled on an Estonian book with the same title, it was published by the Moscow Center for Gender Studies, known for its connections with global feminism, and edited by Rimashevskaia, who served as the head of Russian Academy of Science's Institute of Socioeconomic Problems of Population and who had helped found the Center in the early 1990s. The contents of the book are academic analyses, a reflection by a policymaker on failed domestic violence legislation, interviews with law enforcement officers, a priest, doctors, psychologists, and victims of gender-based violence, and reports from crisis center activists. These chapters show the general acceptance among opinion leaders of the emerging global norms concerning violence against women. By establishing the separation of violence against women into a separate problem, the book accomplished the goal of global feminists and of the authors of *Socio-Legal Protection of the Women: Preventing Violence against Women and Children* (Balibalova, Glushchenko, and Tikhomirova 2001). The experts and opinion leaders in the book acknowledged that domestic violence was not just a private misfortune, but a problem worthy of public response.

In sum, these latter books suggest that Russian activists have been able to keep fruitful tension between the framing of domestic violence in gender-neutral and gendered (feminist) ways.[17] As in other postcommunist contexts (Ishkanian 2004), there was a kind of doublespeak, using the global feminist "gender talk" in some contexts and employing more traditional gender discourse in others. This flexibility with framing problems may be the best tactic to undermine the underlying traditional gender structure, because it revealed the ways that gender is manipulated (Johnson and Robinson 2007). As a whole, the discourse between different activists and scholars developed a frame for the problem that has brought it some wider awareness while simultaneously keeping a global feminist lens (see also Johnson 2009: ch. 5).

Discussion: On Foreign Intervention

In a provocative analysis of the Russian women's crisis center movement up through the 1990s, Julie Hemment (2004a) raised several concerns about foreign intervention, specifically global feminist ideas and the so-called democracy assistance that the United States poured into the region following the Soviet collapse.[18] In what she saw as a context of "liberal triumphalism," Western funds to support the creation of crisis centers helped to privatize—that is, remove from state responsibility—social services just as the transformation of the economy left most Russians in poverty. The role that crisis centers could play in the Western neoliberal project was evident in what Hemment observed to be the main message from crisis counselors to women: do not expect any assistance from the state. Even if this advice reflected real concerns about the Russian authorities' reluctance to help, it served to justify the privatization of state responsibilities to address the wide range of problems related to domestic violence. In her view, even global feminism could be complicit. The transnational feminist movement, Hemment argued, linked the critique of violence against women with human rights, abandoned its radical critique of the structural factors contributing to violence against women in favor of the individualism implicit in human rights. These new global feminist norms, stripped of their call for redistributive justice, were then brought to Russia, supplanting indigenous interest in economic discrimination and forcing women's organizations to shift from self-identified needs to those that international donors were willing to fund. Her concerns echoed others about the de-radicalization of the global women's movement and other segments of postcommunist civil society into professionalized NGOs in response to the new funding environment (e.g., Alvarez 1999; Mendelson and Glenn 2002; Wedel 2001).

In general these concerns, raised by Westerners, have not been echoed in print by Russian activists and scholars directly involved in domestic violence activism. This is also true of the texts in our sample. Since most significant research and activism on domestic violence in the postcommunist period was financially supported by Western donors, this suggests some agreement with the international norms. It might also mean that these activists do not have the liberty to express those concerns. In private conversations, we have heard some unease. For example, an early Russian feminist leader and director leader of the Network Women's Project at Open Society, Anastasia Posadskaya-Vanderbeck, sees the issue of violence against women as being raised by transnational feminists, whereas it was not on the first agenda of the nascent movement under Gorbachev.[19] Another crisis center movement leader asserted that an audit by EU officials for a project grant was worse than the KGB. A feminist scholar who had read grants for one donor's domestic violence project told of the difficulty of working with other committee members who knew little of Russia and who wanted, for example, to fund a hotline in a place where very few people have phones. Non-Russian activists in Russia have voiced some off-the-record frustration with the ethnic Russian dominance in the movement and inconsideration of ethnic concerns.[20] In conversations over the last decade, although many leading feminists expressed some criticism of the funding process, very few were critical of transnational feminism or the conceptualization of domestic violence as a form of violence against women and a violation of women's human rights.

The evolution of Russian writing on domestic violence in our sample also illustrates that the Russian activists have proven more sophisticated in their appropriation and translation of global feminist rhetoric than Hemment's (2004a) analysis predicted. By the middle of the first decade of the new millennium, the Russian feminist scholars/activists succeeded in constructing a new way of thinking about the old problem of domestic violence informed by both global feminist norms and local concerns. The attraction to the notion of economic violence, combined with the common sentiment that the state should continue to provide social support, illustrates that the activists were not tools of neoliberal reformers.

Our analysis also demonstrated that the impact of foreign intervention can be mixed. Some foreign funding designed to support global feminist research ended up supporting de-radicalization of the Russian concept of domestic violence. Funding has worked best (in terms of the feminist conceptualization of domestic violence) when it went to organizations and activists already interested in domestic violence. But this process has created some tactical recycling of research and runs the risk of entrenching these activists as the local experts: the same scholars or activists end up writing the same stuff for funders who know only them, not other activists. Transnational feminist networks appear to have helped spread a concept of economic domestic violence that the Western, especially American, donors would not have chosen. In doing so, the transnational feminist networks have illustrated a commitment to autonomous self-organizing.[21]

Global feminism may have been more successful at setting the terms of the debate in Russia because there was no other strong force offering an alternative way of thinking about women and gender. In contrast, our colleagues studying the new members of the European Union have suggested that the EU's move toward "gender mainstreaming" undermines the more radical, feminist focus on the violence against women (Fábián

2006: 137; Krizsán, Paantjens, and van Lamoen 2005). Ostensibly, gender mainstreaming is a radical move to integrate gender justice concerns throughout the work of governments and public bodies at every step in the policymaking process, but it has also legitimated the elimination of some structures empowered to address women's inequality and focusing more on men than women (Krizsán and Zentai 2006).

Russian Impact on Global Feminism and Beyond

Having examined the impact of global feminist norms, we turn to the impact of Russian activism on global feminist and human rights norms. In examining the global movement addressing violence against women, S. Laurel Weldon (2006) argues that such activism is based on a new commitment to norms of inclusivity and responsiveness. If this is the case, then it would be reasonable to expect that the Russian (and other Eastern European) innovations of global feminist norms concerning domestic violence should have an impact on global feminism and international human rights advocacy. Local and regional innovations, such as the emphasis on economic violence, should begin to be addressed in more recent global feminist documents.

One recent global feminist document is the 2005 Amnesty International (AI) report on Russia titled "Russian Federation: Nowhere to Turn to—Violence Against Women in the Family."[22] After a decade of advocacy on the issue, AI fully committed to the inclusion of gender violence into its human rights work with the inauguration of its transnational Stop Violence Against Women campaign in 2003. Based on AI's research in the Karelia, St. Petersburg, Moscow, and Altai regions, conducted with the assistance of local women's crisis centers, the Russian report acknowledged some progress in these areas, but like an earlier report by Human Rights Watch (1997) it found widespread negligence by state authorities. However, in contrast to the earlier Human Rights Watch study, Amnesty's 2005 report addressed the question of economic violence. AI's definition of domestic violence, in a nod to the Russian definition, states, "[t]he violence may be physical, economical [sic], psychological and sexual (footnote 1.1)." Although Amnesty chose to focus on "physical forms of violence against women in the family," they also acknowledged that

> most of the women who spoke to Amnesty International's representatives had also experienced other forms of gender-based violence, including sexual, psychological or emotional violence and economical [sic] dependency or deprivation, which are no less

harmful to women's ability to fully enjoy their rights than physical violence. (ibid. 2)

Further, AI included some evidence about the extent of economic violence, such as the results from the Gorshkova and Shurygina (2003) survey (Amnesty International 2005: 18). Like Weldon in her (2006) analysis of the global feminist campaign against gender violence, Amnesty appeared to try to balance the global feminist definition with local concerns.

A second piece of evidence of Russian feminist impact on global feminism is the UN special rapporteur's report on violence against women (Erturk 2006), a result of a fact-finding trip to Russia and North Caucasus in December 2004. Erturk became the new rapporteur on violence against women, replacing Radhika Coomaraswamy, who had shaped this position as the global feminist consensus emerged. The UN's report, like Amnesty's, included several findings of Russian authors, such as critiques of Russia's housing and residence permits as obstacles to combating domestic violence, a point raised by Pisklakova and Sinel'nikov in *Violence and Social Changes* (39). More importantly, the special rapporteur also tried to walk the delicate balance of pointing out broader Russian socioeconomic changes while still holding the patriarchal system accountable for the existence of domestic violence in Russia. For example, Erturk included in the report the observation that

> [m]any observers in Russia attribute violence against women to the socio-economic consequences of transition, such as the loss of status experienced by women, increased levels of unemployment, alcohol and drug abuse among men, as well as sexual exploitation. These realities have no doubt intensified the risks of violence for women; however, the loss of status women have experienced is in itself an indication of deep-rooted patriarchal values. (para. 23, 8)

This section suggests that the UN's global feminists have, at least when examining Russia, built upon local understandings of domestic violence. Yet, unlike the Russian authors, the UN's rapporteur did not use the term of economic violence, probably because of the UN's practice of relying on international law and other consensus documents, such as CEDAW and DEVAW, as definitions.

Examples in addition to the UN's special rapporteur's 2005 report demonstrate that including the concept of economic violence is becoming more common. When feminist Minnesota Advocates for Human Rights (MAHR) wrote reports on domestic violence in the Eastern European region in the late 1990s, they did not include economic violence in their working definition. These reports came out of their Women's Program, established in 1993 "to improve the lives of women by using international human rights standards to advocate for women's rights in the United States and around the world."[23] However, in 2000, when MAHR joined the UN's Development Fund for Women (UNIFEM) and the Open Society's Women's Program to establish the Stop Violence Against Women campaign, economic violence was explicitly included.[24] It seems that this choice was a response to the women's groups in the region.[25]

Similarly, economic violence, as a type of domestic abuse, has recently gained recognition in UN documents. The first official mention of economic violence appeared in the final report to the Commissions on Human Rights from the first special rapporteur on violence against women, Radhika Coomaraswamy, who argued that "[domestic] violence is also increasingly defined to include psychological abuse and the withholding of economic necessities from the victim" (2003: 10, para. 30). With a resolution, the General Assembly added a similar concept, "economic deprivation," to DEVAW'S definition of domestic violence (United Nations 2004). Most dramatically, Kofi Annan included economic violence in his speech on the release of the UN's study on violence against women (United Nations 2006), apparently surprising to American observers. The Secretary General's report included "economic violence" in the definition of intimate partner violence (38, para. 113) and as one of the under-documented forms of violence against women (66, para. 222).

Russian activists were not the only ones to employ the concept of economic violence. In addition to other postcommunist societies, it seems to be common in East Asian, Central American, and African societies (for example, it is present in the East and Southeast Asian Regional Program on the Elimination of Violence Against Women 2006). Other recent reports on the global campaign against gender violence have made no reference to economic violence. The World Health Organization's study on domestic violence (García-Moreno et al. 2005) did not use the concept, nor did a recent Human Rights Watch (2006) study of domestic violence in Kyrgyzstan. Still, as ideas circulate more rapidly and freely around the globe, it seems that the postcommunist attraction to the explanatory power of economic violence may have had some impact on quite a few global feminists. In a quick search of more recent documents, in 2009, we found many more references to this notion, including even a reference to "economic abuse" in the definition of domestic violence on the US Department of Justice website.[26]

Over the course of more than a decade, Russian scholars and activists have appropriated and translated global feminist norms concerning domestic violence. Perhaps less fully than the Kazakhstani activists observed by Snajdr in this volume (who created a feminist national origin narrative), the Russians attempted to situate these norms within their own historical and cultural context. Most have endorsed an innovative idea that seems to address Russian contemporary economic conditions, in which people's lives are much more precarious than during recent communist times. The process among activists/scholars has been remarkably collaborative, including not just Russians but North Americans and Nordics and financial support from several Western sources. In sum, global feminist norms—with support from Western donors and transnational feminist networks—seem to have bolstered local activists in a fruitful manner. Russian innovations also appear to have had some impact on global feminist norms, at least reinforcing pressures that global activists were getting from elsewhere to include the factor of economic violence in their construction of domestic violence. The fact that economic violence was not considered by Human Rights Watch or the World Health Organizations is not surprising, because shifting the global consensus, even in the best of circumstances, takes a long time. Local activism has only an indirect influence on international law-making, through NGO forums parallel to the official meetings. From the perspective of global feminists, the postcommunist inclusion in the circulation of global feminist ideas seems a remarkable success, showing that the new global feminism can both push for renewed recognition of women's problems and remain responsive to local concerns.

However, even as Russian feminist activists and opinion leaders recognize domestic violence in new ways, the prospects for significant national reform in Russia appear to have dimmed. In 2006, Russia's President Putin clamped down on nongovernmental organizations, including the large human rights organizations, whose registration was held up by Russian authorities. We can only hope that Russia's remaining democratic procedures will allow these new opinion leaders to have more influence on policymaking and public awareness in the future.

NOTES

The authors are grateful for the feedback from the book's editor, Katalin Fábián, the other chapter writers in this volume, Nanette Funk, and the external reviewer, as well as for financial support from the Brooklyn College Whiting Teaching Fellowship and the City University of New York PSC-CUNY Research Award Program.

1. We reviewed the contents of East View's Russian/NIS databases, including national and regional newspapers, newswires, government documents, and academic journals in social sciences and humanities, almost all of which were in Russian (a handful of sources were in English) from 1994 to 2005 (see http://online.eastview.com/descriptions/index.jsp for description of the databases). In the course of eleven years, we found 1,934 references to various terms for domestic violence, specifically *"domashnee nasilie"* (domestic violence), *"nasilie v sem'e"* (violence in the family), *"semeinoe nasilie,"* (family violence), *"bytovoe nasilie"* (everyday violence), and *"supruzheskoe nasilie"* (spousal violence). "Violence in the family" was by far the most common term, followed by "domestic violence." The latter represents the term most often used by Russian self-identified feminists to represent the feminist concept of violence against women by current or former intimate partners driven by gender inequality. Over time, these feminist activists have joined those who do not identify as feminist in choosing the more inclusive term "violence in the family." This term connotes all violence in the family but has proven more persuasive in the Russian context (see Johnson 2007a, 2007b).

2. Minnesota Advocates for Human Rights (MAHR), "What is Domestic Violence," September 10, 2003, www.stopvaw.org/What_Is_Domestic_Violence2.html (accessed November 18, 2009). As a result, domestic violence (or "family violence" or "abuses in the family") was incorporated into the UN documents that condemn violence against women, such as the General Recommendations 12 (in 1989) and 19 (in 1992) from the Committee for the Convention on the Elimination of All Forms of Discrimination against Women (CEDAW).

3. In 2005, this umbrella organization (called the Russian Association of Crisis Centers for Women, or Association Stop Violence) reported that eighteen of the NGOs in their national network had to close in the previous year due to lack of funding (Amnesty International 2005: 2). ANNA leaders, in the fall of 2005, reported deep concerns that at least some of their member organizations would soon cease to exist.

4. Merry found "that the rights framework does not displace other frameworks [for understanding problems] but adds a new dimension to the way individuals think about problems" (2006: 180–181).

5. These concerns complicate our choice of names to give to women's activism in intergovernmental organizations. The terms scholars and activists use for this activism, such as "global feminism," "transnational feminism(s)," and "international women's movement," and for parts of the world— First World vs. Third World (or even Second World), or postcolonial vs. developing world—can indicate political and cultural commitments or disciplinary backgrounds (Naples 2002: 5–6).

6. Saarinen, personal communication with Johnson, April 22, 2008.

7. Zorica Mrševic (senior research fellow, Institute of Social Science, Belgrade, personal communication with Johnson, December 14, 2006) argued that Russians and the former Yugoslavs "shared the same or similar social/economic/cultural situation and women were exposed to similar if not the same types of violence."

8. Mrševic, personal communication, December 14, 2006.

9. Alexandra Hrycak, personal communication, December 20, 2006. Article 1 of the Ukrainian domestic violence law, in its definition of domestic violence, includes economic violence, which it further defines as "the deliberate deprivation of one

family member by another of the use of living quarters, food, clothing, and other property or funds to which they have a legal right, and which can lead to their death or can harm their physical or mental health" (translated by Hrycak; Zakon Ukrainy pro poperedzhennia nasyl'stva v sim'i [Law of Ukraine for the Prevention of Violence in the Family], Vidomosti Verkhovnoi Rady, 2002, no. 10 p. 70), available at http://zakon1.rada.gov.ua/cgi-bin/laws/main.cgi (accessed Aug. 1, 2007).

10. Heise et al. (1994: 1165), for example, specifically exclude this kind of violence even while examining domestic violence as a neglected public health issue in less developed countries.

11. See, for example, NEWW's online bulletin (1[1], September 1996), www.inch.com/~shebar/neww/neww5.htm (accessed January 9, 2007).

12. The repetition or only a slight modification of earlier works is quite common in our sample. Although problematic in terms of slowing down the development of Russian knowledge and thinking about domestic violence, it reflects the funding environment and represents the tactical use of available funds by crisis centers looking for additional support. Since many donors will not support day-to-day activities, it is essential for organizational survival to be as efficient as possible in using multiple grant opportunities.

13. Both of these Moscow-based crisis centers were founded soon after the collapse of the Soviet Union. While Syostri focused on sexual violence, now including trafficking in women, ANNA has focused on domestic violence (although both have provided assistance for women facing a wide range of violence). Because global funders were more interested in the issue of domestic violence in the late 1990s, ANNA has been more fortunate in getting grants. Both express explicitly feminist orientations and often reference Western feminist theory and practice in their conversations about the work.

14. Zabelina's (2002) survey included 1,528 respondents (both male and female) and covered Tula, Dubna, and the Republic of Komi as well as Moscow. For a discussion of the earlier survey data on domestic violence in Russia, see Johnson (2005).

15. The Gorshkova and Shurgina (2003) survey included 2,100 married people in seven regions (fifty localities) in Russia.

16. For example, Pisklakova and Sinel'nikov (2000:29) mention that "one woman who turned to ANNA for assistance was the wife of a Duma [lower house of the national parliament] deputy, another was the wife of a very famous journalist, and a third was the wife of a successful businessman" (translated by authors).

17. Fábián (2006: 136) argues that "[t]he various resistances toward gender-specific terminology and policy from Central Europe did not originally create, but may have strengthened, a move toward a gender-neutral and child-focused interpretation of domestic violence." The Russian tension between gender neutrality and global feminism suggests that Russian activism has not had the same consequence.

18. See also Olsen (1997), Hemment (2004b), and Ghodsee (2004) for similar critiques. Another analysis employs rational choice arguments about misplaced incentives to please Western stakeholders rather than truly support civil society (Henderson 2003).

19. Anastasia Posadskaya-Vanderbeck, personal conversation with Johnson, New York, June 17, 2004.

20. Most of these comments were off the record, heard by Johnson, while conducting fieldwork in Russia in 1999, 2002, 2004, and 2005, in a variety of cities in the Western half of Russia.

21. Personal conversations by Johnson with scholars/activists (co-founders of the Network East-West Women) Ann Snitow, Sonia Jaffe Robbins, and Nanette Funk, New York, 2006.

22. The report was published both in Russian and in English. The page numbers reflect the English version.

23. Minnesota Advocates for Human Rights (hereafter MAHR), "Women's Program," www.mnadvocates.org/Women_s_Program.html (accessed June 28, 2006).

24. The English-language website is www.stopvaw.org and the Russian www .russian.stopvaw.org.

25. Elisabeth Duban (MAHR consultant), personal communication with Johnson, December 5, 2006; MAHR, "What is domestic violence." MAHR's definition is the following: "Domestic violence is a pattern of abusive and threatening behaviors that may include physical, emotional, economic and sexual violence as well as intimidation, isolation and coercion."

26. US Department of Justice Office on Violence Against Women, "About Domestic Violence," www.ovw.usdoj.gov/domviolence.htm (accessed February 4, 2009).

WORKS CITED

Abubikirova, Natalia, Tatiana Klimenkova, Elena Kotchkina, Marina Regentova, and Tatiana Troinova. 1998. *Directory of Women's Nongovernmental Organizations in Russia and the NIS*, trans. I. Savelieva. Moscow: Aslan Publishers.

Alvarez, Sonia. 1999. "The Latin American feminist NGO 'boom.'" *International Feminist Journal of Politics* 1(2): 181–209.

Amnesty International. 2005. *Rossiiskaia Federatsiia: Nekuda bezhat'—domashnee nasilie nad zhenshchinami* [Russian Federation: Nowhere to Turn to—Violence against Women in the Family], EUR 46/056/2005. London: Amnesty International.

ANNA Crisis Center. 2000. *Nasilie i Sotsial'nye Izmeneniia: Teoriia, Praktika, Issledovaniia* [Violence and Social Change: Theory, Practice, and Research]. Moscow: TACIS/CARITAS.

———. 2001. *Social'nomu Rabotniku o Probleme Domashnego Nasiliia* [To the Social Worker on the Problem of Domestic Violence]. Moscow: Ministry of Labor and Social Development, Department on Children, Women and Family.

Attwood, Lynne. 1997. "'She Was Asking for It': Rape and Domestic Violence against Women." *Post-Soviet Women: From the Baltic to Central Asia*, ed. Mary Buckley, 99–118. Cambridge: Cambridge University Press.

Balibalova, D. I., P. P. Glushchenko, and E. M. Tikhomirova. 2001. *Sotsial'no-pravovaia zashchita zhenshchin: Predotvrashchenie nasiliia v otnoshenii zhenshchin i detei* [Social-Legal Protection of Women: Prevention of Violence against Women and Children]. St. Petersburg: CPB: NII khimmii SPBGU.

Bridger, Sue, Kathryn Pinnick, and Rebecca Kay. 1996. *No More Heroines? Russia, Women and the Market*. London and New York: Routledge.

Coomaraswamy, Radhika. 1996. *Report of the Special Rapporteur on Violence Against Women, Its Causes and Consequences, in Accordance with Commission on Human Rights Resolution 1995/85 (United Nations E/CN.4/1996/53), A Framework for Model Legislation on Domestic Violence,* E/CN.4/1996/53/Add.2.

————. 2003. *Integration of the Human Rights of Women and the Gender Perspective.* United Nations E/CN.4/2003/75, January 6, www.unhchr.ch/Huridocda/ Huridoca.nsf/0/d90c9e2835619e79c1256ce00058c145/$FILE/G0310100.pdf (accessed November 7, 2007).

Drakulić, Slavenka. 1993. *How We Survived Communism and Even Laughed.* London: Vantage.

East and Southeast Asian Regional Program on the Elimination of Violence Against Women. 2006. *A Life Free of Violence: It's Our Right!* UNIFEM, Bangkok, Thailand: UNIFEM. www.unifem-eseasia.org/resources/others/domesticviolence/ PDF/Definition.pdf (accessed November 7, 2009).

Erturk, Yakin. 2006. *Integration of the Human Rights of Women and a Gender Perspective: Violence Against Women: Report of the Special Rapporteur on Violence against Women, Its Causes and Consequences: Mission to the Russian Federation,* E/CN.4/2006/61/Add.2.

Fábián, Katalin. 2006. "Against Domestic Violence: The Interaction of Global Networks with Local Activism in Central Europe." In *European Responses to Globalization: Resistance, Adaptation, and Alternatives,* ed. Janet Laible and Henri J. Barkey, 111–152. New York: Elsevier Press.

García-Moreno, Claudia, Henrica A.F.M. Jansen, Mary Ellsberg, Lori Heise, and Charlotte Watts. 2005. *WHO Multi-country Study on Women's Health and Domestic Violence against Women: Initial Results on Prevalence, Health Outcomes and Women's Responses.* World Health Organization. www.who.int/gender/ violence/who_multicountry_study/en/index.html (accessed November 7, 2009).

Ghodsee, Kristen. 2004. "Feminism-by-Design: Emerging Capitalisms, Cultural Feminism, and Women's Nongovernmental Organizations in Postsocialist Eastern Europe." *Signs: Journal of Women in Culture and Society* 29(3): 728–753.

Gorshkova, I. D., and I. I. Shurygina. 2003. *Nasilie nad zhenami v sovremennykh rossi-iskikh sem'iakh* [Violence against Women in Contemporary Russian Families]. Moscow: Moscow State University Women's Committee.

Heise, Lori, Alanagh Raikes, Charlotte H. Watts, and Anthony B. Zwi. 1994. "Violence Against Women: A Neglected Public Health Issue in Less Developed Countries." *Social Science and Medicine* 39(3): 1165–1179.

Hemment, Julie. 2004a. "Global Civil Society and the Local Costs of Belonging: Defining 'Violence against Women' in Russia." *Signs* 29: 815–840.

————. 2004b. "The Riddle of the Third Sector: Civil Society, International Aid, and NGOs in Russia." *Anthropological Quarterly* 77(2): 215–241.

Henderson, Sarah L. 2003. *Building Democracy in Contemporary Russia: Western Support for Grassroots Organizations.* Ithaca, N.Y.: Cornell University Press.

Heyzer, Noeleen. 1998. "Working towards a World Free from Violence against Women: UNIFEM's Contribution." *Gender and Development* 6: 17–26.

Human Rights Watch. 1997. "Russia—Too Little, Too Late: State Response to Violence against Women." *Human Rights Watch* 9(13): 1–51.

———. 2006. "Reconciled to Violence: State Failure to Stop Domestic Abuse and Abduction of Women in Kyrgyzstan." *Human Rights Watch* 18(9): 1–140.

Ishkanian, Armine. 2004. "Working at the Local-Global Intersection: The Challenges Facing Women in Armenia's Nongovernmental Sector." In *Post-Soviet Women Encountering Transition: Nation-Building, Economic Survival, and Civic Activism,* ed. Kathleen Kuenhast and Carol Nechemias, 262–278. Washington, D.C., and Baltimore, Md.: Woodrow Wilson Center Press/Johns Hopkins University Press.

Israelian, E. B., and T. Iu. Zabelina. 1995. *Kak sozdat' krizisnyi tsentr dlia zhenshchin* [How to Start a Crisis Center for Women]. Moscow: Press-Solo.

Johnson, Janet Elise. 2001. "Privatizing Pain: The Problem of Woman Battery in Russia." *NWSA Journal* 13(3): 153–168.

———. 2006. "Public-Private Permutations: Domestic Violence Crisis Centers in Barnaul." In *Russian Civil Society: A Critical Assessment,* ed. Al Evans, Laura Henry, and Lisa McIntosh Sundstrom, 266–283. Armonk, N.Y.; London: M.E. Sharpe.

———. 2007. "Contesting Violence, Contesting Gender: Crisis Centers Encountering Local Governments in Barnaul, Russia." In *Living Gender after Communism,* ed. Janet Elise Johnson and Jean C. Robinson, 40–59. Bloomington: Indiana University Press.

———. 2009. *Gender Violence in Russia: The Politics of Feminist Intervention.* Bloomington: Indiana University Press.

Johnson, Janet Elise, and Laura Brunell. 2006. "The Emergence of Contrasting Domestic Violence Regimes in Postcommunist Europe." *Policy and Politics* 34(4): 578–98.

Johnson, Janet Elise, and Jean C. Robinson. 2007. "Living Gender." *Living Gender after Communism,* ed. Janet Elise Johnson and Jean C. Robinson, 1–21. Bloomington: Indiana University Press.

Kaselitz, Verena. 2006. "The Networking of European Women's Organizations and Women's Researchers as Transnational Action against Human Rights Violations: Benefits and Obstacles." Paper given at "Gendered Domains: Politics and Democracy in Russia Today," November 16, seminar at Aleskanteri Institute, Helsinki, Finland.

Kay, Rebecca. 2000. *Russian Women and Their Organizations.* New York: St. Martin's Press.

Keck, Margaret, and Kathryn Sikkink. 1998. *Activists Beyond Borders: Transnational Advocacy Networks in International Politics.* Ithaca, N.Y.: Cornell University Press.

Krizsán, Andrea, Marjolein Paantjens, and Ilse van Lamoen. 2005. "Domestic Violence: Who's [sic] Problem." *The Greek Review of Social Research* 117(B): 63–92.

Krizsán, Andrea, and Violetta Zentai. 2006. "Gender Equality Policy or Gender Mainstreaming? The Case of Hungary on the Road to an Enlarged Europe." *Policy Studies* 27(2): 135–151.

Mendelson, Sarah E., and John K. Glenn, eds. 2002. *The Power and Limits of NGOs: A Critical Look at Building Democracy in Eastern Europe and Eurasia.* New York: Columbia University Press.

Merry, Sally Engle. 2006. *Human Rights and Gender Violence: Translating International Law into Local Justice.* Chicago: University of Chicago Press.

Moghadam, Valentine M. 2005. *Globalizing Women: Transnational Feminist Networks.* Baltimore: Johns Hopkins University Press.

Mohanty, Chandra, ed. 1991. *Third World Women and the Politics of Feminism.* Bloomington: Indiana University Press.

Mrsevic, Zorica. 2000. "Belgrade's SOS Hotline for Women and Children Victims of Violence: A Report." In *Reproducing Gender: Politics, Publics, and Everyday Life after Socialism,* ed. Susan Gal and Gail Kligman, 370–392. Princeton, N.J.: Princeton University Press.

Mrsevic, Zorica, and Donna M. Hughes. 1997. "Violence Against Women in Belgrade, Serbia: SOS Hotline 1990–1993." *Violence Against Women—An International Interdisciplinary Journal* 3(2): 101–128.

Naples, Nancy A. 2002. "Changing the Terms: Community Activism, Globalization, and the Dilemmas of Transnational Feminist Praxis." In *Women's Activism and Globalization: Linking Local Struggles and Transnational Politics,* ed. Nancy A. Naples and Manisha Desai, 3–14. New York: Routledge.

Noonan, Norma Corigliano, and Carol Nechemias, eds. 2001. *Encyclopedia of Russian Women's Movements.* Westport, Conn.: Praeger.

Olsen, Frances Elisabeth. 1997. "Feminism in Central and Eastern Europe: Risks and Possibilities of American Engagement." *The Yale Law Journal* 106: 2215–2257.

Pisklakova, Marina, and Andrei Sinel'nikov. 2000. "Mezhdu molchaniem i krikom" [Between Silence and the Scream]. In *Nasilie i sotsial'nye izmeneniia* [Violence and Social Changes]. ANNA Crisis Center: TACIS, CARITAS.

Rimashevskaia, N. M. 2005. *Razorvat' krug molchaniia* [To Break the Circle of Silence]. Moscow: Moscow Center of Gender Studies and Institute of Socioeconomic Problems of Population at the Russian Academy of Sciences.

Saarinen, Aino, Olga Liapounova, and Irina Drachova. 2003. "NCRB: A Network for Crisis Centres for Women in the Barents Region" (Report of the Nordic-Russian Development Project, 1999–2002). In *Gender Research: Methodology and Practice,* ed. Elena Kudriashova, Raissa Danilova, Marina Kalinina, Natalia Koukarenko, Olga Liapounova, Irina Lugovskaia, and Larissa Malik, 1–248. Arkhangelsk, Russia: Pomor State University.

Shelley, Louise. 1987. "Inter-Personal Violence in the USSR." *Violence, Aggression and Terrorism* 1(2): 41–67.

Sperling, Valerie. 1990. "Rape and domestic violence in the USSR." *Response to the Victimization of Women and Children: Journal of the Center for Women Policy Studies* 13(3): 16–22.

———. 1999. *Organizing Women in Contemporary Russia: Engendering Transition.* Cambridge: Cambridge University Press.

Sperling, Valerie, Myra Marx Ferree, and Barbara Risman. 2001. "Constructing Global Feminism: Transnational Advocacy Networks and Russian Women's Activism." *Signs: Journal of Women in Culture and Society* 26(4): 1155–1186.

Sundstrom, Lisa McIntosh. 2005. "Foreign Assistance, International Norms, and NGO Development: Lessons from the Russian Campaign." *International Organization* 59(Spring): 419–449.

United Nations. 2006. Secretary-General Report, "In-Depth Study on All Forms of Violence against Women." General Assembly, United Nations. A/61/122/ Add.1. www.un.org/womenwatch/daw/vaw/SGstudyvaw.htm#more (accessed November 7, 2009).

United Nations General Assembly. 1993. Declaration on the Elimination of Violence against Women (DEVAW). Resolution 48/104 of December 20. http://portal. unesco.org/education/en/files/37319/11024176493Declaration-Elimination-Violence-Women.pdf/Declaration-Elimination-Violence-Women.pdf (accessed November 7, 2009).

United Nations General Assembly Resolution 58/147. 2004. Elimination of Domestic Violence Against Women. http://www2.ohchr.org/english/law/eliminationvaw .htm (accessed November 7, 2009).

Wedel, Janine. 2001. *Collision and Collusion: The Strange Case of Western Aid to Eastern Europe*. New York: St. Martin's Press.

Weldon, Lauren. 2006. "Inclusion, Solidarity, and Social Movements: The Global Movement against Gender Violence." *Perspectives on Politics* 4(1): 55–74.

Zabelina, Tat'iana. 1996. Sexual Violence towards Women. In *Gender, Generation and Identity in Contemporary Russia*, ed. Hilary Pilkington, 169–186. New York: Routledge.

———. 2002. *Rossiia: Nasilie v sem'e—nasilie v obshchestve* [Russia: Violence in the Family—Violence in Society]. Moscow: UNIFEM, UNFPA.

Zabelina, Tat'iana, ed. 2002. *Rossiia: Nasilie v sem'e—nasilie v obshchestve* [Russia: Violence in the Family, Violence in Society]. Moscow: UNIFEM and UNFPA.

Zabelina, Tat'iana and Yevgeniia Israeliian. 1999. *Dostizheniia i nahodki: Krizisnie tsentri Rossii* [Achievements and Findings of the Crisis Centers of Russia]. Moscow: Press-Solo.

CHAPTER 4

Balancing Acts: Women's NGOs Combating Domestic Violence in Kazakhstan

EDWARD SNAJDR

"We hid our neighbor in the basement boiler room of our apartment complex. She lived there for several days. This is how our organization began." Julia sat upright in her office chair as she recalled the pragmatic origins of Podrugi, Kazakhstan's first crisis center and shelter for battered women.[1] Julia's nongovernmental organization, *Podrugi* (Girlfriends), which was officially registered in Almaty in 1998, opened the first domestic violence shelter in the formerly Soviet Central Asian republic.[2] Like other victim service organizations around the globe, Podrugi started out as a small, grassroots network of private citizens who volunteered their time and resources to help women suffering from intimate partner violence (Faier 2002; Kelly 1996; Merry 2005; Mrševic 2000; Wang 1999). In less than three years Podrugi developed into a full-service organization with a permanent staff of eighteen employees who, along with thirteen volunteers, operate a twenty-four-hour domestic violence hotline and a battered women's shelter. In addition to these services, Podrugi provides occasional training for law enforcement and other criminal justice officials around the country. In 2001, Nadezhda Gladyr, Podrugi's executive director, helped to establish a national network of twenty-two NGO-run crisis centers for victims of domestic abuse. A year later, members of Podrugi, along with activists from other women's NGOs in Kazakhstan, also began to collaborate with police officers in the Ministry of the Interior to begin to draft a national domestic violence law.

If one follows Johnson and Brunell's recent characterization of domestic violence policy, discourse, and practice as domestic violence regimes, Kazakhstan appears to be at the level of "moderate reform" (Johnson and Brunell 2006). Podrugi's achievements in the area of victim services suggest the growing presence of NGO participation in shaping domestic violence policy. At the same time, the state, under the leadership of President Nursultan Nazarbayev, has demonstrated a degree of institutional commitment to the problem. In 1998, Nazarbayev created the National Commission for Women and Family—a government agency focusing on, among other things, women's security and well-being. A year later, the Ministry of the Interior established special domestic violence units as part of its national police force.

A key factor in helping NGOs and the state begin to cooperate on addressing the issue of domestic violence in Kazakhstan has been the involvement of the international community, particularly the United States and Western Europe. For example, Podrugi has received institutional support from HIVOS, a Dutch organization championing women's empowerment, and from the Soros Foundation. In early 2000, both Podrugi and the Ministry of the Interior began to collaborate with a training project for which I served as a co-director that was funded by the US State Department and administered by Florida State University.[3] The aims of the project were to develop and implement a curriculum for law enforcement in order to improve their responses to domestic violence and to encourage activists and police to sustain this collaborative training effort after US involvement ended. Podrugi's success in securing external funding and the state's modest effort at creating specialized domestic violence police units were two of the major reasons that the State Department police training project focused on Kazakhstan.

Starting from 2000, the project team brought together both NGO activists and police officers assigned to new domestic violence units to develop a curriculum. By the end of the year, the project team held training sessions in Almaty and then moved to other cities and towns around the country. Each session involved both police and domestic violence activists, including members of Podrugi, the Feminist League and the Women's Information Center, as co-trainers alongside US service providers and law enforcement. During the pilot stages of the project, American participants made significant contributions to the training, but subsequent sessions were revised and managed by local Kazakhstani partners.

Most of the data I present below are from ethnographic field research that I conducted during 2000–2003 while co-directing the training project. This research consisted of interviews and observations among women activists and law enforcement officers, as well as among US police service providers and government officials. During field research I worked as both a traditional ethnographer (i.e., as an "outsider") and as a project collaborator (an insider). This unique position afforded alternating frames of reference and analysis of behavior and information regarding participants of the project and the people with which they worked. On the one hand this was a case of "studying up and over" (Markowitz 2001: 42), whereby many of my ethnographic subjects, namely NGO leaders, were individuals operating in a transnational arena. At the same time, such people move frequently between the local neighborhoods in which they live and work and the more distant and diverse settings of international activism, including conferences, trainings, and demonstrations that they often attend. In contrast to the transnational movement, my "insider" status as a project director afforded unique access as an ethnographer to events and dialogues of which I was a direct participant or subject. Thus, in looking at domestic violence policy and practice in Kazakhstan, along with the emic perspectives of local experts and stakeholders in both the NGO community and law enforcement, I include the views of several participants from the United States.[4] Both local and transnational perspectives can reveal much about the larger frames of the Kazakhstani state's policies and about local civic initiatives, as well as describing the role that international assistance programs can play in shaping local actions and experiences.

While the two primary dimensions of Kazakhstan's domestic violence regime—NGOs and the state—have seen a measure of progress, it is important to recognize that both dimensions involve obstacles that are unique to a multi-ethnic post-Soviet society, including the revival of traditional cultural practices influencing attitudes about gender and directly affecting women's lives, as well as a judiciary that is resistant to reform. In this chapter, I outline how women's activists have engaged the issue of domestic violence in Kazakhstan as a series of negotiations with the post-Soviet state, its society and culture, and the international community. Thus, in addition to describing domestic violence policy in Kazakhstan for comparison with other cases in this volume, I aim to highlight the processes by which activists create and promote local domestic violence policies in the context of specific cultural and political challenges.

Sally Merry (2005) has recently explored the act of translating human rights in traditional gender contexts, arguing that this process involves articulating international principles and concepts within a local framework of traditions and institutions. In her investigation into the question of translating global feminism as human rights discourse, Merry focuses on how the issue of domestic violence requires the work of individual activists moving between and among international arenas and local contexts. In my work with members of Podrugi and their colleagues in other women's organizations, I discovered that this translation process involved more than simply inserting international rights discourse into local vernaculars. It also required balancing political relationships among stakeholders and performing the problem of and solutions to domestic violence within national discourses and local bureaucracies. By performing I mean not only the practice of explaining why domestic violence occurs, but also the political implications and significance of defining, presenting, and understanding the problem in particular ways and for the benefit of specific audiences.

The performative translations put forth by women's activists have aimed to build both discursive and practical bridges across various professional and cultural divides: between police and activists, between urban and rural identities, and between the local and international worldviews. As I will discuss below, women's activists translate domestic violence issues into practices and concepts that draw equally upon local professional sensibilities and perspectives, national and cultural identity politics, and the pragmatic interpretation and exploitation of international rights discourses. NGO practices have emerged from the confluence of grassroots pragmatism among women's activists—who aim for broader social and political change for women in Kazakhstan, the post-Soviet state's nationalist posturing vis-à-vis the large ethnic Russian community, and the limits and restrictions of international development resources. In order to shape domestic violence policy in a postcommunist state, women's activists must perform a series of balancing acts between the principles of global feminism and local ethnic politics, and between institutional norms and NGO-driven reforms. While some of these performances on the part of women's activists appear to be contradictory, I conclude that the pragmatic approaches of Kazakhstan's activist community, which prioritize national identities and highlight political expressions of belonging, may be among its most important strengths in securing future success in aiding victims of domestic violence.

New Women's NGOs in Post-Soviet Kazakhstan

The pragmatism and versatility of Kazakhstan's domestic violence activist community has its origins in the country's dynamic and diverse ethnographic and political landscape. Living among Kazakhstan's eight million ethnic Kazakhs, who make up a 47 percent plurality of the country's citizens are over five million Russians, and several million people belonging to other ethnic groups.[5] This multi-ethnic society continues to grapple with the dramatic move in 1991 away from Soviet domination and toward the often brutal and unforgiving effects of entering the global market economy. With sweeping changes affecting the country, Nazarbayev's postcommunist government, following previous trends of authoritarian rule, tries to balance the relationships between the various ethnic groups through a strong centralized approach to governance. Yet the state has discretely supported a burgeoning Kazakh nationalism, which includes an increased focus on Islam and on the traditional ethnic clans, the *zhuz* (Schatz 2004). Although language reforms have promoted Kazakh (a Turkic language), much of the country still speaks Russian, particularly in urban areas.[6]

While many women in postcommunist Central Asia are embracing new market economies (Kuehnast 1998; Werner 1997) and have benefited from the communist-era education and employment, their representation in state structures and legislative bodies has declined dramatically since communism's collapse (Northrop 2000). They also suffer, along with men, the effects of widespread unemployment and poverty. At the end of the 1990s, over 50 percent of all adult women were unemployed and this number has been rising (Feminist League 1997: 65). Women are also twice as likely to be unemployed as men (National Commission on Family and Women [NCFW] 2000: 74).[7] In rural areas, women still have much less access to education or adequate healthcare. At the same time, traditional pastoralist or Muslim customs affecting women's status and power have persisted and in some areas are enjoying a vigorous revitalization (Doi 2002; Michaels 1998). For example, extended family, patrilocal residence, and bride-price prior to marriage continue to be commonly practiced and openly accepted among both rural and some urban Kazakh families. Moreover, Werner (2003) has reported that kidnapping of brides has increased, particularly in Kazakhstan's heavily Kazakh and Muslim southern regions, despite the state's criminalization of the practice.

Alongside these dynamics, which Kuehnast (1998: 639) describes as the contradictory gender discourses of postcommunism, has emerged a small but growing women's movement that seeks to address a wide range of social, political, and economic issues facing Kazakhstani women (Ruffin and Waugh 1999). While some of these organizations had their roots in the communist-era women's movement, many did not. Even though independent organizations were not allowed under communism, during the Gorbachev period the party-state encouraged greater activism and growth among women's councils (Browning 1987,

1992). Most of these councils, which were the only women-specific and party-mandated organizations during the Soviet period, amounted to little more than consciousness-raising clubs aimed at discussing gender equity (Ferree et al. 1999). Nevertheless, a few women's councils in Kazakhstan provided the basis for more focused activism on behalf of women's rights in the postcommunist period (Konstantinova 1996: 180–181). For example, the Feminist League, Kazakhstan's most visible, vocal, and Western-oriented women's rights group, was founded in 1992 by a group of journalists and artists who had gathered as a women's council during the Gorbachev period to promote women in the arts and media (Feminist League 1999). Other organizations, such as the Women's Information Network, the Association of Single Mothers, and the International Ecological Association Women of the Orient, had all been started by individuals who had been involved with women's councils during late communism. Following the collapse of communism, they began to shape post-Soviet gender politics in Kazakhstan by engaging the state over questions of women's political rights and representation throughout the 1990s.

This politically oriented approach to women's issues, however, was not the path taken by activists who started Podrugi. In fact, prior to 1999, the members of Podrugi had little if any contact with other and earlier women's rights groups in Kazakhstan or elsewhere. Yet through the issue of domestic violence Podrugi activists have become central figures in Kazakhstan's post-Soviet civil society and have made important contributions to shaping new dialogues about women's rights in the country.

Translating Kitchen Activism into Public Action

The six founding members of Podrugi had been a group of friends who lived in an Almaty neighborhood in the early 1980s. Their backgrounds varied—from housewives to highly educated working professionals—but they were socially connected by their common residential community and would meet regularly for tea. None of them had set out with the intention to become full-time activists for women's rights. During the course of one of Podrugi's gatherings, Luba admitted to being abused by her husband. Upon hearing Luba's confession, the others also revealed that they had been, at one time or another, victims of physical or psychological violence at the hands of a spouse or family member. The abuse in Luba's case, however, was so severe that she ended up fleeing her apartment in 1992. The members of Podrugi hid her and her children in the basement of a friend's building.[8]

Luba's experience was not the only case of informal or underground sheltering performed by members of Podrugi. Over the years, others in the group were also forced to seek shelter from their abusers and would find it among their friends. For example, when Tamara married, she began to experience multiple forms of abuse. Her mother-in-law feared that in the event that the couple divorced, Tamara would wrest the apartment away from her only son, leaving the mother-in-law without a place to live. Partially out of this fear, she despised her daughter-in-law. When the husband abused Tamara, his mother did nothing to help the daughter-in-law. In fact, she encouraged these "disciplinary actions." Tamara left the apartment and stayed with Luba for six months.

In dealing with these painful personal experiences of women looking for shelter, Nadezhda's home telephone became a makeshift "hotline." At the time that Podrugi started its work, there were practically no services for women suffering from domestic abuse. Police were technically responsible for the safety of citizens, including victims of violence within the home (Shelly 1996: 139). But both police practice and the attitudes of prosecutors and judges provided little assistance. With the growing access to information that accompanied the collapse of the Soviet Union, the members researched opportunities to get support from international groups interested in helping battered women and learned about how women in other societies had started shelters or crisis centers for victims of domestic violence. In 1996, they decided to create their own crisis center, using Nadezhda's apartment. Shortly after registering the group as an independent NGO in 1998, Podrugi was awarded a grant from HIVOS, a Dutch organization championing women's empowerment, to start a battered women's shelter in Almaty. With several thousand Euro from HIVOS, Podrugi was able to purchase a building for the shelter and rent an apartment for their crisis center office. When they opened the new crisis center facility, much of their work was devoted to explaining to various sorts of people, from police and government officials to ordinary residents, what exactly the organization did. A state-wide Kazakhstani television station, KTK-TV, had an open microphone show based in Almaty. Nadezhda signed up and was given twenty minutes during one of their broadcasts to get the word out about their new crisis center and their plans for the shelter. By 1999, Podrugi opened Kazakhstan's first domestic violence shelter in a modest building that once served as a neighborhood kindergarten. The shelter site was vandalized before renovation work was complete. Activists never found out who caused the damage, but they learned from nearby residents that rumors had been circulating in the area that a "woman's house" was going to be operating there, which people interpreted to mean a brothel.[9]

By 2001, Podrugi had moved their crisis center to a three-room apartment at a secret location in one of Almaty's suburbs, and began offering a twenty-four-hour hotline. But moving from citizen volunteers to full-time service providers with no professional training proved challenging. Nadezhda recalled that

> We did not know the half of running a shelter. At first, we allowed women only fourteen days to stay. Two weeks, that was all. We now know that this is so little time to figure things out. So we have revised the stay to up to two months (interview with Gladyr, March 3, 2002).

Another unforeseen problem was how best to meet the needs of children who often accompanied their mothers to the shelter. With only sixteen beds in the facility, a woman with four kids took up a third of the available space. Another Podrugi staffer, remembering the shelter's early days, reported that "Our shelter was bare-bones at first. Now we have toys and furniture for children. We created spaces that kids can enjoy and in which they can feel safe" (interview with Aigul, April 25, 2003).

While Podrugi was piecing together the vital services that victims of battering actually required, the Kazakhstani government established domestic violence units in police departments around the country. These special units of the Ministry of the Interior were quite small. The domestic violence unit in the Almaty City police—the country's largest—had a staff of only six officers. Other units around the country consisted of one or two officers, reassigned from some other division or unit. For example, in the Petropavlovsk region in northern Kazakhstan, a police captain who had worked with juvenile crime division was designated to be the domestic violence officer for the entire region, with a population of over 700,000 people.

This surprisingly positive but limited effort on the part of the state was not coordinated with any other governmental entity. It was also accomplished without consultation with key women's organizations such as the Feminist League or the Women's Information Center. Furthermore, police officers who were assigned to these units received little if any formal training. The government's assumption appeared to be that these specialized officers' experience with juvenile crime would be sufficient to address the issue of intimate partner violence in the home. In fact, these units' initial mandate, according to the colonel who was appointed to oversee the Almaty unit, was simply to gather data on crimes against women and specifically on crimes involving spouses and families. Most of the officers assigned to the special domestic violence unit took on this new responsibility on top of their previous duties (interview with Shopshekbayeva, February 2, 2000).

Several women's organizations interpreted the creation of domestic violence units in the Ministry of the Interior as a half-measure on the part of Nazarbayev's government. They argued that by forming these units the state wanted to appear to more comprehensively fulfill its commitment to the Convention on the Elimination of All Forms of Discrimination Against Women (CEDAW). As a signatory state of CEDAW, Kazakhstan had also established the National Commission on Family and Women, whose main task was to submit an annual report to the UN CEDAW committee on the status of women and children in the country. Regardless of why these units were created and whether the government was serious about supporting their work, Podrugi activists reached out to them within months of their formation. Podrugi started with the obvious step of providing the police with the organization's hotline number and told them about their shelter and crisis center (interview with Gladyr, March 3, 2002).

Yet Podrugi quickly realized that the new police units lacked the training to assist the NGO's work with victims of battering. For example, when Nadezhda told the colonel about her shelter, she was at first enthusiastic and hopeful that the police officers would help victims who were in danger get to the facility safely. However, on more than one occasion, after delivering a victim to Podrugi, the officer later revealed to the victim's husband where his wife was staying. One captain even gave the shelter's address to a particularly aggressive batterer. Podrugi activists quickly realized that if police were going to aid them in their work, they would require training beyond what the state was providing these police officers. Such specific training did not need to be elaborate or lengthy, and after initiating several meetings with the domestic violence unit in Almaty, Nadezhda convinced the colonel to allow her staff to train the police officers. As a sign of good faith, the officer who had revealed the shelter's location was later reassigned to another department at the request of the unit's commander.

Despite the fact that NGO-driven victim services and nascent law enforcement responses were starting to connect in the late 1990s, these collaborations had no impact on the rest of the justice system. The only punishments that courts enforced on abusive husbands—that is, if such cases were even to get as far as a courtroom—came in the form of relatively small fines. In terms of preparing a case against a batterer, women were required by the court to pay for their own medical exams in order to submit evidence about the crime. Nevertheless, Podrugi activists and local police in Almaty began to work together at the level of community intervention and in the context of US-funded police training.

Transforming Global Feminism into Local Practice

In the initial months of the US-sponsored training project, American team members thought it important to provide Kazakhstani project participants with expertise on the utilization of human rights discourse for local activists and law enforcement. We quickly discovered, however, that Kazakh women's activists, and many state officials for that matter, were well-versed in the language of human rights. In fact, several NGO activists and police officers pointed out to us that the United States had still not signed onto CEDAW, as Kazakhstan had already done by 1998. Nevertheless, ensuring that the government of Kazakhstan abided by the protocol outlined in CEDAW became a priority goal among several women's NGOs, including the Feminist League and the Women's Information Center. Both of these organizations provided Podrugi with political allies in their work on domestic violence, since activists from each group had prior experience working alongside, as well as critiquing, state officials. For example, the Feminist League exploited Kazakhstan's signature status on the UN's CEDAW convention as an opportunity to help formulate and revise the state's strategy to improve the status of women and to address, in particular, the issue of violence against women. To achieve this, women's NGOs submitted a critique—or what is known as a shadow report—of the official report that the NCFW presented to the UN. A significant portion of this shadow report highlighted the situation of violence against women in Kazakhstan, a problem that previously had little data available. With Podrugi's cooperation, however, the Feminist League could now include some real numbers for at least the city of Almaty. In 2000, 1,028 calls were made to Podrugi's hotline and sixty-four women sought protection at their shelter (Podrugi 2003). Prior to these numbers, the only statistics regarding domestic violence among residents in Almaty were the result of a survey commissioned by the NCFW which suggested that nearly 30 percent of all women experienced domestic violence at some point in their life (NCFW 1999). A recent survey conducted by the Ministry of the Interior (with cooperation from Podrugi) reported that 70 percent of respondents experienced violence in the home each year (UNIFEM 2005).[10]

Interestingly, in 1998 the NCFW asked the Feminist League to help them write the country's official CEDAW Report. In this sense, the Feminist League created a civic-state relationship that was mutually beneficial, albeit with a marginal government agency. In fact, the organization found itself on both sides of state policymaking. On the one hand, it assisted the National Commission in presenting data regarding women's employment, education, and health services. On the other, it offered an openly critical analysis of, and legislative recommendations to address, traditional and patriarchal marriage customs, workplace inequality, and the pervasiveness of forms of violence against women (Feminist League Commentary 2000)

Kazakhstan's ratification of CEDAW provided Podrugi and other women's NGOs with an internationally legitimated agenda, and it gave them a platform upon which to build stronger relationships with international women's organizations and Western feminist groups. Although members of the Feminist League and other women's NGOs had attended the Beijing Summit in 1995 and had traveled to dozens of conferences sponsored by the European Union and the United States, their pragmatic partnership with the Commission on Family and Women brought a dialogue about global feminism home. Even though several Podrugi activists visited the United States through the Sister Cities program for training on practical issues such as running a domestic violence hotline and the administration and expansion of an issue-based NGO, their work with the Feminist League encouraged them to apply their knowledge in an attempt to draft a national domestic violence law in collaboration with Kazakh law enforcement.

In addition to using international human rights discourses such as those articulated by CEDAW to apply pressure on the state to address domestic violence, NGOs have found other international discursive frameworks to be vital to public outreach efforts. For example, Podrugi and other women's organizations have capitalized on the international campaign Sixteen Days of Activism against Gender Violence, first developed in 1991 by the Center for Global Women's Leadership at Rutgers University. (See chapter 8 in this volume for other examples of NGOs joining from postcommunist states.) In 2002, between November 25, the International Day against Violence against Women, and December 10, International Human Rights Day, Podrugi, along with the Women's

Information Center and the Feminist League, organized a series of public information events about domestic violence with support from the Soros Foundation Open Society Foundation (OSI). The international campaign, which is designed to coordinate NGO activities around the globe, provided Podrugi with a high-profile discursive frame within which it could open dialogue with both the government and local communities about gender violence. This campaign has helped to structure the public face of the women's movement in general and Podrugi in particular by providing an annual (and therefore cyclical) discursive platform. Its first events in 2002, which included public service radio announcements and pamphlet campaigns, have developed into tightly coordinated seminars and meetings involving high school students, activists, and domestic violence police officers from the Ministry of the Interior (Podrugi 2002, 2004).

Transforming global feminism into local practice has been an incremental process for domestic violence activists in Kazakhstan. On the one hand, the language of human rights is a familiar discourse for both activists and government officials, including police officers. But how it is used to frame the problem as a critical public dialogue depends upon how activists implement the discourse. On the other hand, although it has provided Podrugi with a set of benchmarks through which it may critique the state, it has also focused the organization's attention on following the lead of other organizations in Western Europe and North America. In training sessions with police, however, women's activists have demonstrated a significant degree of creativity in terms of how and in what ways they define the problem of domestic violence and reach out to police officers in hopes of gaining partners to combat it.

Performing the Problem of Domestic Violence in a New Nation

Gulsara, a lawyer from the Women's Information Center, a group closely aligned with the Feminist League, and who was partnering with Podrugi to train police officers, stood silently before the group of officers sitting in rows of chairs and folding tables in the dark function room of the modest Brezhnev-era hotel in the center of Astana, Kazakhstan's new capital city.[11] The television screen behind her glowed blue, and then it flashed images of Kazakhstan's diverse landscapes: vast, rustic steppes, steep canyons, and quiet birch forests. These scenes of nature and wilderness were replaced first by the bright and elegant profiles of mosques, and then shifted to lingering images of the intricate faces of village residents and vivid pictures of handmade rugs, traditional yurts, and ceremonial costumes. Over these portraits of Kazakhstan's natural and cultural geography, Gulsara spoke authoritatively about past traditions and customs of Kazakh culture. The traditions she described recalled a pastoralist community that seemed not to suffer from broken homes or abusive husbands. Then, in contrast, Gulsara announced to the audience that

> [g]ender inequality has its origins when Kazakhs shifted from pastoralist subsistence to sedentary agriculture. These changes were the result of domination by Muslim invaders and later the influence of Russian colonists. If one goes back far enough into the past, we see a society in which women were warriors alongside men, and they knew how to fight and how to raise horses. In this traditional culture wives were never beaten.

Podrugi's participation in the training program was as much an exercise in performing identities, that is, displaying the organization's willingness to promote positive images of ethnicity and heritage, as it was an effort to convey the technical knowledge of victim advocates or shelter staff about the problem of domestic violence in the country. Such a performance demonstrates the tactical approach that activists take toward Kazakhstan's increasingly contentious identity politics.[12]

Podrugi activists had carefully planned their presentations to encompass a broad range of issues around domestic abuse, including a particular interpretation of the history of the problem. Rather than viewing the past as a time steeped in patriarchal power and abuse, when communities condoned battering or ignored the violence occurring within homes (an approach one often sees in training programs in Western countries), to the contrary, police officer training in Kazakhstan often resembled a college seminar in cultural anthropology complete with detailed descriptions of subsistence strategy (in this case, pastoralism), marriage practices, family structure and tribal-level decision-making models—but infused with the rhetoric of nationalist revival. Gulsara crafted a set of cultural lessons that articulated a national ethnic (Kazakh) community whose members could take pride in the past rather than shamefully dwell on its contemporary record of purportedly widespread gender-related violence. Of course, this act of cultural translation relied on essentializing the pastoral culture, using ethnographic materials that were part of the state's mission to promote Kazakh identity in the face of more than eighty years of Soviet (and Russian) rule.

Gulsara's presentation, which essentially ethnicized the origins of domestic violence in Kazakhstan, contrasted sharply with the initial approach of Podrugi trainers during the first pilot sessions of the project. Earlier, even prior to introducing the services that currently existed in Almaty for victims of battering, activists focused aggressively on educating officers in feminist theory. This involved introducing them to economic models of gender inequity, presenting data on unequal political representation and earning power, and of women's officially disregarded domestic production and reproduction. Much of this explicitly feminist theoretical training was delivered by members of the Feminist League, who had developed this material from its participation in international feminist conferences, including its participation in the Beijing Conference in 1995. Podrugi members had asked the Feminist League to help them present material on gender issues for the police training. Such material included detailed yet ultimately abstract graphs and charts, delivered in a lecture format with few attempts to elicit questions from trainees. Podrugi activists then used to close this gender module by briefly describing their shelter services and providing police officers with the hotline number.

By the third training session in March 2001, only a couple of months into the project's second year, Podrugi activists reorganized their gender module to emphasize the experience of victims of violence and to demonstrate what kind of help their organization could provide women in need. For example, in place of theoretical material, Nadezhda began the module with a role-play exercise directly involving the participation of trainees. Officers were asked to be not police, but a mother or father, a neighbor, a boss or co-worker, a doctor, and a judge. Role-play participants then read from text cards created from the actual experiences of women whom Podrugi had helped in the past. Nadezhda played the part of a victim.

"There is nothing I can do for you, ma'am" read one officer, acting as a local judge during a training held in Almaty. "Your husband has a right to see his children, and his family has promised me that they will take better care of them than you," he announced. Such exercises had remarkable effects on trainees, who excitedly recounted their own knowledge of similar scenarios from their work, among their families, or in their own neighborhoods.

In addition to role-playing, Podrugi activists employed their growing knowledge of police practices to connect with officers and to get them to see their utility and symbolic power in local communities. For example, during one segment of the training, Nadezhda readily acknowledged the limitations of official law enforcement procedures in cases of domestic disturbances, many of which involved some form of violence or abuse. Police had complained in previous training sessions that their own official procedures limited their ability to address domestic disputes. For example, one officer noted during a training session in 2001 that the police were not allowed into a private residence unless there were clear signs of criminal activity. Regardless of whether this was indeed an accurate assessment of police powers, Nadezhda suggested that in cases where officers could not find cooperative witnesses, responding police units should at least leave information about the hotline in the building's vestibule.

One of the most intense but perhaps enlightening components of the police training was unwittingly developed by activists who encouraged officers to ask a visiting judge and prosecutor about the judiciary's frequent rejection of police cases regarding husbands who have physically abused their spouses. On one occasion during a training held in Astana, a lieutenant boldly argued with a local judge about the lack of cooperation that police perceive on the part of the courts to support charges against husbands who have behaved violently in their homes. Shifting the dialogue about domestic violence from didactic presentations to discussions/debates among stakeholders proved to be a strategy that encouraged the participants to the discovery of common ground and opportunities for cooperation among police and women's activists. Moreover, by acknowledging that other elements of the justice system or social service agencies contributed to the obstacles that victims of violence faced, Nadezhda avoided directly blaming law enforcement, which in turn encouraged a discussion of how these other institutions could cooperate with NGOs.

Nadezhda's performances as a police trainer were based on her experience with them as a victim. In this sense, her brave expressions of personal intimacy fostered a growing sense of respect among trainees, which in turn increased her pedagogical authority. She did not view police in an adversarial perspective, but rather as being unaware of their own powers of victim assistance. Her personal experience with domestic violence provided her with some insight into how to reach out to these civil servants. During her personal ordeal with an abusive partner, Nadezhda recounted, she found some of the local police to be sympathetic to her situation. She described how they attempted to resolve the problem in informal ways, an approach that Podrugi members had followed during its early days of providing assistance to victims of violence. She herself had asked for help, but pleaded with officers in the aftermath of one beating not to send her husband to jail:

> The neighbors had called the police. And they arrested D. They asked me "What do you want us to do?" I told them "I want him gone from my life, but please do not throw him in prison!" The police then threatened him with prison—really tried to scare him. Then they informed him that I was not filing charges against him. They then made him sign a paper agreeing never to talk to me.

Nadezhda encouraged the police trainees to try similar *ad hoc* approaches when handling domestic disputes and cases of battering.

These revised presentations by Podrugi and other NGO trainers, designed to engage with police, highlighted the powerful civic role of law enforcement in contemporary society. For example, when presenting the case of a problematic victim of abuse, a woman who was uncertain about what she wanted, Gulsara challenged the police trainees, who had first interpreted the situation as a waste of their time, by reminding them that "If you say: This is not my business, you may very well force the woman into a corner. She may commit suicide, or even murder."

Relationships between NGOs and state representatives certainly take time to develop. However, through the training program, the process of NGOs and state collaboration unfolded not from the top down, but from across the rank and file. This type of coordination has appeared to produce local-level transformations in police practice. For example, the project team later learned that after one Almaty training in 2002, the district police officers who had been through the program had created, over a period of several months, their own crisis center facility and had invited Podrugi activists to train each officer in the department. Other mid-level relationships continue to play vital roles in linking police with activists. For instance, the hotline workers at Podrugi's crisis center are now routinely informed of who is on duty at the local precinct.

Discovering Surrogate Solutions

Despite its recent initiatives to enhance and improve responses to domestic violence, since 2001 the state has backpedaled on (or perhaps simply neglected) its commitment to the problem, particularly in the sphere of law enforcement. Members of Podrugi reported in 2003 that two of the primary police collaborators, both of whom had participated in the development and delivery of law enforcement training, were reassigned to other divisions within the Almaty police department (Podrugi 2003). In addition to police personnel changes, and perhaps more importantly with regards to official institutional practices, a draft domestic violence law has yet to be approved by Kazakhstan's *majilis* (legislature). This draft was prepared in 2002 but has been languishing due to resistance on the part of lawmakers to pass the bill, who argue that the current criminal code is adequate to arrest and punish offenders.

Yet, several small measures of support for addressing domestic violence have come in the form of state-level action. For example, in 2002, Nadezhda received the Anniversary Medal commemorating ten years of Kazakhstan's sovereignty for her work in promoting services for women who experience violence. Her colleagues, Evgeniia, from the Feminist League, and Gulsara, from the Women's Information Center, also received this prestigious state award that same year. While such a gesture is more symbolic than substantive, the state's acknowledgement of women's activists is, nevertheless, a source of internal legitimacy and a form of public consciousness-raising. Additionally, the state's continued willingness to collaborate with the Feminist League, and thus indirectly with members of Podrugi, on the CEDAW reporting process, indicates a sustained commitment not only to keep the issue of violence against women on the national agenda, but more importantly, to include civil society in the national discussion.

Moreover, in contrast to the ethnicization of domestic violence promoted by NGO activists such as Gulsara in training sessions, women's activists also perform a sort of ethnic disappearing act when it comes to representing their organization among the international community. In the international context of filing progress reports and documentation of its work with victims, Podrugi, as a Kazakhstani organization, highlights the multi-ethnic character of its staff. It demonstrates through statistics and records how the NGO serves women of all ethnic groups and that it aspires to support and to fight for global standards on combating violence against women. Ethnicity thus serves activists as a surrogate theme, which may be ambiguously performed in order to promote, on the one hand, local solidarity with Kazakhstan's ethnic revival and, on the other, international solidarity with the global women's movement.

At the same time, while these NGO collaborations with the state have yielded positive measures in terms of public awareness and limited training for police, it is also problematic that the state places much of the burden of research and policymaking on small and under-funded NGOs. Still, the state does not hesitate to share credit with these organizations on the international stages of UN committees and government websites.

Nevertheless, these surrogate strategies are not limited to state-NGO relationships; they also include NGO and international collaborations in which the problem of domestic violence takes on a new type of performance in order to secure new opportunities for funding. For example, the Women's Association of Petropavlovsk (WAP), one of Podrugi's newest partners in the Union of Crisis Centers, received a grant in 2003 from the American Bar Association's CEELI program to help provide services to victims of human trafficking.[13] WAP began as a local business organization for women seeking to participate in Kazakhstan's postcommunist market economy. It views its work on violence against women with a broad scope and mission, thus providing a haven for both battered women and victims of trafficking. While not as much of a stretch as WAP's "shelter" for victims of trafficking, Podrugi's campaign to educate the public about domestic violence has incorporated working with local women's micro-development programs in Kazakhstan's southern regions. In rural areas where women suffer significant poverty and a severe lack of services and resources, a few Kazakhstani women's NGO have started grassroots women's collectives in several villages outside of Almaty to promote education and skills-training for female residents (Zellerer and Vyortkin 2004). Within the framework of such programs, Podrugi activists and members of other victim service organizations have conducted seminars about domestic violence in several villages outside of Almaty, identifying the problem of domestic abuse as a factor in discouraging economic opportunities for women. Podrugi was invited by the leaders of other women's NGOs, including the Ecological Association Women of the Orient, after members of the organization learned about their work in Almaty. While the development effort is small in scale, the new women's collectives in these villages offer Podrugi activists an attentive audience, willing to share their experiences with urban educated women and to gain insight from their work in the city.

There are perhaps two lessons to be learned from the case of domestic violence activism in Kazakhstan. First, there is a confluence of unpredictable factors, which include local initiatives and international cooperation, coupled with the availability of resources and a willingness on the part of the United States and West European states (such as the Netherlands) to provide assistance. In terms of sustaining the momentum and accomplishments of victim service advocates, this dynamic context is particularly challenging when it comes to resources for long-term planning and coordination. Second, the local level collaborations among women's organizations, police, and international assistance providers demand flexibility and do not suggest any long-term structural changes in terms of domestic violence policy.

There remain other divides and conflicts for which space does not afford a more in-depth discussion here. These issues include significant differences between the Russian North and the predominantly Kazakh South. In the South, the problem of mothers-in-law abusing their daughters-in-law and extended family networks that trap women seeking to flee are serious problems. Women in this area may be reluctant to seek assistance from a shelter, let alone be able to leave their families. In the North, some practitioners consider the problem of abuse in Russian households to be even more extensive and more under-reported than in Kazakh areas (Snajdr 2007). Additionally, strategies to assist battered women have emerged within a Muslim-oriented women's movement that is not willing to cooperate with either the current domestic violence community led by Podrugi or the local police (Snajdr 2005). This organization views both the state and feminist-oriented NGOs as not acting in the best interest of the Kazakh religious and ethnic community.

The problem of domestic violence movements in postcommunist states depends not only on internal, ethnic politics and policies but on decisions and resources beyond national boundaries. In order to continue working on this serious women's issue and to provide effective help, activists need not only to hold the state accountable to its international commitments to human rights policy, but also to push for more cooperation and coordination with local law enforcement and the courts. At the same time, as funding for women's issues become increasingly scarce, Podrugi and other service organizations need to exploit the small funding opportunities that still exist and lobby the state to increase assistance for victims of battering. All of these challenges will no doubt require the ability to perform the problem as a national issue and one that can be defined and addressed within the framework of a post-Soviet political arena.

NOTES

1. Julia, Luba, and Tamara are pseudonyms. For reasons of privacy and respect for their work, I do not want to reveal the real names of the individuals involved in the incidents described here.

2. Although the official language of the country is Kazakh, Russian is still spoken throughout Kazakhstan and widely used by NGOs. Many women's NGOs have names that may be referred to either in Russian or Kazakh, but most are identified in UN reports using their Russian forms. With the exception of Podrugi, which is referred to as such even in Kazakh, I will use English translations for all other Kazakhstani NGOs discussed in this chapter.

3. The other project team members included Evelyn Zellerer and Dmitriy Vyortkin. The project was funded by the Bureau for International Narcotics and

Law Enforcement Affairs (INL), US Department of State (grant #S-OPRAQ-98-H-N163). This training project was part of a multi-year initiative on the part of INL to improve law enforcement responses to domestic violence throughout the states of the former Soviet Union and parts of Eastern Europe. In addition to Florida State University, other grantees included Winrock International, Connect Russia-U.S., and the University of South Carolina. These other grantees developed projects for Russia, Ukraine, and Moldova.

4. *Emic* refers to the native's point of view, generally indicating a cultural insider's perspective.

5. There are officially 132 ethnic groups in the Republic of Kazakhstan. In addition to Kazakhs and Russians, there are also Ukranians (3 percent), Germans (3 percent), Uzbeks (3 percent), Tatar (2 percent), and Uighurs, Kyrgyz, Tajiks, Turkmen, and Koreans (who together comprise 7 percent of the country's total population of some 17 million).

6. For more detail regarding the political, economic and cultural aspects of Kazakhstan's transition from communism see Ro'I (1995), Schatz (2004), and Svanberg (1999).

7. According to data from the national Committee on Family and Women, a total of 644,600 women were unemployed compared to 323,200 men for the year 1999 (NCFW 2000: 74).

8. Women's activists from the United States who worked with our project team readily acknowledged that underground sheltering was a common grassroots response to domestic violence prior to the development of shelters and crisis center in the mid-1980s. Some of our project consultants also revealed that they were aware of current cases in the United States of "going underground."

9. Prostitution is a growing criminal industry in Kazakhstan and one that offers young rural women opportunities to earn money in the city.

10. There are still very few statistics available on the scope, range, and frequency of domestic violence in Kazakhstan, a problem that both the Ministry of the Interior and victim advocates are trying to solve.

11. Nazarbeyev moved Kazkahstan's capital from Almaty to Astana (a city previously called Akmola) in 1997. Several theories have emerged to explain this move, including that it was an effort on the part of Nazarbeyev to impose more control over the Russian-dominated northern part of the country, or that the transfer was a strategic decision to move the governing center away from Kazakhstan's border with China. The government's official explanation has been that Astana provided a more central location for the new state's capital city.

12. This flexibility is no doubt similar to the Polish domestic violence movement's strategies to align with shifting political arenas. Johnson and Brunell note that "when the [Polish] government shifted to the right, domestic violence activists, within and outside the state, made a compelling argument that the Church's strong commitment to family should extend to social policies affecting the family" (2006: 581).

13. CEELI stands for the Central and East European Law Initiative, a program of legal assistance and training promoting democracy and the rule of law that was created by the American Bar Association in 1990 following the collapse of communism in East Europe. The program is funded by USAID and now includes Eurasia.

WORKS CITED

Browning, Genia. 1987. *Women and Politics in the USSR: Consciousness Raising and Soviet Women's Groups.* New York: St. Martin's Press.

———. 1992. "The Zhensovety Revisited." In *Perestroika and Soviet Women,* ed. Mary Buckley, 97–117. Cambridge, UK.: Cambridge University Press.

Doi, Mary. 2002. *Gesture, Gender, Nation: Dance and Social Change in Uzbekistan.* Westport, Conn.: Bergin and Garvey.

Faier, Elizabeth. 2002. "Domestic Matters: Feminism and Activism among Palestinian Women in Israel." In *Ethnography in Unstable Places: Everyday Lives in the Context of Dramatic Political Change,* ed. Carol Greenhouse, Elizabeth Mertz, and Kay B. Warren, 178–209. Durham, N.C.: Duke University Press.

Feminist League. 1997. *Report on the Status of Women, Republic of Kazakhstan.* Almaty: Malvina Publishing House.

Ferree, Myra Marx, Barbara Risman, Valerie Sperling, Tatiana Guirkova, and Katherine Hyde. 1999. "The Russian Women's Movement: Activists' Strategies and Identities." *Women and Politics* 20:83–109.

Johnson, Janet Elise, and Laura Brunell. 2006. "The Emergence of Contrasting Domestic Violence Regimes in Postcommunist Europe." *Policy and Politics* 34(4): 575–595.

Kelly, Liz. 1996. "Tensions and Possibilities: Enhancing Informal Responses to Domestic Violence." In *Future Interventions with Battered Women and their Families,* ed. Jeffery L. Edelson and Zvi C. Eiskovits, 67–86. Thousand Oaks, Calif.: Sage.

Konstantinova, Svetlana. 1996. "Russia's Portrait in the Women's World Gallery." *SAIS Review* 16:175–185.

Kuehnast, Kathleen. 1998. "From Pioneers to Entrepreneurs: Young Women, Consumerism, and the 'World Picture' in Kyrgyzstan." *Central Asian Survey* 17(4): 639–654.

Markowitz, Lisa. 2001. "Finding the Field: Notes on the Ethnography of NGOs." *Human Organization* 60(1): 40–46.

Merry, Sally. 2005. *Human Rights and Gender Violence: Translating International Law into Local Justice.* Chicago: University of Chicago Press.

Michaels, Paula. 1998. "Kazak Women: Living the Heritage of a Unique Past." In *Women in Muslim Societies: Diversity within Unity,* ed. Herbert L. Bodman and Nayereh Tohidi, 187–202. Boulder, Colo.: Lynne Rienner.

Mrševic, Zorica. 2000. "Belgrade's SOS Hotline for Women and Children Victims of Violence: A Report." In *Reproducing Gender: Politics, Publics and Everyday Life after Socialism,* ed. Susan Gal and Gail Kligman, 370–392. Princeton, N.J.: Princeton University Press.

National Commission on Family and Women (NCFW). 1999. Violence against Women Survey. Almaty, Kazakhstan.

———. 2000. *"Women of Kazakhstan."* Almaty, Kazakhstan: Malvina Publishing House.

Northrop, Douglas. 2000. "Languages of Loyalty: Gender, Politics and Party Supervision in Uzbekistan, 1927–41." *Russian Review* 59(2): 179–200.

Podrugi. 2003. *Annual Report*. Almaty, Kazakhstan.

———. 2004. *Annual Report*. Almaty, Kazakhstan.

Ro'I, Yaacov. 1995. "The Secularization of Islam and the USSR's Muslim Areas." In *Muslim Eurasia: Conflicting Legacies*, ed. Yaacov Ro'I, 5–20. London: Frank Cass.

Ruffin, M. Holt, and Daniel Waugh, eds. 1999. *Civil Society in Central Asia*. Seattle: University of Washington Press.

Schatz, Edward. 2004. *Modern Clan Politics: The Power of "Blood" in Kazakhstan and Beyond*. Seattle: University of Washington Press.

Shelly, Louise. 1996. *Policing Soviet Society: The Evolution of State Control*. London: Routledge.

Snajdr, Edward. 2005. "Gender, Power and the Performance of Justice: Muslim Women's Responses to Domestic Violence in Kazakhstan." *American Ethnologist* 32(2): 294–311.

———. 2007. "Ethnicizing the Subject: Domestic Violence and the Politics of Primordialism in Kazakhstan." *Journal of the Royal Anthropological Institute* 13(3): 603–620.

Svanberg, Ingvar, ed. 1999. *Contemporary Kazakhs: Cultural and Social Perspectives*. New York: St. Martin's Press.

UNIFEM. 2005. "Kazakhstan: Crisis Centers Implement Higher Professional Standards in Responding to Violence against Women." www.unifem.org/gender_issues/voices_from_the_field/story.php (accessed February 26, 2009).

Wang, Xingjuan. 1999. "Why are Beijing Women Beaten by their Husbands? A Case Analysis of Family Violence in Beijing." *Violence Against Women* 5: 1493–1504.

Werner, Cynthia Ann. 1997. "Marriage, Markets and Merchants: Changes in Wedding Feasts and Household Consumption Patterns in Rural Kazakhstan." *Culture and Agriculture* 19(1–2): 6–13.

———. 2003. "Women, Marriage, and the Nation-State: The Rise of Non-Consensual Bride Kidnapping in Post-Soviet Kazakhstan." In *The Transformation of Central Asia: States and Societies from Soviet Rule to Independence*, ed. Pauline Jones Luong, 59–89. Ithaca, N.Y.: Cornell University Press.

Zellerer, Evelyn, and Dmitriy Vyortkin. 2004. "Women's Grassroots Struggles for Empowerment in the Republic of Kazakhstan." *Social Politics* 11(3): 439–464.

CHAPTER 5

From Soviet Liberation to Post-Soviet Segregation: Women and Violence in Tajikistan

MUBORAK SHARIPOVA AND KATALIN FÁBIÁN

The West is relatively oblivious to the status of women in Tajikistan, who continue to carry the burdens of the 1992–1997 civil war: poverty, disease, increasing criminal activity, and violence. Because of Tajikistan's relative anonymity outside of Central Asia and its very recent history as an independent country, it is worth studying because it can offer many important insights into how the postcommunist transition has affected women's status and how local and global forces interact regarding increased violence against women. The officially sanctioned structural violence during the Soviet era (1917–1991) transmuted to a widespread and public violence during the civil war. After the civil war, the outright atrocities transformed into a wide undercurrent of violence against women in the private sphere that included forced marriages, beatings, confinement in the home, and increasingly limited access to education and employment. During this trend of increased gender inequality and segregation, both international organizations working in Tajikistan and global economic trends (such as travel and migration) spread new concepts and mechanisms to enhance gender equality and decrease violence both in the private and the public spheres.

This expansion of violence against Tajik women is a stark reminder that domestic violence is intrinsically connected to broader political, economic, and social trends. Although the international environment has greatly assisted in allowing voices from Tajikistan to raise their concerns, global political, economic, and military considerations also absolved the postcommunist Tajik governments from seriously addressing domestic violence. The losses that generations of Tajik women experienced during the Soviet and post-Soviet political and social upheavals continue to be generally unrecognized, unrecorded, and rarely considered.

The research for this chapter was based on interviews with local women (n=900) and participatory research for extended periods in Tajikistan during 1998–2000,[1] and regular trips there until 2009. We explore the gender-specific transformation processes of the post-Soviet Tajik society and examine their implications on violence against women. In analyzing women's social and political status and violence against women in Tajikistan, we focus on the contemporary situation after the civil war, although we very much recognize that women's situation was profoundly influenced by the period before the collapse of the Soviet Union in 1991 and the immediate post-Soviet period during the civil war.[2] The main segment of the essay details the findings of the 1999 survey on violence against women supported by the United Nations World Health Organization (WHO).

Our analysis of the interviews and the interviewers' diaries demonstrates the widespread nature of violence against women in post-Soviet Tajikistan. As the country struggles to overcome the heavy losses of the civil war, our research and much corroborating evidence show that domestic violence has dramatically increased because of interlocking political, economic, and cultural forces (Haarr 2007). The increased subjugation of girls and women after the civil war can be attributed to wartime conditions of extreme economic deprivation and life-threatening political instability, conditions where traditional and Islamic institutions and international humanitarian assistance provided some refuge and consequently emerged as much stronger influences on contemporary politics and gender relations.

Tajikistan is experiencing a religious renaissance and a revival of traditional norms that are, at least in part, shedding a previously enforced Soviet rule. As both the Soviet period and the contemporary political turning points in Tajik history were accompanied by a spread of violence, it is sadly not entirely surprising that gender violence has also been pivotal to the contemporary political, economic, and social transformation (Harris 2004).

In today's Tajikistan gender norms and the status of women are at the heart of the sociocultural and economic changes, exactly as they were when Soviet rule was established.[3] Although Tajikistan shares much with the other post-Soviet republics, each new Central Asian state produced a different response to the new challenges of modernization and Islam in the newly interconnected, global era (Goldberg et al. 2008; Spechler 2004). Both during and after the Tajik civil war, women's bodies became the symbolic and often actual conflict zone between the traditional and new globalizing forces, reflecting the early Soviet-era dramatic political and social transformations. What makes the Tajik case particularly worth studying is that it reinforces observations regarding women's precarious situation during major political transformations worldwide. It also serves as a crucial reminder that domestic violence is deeply embedded in the gender inequality of long-standing historical, political, and economic practices.

Gender Inequality in Contemporary Tajikistan

The Republic of Tajikistan is located in the Central Asian region of five post-Soviet countries.[4] According to the 1994 constitution, Tajikistan is a sovereign, democratic, and secular state, with a republican form of governance, where women and men have equal rights.[5] Despite such grand declarations, Tajikistan has struggled intensely with its newly gained sovereignty. In addition, it has found implementing free and competitive elections a difficult process. Most importantly from our perspective, inequality between the sexes in Tajikistan has grown dramatically, and increasing inequality has contributed to a growing trend of violence against women.

Economic Inequality

One possible reason for the wide discrepancy between men's and women's position in Tajik society is that the country remains one of the world's poorest, with its US$280 GDP per capita. Of the 179 countries in the 2008 Human Development Index, Tajikistan ranks 124th (UNDP 2008). When it was part of the Soviet Union, Tajikistan was one of its poorest republics. The Tajik population is over seven million and is growing rapidly.[6] The economy is based on subsistence agriculture, assistance from international donors, and barter with neighbors, plus three commodities that make up 80 percent of all foreign exchange earnings: aluminum, cotton, and illegal drugs (Gleason 2003: 83). The regional economic crisis of the 1990s and the civil war in 1992–1997 further exacerbated poverty, and the persistent impoverishment had many specifically gendered consequences.

Lack of employment opportunities pushed over 25 percent of the 3.7 million-strong Tajik labor force to migrate out of the country (IFES 2006).[7] More than 200,000 professionals left due to the war and its aftermath, resulting in ill-equipped and poorly managed hospitals and schools. As many men emigrated, became displaced, or died in the civil war, women took on the principal roles of breadwinner and head of household.[8] Many women quit their former jobs and became "businesswomen," engaging in small-business activities, such as buying and selling goods in the local bazaars or making "shuttle-business" trips to the former Soviet successor states and other neighboring countries

(Sharipova 2000).[9] Girls left school to help out at home or work for some meager payment.[10]

However, in many cases the new jobs had adverse health consequences, as the girls and women often had to carry and haul heavy loads.[11] Women's new business ventures often also sparked humiliation and sexual harassment by racketeers, train conductors, drivers, militia, and criminals. Prostitution and human trafficking circles developed, with young women being sent to the countries of the Gulf States (International Organization for Migration [IOM] 2001; Mirzoeva 2004; Sulaimanova 2004). To avoid rape and the associated humiliation of the family, parents forced their daughters to marry the first person who asked.[12] Arranged marriages involved girls as young as ten, some of whom became second or third wives to men much older than they were, simply to avoid shame from the loss of *namus*. (*Namus* is an Arabic word meaning reputation, fame, and honor. In this context, "loss of *namus*" means "blow to chastity.")[13] Drug dealers also exploited females, increasingly using them as "mules" for smuggling.[14] These phenomena contributed to the justification of state-mandated discriminatory practices against women such as routine strip-searches and gynecological exams when crossing national borders (Vandenberg 2001).

Political Inequality

Tajik women not only had to cope with local economic problems directly undermining their households and communities during the civil war, but also needed to step up as some of the main actors in conflict resolution and peace-building. Although some indicators since the end of the civil war show improvement in women's representation in public life in Tajikistan, the ratios of women in decisionmaking positions have remained persistently low. A study of gender and livelihoods carried out by the Aga Khan Foundation about Badakhshon women explained that the decrease in female representation in politics was because women had been compelled by economic and emotional difficulties to withdraw from leadership positions and to return to domestic support roles to help their families survive.[15] "With their energies occupied elsewhere, women no longer had time to participate actively in public decision-making arenas, even at the local level and [. . .] many women felt that this lack of political representation had negatively affected women's status in society" (Kanji and Gladwin 2000).

Women's political representation in the Tajik parliament first decreased from a share of 30 percent (quota) during the Soviet era to

3 percent among parliamentary deputies and 7 percent of senior posts within government ministries (Falkingham 2000: 7). In 2000, only five women headed city or regional governments (*hukumats*), although women held positions as deputy chairs in 45 of the total 64 local administrations. Women were in charge of 28 of the country's 342 village (*jamoat*) councils.

As one counterweight to these trends of increasing gender inequality, the OSCE, USAID, and many other international organizations supported political debates and discussions between various Tajik women's NGOs, parliamentary leaders, and representatives of political parties in the early 2000s. The halting but still significant encounter of Tajik society with these various international organizations finally started to challenge the broad acceptance of women's inferior position in decisionmaking. Under the watchful eyes of international observers and dependent on foreign aid at the time, the Tajik government decided to reintroduce a quota system to ensure women's formal representation in all governmental and political structures (Asian Development Bank 2000). After the second (highly contested) Tajik elections in 2005, women gained 17.5 percent of the seats in *Majlisi Namoyandagon*, the lower chamber of legislature, and 23.5 percent in *Majlisi Milli*, the upper chamber. Women also earned 11.5 percent of seats in local legislatures (Inter-Parliamentary Union 2005; Rakhmanova 2007; UNDP 2007/08).[16]

Despite these encouraging increases in women's representation and the limited democratization, Tajik people, and especially women, still have very limited access to the legislative machineries that could protect them from discrimination, violation of their rights, and widespread crime and corruption. Very few, if any, Tajik women would be in a position to safely rely on the judicial system to defend their reproductive rights, right to work and to education, and freedom of expression.

Women become further marginalized in their own society by a combination of powerful structural forces: a) poverty; b) the high level of corruption; c) the emerging conservative norms; d) the absence of functioning democratic institutions and processes to protect women's rights; e) the general lack of awareness about women's rights and gender issues in governing bodies and Tajik society. It should be noted that in 2004, and under government pressure, Hikmatullo Tojikobodi and Eshoni Abdukhalil, the religious leaders of the Tajik Department of Ulems, issued a decree that prohibited women from attending mosques to pray (Rotar 2006). These steps not only limited women's freedom of religion but also narrowed their resources for physical survival, because these places of worship also serve as community welfare institutions (Singerman 2004). The Ulems' decree of 2004 effectively completed women's political and economic segregation with spiritual segregation. While women were helping their families to survive and engaging in peaceful reconstruction, two different processes led to their renewed exclusion from the political sphere and denied them their fair share of the nation's economic resources.

The Reasons for Women's Decreasing Social Status in Tajikistan

There are at least three main sociopolitical and cultural reasons for the contemporary dwindling role of Tajik women in public life. First, the distribution of previously nationalized assets detrimentally affected women in Tajik society. Second, the lack of a functioning democracy curtailed the possibility of speaking up and acting to reveal the corrupt practices. Third, the revival of traditional institutions has further exacerbated women's "protected" but extremely dependent position in post-Soviet Tajik society. As Tajik society fell back on the support of traditional institutions such as kinship, gender roles became further bifurcated. These three main processes are complementary and are all responsible for the increased restrictions on women's political and economic opportunities, the erosion of women's leadership, the enhanced seclusion of women, and their greatly reduced social status.

First and foremost, the unequal and corrupt process of distributing the vestiges of the Soviet economy contributed greatly to women's decreasing social status in Tajikistan. The postcommunist elites, such as warlords and nationalist and Islamic leaders, privatized previously nationalized assets during the civil war and its immediate aftermath. Due to lack of information, political skills, and basic resources, women had little chance to participate in the rapid redistribution of previously public goods. Supported by international financial institutions such as the World Bank, the state liberalized the economy and many of the social services by massive deregulation and privatization. The abrupt wave of privatization produced massive negative social and gender-specific consequences.[17] Unbridled privatization resulted in high levels of unemployment, deep poverty, and the feminization of poverty. These outcomes continue to characterize the contemporary economic crisis.

Even a decade after the civil war ended, the situation for women has not improved significantly. In 2007, fewer than two-thirds of the population had access to safe drinking water (UNICEF 2008). The infant mortality rate (110.76 deaths/1,000 live births in 2005) and maternal mortality rate (100 deaths per 100,000 births) are still among the highest in the world (UNICEF 2006). While the state is unwilling and/or unable to address and solve the mounting social problems, corruption and the emerging religious revival threaten even the maintenance of the fragile peace. The breakdown of the state or further religious radicalization could have disastrous consequences, especially for the already vulnerable populations.

The second main factor that has profoundly contributed to Tajik women's decreased social status is the difficult post-Soviet cultural process of redefining national identities in the newly independent country. This process strengthened the patriarchal values and traditions and did not incorporate women's crucial role in the society (Whitsel 2009). Acceptance of men's dominance is deeply rooted in the consciousness of most Tajik people, particularly in the rural areas. Contemporary Tajik decisionmakers do not consider the traditional value-orientations as a threat to women's status, nor does mass media discuss the value and importance of gender equality.[18]

Violence against Women in Contemporary Tajikistan

With Tajikistan's violent transformation from a Soviet Republic to an independent country, domestic violence took on even broader meanings than it did in most Western conceptualizations. Our analysis of the 1999 WHO survey and additional gender-specific data discloses the long-standing historical aspects of violence against women, such as the structural violence during the Soviet era and the damage of the civil war and its aftermath. These data also reveal the interconnected political, social, and cultural factors that combine and reinforce one another in the spread of violence against women in Tajikistan.

There are no data on violence against women during Soviet times because the issue was taboo—it was nameless and unacknowledged (Johnson 2007). Yet Tajik society was tainted with violence. In interviews conducted between 1998 and 1999, the majority of both old and young Tajiks viewed violence against women as a normal part of their daily lives (Sharipova 2002; WHO 1999). Domestic violence was a widespread mechanism to preserve women's sense of inferiority and was an accepted means of controlling their behavior.

The Tajik civil war put a sudden and dramatic end to earlier aspirations toward political and economic reforms.[19] The prevalence of societal and domestic violence against women appears to have been exceptionally high during the civil war period. There are no official data on how many women were killed or wounded during military actions, how many became refugees or internally displaced, and how many were raped. Many displaced and refugee Tajik women were exposed to violence and discriminatory treatment based on their gender and ethnicity in refugee camps and in locations to which they fled.[20] But the common perception during the height of the civil war was that women were less vulnerable to physical abuse than men.

To produce a record of the violence women face, the World Health Organization sponsored a survey titled Violence against Women in Tajikistan in 1999, soon after the end of the civil war. This WHO study found that two in three women reported being beaten by a non-family member and that these beatings took place most often at school and in the street (WHO 1999). Survey participants reported that during the civil war, combating parties exacted vengeance by humiliating and raping the women on the opposite side.[21] The results of the WHO survey showed that immediately after the civil war the number of health-threatening psychological disorders connected with post-traumatic stress, such as suicide and suicide by self-immolation, were on the increase (Muhammadiev 1998, 2000).[22] Researchers also noted an increase in organized crime, vagrancy, alcoholism, and drug addiction, and epidemic proportions of contagious diseases (e.g., malaria, tuberculosis, and AIDS).[23]

Despite the many trials and tribulations that challenged cooperation between Tajik and international organizations in the post-Soviet period, the Violence against Women in Tajikistan research project successfully brought together different actors to survey the nature and scope of violence against women. In this segment, we use excerpts from this project to substantiate our claims. We have also updated the 1999 study with contemporary and on-site observations in Tajikistan.

Preparations and Methods of the Survey

The first stage of the WHO-sponsored research project was to design a questionnaire with open questions about women's rights and violence against women. A separate survey was also prepared for specialists, social and health officials, and local NGOs working with women in three regions: Khatlon (comprising 35.1 percent of the Tajik population); Soghd (30.5 percent); and the Regions of Republican Subordination (21.8 percent), which includes the capital, Dushanbe. Only Badakhshan (3 percent) was not included in the study, because of the extreme difficulty of reaching this mountainous region combined with a lack of finances.

Although this omission was regrettable, it probably did not skew the results of the survey because the region's population is so small.

We collected data from various national ministries and local government offices, schools, medical establishments (including maternity wards), mosques, and workplaces. The results of the preliminary surveys from 1997 were used by the NGO Open Asia as the basis for a conference on domestic violence, the first of its kind in Tajikistan. The 1998 conference brought together academics and representatives of various governmental agencies and NGOs, especially women's NGOs, and religious leaders from around the country to debate various aspects of violence against women. The information we gathered at this conference helped us create the final questionnaire, which was produced in both Russian and Tajik and was supervised by WHO experts on violence against women. The questionnaire covered socio-demographics, opinions on and experiences of violence, and health status (WHO 1999).

Nine hundred women and girls (aged 14–65 years) were interviewed.[24] The interviews, plus the interviewers' daily journal entries and additional focused interviews with victims of violence and their responses to open questions, provided the qualitative data.

Translating Concepts Related to Domestic Violence

There was no common concept of violence against women in Tajikistan prior to the study. Even obvious forms of physical abuse such as beating were defined differently; for example, *zadan* (to beat), *kuftan* (to beat with fists or kick), *laghadkub kardan* (to kick), and *zur ovardan* or *zurovari* (to use violence). It was exceedingly difficult to find a single Tajik word to define the whole concept of violence and its different forms.[25]

In the opening speech of the 1998 conference, Tajik language experts and Persian-speaking Iranian and Afghan attendees suggested the Tajik word *"khushunat"* for violence (Sharipova 1998). *Khushunat* covers all kinds of aggressive and violent behaviors. In retrospect, this word choice may be obvious, but at the time it was difficult to find an appropriate bridge between meanings. Tajik National Radio repeatedly broadcast the presentations of the 1997 conference, and consequently many comments and calls came from all over the country in support of the "mission against violence."

The WHO study focused on physical violence (such as beating) and sexual and psychological violence (forced marriage, cruel treatment, restriction of personal freedom, threatening with a weapon, etc.). It did not include other types of violence or state-supported violence (such as child marriage or forced deprivation of schooling) and did not recommend separating economic violence—which was emerging in various postcommunist contexts (see chapters 3 and 7 in this volume)—from the three already well-established forms of violence.

The draft questionnaires (in Tajik, Russian, and English) included questions about women's opinion of violence in general and its scope. The interviewees were then asked more direct questions about whether they experienced certain types of violence in their girlhood and adolescence. To measure the frequency of violence, we used three- to four-value ordinal scales, from "it happens every day" through "it happens every month" and "it has happened sometimes," to "it only happened once." Questions such as "Were you beaten in your girlhood by your father, brother, or other relatives?" used a three-value ordinal scale where the two last categories, "it happened sometimes" and "it happened only once," were aggregated into "it happened sometimes." In questions such as "Have you ever been forced to have sex by your husband?" the full four-value ordinal scale was used. For the purposes of the WHO survey, the exposure to violence separately examined the cases in which a) the perpetrators were parents, husbands, or relatives, and b) those when the perpetrators were not relatives, that is, strangers, teachers, etc.

The debates between the interviewing staff and the WHO experts keenly demonstrated that terminology to describe violence, the issues of violence against women in general, and domestic violence in particular have all been very obviously missing in Tajikistan. Some Tajik concepts of violence differed from the associated Western meanings. For example, Tajik interviewers, and especially interviewees, did not see a forced sexual act by a husband as sexual violence but considered it as a normal act that sometimes occurred between spouses. Similarly, Western experts considered many aspects of the traditional *adat* (such as arranged marriage, prohibition to continue education, or restrictions on meeting friends or relatives) as restrictions on personal freedoms and as forms of psychological violence. These differences of interpretations between Tajik and international experts remained difficult to bridge.

Because violence was taboo during Soviet rule, the women interviewees, interviewers, and scholars were not used to speaking about the topic. The interviewers faced many linguistic and conceptual problems in defining violence against women and children, and in differentiating between physical, psychological, or sexual abuse, sexual harassment, incest, rape, human or women's rights, reproductive rights, choice in contraception, etc. Many Tajik women did not understand these "foreign concepts," while others felt that they should not utter such taboo words. Polygamy (or more accurately polygyny, with the husband having more than one wife), was addressed only to a limited extent (for a broader discussion, see Tabyshalieva 2000).

Problems during the Field Survey: Physical Safety and Gaining Trust

The 1999 WHO study hired twenty-one interviewers, three supervisors, and six experts on violence against women to conduct the research and field surveys in Tajikistan. The interviewers were legitimately concerned about their own physical safety and the high emotional demands of their job. To increase the safety of the staff, each project participant received an official letter stating that they were representatives of a WHO project working on women's health issues. Indeed, this euphemism and the WHO letter proved to be of significant help in many cases, especially in the most severely war-affected regions.[26]

To obtain truthful information we needed to establish contacts based on mutual trust. Interviewers had to make significant efforts to help the respondents overcome their fear of speaking about very private and confidential issues.[27] Women were uncomfortable responding to the questionnaire in their homes, and they especially avoided the presence of other family members during the interviews. Consequently, most interviews took place in more neutral locations, such as health centers, but even these places posed problems of privacy and access.

The interviews showed that the higher a woman's social status, the more difficult it was for her to admit that she was a victim of violence.[28] Interviewers also pointed out that interviewees "[considered] sinful, embarrassing, and no good [imprudent] to complain about one's husband or to tell others about family problems." It became obvious that rape in marriage was the most forbidden topic of discussion. Respondents often did not want to directly recognize the severe problems they or their families faced because of domestic violence. Considering the reluctance of the interviewees, the rates of violence the survey recorded have been stunningly high. As a diversion from these difficult themes, some women eagerly turned the discussion to financial problems.

Women's Socioeconomic Conditions

The difficult economic and financial conditions of the women respondents were some of the most frequently mentioned themes in the interviews and staff journals. Reflecting on the Tajik postwar situation, one interviewer noted that the respondents were just happy to receive the scant payment of one somoni (about US$0.50 at that time) that the WHO offered for the interview because they did not have enough money to buy bread. Another respondent stated that she had not eaten hot food for months. In the regions where severe military conflicts took place, the economy was in shambles and health care was extremely precarious. The interviewers noted the grossly unsanitary conditions that emerged due to the deterioration of the social infrastructure and the increase of poverty. Potential respondents would beg the interviewers, "Please interview me and [the payment] will help me to get rid of fleas and lice." The interviewers also witnessed extremely unhealthy conditions in maternity hospitals. For example, one interviewer noted that "I could not watch the filthy conditions in the place where women deliver babies. Now I understand why our children are so often sick."

In rural areas, women and their families lived in very crowded conditions. Several families often lived together, resulting in twenty to thirty people living under one roof. The people who lived in such crowded places were mainly returning refugees who found their houses ruined and their families dispersed, killed, or in ill health. The returnees frequently tried to survive together in those relatives' houses that had remained intact after the war.

Social expectations and economic needs forced single women to marry. Widows had to marry just to escape public condemnation for being a single woman.[29] Alternatively, they needed a "man-defender" at home to protect them. Interviewers pointed out the women's lack of confidence and the uncertainty of their future. One survey respondent said, "I cannot be sure of anything, I am scared and always feel uneasy or alarmed" (diary of a WHO interviewer). Interviewers especially pointed out that old, long-forgotten traditions and customs were becoming widespread again in postwar Tajikistan. The spread of polygamy, the lowering of the legal age of marriage, forced marriages, and other specifically misogynist practices were increasing alarmingly.

The spread of polygamy after the civil war was directly connected to the loss of life in the five-year conflict that left behind many widows and few marriageable men. One interviewee stated, "A woman has to put up with a man's mockery or abuse for not to be [sic] abandoned by him. A man would say to a woman: if your behavior is bad—keep in mind that there are many widows nowadays and it is very easy to change one wife for another." Similarly, an interviewer wrote in her diary another interviewee's story: "I am only nineteen but I am afraid to become a spinster. I want anyone to marry me." Yet another recalled a woman saying, "I wanted to study very much, but my family forced me into marriage." The interviews and the diaries support one another in showing the extreme social pressure Tajik women suffered: "She had a walk with her fiancé and his sister called her a prostitute for this. She poured gasoline over herself and lit it"; "A mother did not allow her daughter to meet and be friends with neighbor boys, saying that after that nobody would marry her" (dairies of WHO interviewers).

After the civil war, women were often left behind without social or psychological support. Interviewers frequently mentioned that while women had difficulties expressing their mental anguish, they spoke much about loneliness. In their journals, the interviewers also referred to most women not understanding that they were exposed to violence and that they were entirely unaware of their rights.

Findings on Violence against Women in Tajikistan

The findings of the WHO study are based on both qualitative and quantitative data on the prevalence of different forms of violence against women in Tajikistan. They reveal a high prevalence of physical, sexual, and psychological violence against women and girls. One in three women reported experiencing some form of abuse: 35 percent of women interviewed reported experiencing physical violence perpetrated by family members during girlhood and adolescence, 34 percent experienced physical violence from non-family members, and 44.5 percent reported having experienced psychological (emotional) violence during girlhood or adolescence. These data have been confirmed by repeated studies, although none have yet been performed on as broad a spectrum of the population as the 1999 WHO survey. For example, in a standardized interview of 800 men and women based on a national sample and focus group discussions among 80 women, 61.5 percent of women and 59.8 percent of men stated that physical violence against women is widespread or very widespread (Shoismatulloev 2005).

During womanhood (defined as age fifteen and up), approximately 50 percent of the women had experienced one of the three forms of violence by a family member. Most frequently, husbands and in-laws violated women's choices in sexual and reproductive matters. One in four (24 percent) women reported that someone had either attempted or succeeded in forcing them to have sex against their will. One in two married women (47 percent) reported that their husbands forced them

TABLE 5.1. PREVALENCE AND PERCEPTION OF
VIOLENCE AGAINST WOMEN IN TAJIKISTAN, 1999 AND 2005

TYPE OF VIOLENCE AGAINST WOMEN	PERPETRATOR [1999 DATA]		NATIONAL PERCEPTION (STANDARDIZED INTERVIEW, 470 WOMEN) [2005 DATA]				
	Family Members	Non-Family Members	Very Wide-spread	Wide-spread	Not So Wide-spread	Not Wide-spread	Difficult to Answer
Psychological Violence	44.5%	21%	33.0%	37.3%	20.5%	5.6%	3.5%
Physical Violence	35%*	34%*	21.2%	40.3%	27.8%	6.7%	4.0%
Sexual Violence	0.5%	7%	9.9%	18.4%	36.0%	26.5%	9.2%
Women who did not experience any violence	41%	54%					

*Based on three-value ordinal scale
Source: Shoismatulloev 2005 and WHO 1999.

to have sex. Women were asked to recall three pregnancies: the first, the one before last, and the last. More than 5 percent of all pregnancies were attributable to rape (see Table 5.1).

The most common form of domestic violence, however, is forcing a woman to have a baby every year, regardless of her desire or health. Violence directly affects women's reproductive rights, and it may limit or eliminate her freedom to use contraception or even to negotiate its use. In the interviews, many married woman revealed they were afraid to even raise the issue of contraception for fear of being beaten.[30]

Traditional norms have also institutionalized certain forms of violence against women, such as girls' and widows' forced marriages, elimination of reproductive choices through violence, rape within marriage, and forced pregnancies. In the WHO survey, more than 22 percent of women were forced to marry and another 5 percent were married because of the fear of public opinion that condemns unmarried girls of marriageable age to being spinsters (WHO 1999). Child marriages have increased steadily since 1995. At the beginning of the civil war, the age of consent for girls was lowered to seventeen, although many girls are married before their sixteenth birthday in religious ceremonies.[31] Married women (barely old enough to be called "women") under seventeen frequently have one or even more children in Tajikistan.

The WHO research also documented various forms of domestic violence with connections to traditional norms in Tajikistan, such as parents,' relatives,' husbands,' in-laws,' and other relatives' cruel treatment toward women, restrictions on girls' studying and working outside the home, being forbidden to meet with or visit other people before and after marriage, strict regulation of responsibilities, economic dependence and control of expenses, being refused help with housework, and having limited input in important decisions in the parents' and husband's family.

Further repression comes in the form of polygamy which, although prohibited by both Soviet and post-Soviet Tajik laws, is becoming more widespread (Greenberg 2006; Zakirova 2002). Among our survey's respondents, 10 percent entered into *nikoh* (a traditional registration of marriage in Islam), which is an unofficial polygamous marriage. In polygamous marriages, women are more likely to face abuse, including sexual abuse.[32] In our study, 47 percent of all married respondents had been sexually abused by their husbands. When the figures were broken down by marriage type, we discovered that 42 percent of women in a monogamous marriage were sexually abused by their husbands, compared to 62 percent of women in a polygamous marriage.

We concluded from these interviews that in Tajik society conservatism and support for patriarchy related to violence against women. We then proceeded to examine how the most important traditional Tajik institutions, such as *avlod* (kinship) and *adat* (Islamic law), have contributed to the spread of violence against women.

Growing Traditional Influences

As material and physical insecurities increase, family, tribal, and regional ethnic relations are becoming stronger, while trust in governmental institutions remains low (Dadabaev 2006). *Avlod*, the traditional extended kinship network, merits special attention in a discussion on gender inequality and violence against women.

Avlod is one of the most powerful Tajik traditional institutions that have laid the foundations of the paradoxical nature of women's social status.[33] On the one hand, these traditional institutions protected women from some of the most dire and direct interventions of the Soviet state and the ravages of the civil war, and they placed the burden of material provision and economic security squarely on men's (father's, brother's, husband's) shoulders. On the other hand, this so-called protected status also resulted in women's isolation and economic dependence. *Avlod* not only provides significant physical protection but also offers the considerable emotional security of a sense of belonging, and it often provides social and economic support. Amid the very insecure political and economic circumstances during and immediately following the civil war, when the government provided at best negligible social assistance and health care, Tajik society survived to a great extent due to the informal *avlod* structures, which continued to carry out their traditional functions of protection during these difficult times.

In traditional institutions such as *avlod*, two main rules are dominant: the subordination of the young to the older generation, and women's submission to men (husband, father, brother, uncle, other male relatives).[34] These hierarchies arise from the traditional belief that women, like children and young people, are physically and emotionally less developed than men. Their perceived need for protection provides the basis for men's control and power over women's and children's behavior. The traditional norm of exclusive male inheritance has further underlined women's and children's full economic dependence. In addition, these exclusive male inheritance rights extend beyond material goods, such as household ownership, to cultural capital, such as the inheritance of political power.

Women's status in *avlod*, especially in rural areas, has been rather low, although wealth, education, personal initiative, or the father's/husband's status in the social hierarchy make their position more nuanced and complicated. However, *avlod* represents a strict patriarchal ideology that oppresses a woman as an individual and deprives her of initiative, education, and development. Heads of *avlod* control the members' conduct and enforce traditional marital norms that decree that women and girls should be obedient, calm, patient, and forgiving. According to *avlod*, a woman's husband and his relatives control her every move. This control preserves women's seclusion in society, which further determines whether they can leave their home alone or only with a chaperone, and where they are allowed to go. *Avlod* controls women's income-generating activities, restricts marriages between different religions and ethnicities, and decides at what age and to whom a girl should be married. Traditional norms prohibit most women and girls from establishing social contacts outside of their extended family, especially those involving men, and authorizes segregation in public facilities such as mosques and most entertainment places. In addition, *avlod* denies women's right to political and social activity, the need for women's representation in the national and local governments, and their access to economic and social capital.

However, although oppressive, *avlod* also provides women and children with significant moral and financial support and security. This sense of security is the main reason both girls and their parents consider marriage as a main avenue for their future. One in six women reported in the WHO survey that they were married because they wanted physical protection and some sort of economic support in the highly unstable Tajik political environment. The sense of externally validated security that *avlod* provides is why many women would not consider leaving their family, even if they are in grave danger at home from various forms of domestic violence. Women see themselves as "respected as long as they are under the wing of male protection," because "it is a sin for a woman to divorce" and because their status in local society is "only recognized through a male member of the family" (excerpts from interviews). Interviewees frequently repeated the popular saying: "You have a husband, you are respected."

Avlod members, especially women, can expect to suffer ostracism if caught in the "wrong" kind of sexual activity, such as premarital sex or adultery. Sexually explicit behaviors bring the most heavy-handed punishments, such as parents killing their daughters or relatives torturing women for "dishonoring" their family or *avlod*. Consequently, family conflicts often arise because of suspicions about "unchaste" sexual behavior and can end in tragedy. In a related study on violence against women and children, only 14 percent of parents said that they were willing to support their daughter if she lost her virginity before marriage and 5 percent stated that they would kill her (Sharipova 2002). These responses further underline that violence against children is linked to violence against women.

Although a girl child is looked down on as a liability, she is also seen as family property and a potential source of income. A bridegroom must pay a *kalym* (bride-price) as a "gift" to his future wife's family. The girl's parents and relatives determine the sum of the *kalym* as the price of her dignity, virginity, physical potential to serve the husband's family and bear children, and her "professionalism" in managing housework, etc. In some cases, the bridegroom has to pay additional payments to *kalym*, for example "the cost of mother's milk," or the price for "mother's care." A girl child is basically regarded by her parents as a very profitable item; they try "to sell" her for more money, depriving her of a childhood and, just as importantly, a free choice. The strictly gendered social expectations are why parents bring up their daughters in a dramatically different way from how they rear their sons.

Exactly because of the interlocking social and economic support prevalent in traditional social structures (such as *avlod* kin networks) and Islamic charities, the impact of and respect for these institutions increased during and after the civil war. Islam's influence is indisputably growing in Central Asia,[35] but religion is only one influence among many, starting with the family and extending to kin networks, regional loyalties, and allegiance to the newly independent states, as well as political affiliations. Due to the dearth of health and welfare services, many women turned to Islam and its religious institutions for psychological and material help. Although religious education is not officially recognized, it is becoming more valued, often at the expense of public education. Traditional and Islamic institutions undoubtedly provide a sense of belonging and security, but they have also brought more patriarchy into Tajik society.

The Tajik government has been alternating between ignoring (and thus supporting) and controlling/oppressing Islamic institutions. Official legislation has started to lose ground to *adat,* an Islamic or common law.[36] The very issues the government has recently tackled show an increasing symbolic and actual power of Islam in politics and everyday life. On a symbolic level, and like many countries struggling to establish a balance between secularism and religious freedom, the Tajik government took steps to limit religious appearance and activity, for example by banning (Islamic) headscarves in schools in 2005. However, on a more profound legal and economic matter, the Tajik parliament held series of heated debates in 1996 about paragraph 33 of the Constitution, which forbids polygamy. The legalization of polygamy proved to be an ongoing crucial and divisive social issue and a source of further decline in gender equality in contemporary Tajikistan (Zakirova 2002).

Islamic religious leaders support polygamy. Some high-ranking scholars in the Tajik Academy of Science have voiced support for this system, and Tajik scholars tend to view it as not causing any harm to women. For example, Abdulloev argues that "[v]iolence is more common in the West than in the Muslim countries" because of the "social and moral consequences of irresponsible freedom of Western women" (Abdulloev 2000: 1–2). Although he speaks out against the cruelest forms of physical violence, he accepts those oppressive forms of patriarchy that are among the root causes of violence against women, saying that "in our society religion teaches a man to be honest and conscious, making him feel proud of being a man, and this in its turn protects women from violence"; and that "the real causes of violence are slogans proclaiming freedom and equality" (Abdulloev 2000: 6–7).

State Response to Gender Inequality and Violence against Women

In post-Soviet Tajikistan, official discourse on women focused nearly exclusively on motherhood and only marginally concerned "women and family" issues. Following the Tajik government's mandate, the national Women's Committee organized official annual contests for "Best Mother of The Year" (Sharipova 2000). Moreover, post-Soviet Tajik national debates centered on legalizing polygamy and conserving women's traditional role by controlling their behavior in public and domestic spheres (Zakirova 2002).

After the civil war, the weak post-Soviet Tajik government desperately needed international support and approval. A member of the United Nations since 1992, the Tajik government clearly wanted to prove its good intentions after the civil war. The government speedily ratified most human rights conventions, including the UN's Convention on the Elimination of All Forms of Discrimination against Women (CEDAW), the Beijing Platform, and other international conventions and declarations on women's issues.

Tajikistan signed and ratified CEDAW on October 26, 1993. It also signed the Optional Protocol on September 7, 2000. However, Tajikistan was late in submitting its first CEDAW report in 2007 (Braun 2007; UN Division for the Advancement of Women, Economic and Social Affairs 2008) and the Optional Protocol has not yet been ratified as of late 2009 (United Nations 2009). The 1999 Presidential Decree on Improving Women's Role in Tajik Society established a National Plan of Action to Decrease Violence against Women. This plan became part of the broader National Plan of Action on Improving Women's Status in Tajikistan (2000). Emerging from internationally funded and coordinated awareness-raising, the Tajik legislature adopted the Gender Equality Law in March 2005. The government also amended the Civil Code and the Land and Family Codes to underline the rejection of domestic violence, and a consultative process has started on the Draft Law on Domestic Violence (UN Tajikistan Information Platform 2007a, 2007b). As in many other post-Soviet republics, despite the legal changes, the national plans, and the (pending) ratifications of international treaties, much governmental action remained only on paper (Avdeyeva 2007).

State complicity and lack of local government resources added to the failure to protect women from all types of violence. The Tajik Criminal Code of 1998 criminalizes rape and defines its punishment as three to twenty years of imprisonment, or even death in special severe cases (Criminal Code of Tajikistan 1999). There are still no legislative mechanisms defining and punishing marital rape in Tajik law; in fact, Tajik legislation on rape, sexual assault, sexual harassment, and some of the provisions covering other forms of abuse, such as beating, torture, and injury remain unchanged from Soviet times. They are rarely, if ever, implemented.

Meaningful implementation of laws against domestic violence is being delayed by many factors. First, Tajikistan is an intrinsically patriarchic society, where an older man—such as a husband, father, or adult brother—and his status determine a woman's place and rank in society.[37] Second, impunity and permissive Tajik attitudes toward violence lower the potential of reducing violence against women. Third, many forms of violence, especially psychological abuse, are not considered to be violence, especially by those who argue that any tradition is valuable in itself. Fourth, and perhaps most important, political, economic, social, and cultural factors intertwine to place women in an inferior place in Tajik society. These interlocking systems strengthen one another, leading women to believe that domestic violence is a "normal" part of life. The few, albeit powerful, disruptions to the increasing influence of traditional interpretations of gender roles have come from various international organizations: both states and their alliances, and numerous internationally connected NGOs.

The Effects of International Organizations and International and Local NGOs on Fighting Violence and Improving the Status of Women in Tajikistan

Counterintuitively, the otherwise very difficult social and political landscape in Tajikistan have worked to the advantage of those addressing gender issues. Because the country needed external support to rebuild itself and to reemerge on the international stage, government officials were more willing to sign international treaties as an indication of goodwill. Consequently, international governmental and nongovernmental organizations (IGOs and INGOs) were much less likely to encounter harassment and red tape when setting up gender-related activities, such as awareness-raising programs on gender issues, and in various attempts to develop more efficient legislative norms for protecting women (Sharipova's interviews in Dushanbe, 1999–2002, Spindler 2008).

Armed with the WHO and other UN-sponsored research data, international organizations (IOs) have begun to cooperate with locals and have initiated and supported NGOs to implement programs to tackle the manifold issues of violence against women. In the early 2000s, hundreds of Tajik NGOs, civil society activists, officials and experts, journalists, and other professionals have worked on gender issues in Tajikistan. Most of the programs that these Tajik organizations were involved in have been financially and technically supported by international organizations.[38]

The Civil War Era

During the civil war, hundreds of such IGOs, INGOs, and local NGOs (such as women's support groups) came to help rebuild the country by providing generous humanitarian assistance. International humanitarian assistance was instrumental in keeping at least a semblance of normalcy in Tajikistan. UN organizations were some of the first to provide humanitarian assistance to the Tajik people. For example, the UN Mission of Observers in Tajikistan (UNMOT) was established in 1994 (it was replaced in 2000 by the United Nations Tajikistan Office of Peacebuilding [UNTOP]), and the Special Representatives of the UN Secretary-General were established in 1996. Other international organizations, such as the Organization for Security and Cooperation in Europe (OSCE) and the Organization of the Islamic Conference (OIC), also actively helped maintain peace in 1997 (Taylor 2002).

Due to the pervasive instability during the civil war, international organizations often lacked reliable access to both the government and the opposition. The international organizations needed to engage at least minimally with the fighting parties in order to successfully pursue their humanitarian assistance programs. They could rarely dedicate resources to a careful study on the nature of the armed groups in the areas in which they worked, but they needed reliable information. Their major constraints have been a shortage of material resources and a lack of time. In some cases, IGOs and NGOs were justifiably concerned that any investigation into the nature of the fighting parties could jeopardize the perception of their organizations' impartiality and generate skepticism about their motivations (Centre for Humanitarian Dialogue 2003).

Even when the civil war ended and the lacuna of political institutions was slowly disappearing, relations between international organizations and the Tajik government, opposition parties, and emerging local NGOs often remained weak and unreliable.

Instead of closing their eyes to human rights violations, as many strategically interested states have done, international organizations were and have remained in a privileged position to use their leverage and the goodwill generated by their humanitarian aid to assist the improvement of women's situation in Tajikistan. Many INGOs decided to actively engage with gender issues in Tajikistan: for example, the UN agencies UNIFEM, United Nations Population Fund (UNFPA), UNDP, UNICEF, UNESCO, the UN's Office of the High Commissioner for Human Rights (OHCHR), WHO, and the EU Delegation, OSCE; various INGOs, such as the Aga Khan Humanities Project (AKHP), CARE, the Open Society Institute (OSI), OXFAM, the Swiss Cooperation Office–Consular Agency (SCO), *Deutsche Welthungerhilfe*/German Agro Action (DWHH/GAA) as well as various states' foreign assistance agencies, such as USAID, and the Swedish International Development Cooperation Agency (SIDA).

For many reasons, a significant portion of the personnel in the international governmental organizations (IGOs) and NGOs were women. First of all, the international organizations (IOs consisting of both INGOs and NGOs) had few other options but to hire women in Tajikistan because so many men had been killed, permanently disabled, or fled the country during the civil war. Second, the IOs decided to hire local women to assist in their humanitarian activities that relied on close familiarity with the environment. Third, women became more engaged in international humanitarian activity because such a prominent public activity was perceived as less dangerous for women than for men. The fourth factor that played a crucial role in women's engagement in international programs was the institutional weakness of the Tajik government and the main opposition parties. Women's relatively high engagement in the international humanitarian programs led to more gender-aware trends in building civil society and in developing local NGOs' programs on gender issues.

Possibly as a sign of spillover from the externally induced governmental-level openness toward gender issues, women were in charge of 224 (19.8 percent) of the 1,130 NGOs that were registered in 2005 in Tajikistan (UNDP 2006). Many of these NGOs replicated globally resonant themes in their operations, such as services to victims of domestic violence and trainings for women's business skills (Simpson 2006). Even if these are needed and useful services, the donor-driven nature of many NGOs raises the question of a new type of colonial relations with international organizations. With postcolonial gender studies arguing that colonial states redefine gender relations to strengthen their power (Edgar 2006; Northrop 2004), Western support for NGOs' focus on domestic violence becomes problematic. The attack on domestic violence as a foreign construct becomes especially viable when newly established nations, such as Tajikistan, claim to return to and reestablish precolonial (pre-Russian and pre-Soviet) traditions.

The Effect of International Organizations on Domestic Violence

International organizations initiated the Tajik political discussion on the development of legislative framework on gender equality and domestic violence. For example, UNIFEM developed a gender-sensitivity training program that contained such activities as strengthening the coordination between the Tajik government and NGOs to eliminate domestic violence and to build their capacities to prevent domestic violence (UN Tajikistan Information Platform 2007a, 2007b).

As generous and well intended as the international assistance to women in Tajikistan was, it also produced many problems that created formidable barriers against a successful implementation of the gender-sensitive antiviolence programs. First and foremost, the abovementioned crucial changes in gender-sensitive legislation passed in the Tajik legislature not because the government wanted to support democracy or to improve women's role in the society, but because they could thus avoid the expected intense opposition of the Islamic and other more traditional forces, exactly because of prevailing antidemocratic trends. In the absence of transparency related to governmental actions and the activities of international organizations, the dearth of free media, freedom of speech, and weakness of the political opposition, the government was in a position to "please" international donors by passing Western-oriented, top-down programs, most of which had no connection with Tajik women's NGOs. Moreover, as a male member of the Academy of Science of Tajikistan said, "violence against women is not a woman's issue, it is mainly a man's issue" (Sharipova's personal communication, Dushanbe, 1999).

Many of the international organizations listed above have encountered serious obstacles to establishing a collaborative approach with a wide range of Tajik civil society. Access to and dialogue with Tajik formal and informal groups would have strengthened the international organizations' potential for success. Especially in the case of programs on domestic violence, such communication and access to the target groups would have been essential in the war-ravaged and increasingly traditional Tajik society.

Most Tajik men and the large majority of rural-based social organizations have not supported the collaboration of international organizations with (mainly urban) Tajik women's NGOs. Men's vocal opposition often became intimidating and physically violent. Female NGO activists were frequently threatened and have been beaten in many cases (speech by Ms. Nasreddinova Latofat, chairperson of the Tajik Women's Committee at the annual reporting meeting, January 2000). Even the high-ranking and respected scholar Sherzod Abdulloev, head of the Department of Religious Studies of the Tajik Academy of Science, wrote, "Many of our fellow citizens are the followers or adherents of the Western way of life, and they get on the fishhook of the enemies of Islam, who use for their lures such popular slogans as 'democracy and women,' and 'women in democratic society,' and 'women and violence'" (Abdulloev 2000: 1). Soviet-era history appeared to be repeating itself in contemporary times, as women in Tajikistan once again became live shields between foreigners and the deeply patriarchal local society and its Islamic and traditional forces.

International organizations' lack of access to informal parts of Tajik society have significantly diminished their achievements in supporting peace and democracy building, especially in relation to gender equality. Gender-specific activities of international organizations have focused on formal organizations, such as the Tajik parliament, local governments, NGOs, mass media, schools, and hospitals. The approach of international organizations has been a replication of their own home environments where these formal institutions would carry the most weight in decisionmaking. It is also indisputably difficult to gain reliable access to the informal and (to Westerners) culturally less familiar organizations that form an important part of Tajik society. International organizations' lack of awareness, information, and access to less formal but extremely influential organizations such as *avlod* (kin networks) and Islamic institutions, where the majority of Tajik women get together and where perceptions of Western activities are shaped, has resulted in these informal organizations' being left out from the concerns and programs of international organizations.

There is a not entirely hidden political contestation between the IOs and the local traditional forces, often trapping individuals and organizations who wish to both honor local traditions and also challenge gender inequality and the oppression of women. Islamic organizations' opinion of IOs' activity strongly affects public opinion and cooperation with the IOs. International humanitarian organizations work, and thus compete, in the same sociopolitical field with the local Islamic organizations. Islamic movements often claim that IOs are not transparent because of their dependence on Christian or other missionary religious donations. In the eyes of Islamists, international organizations have had a hidden political and religious agenda and have not honored the premise of neutrality (Centre for Humanitarian Dialogue 2003).

One obvious and painful example of the closed nature and inflexibility of the international organizations is the foreign donors' very complicated system of grant applications. Nearly all international organizations (both IGOs and INGOs) maintain the condition that local applicants include their official registration in order to receive a grant. This condition may seem simple and self-explanatory in Western Europe and North America, but even the concept of an NGO was new to all post-Soviet societies, since nongovernmental initiatives had previously been prohibited. In addition, registering an NGO has been an exceedingly difficult bureaucratic process and a considerable financial burden in Tajikistan (USAID 2008).

Even more difficult than the official registration of an applicant NGO is the requirement for proficiency in English when applying for and receiving grants. With more than 70 percent of the Tajik population living in rural areas and with Soviet education placing little emphasis on teaching and learning English, it should have been obvious to the international organizations that precious few Tajiks would be familiar with writing grant proposals and even fewer would be able to communicate in English—with the exception of a very closed circle of the earlier Communist elite.

The requirement for English grant-writing skills meant that the urban middle classes came to dominate the NGO sector (Asian Development Bank 2000). The English translators for the international organizations most often came from Russian-speaking or Russified Tajik backgrounds. The translators, who served as crucial links between Tajiks and the international organizations, were mainly from urban, Russian-speaking elite groups and did not know either the Tajik language or, more significantly, the Tajik realities in rural areas. Consequently, these centrally placed translators became by default the "experts" on Tajik society, probably directing the international organizations even further away from their original intent and from the more efficient participatory approaches.

One of the most perplexing questions about this series of miscommunications is why the international organizations did not anticipate these problems when they had faced them already in postcommunist

Central Europe and in Eastern Europe since the mid-1990s (see Carothers 1999; Carothers and Ottaway 2000; Wedel 1998). In addition, social scientists of the Central Asian region have long advocated taking informal organizations into account when engaging in local politics and societies (Anderson 1997; Collins 2004; MacFarlane 1999).

Finally, in 2003, the Gender Theme Group started to coordinate the UN agencies and the other international organizations and donors. The Group's mission is to lead, strengthen, and support the gender mainstreaming process to coordinate the various and often rather disparate gender mainstreaming strategies among the UN agencies and the international organizations, and particularly to assist the Tajik government in integrating gender equality priorities into the National Development Strategy and Poverty Reduction Strategy (NDS/PRS; Gender Theme Group 2007).

Since 2006, the Gender Theme Group has produced a map of gender-related projects and interventions in Tajikistan. They have also procured a budget of tens of millions US dollars for the nine gender-issue target areas:

1) Strengthening the Tajik national capacity to promote gender sensitive policy and resource allocation

2) Preventing violence against women

3) Promoting equal rights and opportunities among the sexes

4) Improving women's access to resources and assets

5) Strengthening public awareness of gender equality

6) Participating on equal levels

7) Improving national legislation to reflect gender equality

8) Promoting equal participation in the decisionmaking process

9) En-gendering indicators and methodologies for gender-sensitive analysis (Gender Theme Group 2007)

Linking various cultural, economic, and political aspects of women's role in Tajik society may allow for these programs and related legislative changes to be adapted to local environments and gain local support, and thus be more successful.

Tajikistan is transitioning to civil order, but the current situation can still be characterized as a time of political and economical instability. Poverty and lack of social security have a significant impact on the low status of women. Lack of state support, high levels of unemployment and underemployment as well as of migration, limited access to education, and women's becoming heads of households all contribute to the increasing gender gap in education and health status. Many other powerful recent historical and political factors have also contributed to the increase of violence against women; these include the civil war, the very recent introduction of the culture of human rights, the failure of democracy, corruption, the lack of independent mass media, the dearth of (legislative) institutional mechanisms for the protection of women, the generally conservative sociocultural environment with its revival of religious and traditional norms, the absence of a real political will to raise women's status in Tajik society, the shortage of women's political and economical opportunities with the consequent scarcity of women's leadership, and even the dearth of theoretical work on gender as it plays out in Tajik circumstances and missing gender disaggregated data.

The WHO survey and the broad study of the literature have revealed a high prevalence of physical, sexual, or psychological violence experienced directly by women and girls in Tajikistan. Various groups and governments have used the decades of violent conflict in Tajikistan to make people believe that violence is justified and that it can help achieve political, economic, and other goals. In the beginning of the Soviet era the Communists faced strong resistance in nearly all colonized countries. Their rule and way of management relied largely using violence to intimidate people into acquiescence. Thus, violence became "legitimated" by the Soviet state and became the norm, an everyday affair in interpersonal relations, including gender relations inside and outside of the family. It appears that it was this political violence (intimidation, repression, war, etc.) that spread widely in Tajik society during Soviet and post-Soviet times, and it continues to play a crucial role in spreading gender violence in the domestic sphere.

Although Soviet attempts to eradicate religion and the strong policy supporting women's emancipation left their marks on gender roles in Tajik society, the results were not exclusively positive. Tajik women during Soviet times were exposed to new forms of violence, which did not disappear with the fall of the Soviet system. After the collapse of the USSR and the ensuing Tajik civil war, the economic and political crisis, combined with the revival of tradition and religion, led to the further escalation of violence toward women and unraveled nearly all the Soviet era's achievements on gender equality. Moreover, the rapid change in political and economic systems in Tajikistan failed to address the historical and sociocultural aspects of victimization of Tajik women during Soviet and post-Soviet times. On the contrary, these developments only created new sources of tension and new excuses for violence against women. Soviet modernization and female emancipation were not deeply rooted in Tajik society, but post-Soviet developments seemed only to worsen the status of women in Tajikistan instead of improving it.

Gender policy in Tajikistan (if one can speak of such policy) is mostly supported by programs of various (usually Western-oriented) international organizations. However, even these efforts have been weakened by a failure to support democracy-building, which has manifested itself as IOs' lack of access to current sociopolitical debates, continued socio-economic and political instability, the absence of social security, and massive corruption. Gender policy on women's access to decisionmaking, work and work-related rights, reproductive and sexual health and rights, access to education and social security, and even access to nutrition, has in fact declined in Tajikistan.

Women's segregation has been furthered in Tajikistan's contemporary conservative sociocultural environment with the revival of religious and traditional norms. The revival of traditional Islamic law and traditions of gender discrimination has spread such phenomena as polygamy and child marriages, unregistered marriages, and bride price, and has increased the prevalence of violence against women in Tajikistan. The issue of violence against women has been taboo because people believed that somehow, by tolerating or enduring violence, the problem would not exist. The cumulative impact of these developments for women in Tajikistan has been devastating, and women remain the poorest and most marginalized group in Tajik society.

NOTES

1. Muborak Sharipova is the author of the first study on violence against women in Tajikistan, *Report on Violence against Women in Tajikistan: Analysis of Qualitative Data,* published in 2000. The study was supported by the WHO, the Swiss Agency for Development and Cooperation, the UNDP, and the Italian government.

2. According to UN and Tajik official reports, 50,000–100,000 civilians perished during the civil war (Human Rights Watch 2003; Jonson 2006). The economic cost of the war is estimated at US$7 billion (UNDP 1995).

3. Studying women's issues in Central Asia and in the Soviet Union in general began with what was called the *zhenskii vopros* (the "woman question") in Russian late-imperial-period discussions of women's rights and roles (Stites 1978; Togan 1999).

The "woman question" became shorthand for the ongoing inequality of women in Soviet times. The partial acknowledgement of this gender inequality did not lead to a development of women's studies; however, gender analysis appeared as a result of Western influences (see Kamp 2009).

4. Kazakhstan, Kyrgyzstan, Tajikistan, Turkmenistan, and Uzbekistan are included under the term "Central Asia."

5. Tajikistan (*Jumhurrii Tojikiston* or *Tocikiston* in Tajik) became part of the Russian Empire in 1868. In its tumultuous early days it was called the Bukhara Emirate (1917) and was part of the Central Asian Emirate. Tajikistan became a Soviet Republic in 1918 but was incorporated into Uzbekistan in a piecemeal fashion between 1924 and 1929. It gained its independence as Tajikistan on November 9, 1991.

6. Since 1980 the number of inhabitants has doubled. The 2007 estimate of population growth was 1.895 percent and the birth rate was 27.33 births per 1,000 of population. The fertility rate per woman for 2007 is estimated at 3.09. The population is very young: the median age is 21.3 years and people under fifteen represent 38.8 percent of the total population (UNICEF 2008).

7. An estimated 700,000 people became refugees or became internally displaced during the civil war (UNDP 1995).

8. In 2000, 5 percent of all households consisted of single mothers with children (UNDP 1995).

9. In 2007, 60 percent of the population, most of them women and children, lived below the poverty line (US Central Intelligence Agency 2008). Food insecurity reached dramatic proportions both during and after the civil war, producing high rates of malnutrition and child and maternal mortality. The rapidly increasing prices of basic goods and services—food, clothes, health care and medicine, childcare and education, transport, electricity, water, communication—further damaged the population's quality of life, and especially affected women and children.

10. There have been significant gender disparities in educational achievements. In 2000, there were 63 girls per 100 boys in general secondary schools, whereas in 1990 there were 104 girls per 100 boys. Poverty and fear of harassment have restricted girls' access to school, and educating girls became less of a priority. More than 20 percent of girls drop out after primary school in Tajikistan (UNICEF 2006). The gender gap in higher education has also widened, from 58 women per 100 men in 1990 to just 34 women per 100 men in 1998 (Falkingham 2000: 10).

11. "Women often end up in hospitals with traumas, broken bones, hernias, prolepsis of internal organs, and STDs." Sharipova's interview with physician Shoira Yusupova, in Dushanbe, Tajikistan, November 22, 1999.

12. During the civil war, the militia forced young women to marry. Some women were forced into sex and consequently bore children. In order to avoid scandal, some women reported the incident as forced marriage, even if the act of marriage did not actually take place (WHO 1999).

13. Women who had been raped in Tajikistan were often rejected by their own families and their broader communities.

14. Interviews in prison with female drug traffickers in *Living Containers* (Sharipov 2002).

15. Badakhshon refers to the Badakhshon Autonomous Region (BAR), the mountainous region in Tajikistan.

16. As of 2005, the percentage of female managers in local administration was 15.5 percent and the ratio of women in government ministries was 7.3 percent, while 12.3 percent of managerial personnel of the president's office were women (Rakhmanova 2007). In 2006, women accounted for 27.3 percent of parliamentary seats in neighboring Afghanistan, thanks to the women's quota established in the new constitution, and 22.5 percent of parliamentary seats in Pakistan. In Uzbekistan, women hold 17.5 percent of seats in the parliament, while in Turkmenistan women occupy 16 percent, according to the Inter-Parliamentary Union (IPU) at www.ipu.org/wmn-e/classif.htm.

17. Since 1992, the Tajik social sector has suffered from severe financial constraints. Total spending on the social sectors in 1998 amounted to just over 7 percent of GDP, compared with 20 percent in 1992 (Falkingham 2000: 9). One illustration of the unbridled nature of liberalization was the privatization of many public buildings, such as schools and kindergartens. Many women were forced to trust the supervision of younger children to older ones or to leave them unsupervised. Cases of child abandonment, the appearance of street children, school dropout rates and truancy, child labor, begging, pickpocketing, child prostitution, and children's involvement in the network of adult criminal gangs have all risen. For an additional gendered critique of World Bank structural adjustment policies, see Brym et al. 2005.

18. Anti-Soviet and anti-Russian sentiments emerged as crucial components when confirming Tajik national identity. For example, in 1989, the first law that the Tajik legislation drafted during perestroika was the Law on National Language, intended to "promote and safeguard" the national language and identity against Russification. Although the draft was discussed at the national level, the lawmakers disregarded the role of women in maintaining the Tajik language and keeping national traditions alive during the seventy years of Soviet rule and the preceding forty years in the Russian Empire.

19. Triggered in 1992 by conflicts between the pro-communist forces on one side and a coalition of pro-democratic and pro-Islamic groups on the other, the civil war ended in June 1997 when the UN, Russia, and Iran brokered a power-sharing peace agreement (Taylor 2002; UN Secretary General 1997).

20. Tajik refugees often could not obtain legal refugee status in Russia, Uzbekistan, Turkmenistan, or Kyrgyzstan. Without legal status the refugees were denied the protection of domestic and international legislative mechanisms. Human Rights Watch (HRW) reported numerous cases of Tajik refugee women being raped in refugee camps in Afghanistan (Human Rights Watch 2003).

21. The Organization of Security and Cooperation in Europe (OSCE), the UN High Commissioner for Refugees (UNHCR), and HRW all documented numerous cases of rape during the civil war (Human Rights Watch 2003; UNDP 1995; Zuhurova 1999).

22. In 1998, the National Burns Centre in the capital Dushanbe reported that during the civil war they received an average of thirty bodies of women every month who had committed suicide by self-immolation. Self-immolation was seen as turning against oneself in times of utmost desperation (Sharipova's interview with the Director of the National Burns Centre, Dushanbe, Tajikistan 1998). The 1998 Conference on Violence against Women in Tajikistan, organized by the Dushanbe-based Open Asia Foundation, included a discussion on the roots of self-immolation in Tajik society in which the participants argued that self-immolation was women's protest against violence (Odinaeva 2009; Sharipova 2000).

23. Before 1991, drug addiction and drug use were not registered in Tajikistan because drugs were also a taboo during the Soviet regime. According to the Tajik Health Ministry, there were 8,000 officially registered drug users in 2007. However, the Tajik Drug Control Agency estimated that the real numbers are closer to 55,000–75,000 (UN Office for the Coordination of Humanitarian Affairs 2007).

24. Each interviewer received a manual of terms and definitions as a guideline. Interviewers were asked to spend ample time with each respondent to explain the aims of the survey and what the different types and forms of violence in it meant. All interviewers and their supervisors had to keep diaries, which were added to the collection of records for qualitative data. To limit under-reporting, a section of the questionnaire also asked about perceptions of violence and the extent of violence among other family members and acquaintances. The crosscheck on the perceptions of violence allowed the interviewees a greater freedom of expression if they were reluctant to share their own experiences. The research team expected significant reluctance to share personal experiences, partially because a wide range of highly vulnerable groups of women were included in the survey, such as the displaced and the refugee returnees, those residing in areas where the civil war raged, war widows and women who were head of households, and women engaged in different forms of marriage (both religious and official) and polygamy.

25. During an early workshop between the staff conducting the interviews and the international experts assisting with the preparations, the staff debated with experts on how to apply the concepts and vocabulary of violence against women in the Tajik and the Russian surveys. In this workshop the definition of the concept of violence against women, as it is used in the UN Convention on the Declaration on Eradication of Violence against Women (CEDAW), was adapted to the specificities and local dialects of Tajikistan. One objective of the workshop was to give specific definitions to each type of violence so we could then offer the specifications of each when talking with various Tajik communities.

26. In some cases, armed men stopped the interviewers. The armed men often did not belong to any official military forces, but they felt free to interrogate the staff about the purpose of their visit to the given district/region. In such cases, the interviewers had to lie that they were doctors visiting sick people. In other cases, the WHO letters helped. The interviewers mentioned that both the general population and local government officials showed very positive attitudes toward the WHO. One interviewer working in Gharm region (where a major armed conflict took place) wrote in her diary that on the day before her arrival, the guard who had worked for the internationally funded Women's Center where she conducted interviews was killed. The interviewer noted: "I was afraid very much that the *mojaheddins* (armed opposition groups) would discover what I was asking my respondents about."

27. One of the interviewers commented, "At the beginning, some respondents did not give their consent to fill out the questionnaire. Their main reason was fear. It usually took quite a long time to make them believe that their answers would be confidential. The questions about violence just scared some women respondents. They tried to tell me that they never saw or knew anything like that."

28. An interviewer stated, "It was especially difficult to question women of higher social status and to get frank answers to the questions from them, especially when the questions were connected with violence against them. In families with notably

high social status, the forms of violence were hidden. We discovered that in such families the psychological forms of violence prevail, which sometimes were very rude and vulgar."

29. A widowed woman often loses most of her rights to her husband's property. She can be thrown out of her deceased husband's home. The "best case" scenario for a widowed woman is that she has a son, because then she will be responsible for the property until her son comes of age. When the son reaches adulthood, his mother is expected to take care of the household until he marries, when the wife or wives will be expected to obey her and take care of the elderly woman.

30. Among those who had had an unwanted pregnancy, husbands or other relatives forced 7 percent to have the child; 5 percent wished to terminate the pregnancy but did not because of "fear of god and public opinion"; and 7 percent did not even know what they could do besides accepting the baby when they became pregnant. When women were asked about their reasons for wanting to terminate the pregnancy, 2 percent stated that the pregnancy was a result of rape; 6 percent said that their husband, mother, mother-in-law, or other relatives forced them to continue with the pregnancy. In addition, 9 percent confided that they did not use contraceptives because their husbands did not want them to do so and they were afraid of condemnation; and 8 percent did not use contraceptives because of religious teachings.

31. Various official documents refer to seventeen as the age of consent in Tajikistan, such as the AIDS/HIV information site, www.avert.org/aofconsent.htm and the US Embassy in Tajikistan http://dushanbe.usembassy.gov/marriage_in_ tajikistan.html. However, interviews and the US Embassy information also confirm that girls younger than seventeen often marry, with only the religious ceremony marking the event.

32. Because polygamy is not legal in Tajikistan, men usually do not want to officially register their second or third marriages. Consequently, in the case of divorce from the second, third, or fourth wife, the husband's family can avoid the division of property. The divorced or widowed daughters-in-law are often driven out of their husband's house for trivial reasons. Under these circumstances, the wives cannot even take their own things with them. Once out of the family compound, the woman and her children lose all rights to the house and other properties. In addition, children born in unregistered marriages are not registered either, and do not receive prenatal or postnatal medical care. The long-term consequences can be dire for unregistered children. Without official papers they have trouble attending school and they can encounter many difficulties when trying to marry officially or find a job. If children born in unregistered marriages die, their deaths are not registered.

33. *Avlod* (kinship or extended family) is the basis of Tajik traditional social institutions. *Avlod* consists of family members of at least two generations who live together, most often the parents and their unmarried children. A married son would also join this compound with his wife (or wives) and children. Extended families have common ownership of the house, land, and cattle. The men (father or/and grown son(s)) are the decisionmakers and are considered to be responsible for the wellbeing of the family. Usually the oldest or most authoritative man becomes the head of the extended family and *avlod*. All the relatives of this extended family are part of the kinship and create a broad and deep-reaching traditional institution (for more about Tajik family structure and the *avlod* see Bushkov 1991).

34. Experts such as Tyomkina (2005) point out that the norms of absolute respect to elders and the unquestioned authority of husbands are becoming more flexible

in many Tajik families, but the norm of obeying the husband's authority in society remains very strong.

35. Many other examples show how the revival of Islam and tradition are becoming faster, deeper, and stronger; for example, the appearance of the new Islamic political groups, such as *Hizb-ul Tahrir* (The Party of Reform) and the growing presence of *Hizb-i Nehzat-i Islam* (Islamic Renaissance Party) (Roy 2000).

36. "*Urf u Odat*" or "*Adat*" are a collection of Tajik traditional norms, rules, and customs.

37. The Tajik saying "*Shu dori—obru dori*" (If you have a husband, you have respect) is still very much standard, even though many widows have managed to become economically independent and have gained respect in society because of their business activities, hard work, and skills. Widows have fought their very unfavorable social environment ardently, simply because they had so much at stake. In eking out a living alone, many widows have learned not to hide behind a husband's shoulders, not to care about what others say about them, and to fight for their and their children's survival. However, only men are considered to be the leaders in extended families, and a woman usually has to entrust her right to protection to a man. These social pressures also increase the chances of psychological abuse of females in a family.

38. Follow-up activities started in 2001 as a direct result of the WHO research project. Local NGOs in the city of Kurgan Turbe created a crisis center called *Gamkhori*. At the beginning of 2004, the Kurgan Turbe Project assisted the Tajik government's Committee on Women and Family Affairs to establish *Bovari* (Trust), another crisis center in the capital Dushanbe. These two crisis centers provide psychological counseling and legal and medical aid for the two cities as well as nearby districts. The overall goals of these crisis centers are to reduce both the level of violence against women and to provide access to welfare services for survivors of violence. In addition, they have attempted to change the general attitude to violence against women and organize effective lobbying campaigns on the issue at the national level. Eight NGOs founded the Association of Crisis Centers of Tajikistan (Gulrukhsor Women's Center, Women of Science Tajikistan, the Tajikistan National Association of Businesswomen, *Modar, Nachoti Kudakon* (city of Kuliab), *Bonuvoni Khatlon* (city of Kurgantiube), *Chashman Khaet* (city of Khudzhand), *Zankho Ziddi Zurovari* (city of Istravshan). The Association of Crisis Centers was registered in December 2006, and its mission was to provide social services to victims of violence and to improve the social, political, and economic status of women in Tajikistan by working to reduce violence in the community and enhance gender equality (Gender Theme Group 2007; Modar 2008). However, the Association of Crisis Centers fell apart within two years, replicating the short period that has been characteristic of similarly coordinated efforts among NGOs.

WORKS CITED

Abdulloev, Sherzod. 2000. *Islam and Eradication of Violence Against Women*. Prepared for the WHO Study. Dushanbe, Tajikistan: unpublished manuscript.

Anderson, John. 1997. *The International Politics of Central Asia*. Manchester, UK: Manchester University Press.

Asian Development Bank. 2000. *Women in Tajikistan: Country Gender Assessments*. www.adb.org/documents/books/country_briefing_papers/women_in_tajikistan/ (accessed November 7, 2009).

Avdeyeva, Olga. 2007. "When Do States Comply with International Treaties? Policies on Violence against Women in Post-Communist Countries." *International Studies Quarterly* 51(4): 877–900.

Braun, Sylvia. 2007. "NGOs Are Important for CEDAW—Take Part." *Activities and Initiatives of Women Worldwide: IWTC Women's GlobalNet: 316.* The International Women's Tribune Centre (IWTC). www.iwtc.org/316.html (accessed November 7, 2009).

Brym, Robert J., Stephanie Chung, Sarah Dulmage, Christian Farahat, Mark Greenberg, Manki Ho, Khadra Housein, Dina Kulik, Matthew Lau, Olivia Maginley, Armen Nercessian, Emilio Reyes Le Blanc, Adrian Sacher, Nadia Sachewsky, Alex Sadovsky, Stephen Singh, Shankar Sivananthan, Nick Toller, Sara Vossoughi, Krista Weger, and Tommy Wu. 2005. "In Faint Praise of the World Bank's Gender Development Policy." *Canadian Journal of Sociology/ Cahiers Canadiens de Sociologie* 30(1): 95–109. www.cjsonline.ca/articles/ brymeta105.html (accessed November 7, 2009).

Bushkov, Valentin. 1991. "Tadjik Avlod Thousands of Years Later." *Vostok* 5: 72–81.

Carothers, Thomas. 1999. *Aiding Democracy Abroad: The Learning Curve.* Washington, D.C.: Carnegie Endowment for International Peace.

Carothers, Thomas, and Maria Ottaway, eds. 2000. *Funding Virtue: Civil Society Aid and Democratic Promotion.* Washington, D.C.: Carnegie Endowment for International Peace.

Centre for Humanitarian Dialogue. 2003. *Humanitarian Engagement with Armed Groups: The Central Asian Islamic Opposition Movements.* Geneva: Centre for Humanitarian Dialogue.

Collins, Kathleen. 2004. "The Logic of Clan Politics: Evidence from the Central Asian Trajectories." *World Politics* 56(2): 224–261.

Criminal Code of Tajikistan. 1999. Dushanbe.

Dadabaev, Timur. 2006. "Public Confidence, Trust, and Participation in Post-Soviet Central Asia." *Central Asia–Caucasus Institute Analyst.* www.cacianalyst.org/ ?q=node/3977/print (accessed November 7, 2009).

Edgar, Adrienne. 2006. "Bolshevism, Patriarchy, and the Nation: The Soviet "Empancipation' of Muslim Women in Pan-Islamic Perspective." *Slavic Review* 65(2): 252–272.

Falkingham, Jane. 2000. *Women and Gender Relations in Tajikistan.* Country Briefing Paper: Asian Development Bank. www.adb.org/documents/books/country_ briefing_papers/women_in_tajikistan/ (accessed November 7, 2009).

Gender Theme Group. 2003. *Tajikistan—on the Way to Gender Equality.* www.untj .org/files/gender/Advocacy_event.pdf; and www.untj.org/files/gender/mandate .pdf (accessed November 7, 2009).

———. 2007. "2006 Report on Joint Activities." *UN Tajikistan Information Platform.* www.untj.org/?c=21&id=41 (accessed November 7, 2009).

Gleason, Gregory. 2003. *Markets and Politics in Central Asia: Structural Reform and Political Change.* London and New York: Routledge.

Goldberg, Itzhak, Lee Branstetter, John Gabriel Goddard, and Smita Kuriakose. 2008. *Globalization and Technology Absorption in Europe and Central Asia: The Role of*

Trade, FDI, and Cross-border Knowledge Flows. The World Bank: World Bank Publications.

Granick, David. 1987. *Job Rights in the Soviet Union: Their Consequences.* Cambridge: Cambridge University Press.

Greenberg, Ilan. 2006. "After a Century, Public Polygamy Is Re-Emerging in Tajikistan." *The New York Times.* November 13.

Haarr, Robin. 2007. "Wife Abuse in Tajikistan." *Feminist Criminology,* 2(3): 245–270.

Harris, Collette. 2004. *Control and Subversion: Gender and Power in Tajikistan.* London: Pluto Press.

Human Rights Watch. 2003. *Anatomy of Civil War in Tajikistan: Ethno-social Processes and Political Struggle, 1992–1995.* Central Asia and Central Caucasus Press AB, Sweden. www.ca-c.org/datarus/st_08_bush.shtml (in Russian; accessed November 7, 2009).

Human Rights Watch. 2005. Uzbekistan: *Andijan Crisis Aftermath.* www.hrw.org/campaigns/uzbekistan/andijan/ (accessed November 7, 2009).

International Foundation for Electoral Systems (IFES). 2006. *Political Engagement and Enfranchisement of Labor Migrants from Tajikistan.* www.ifes.org/publications-detail.html?id441 (accessed November 7, 2009).

International Organization for Migration (IOM). 2001. *Deceived Migrants from Tajikistan: A Study of Trafficking in Women and Children.* www.iom.tj/publications.html (accessed November 9, 2009).

Inter-Parliamentary Union (IPU). 2005. *Women in National Parliaments.* www.ipu.org/wmn-e/classif.htm (accessed November 7, 2009).

Johnson, Janet Elise. 2007. "Domestic Violence Politics in Post-Soviet States." *Social Politics: International Studies in Gender, State, and Society* 14(3): 1–26.

Jonson, Lena. 2006. *Tajikistan in the New Central Asia: Geopolitics, Great Power Rivalry and Radical Islam.* London: I. B. Tauris.

Kamp, Marianne. 2009. "Women's Studies and Gender Studies in Central Asia: Are We Talking to One Another." *Central Eurasian Studies Review* (CESR) 8: 4–14.

Kanji, N., and Gladwin, C. 2000. *Gender and Livelihoods in Gorno-Badakshan.* Dushanbe: The Mountain Societies Development and Support Program.

MacFarlane, Neil. 1999. *Western Engagement in the Caucasus and Central Asia.* Washington, D.C.: Brookings Institution Press.

Mirzoeva, Gulchehra 2004. Armed Conflict and Human Trafficking in Tajikistan. NGO Modar. http://modar.tj/index.php?option=com_content&task=view&id=90&Itemid=15 (accessed November 9, 2009).

Modar. 2008. Association of Crisis Centers in the Republic of Tajikistan http://modar.tj/index.php?option=com_content&task=view&id=67&Itemid=15 (accessed November 20, 2009).

Muhammadiev, Davron. 1998. *Social and Demographic, Ethnic and Clinical Characteristics of Tajik Women Who Committed Auto-Aggressive Actions Via Self-Immolation.* Dushanbe, Tajikistan: Tajik State Medical University.

———. 2000. Diagnosis and Prophylaxis of Suicides (Self-Immolation) Among Tajik Women (Social, Demographic, Ethnic/Anthropologic, Cultural, and Medical

Aspects). *Report Prepared for the VAW Tajikistan Study*. Unpublished manuscript prepared for the WHO Study. Dushanbe, Tajikistan.

Northrop, Douglas. 2004. *Veiled Empire: Gender and Power in Stalinist Central Asia*. Ithaca, N.Y.: Cornell University Press.

Odinaeva, Mukammal. 2009. *Female Suicide "Epidemic" in Tajikistan*. Dushanbe: UNHCR and Refworld. www.unhcr.org/refworld/country,,,,TJK,4562d8cf2,4a0d 1f3b1e,0.html (accessed November 20, 2009).

Rakhmanova, Malika. 2007. "Tajikistan Ranked 62nd in 2006 in Terms of Percentage of Women in Parliament." Asia-Plus Information Agency. March 3. www.asia-plus.tj/en/news/50/16244.html (accessed November 20, 2009).

Rotar, Igor. 2006. Tajikistan: Council of Ulems—An Instrument of State Control. *Forum 18 News Service*. www.forum18.org/Archive.php?article_id=796&pdf=Y (accessed November 7, 2009).

Roy, Olivier. 2000. *The Foreign Policy of the Central Asian Islamic Renaissance Party*. New York: Council of Foreign Relations Publishers. www.cfr.org/content/ publications/attachments/Roy.pdf (accessed November 7, 2009).

Sharipov, Kholmurod. 2006. *Otashnihodon*. [Those Who Attend the Hearth]. Dushanbe: Ifron.

Sharipov, Orzu. 2002. *Living Containers*. Open Society Archives. www.osaarchivum .org/filmlibrary/browse/country?val=69 (accessed November 7, 2009).

Sharipova, Muborak. 1998. Opening Remarks: Speech at the First National Conference on Violence Against Women in Dushanbe, Tajikistan.

———. 2000. *Report on Violence against Women in Tajikistan: Analysis of Quantitative and Qualitative Data*. Copenhagen, Denmark: WHO Regional Office for Europe.

———. 2001. Prevalence and Risk Factors of Violence against Children in Tajikistan: Results of the National Survey. Dushanbe: Open Asia.

———. 2002. "Theoretical and Practical Problems of Violence Against Children Based on National Surveys Implemented in Tajikistan." Ph.D. thesis. Moscow: Russian Academy of Science, Institute of Sociology.

Shoismatulloev, Shonazar. 2005. *Violence against Women: Past and Present*. Dushanbe.

Simpson, Meghan. 2006. "Local Strategies in Globalizing Gender Politics: Women's Organizing in Kyrgyzstan and Tajikistan." *Journal of Muslim Minority Affairs* 26(1): 9–31.

Singerman, Diane. 2004. "The Networked World of Islamist Social Movements." In *Islamic Activism: A Social Movement Theory Approach,* ed. Quintan Wiktorowicz. Bloomington: Indiana University Press.

Spechler, Martin. 2004. "Central Asia on the Edge of Globalization." *Challenge* 47(4): 62–77.

Spindler, Amy. 2008. *Thirsty for Knowledge: A Case Study of Women's Empowerment and Social Capital through a Development Assistance Program in Rasht, Tajikistan*. Washington DC: Mercy Corps.

Stites, Richard. 1978. *The Women's Liberation Movement in Russia*. Princeton: Princeton University Press.

Sulaimanova, Saltanat. 2004. "Migration Trends in Central Asia and the Case of Trafficking in Women." In *In the Tracks of Tamerlane: Central Asia's Path to the 21st Century*, ed. Daniel L. Burghart and Theresa Sabonis-Helf, 377–400. Washington, D.C.: National Defense University.

Tabyshalieva, Anara. 2000. "Revival of Traditions in Post-Soviet Central Asia." In *Making the Transition Work for Women in Europe and Central Asia*, ed. Marnia Lazreg, 51–57. World Bank Technical Paper no. 457. Washington, D.C.: The World Bank.

Taylor, Russell. 2002. "Time to Reflect." *UN Chronicle*. http://findarticles.com/p/articles/mi_m1309/is_4_39/ai_96951759/ (accessed November 9, 2009).

Togan, Isenbike. 1999. "In Search of an Approach to Women's History in Central Asia." In *Rethinking Central Asia: Non-Eurocentric Studies in History, Social Structure, and Identity*, ed. Korkut Erturk, 163–193. Reading, UK: Ithaca Press.

Tyomkina, Anna. 2005. "Gender Order: Post-Soviet Transformation in North Tajikistan." In *Gender: Tradition and Contemporaneity: Collected Articles on Gender*, ed. Safia Kasimova, 27. Dushanbe.

UNICEF. 2006. *Tajikistan: Country Statistics*. www.unicef.org/infobycountry/Tajikistan_statistics.html (accessed November 9, 2009).

———. 2008. *Tajikistan*. www.unicef.org/infobycountry/Tajikistan.html (accessed November 9, 2009).

United Nations. 2008. Rights and Dignity of Persons with Disabilities (Enable). *Countries that have ratified the Convention*. www.un.org/disabilities/default.asp?navid=18&pid=257 (accessed November 9, 2009).

———. 2009. Chapter IV Human Rights: 8.b Optional Protocol on the Convention on the Elimination of All Forms of Discrimination against Women. *Treaty Collection*. Status at 08-11-2009. http://treaties.un.org/Pages/ViewDetails.aspx?src=TREATY&mtdsg_no=IV-8-b&chapter=4&lang=en (accessed November 20, 2009).

United Nations Development Program (UNDP). 1995. *UNDP Human Development Report: Tajikistan*. www.undp.org/rbec/nhdr/tajikistan/chapter7.htm (accessed April 19, 2008; no longer available).

———. 2006. *Parliament Needs Assessment Study*. Dushanbe, Tajikistan. www.reliefweb.int/rw/res.nsf/db900SID/OCHA-6PX63S?OpenDocument (accessed November 7, 2009).

———. 2008. *UNDP Human Development Report: Tajikistan*. http://hdrstats.undp.org/countries/data_sheets/cty_ds_TJK.html (accessed April 24, 2008; no longer available).

United Nations Division for the Advancement of Women, Economic and Social Affairs. 2008. *States Parties for the Convention on the Elimination of All Forms of Discrimination Against Women (CEDAW)*. www.un.org/womenwatch/daw/cedaw/states.htm (accessed November 9, 2009).

United Nations Office for the Coordination of Humanitarian Affairs. 2007. *Tajikistan: Afghan narcotics fuel drug addiction.* IrinNews: Humanitarian News and Analysis. www.irinnews.org/report.aspx?ReportId=72937 (accessed November 9, 2009).

United Nations Tajikistan Information Platform. 2007a. Gender Theme Group meeting, July 6. www.untj.org/?c=21&id=87&a=1688 (accessed November 20, 2009).

————. 2007b. Meeting on Draft Domestic Violence Legislation, October 24. www .untj.org/?c=21&id=87&a=1783 (accessed November 20, 2009).

US Agency for International Development (USAID). 2008. *Tajikistan: 2007 NGO Sustainability Index.* www.usaid.gov/locations/europe_eurasia/dem_gov/ ngoindex/2007/tajikistan.pdf(accessed November 9, 2009).

US Central Intelligence Agency (CIA). 2009. "Tajikistan: Economy Overview." *World Factbook.* www.cia.gov/library/publications/the-world-factbook/geos/ti.html (accessed November 7, 2009).

Vandenberg, Martina. 2001. Women, Violence, and Tajikistan. *Eurasia Policy Forum.* www.eurasianet.org/policy_forum/vand022001.shtml (accessed November 9, 2009).

Wedel, Janine. 1998. *Collision and Collusion: The Strange Case of Western Aid to Eastern Europe, 1989–1998.* New York: St. Martin's Press.

Whitsel, Christopher. 2009. "Family Resources, Sitting at Home and Democratic Choice: Investigating Determinants of Educational Attainment in Post-Soviet Tajikistan." *Central Asian Survey* 28(1): 29–41.

World Health Organization (WHO). 1999. *Violence against Women: Pilot Survey in Tajikistan.* Copenhagen, Denmark: WHO Regional Office in Europe.

Zakirova, Nargiz. 2002. *Tajik Women Want Polygamy Legalized.* Institute of War and Peace Reporting (IWPR). www.islamawareness.net/Polygamy/poly_m_ news0003.htm (accessed April 6, 2008; no longer available).

Zuhurova, Zarafshon. 1999. "Women and War: From Healing to Empowerment." Informal Paper distributed at the Organization for Security and Cooperation in Europe (OSCE) Supplementary Implementation Meeting on Gender Issues, Vienna, June 14–15.

CHAPTER 6

The Politics of Awareness:
Making Domestic Violence Visible in Poland

THOMAS CHIVENS

In July of 2005, the Polish government passed an Act to Counteract Domestic Violence.[1] Taking effect on November 21 of that year, it legally defined domestic violence for the first time in Poland. The act delegated administrative responsibilities to regional and local governments to provide support and treatment for victims and perpetrators and imposed obligations on the Council of Ministers to develop a national program to stop family violence. In addition, the law obliged the Ministry of Labor and Social Policy to determine standards for those intervention efforts, to monitor the development of the national program, and to establish and finance research and awareness-raising efforts, educating Poles on the causes and consequences of violence among family members (Open Society Institute 2007).

The legislation marked a concrete legal recognition of domestic violence as a social problem in Poland, and in doing so provided a glimpse into how the Polish state imagined the policing of families at the start of the twenty-first century. Yet, more than three years after taking effect, its meanings and practical consequences are difficult to discern. Answers regarding how and to what extent the law is implemented are unsettled, while concerns about whether the provisions of the law effectively address domestic violence against women are the subject of significant debate (Mrozik et al. 2007). Starting with a description of the 2005 law, I explore the field of domestic violence intervention that preceded it. I draw on the unsettled nature of domestic violence policy in Poland to seek a better understanding of "awareness" as it pertains to domestic violence against women, a process best understood as ongoing, unstable, and contested.

It is often observed in discussions of domestic violence that the absence of awareness effectively produces a concomitant silence in terms of public action (a lack of social education or a tacit acceptance of violence against women) and state interventions (a lack of education in judicial and policing systems, or the absence of statistics, tracking, or support; see Fineman and Mykitiuk 1994). Lack of awareness constitutes a silence that compulsively repeats the absence of protection for battered women, an absence that unfolds unevenly in its intersections with racial, class, national, sexual, or other historically formed identifications and inequalities (Sokoloff and Pratt 2005). While techniques and strategies for producing awareness are familiar to domestic violence intervention expertise in all their contemporary forms, the work of awareness (and what that work consists of) becomes particularly clear in contexts where an absence of awareness is designated in advance, as has been the case in formerly communist countries of Eastern Europe. That is, the work of awareness is especially relevant to analyze in postcommunist state transitions such as in Poland because calls for awareness are juxtaposed to claims that prior to 1989 domestic violence against women was not systematically recognized or named, either in law or in policing practices (Fábián 2006; Hemment 2004; Johnson 2007; Marcus 2002; United Nations Development Program 2007).

While the politics of domestic violence awareness are resolutely concerned with locality, work to refashion gender-inflected public/private boundaries has little use for larger geographic origins or destinations aside from designating obstacles for effective intervention (such as cultural or national forms of masculinity, motherhood, or religion), or as provisional reference points for naming the origins of model programs (Kwaitkowska 1998; Shepard and Pence 1999; Walentyna 1994). Instead, domestic violence awareness is constituted by locally and transnationally linked circuits of intervention that attempt to render violence against women vocally and visibly problematic, and draw on a relatively standard set of representational modes and techniques for achieving recognition and change (such as victim stories, advertisements, instructional manuals, informational brochures, presentations of data or their absence, as well as local, national and international monitoring, research, and educational programs).

To understand the emergence of domestic violence policy in postcommunist Poland, then, is to attend to the assembly of particular strategies and material forms that awareness-raising work has taken, in addition to stories, struggles, intervention infrastructures, or laws they have sought to produce. Descriptive attention to the practice of awareness-raising itself provides an important complement to understanding the complex vectors of social change charted in this volume. As Janet Elise Johnson and Gulnara Zaynullina point out in this volume, the relative absence of languages for describing abuse prior to the 1990s place significant stake on the production and circulation of knowledge about what constitutes domestic violence. Much ultimately rests on how awareness-raising practices understand and identify which norms ought to be taken up as problems, and how obstacles to change are framed.

Poland's 2005 Law to Counteract Domestic Violence

Although law in the name of domestic violence did not exist in Poland prior to 2005, a range of intervention protocols, research practices, and support services developed in the 1990s, constituted through (but not reducible to) always-local transnational networks, and composed of state and nongovernmental organizations (Aulette 1999; Brunell 2005; Fábián 2006; Minnesota Advocates for Human Rights 2002; Nowakowska 1999, 2000). As Urszula Nowakowska noted in her edited volume *Polish Women in the 90's: The Report by the Women's Rights Center,* Poland's 1997 Criminal Code defined domestic abuse most directly in section 207 under "Crimes against Family and Custody" (Nowakowska 2000: 149):

> Whoever abuses physically or psychologically a member of a family or an intimate relation, or any other permanently or temporarily dependent person, or a physically or mentally disabled person, or a juvenile may be found guilty and sentenced to a minimum of three months and a maximum of five years in jail (Law of June 6 1997 Polish Criminal Code, Section 207).

Although "abuses" (*znęca się*) need not be interpreted to mean repetitive and ongoing abuse, it often had been, as Monika Płatek, Poland's Violence Against Women monitor for the United Nations Development Fund, observed several months before the 2005 law was passed (Płatek 2005: 6).

Płatek suggests two main reasons the former criminal code was not effectively enforced to assist victims of domestic violence. While it *could* be interpreted to protect women from domestic violence even without any legislative changes, domestic violence was generally viewed as a "family matter" by the courts (ibid. 6). Related, imprisonment was the most obvious punishment available under the 1997 Criminal Code, which the court system felt was not "appropriate" to matters of family (ibid. 7). While alternative modes of intervention may indeed have been available under the 1997 Criminal Code, the core problem was a marked lack of "political will" (ibid. 7). The lack of any formal set of juridical protections prior to the 2005 law was itself a tacit decision by the state to not treat domestic violence as a serious social problem (Nowakowska 2000). This was most dramatically registered by lengthy and cumbersome court procedures to determine cases, with 90 percent of convictions receiving suspended sentences (Minnesota Advocates for Human Rights 2002: 48).

In contrast, Poland's 2005 Law to Counteract Domestic Violence represented a complex intervention into the potential treatment of domestic violence victims and perpetrators. It could be understood as a recognition of certain aspects of the field of intervention that developed through the 1990s (with respect to what was specifically included in the law, such as "social awareness," "victim advocacy" and "education programs"), as well as a critical commentary on those intervention efforts (with regard to what was pointedly left out of the law, such as a specific focus on gender or women, or the creation of immediately effective restraining orders to protect victims).

Composed of seventeen articles, the law specifically addresses three broad themes: actions included in the scope of family violence intervention; rules for treating people affected by family violence; and rules for treating people using family violence (Article 1). In specifying its legal reach, the 2005 law defines "family members" as those "living jointly in or running a common household," as well as "next of kin" as defined in the 1997 Criminal Code (Article 2.1).[2] Family violence itself is defined as a "single or repetitive" violation of family members' "rights or personal goods" that "exposes those persons to danger of loss of life, health, destroys their dignity, personal inviolability, freedoms, including sexual freedom, harms their physical and psychic health, as well as causes suffering and moral damage to persons affected by violence" (Article 2.2).

The third and fourth articles outline provisions for assisting victims and perpetrators respectively. For victims, medical support is to be provided, along with psychological, legal, and social counseling. Likewise, people "affected" by family violence are entitled to "crisis intervention support" (Article 3.2). While immediate, *ex parte* restraining or protective orders are not part of the 2005 Law to Counteract Domestic Violence, the law does provide for "protection against further harm through the prevention of the perpetrators of violence from living in the common flat with other family members, as well as through a ban on contacts between the perpetrator and the aggrieved person," (Article 3.3). Additionally, "assurance, on request, of safe shelter in a special center to support victims of family violence" is provided for (Article

3.4). The fourth article, conversely, outlines responses provided for perpetrators of family violence: With regard to those "who use family violence," the statute provides means "that prevent their contact" with the injured parties, and provides for their "participation in corrective-educational programs" (Article 4).

Details of how the response infrastructure will be established form the bases of articles six through nine. Local administrative units (*gminy*) are required to develop "local prevention systems," counseling and shelter services and local support centers (Article 6.2). Counties (*powiaty*) are required as well to create and run "crisis centers" for victims of domestic violence (Article 6.3). Government initiatives to support victims of domestic violence and to implement educational programs for perpetrators are also to be implemented at the county level (Article 6.4) and paid for by the state budget (Article 6.5). Larger administrative units, voivodships (*wojewody*), are charged with tasks of generating new intervention programs, developing support systems for victims and the educational programs for perpetrators, and providing training for those whose work intersects with domestic violence intervention (Article 6.6). More specifically, voivodships are charged with "drawing up instructional materials, recommendations, and procedures" for crisis intervention centers and for those who intervene in cases of domestic violence, and also for monitoring domestic violence (Article 7.1 and 7.2). In further specifications, "crisis intervention" is to be understood as "a complex set of interdisciplinary actions taken toward persons and families in a state of crisis. Crisis intervention aims to restore mental balance" and the ability to manage independently, and seeks to prevent the reaction to crisis from resulting in a chronic state of psycho-social" incapacity, which modifies the March 12, 2004 Act on Social Aid (Article 16.1).

According to Article 9, the Minister for Labor and Social Policy is responsible for "directing and financing" research into domestic violence, organizing "social awareness" campaigns, and monitoring the implementation of a National Program to Prevent and Counteract Domestic Violence (a program which itself is to be established by the Council of Ministers in Article 10). Article 9 calls for state and local government agencies to cooperate with "NGOs, churches, and religious unions within the scope of helping victims of violence, influencing persons who use violence, as well as raising social awareness of the reasons and results of domestic violence" (Article 9.1). Article 10 very generally outlines the National Program to Prevent and Counteract Domestic

Violence. The goals of the National Program, adopted by the Council of Ministers, are to provide assistance to victims of violence, to "take corrective and educational actions" for perpetrators, and, more generally, to raise "social awareness" (Article 10). Article 12, subsequently, legally requires officials whose work is in any way related to domestic violence to report cases to the police or prosecutor.

The final articles of Poland's 2005 Law to Counteract Domestic Violence cover a range of specific issues, including attention to separating perpetrators and victims. Although neither civil protection orders nor any new powers of policing are introduced, Articles 13 and 14 interpret the powers of the court to separate victims and perpetrators under the 1997 Criminal Code. Specifically, Article 14 states that "[i]f evidence appears at the time of arrest against the person who is accused of committing the crime," the courts may choose not to arrest the suspect, but instead place "the person under police supervision with the understanding that the person" will leave their residence "in a time period defined by the court" and that the perpetrator has a place to go (Article 14.1). This may be extended to require the perpetrator to refrain from "being in touch with the aggrieved person in a determined manner" (Article 14.2). Though police surveillance provisions are available if there is no temporary arrest, this option is made available only if the perpetrator has a specified place to go.

Without a policy of mandatory arrest, eviction, or comprehensive restraining orders, how contact might be limited is ultimately left up to courts on a case-by-case basis. Indeed, the stated object of intervention in Poland's current law leaves open difficult questions of what "domestic" or "family" ultimately designates, who is to be protected, why, and how; all are questions that remain unresolved at a basic level from the standpoint of Polish domestic violence policy.

Legal Fragility

The legislator and lawyer Sywia Spurek noted in a commentary on the law that although it may not have met "expectations" for protecting women from domestic violence, "what is important is the fact that we have the Act and it is legally binding. And being a separate Act, it may be amended" (Spurek 2008).[3] What, though, were "expectations," and how were they left unmet? Dissatisfaction with the current law from the perspective of women's rights advocates stems from two broad standpoints. From one vantage point, the law itself suffers from inadequate implementation. Questions of "restraining orders" and effective court procedures are of particular concern. From another vantage point, though, critics point to an absence of measures to effectively protect women from domestic violence to begin with, raising questions about what, exactly, the law targets (Mrozik et al. 2007).

In a short summary of the legislative history of Poland's 2005 Law to Counteract Domestic Violence, Sylvia Spurek writes that the first drafts of the law were prepared in 2003 by "Government Plenipotentiary for the Equal Status of Women and Men, Izabella Naruga-Nowacka, in cooperation with nongovernmental organizations" (Spurek 2008: 1).[4] Further work was completed when Magdalena Środa became plenipotentiary and Naruga-Nowacka became deputy prime minister. Sywia Spurek, a lawyer, legislator, and legal expert working for the plenipotentiary, describes her participation in the initial drafting phase as an effort "to ensure the victim's right to be safe" (ibid.). Based on an Austrian model for domestic violence intervention, itself inspired by a model of intervention from Duluth, Minnesota, the goal was to be accomplished through "restraining orders, which could enable isolating the perpetrator from the victim" (ibid.). The premise was to extend powers of immediate protection orders to the police, allowing for immediate eviction for ten days, and an ongoing restraining order that would last three months (ibid.: 2).

According to Agnieszka Mrozik, the initial drafting, which did not make it to parliament intact, was directed at four primary assumptions: domestic violence is a crime; the state is responsible for preventing domestic violence and punishing perpetrators; perpetrators are to be held responsible; and victims have a right to safety (Mrozik 2005). In addition, the initial drafting included a ban on corporal punishment for children. Though drafted by the Government Plenipotentiary for the Equal Status of Women and Men, it was developed in consultation with nongovernmental organizations. Specifically, the Women's Rights Center (*Centrum Praw Kobiet*), the League of Polish Women (*Liga Kobiet Polskich*), the Nobody's Children Foundation (*Fundacja Dzieci Niczyje*), the Blue Line (*Niebieska Linia*), *Victoria,* and Amnesty International were consulted during the drafting process. Indeed, the definition of domestic violence proposed by nongovernmental organizations was ultimately accepted in the 2005 law (Mrozik 2005).

The provisions for immediately effective evictions and restraining orders, which account for the particular challenges posed by cases of domestic violence, were highly controversial and ultimately dropped before the law was formally presented to parliament in January of 2004

(Spurek 2008). Spurek explains that a decision was made that it would be "better to have the law even without these regulations than not to have any law" (ibid.: 3).

Rather than focusing on the right of victims to safety and security as a human right, members of parliament from conservative political parties (including Civic Platform, Law and Justice, and the League of Polish Families) argued that eviction and restraining orders would violate constitutional rights to property. Stanislaw Gudzowski, from the League of Polish Families, considered the project an "idea of frustrated feminists who aimed at bringing up the next generations of deviants—victims of stress-free education" (Mrozik 2005a). Other critics of mandatory evictions and restraining orders such as Antoni Stryjewski argued that the measure would increase homelessness (ibid.).

The draft considered by the Polish parliament was already significantly weakened before it arrived for deliberation; it included no comprehensive restraining order policy and no new powers of policing (Spurek 2008). Likewise, a proposed ban on corporal punishment was rejected on the grounds of a "right" to punish one's children, asserting that the art of governing children would remain a matter of family privacy and therefore beyond the scope of state intervention (ibid.: 3). Thus the process of formulating the law reveals its instabilities, in part an attempt at acknowledging violence regardless of its modification as private by providing support for victims and perpetrators, while also reinforcing the concept of family as a space of violence set apart from the law by virtue of what is left silent. Many feminist-oriented critics, though, agreed that although the law may not adequately address domestic violence against women, it marks a significant improvement, at least at the level of law, over the previous treatment of domestic violence cases (Mrozik et al. 2007).

Silences in Practice

In November of 2005, just before Poland's Law to Counteract Domestic Violence took effect, parliamentary elections brought in a new conservative government. With the resignation of the former ministers, the Plenipotentiary for the Equal Status of Women, headed at the time by Magdelena Šroda, was abolished on November 3. It was replaced by the Department of Women, Family and Anti-Discrimination, located in the Ministry of Labor and Social Policy, with Ms. Joanna Kluzik-Rostkowska as the department's first director. On January 16, 2007, in New York, Ms. Kluzik-Rostkowska represented Poland to the

United Nations Committee on the Elimination of Discrimination Against Women (CEDAW), discussing her country's efforts to achieve gender equality (Kluzik-Rostkowska 2007).

Although the UN committee experts had expressed concern over the department's mission to focus on gender issues in labor policy, Ms. Kluzkik-Rostkowska's official comments underlined successes made in the intervention of domestic violence, emphasizing the theme of domestic violence against women on several occasions. In addition to Poland's recognition of CEDAW, from the moment Poland joined the European Union on May 1, 2004, she reported, "it has been implementing one of the European Union's horizontal policies: gender mainstreaming— the systematic inclusion of gender-equality strategies and endeavors with the use of special EU-funded resources" (ibid.: 1). She highlighted the 2005 Law to Counteract Domestic Violence, noting that "[f]rom the standpoint of the victim of domestic violence, the most important thing is the provision ordering the perpetrator out of a jointly inhabited dwelling and banning that individual from approaching the victim of or witness to the violence" (ibid.: 6). She continues,

> Given the awareness of the scope and weight of the phenomenon of domestic violence, including that against women, the Polish government has been undertaking systematic endeavors of an inter-institutional and often international nature to strengthen cooperation of all institutions able to contribute to the limitation of violence and lend support to the crime victims. (ibid.: 6)

In addition to the National Program to Counteract Domestic Violence, established by the 2005 law, a government program to reduce crime and antisocial behavior, Safer Together, also targets "domestic violence, including that directed against women," as one of its priorities (ibid.: 7).

As a third line of support for domestic violence intervention, Kluzik-Rostkowska reported on Poland's commitment to participate in the European Union program, Daphne III, to address violence against "children, juveniles, and women," which covers the period from 2007 to 2013 (ibid.: 7). Daphne III, she noted, would provide program support for institutions that meet those objectives, particularly by instituting awareness-raising practices. In conclusion, she stated, "preventing domestic violence, including that directed against women, as well as prosecuting its perpetrators, is one of the priority statutory tasks of the police," noting a statistical increase in the number of home interventions and arrests in recent years and increased reporting, particularly since 1998 when police recordkeeping practices were first introduced (ibid.: 8).

The speech is instructive on several fronts. Repeated mentions of "women" are curious throughout the CEDAW address insofar as this appears to be a redundant over-correction, answering in advance a perceived criticism about what domestic violence ultimately designates, in practice, from the standpoint of the Polish state. Without question, it signaled recognition that the Polish government understood the importance of appearing to address domestic violence against women.

During the same meeting in New York, a coalition of NGOs from Poland, led by Wanda Nowicka, Magdalena Pocheć, and Stana Buchowska, presented a markedly different interpretation of the state of domestic violence intervention policy as of January 2007. Representing Poland's Federation for Women and Family Planning, La Strada Foundation, Profemina Foundation, PSF Women's Center, and the Women's Rights Center, their statement to CEDAW noted that "gender equality has never constituted a priority of any Polish government" (Nowicka et al. 2007). With regard to domestic violence against women in particular they identified nine ways that Poland's government policies demonstrated a "lack of continuity" and coherence (ibid.: 1).

First on the list of deficiencies was the extent to which domestic violence is legally understood to be gender neutral. Secondly, cases of domestic violence against women continue to require lengthy procedures, during which time women often have to live with their abusers. Related to this deficiency, restraining orders, to the extent that they do exist, either "take too long" to get or are otherwise "ineffective" (ibid.: 2). Data collection is "insufficient" and "imprecise," and fails to take account of "refusals to initiate criminal procedure as well as accurate gender disaggregated data on killings resulting from domestic violence" (ibid.: 2). Additionally, there is a general lack of adequate services, limited access to free forensic examination, and too few shelters to meet demand (ibid.: 2).

Noting a lack of information on what practical changes the law may or may not have had, in October of 2007 the Feminoteka Foundation (*Fundacja Feminoteka*) in Warsaw presented a report supported by the Heinrich Böll Foundation study and authored by Agnieszka Mrozik, Ewa Rutkowska, and Iwona Stefańcyzk titled "Who Are We Protecting From Violence? Two Years of the July 29, 2005, Law to Counteract Domestic Violence: A Critical Report." Prepared in collaboration with collection of domestic violence advocates, experts, and state and non-governmental organizations, the report attempted to address how or whether the legal provisions made possible by the 2005 law were implemented at any level. Among their findings: the measures to separate victims from perpetrators are rarely implemented, and rates of suspended sentences remain at 90 percent (Mrozik et al. 2007: 11).

Importantly, the report highlights the relative absence of statistical information, which continues to present a significant problem for understanding domestic violence and its interventions in Poland (Gruszczyńska 2007). "Who Are We Protecting from Violence?" provides theoretical appraisals, discussions and recommendations, and resources, listing twenty-one nongovernmental organizations in Poland currently addressing domestic violence in some form" (Mrozik et al. 2007: 95–99), out of roughly three hundred organizations in Poland dedicated to women's issues (Fuszara 2005: 1064). However, the most notable finding is that, after being in effect for two years, there is an "absence of information regarding how the law is functioning at either local or national levels" (Mrozik et al. 2007: 6).

"Who Are We Protecting" is a report of absence. The absence of inquiry touches on a number of questions: Had court decisions against perpetrators of domestic violence against women changed? Were national funding for programs to support victims or perpetrators, the presence of new awareness campaigns, and the creation of "interdisciplinary" networks to intervene in domestic violence at all administrative levels established, and what were they doing (ibid.: 6)? On November 27, 2007, the Warsaw section of Poland's largest daily newspaper, *Gazeta Wyborcza*, printed a story by Magdalena Dubrowska with the instructive title, "The Battered Women's Law." Dubrowska's article, which ran during the international campaign, Sixteen Days of Activism Against Violence Against Women, outlined Feminoteka's findings. It also coincided with a summit organized by Feminoteka to bring together police officers, prosecutors, academics, and government officials to discuss obstacles and potentials for more adequate domestic violence intervention in Poland.

The debate placed in clear view the difficulties of producing an effective infrastructure for domestic violence intervention, as well as the challenges posed by the interdisciplinary language of the 2005 Law to Counteract Domestic Violence; it pointed to the future/ongoing potential for collaborative intervention, and provided at the very least a reminder of the importance of inter-institutional dialogue, however sporadic, provisional, partial, or slow-moving infrastructural change may be (Piotrowska 2007). At the same time, this debate raises important questions about what constitutes a "policy" of domestic violence intervention, to whom is it ultimately directed, and how a field of intervention might, or might not, come to life.

Violence, Activism, and International Circuits of Re-Modeling

When I arrived in Warsaw in the fall of 2000, one of the very first business cards I was handed had on it the words, *"Duluth Koordynator."* It was given to me by a woman named Renata (a pseudonym) with whom I worked off and on over the next year and a half. Renata was in her mid-twenties and was employed by one of the many NGOs in Warsaw aimed at fostering support for women's issues following the turbulence of 1989. Renata spoke impeccable English with a slight British accent, and provided invaluable assistance as I was learning to speak Polish at the beginning of my fieldwork. In one of our first encounters, Renata told me that she was translating the Domestic Abuse Intervention Project (DAIP) training manual, known colloquially as the Duluth Model, into Polish. I mentioned that I had never been to Duluth, but that while learning to facilitate batterers' treatment programs in North Carolina in 1997, I had learned a modified form of the Duluth manual. After a short silence, she smiled saying that she hadn't realized Duluth was the name of a city, an easy point to be unaware of given that, beyond the name, models such as Duluth's rely precisely on their transferability, not their rootedness in one or another location.

From 2000 to 2001 we worked together on projects of translating, as well as researching police implementation of domestic violence recording procedures, research that indicated much room for improvement. She also invited me to attend training programs for police officers in Poland run by her NGO that drew heavily upon the Duluth Model for domestic violence intervention. Training programs were run sporadically by organizations depending on funding sources. At different times, the American and British Embassies, the Ford Foundation, the Stefan Batory Foundation, and certainly others provided support for nongovernmental agencies concerned with women's rights issues. One of the more effective strategies of awareness raising was to encourage victims of abuse to travel, along with training programs, to share their stories first hand with members of parliament or local police officers and prosecutors.

Shortly before I had arrived in Warsaw, Renata's NGO had taken part in an anti–domestic violence program in Budapest organized by the

Domestic Abuse Intervention Project in Duluth, Minnesota. NGO representatives, along with police officers and prosecutors, attended the program organized with the goal of training community teams composed of
police officers, prosecutors, and nongovernmental workers from former
communist bloc countries. These teams would then return to their local
communities to implement Duluth's Coordinated Community Response.
Additionally, nongovernmental trainers would travel to communities
within their particular countries to train others in the development of
Duluth's Coordinated Community Response system.

The international routes through which gender emerged into political debate represented a striking and complex achievement in transnational politics. Reflecting on their work to train police officers around
the world in a model for domestic violence intervention developed first
in the 1980s in Duluth, Minnesota, the creators of the internationally
renowned model for governance known as the Duluth Method for stop-
ping violence against women write,

> The Domestic Abuse Intervention Project (DAIP) . . . [has] con-
> ducted more than 600 training sessions and seminars in the United
> States and at least five countries. Communities in the United States,
> Scotland, New Zealand, and Germany have adopted aspects of
> Duluth's community intervention model. However, when the
> "Duluth Model" phrase is used in these different communities, it
> can take on different meanings. For example, it may be understood
> as the men's curriculum, the use of a mandatory arrest policy, the
> use of a tracking system to monitor the criminal justice system, or
> interagency coordination. (Shepard and Pence 1999: 4)

The image of security delivered by the language of the Duluth model is
very different from a socialist vision of guaranteed employment, political participation, retirement benefits, housing, or food. With a narrow conception of the economic as a possible source of violence, and
a theory of violence as an instrument for achieving male power and
control, the Duluth Model becomes a useful means for critiquing and
intervening in a form of domination that does not generate a critique of
work, housing or families. Central, though, to the model is the growth
of awareness across all levels of the field of intervention—raising awareness of police officers, of violent men, of the public, of judges, of prosecutors, and more.

It would not be surprising if the DAIP training efforts comprised a
small and fleeting moment in domestic violence intervention expertise

in Poland, particularly as funding routes from the European Union became more available, as well as exchanges with domestic violence expertise from Britain and Austria or the Netherlands. Likewise, several Polish police officers I worked with spoke often about the importance of constructing Polish models and reporting systems. In their view, the most pressing issue was to refocus from violence against women (which they equated with the "American model") to violence against children. Most striking was the ease with which the infrastructure developed to intervene in one crisis could remain relatively intact at the same time it was redirected. As I completed research in Poland in late 2001, a new state campaign was underway, called "A Childhood Without Violence." What remained (and remains) unclear is the extent to which this marked an extension of the previous campaign to stop violence against women or (even if unintentionally) its relative erasure.

Educational Circuits as Cultural Intervention

Reference to Polish sayings such as "If you don't beat her, her liver will rot" or "If you love her, you beat her" are often used to provide evidence of lack of awareness of domestic violence, particularly in rural Polish communities (Nowakowska 2000). More specifically, they provide evidence of cultural obstacles to intervention. For example, in a 1998 essay on the predicaments of domestic violence in Poland Anna Kwiatkowska asked "why people tolerate acts of violence in Poland and to what extent this is connected to Polish culture" (Kwiatkowska 1998: 68). In doing so, she identified three overarching themes that she suggested constitute a "Polish specialty" with regard to domestic violence in Poland. These themes, she argued, contributed to attitudes that complicate postcommunist state interventions, attitudes that at once venerate Polish women and deny them political recognition and intervention: the Roman Catholic Cult of the Virgin Mary, the heroic image of the Mother Pole as martyr who suffers as national guardian, and the legacy of "fake" egalitarianism of the Communist Party (ibid.: 69).

Accounts of "culture" are generally mobilized as demonstrations of obstacles to effective intervention in Poland, with consequences that may reach into the fabric of all agencies that constitute a field of intervention. What remains beyond the view of these accounts, though, is the work of writing culture itself as part of a wider field of intervention composed of social research and rapporteurs. Out of view, in other words, is how "intervention" is itself a cultural practice, one that draws upon the concept of culture at specific moments of reporting. Injunctions to report, to capture, or otherwise to stabilize a given moment or locale may be composed of any number of complex origins in discussions of violence. Reports and evaluations are crucial to the participation in contemporary awareness politics. When successful, reports straddle a fine documentary line between describing and transforming worlds.

Reports issued by human rights–monitoring international agencies inadvertently imply a dichotomy between an international community of astute observers who cast a morally concerned eye, and a national specialty under review, even though country reports are often prepared by local NGOs. The appearance of this dichotomy lends rhetorical force to those who feel "Polish culture" has become the object of concern of those who claim higher moral or civil ground, whether in the guise of anti-feminisms more generally, or in specific attacks on domestic violence intervention strategies.

One of the early, and most articulate, voices of rage can be found in statements made by Kazimierz Kapera, the director of the Plenipotentiary for Family Affairs from 1997 to 1999 in the government of Jerzy Buzek. In response to then-emerging programs to raise awareness about domestic violence, Kapera "recommended that the scarce money for family services not be spent on programs for battered women but rather on programs that strive to keep families together," asserting that a nationwide anti-violence awareness campaign "tarnishes the image of Polish men" and "portrays the Polish male 'as an alcoholic, a wife abuser, a primitive pervert raping her [his wife] and sexually abusing children'" (Family Violence Prevention 1998). Kapera refused to "recognize the very existence of the problem," criticizing "the campaign against domestic violence as aimed against the family and as irrelevant, since . . . husbands are kind and they treat their wives gently" (Nowakowska 1998).

The subtext of much resistance to domestic violence awareness initiatives invokes feminism as a politically correct disease and an import from an international West (Kołakowska 2000; Renne 1997). The first awareness campaign in Poland emerged in 1997 as part of a broader Stop Domestic Violence campaign, directed by the Blue Line (*Niebieska Linia*) NGO operating then under the government-based State Agency for Solving Alcohol Related Problems, PARPA (*Państwowa Agencja Rozwiązywania Problemów Alkoholowych*). To raise awareness and initiate public discussion on domestic violence, the campaign displayed posters in twenty-two cities throughout Poland, making extensive use of news and advertising media, from newspapers, television, and radio, to brochures, leaflets, and large, publicly visible posters. Its goal was to advertise the introduction of a National Emergency Service for victims of domestic violence and initiate public discussion of domestic violence for the first time in Poland. The images of a battered women and child with a caption, "Because the soup was too salty," had a particularly enduring effect (see figure 8.5).

A criminologist involved with the campaign lamented to me:

> You know, this campaign called "Stop Domestic Violence," its goal was to make society see that domestic violence was a problem, and it started debates in every local government about what to do . . . I think our records showed that 50 percent of the people in Poland saw these campaign billboards, and of those, about 70 percent think it was called "the soup was too salty." (Interview, September 2001)

Jokes emerged in popular magazines, with pictures of bruised and bleeding men with various captions like "Because he forgot to bring her flowers."

As an awareness-raising campaign, it was a striking success. According to PARPA, the campaign succeeded in establishing a hundred points of contact for victims, trained 2,500 professionals, and hosted ten awareness-raising conferences. The National Emergency Service included telephone support lines to establish a base for rendering domestic violence statistically legible, as well as for researching the effectiveness of its own intervention efforts, created "Blue Card" procedures for police officers to keep track of domestic violence incidents, and domestic violence intervention training for professionals. In the first year following the awareness-raising campaign, the Blue Line hotline received 5,000 phone calls, up to 7,000 by 1999, and 13,500 by 2004.[5] Statistical infrastructures and surveys developed during the late 1990s and into the present provide constant reminders of the damage caused by domestic violence and of the importance of continuing to develop an infrastructure for adequate understanding and interventions.

Though the 1997 Blue Line campaign was directed by state agencies to bring domestic violence into social view, it also sought to educate professionals working for the state. The Blue Line organization was not alone in this endeavor, with other NGOs such as Warsaw's Women's Rights Center and the League of Polish Women also conducting training programs to educate police officers, prosecutors, and victims' advocates. Education was the key cultural form of awareness-raising. It was necessary to teach the public about domestic violence, but also to train police officers, judges, and legislators, and ultimately to train others to become trainers. For this to take place, though, it would presuppose an apparatus of expertise capable of raising awareness in contextually appropriate ways, depending on whether one was positioned, for example, as a police officer, lawyer, legislator, judge, victim, perpetrator, or nongovernmental rights worker. In other words, a lack of awareness is not simply an absence of knowledge. Instead, even without the obstacles of other "cultures," there are multiple ways to lack awareness of domestic violence, each of which calls for the creation of different strategies for raising it, and all of which, together, might best be seen as a project of cultural production.

Technical Dilemmas: Assembling Awareness

There is no easily discernible center, or direction, from which awareness definitively originates. Indeed, the work of awareness is at its most effective when it succeeds in destabilizing the very fiction of an originating point, such as "the West." This does not mean that domestic violence expertise comes from nowhere. Popular models of domestic violence intervention circulate with geographic names, whether from Austria, Duluth, Australia, Cleveland (England or the United States), and many others. Likewise, discussions about what domestic violence is, questions surrounding which intervention procedures are most effective, or how obstacles can be overcome travel along routes of exchange that in many ways mirror the politics of international development aid. In this regard, domestic violence intervention efforts in Poland have come to life as part of postcommunist transnational circuits of social expertise, gender activism, training programs, and funding from government and private organizations that have tended to flow in particular directions.

However, following these routes as a description of domestic violence intervention in Poland would reify the very colonially informed, social-evolutionary dichotomies that are potentially destabilized by awareness politics (implied in directional distinctions like East/West). Following those routes as a description of how domestic violence intervention policy has emerged in Poland would effectively gloss over the politics of gender and violence, power and control, to which intervention experts are responding in the first place. Place names, indeed, are only relevant insofar as models of domestic violence interventions circulate in a competitive marketplace of state machinery, legal expertise, and activist labor. Intervention models aren't descriptive of, or necessarily linked with, territorial boundaries within which meanings are stabilized and could be filled in—even at the same time that attention to locality, in the sense of making *domestic* violence visible, is of utmost importance in understanding how models work and what they do.

In contrast, questions of silence, reporting, voice, and representation are the technical problems faced by the politics of awareness, and these comprise the substantive obstacles to the emergence of domestic violence policy in Poland. Awareness as a political practice takes relatively regular forms with regard to domestic violence intervention, from the creation of statistical databases, distribution of information, lobbying for legal changes, advertising, and researching the effectiveness of the practices themselves. Unlike political practices such as consciousness-raising, redistributive class politics, collective organizing, solidarity, or other historical modes of political change, awareness politics seek social change by obtaining recognition and rights for victims through pedagogy (whether directed at individuals, judges, police officers, legislators, hospital workers, or those responsible for interagency coordination; Daniels 1997; Fraser 1996; Gordon 1988; Pleck 1987). As a form of political intervention, awareness-raising is linked to what could be thought of as a mobile, late civil human rights activism. The viability of domestic violence awareness-raising as a mode of social change (and what its visions of change are) often exist in a tense relationship to the ordering power of funding opportunities. At the same time, awareness politics make effective use of marketing in the struggle to determine what crime consists of and how governmental response might be arranged.

And yet, perhaps because awareness politics are highly individualized, mobile, and flexible, they appear also easily appropriated or refashioned in contrary or counterintuitive ways. As such, a focus on domestic violence "against women" as the target of awareness practices is always at risk of disappearing from view through the same machinations that have rendered it visible. Even in the best of circumstances, intervention's failure is familiar territory to students of domestic violence, regardless of locale. There is nothing unique in this about the difficulties that Polish anti–domestic violence activists and state workers face; the fact of an anti–domestic violence law is by no means a guarantee of its effectiveness.

Failures to Appear

In the early 1980s, when Wini Breneis and Linda Gordon reviewed the state of literature on family violence in the United States, they wrote: "Only a few decades ago, the term 'family violence' would have had no meaning: child abuse, wife beating, and incest would have been understood but not recognized as serious social problems" (Breneis and Gordon 1983: 490, cited in de Lauretis 1987: 33). Since then, meanings of domestic violence, as well as international responses, have accelerated, along with awareness, and the instabilities of what it pertains to. In 2005, the US State Department report on Human Rights in Poland explained:

> Violence against women [in Poland] continued to be a problem. Police statistics indicated that approximately 80,185 women were victims of domestic violence during 2003. Women's organizations asserted that the number of women suffering from domestic abuse was probably much higher because battered women usually refused to admit abuse even to themselves. (US Department of State 2005)

Who controls what one is to become aware of is an ongoing and contested domain, and may remain unsettled even as the apparatus to produce awareness continues to take shape. Specific terms used to identify or modify violence may indicate how violence is understood and acted upon—whether the violence is modified as home, domestic, family, private, against women, etc.—and Poland's anti-domestic violence efforts have, for example, tended to displace the category of "women" with "children."

However, the flexibility of awareness politics consists not simply in the politics of terminology, but in the apparatus of objectification itself, in which recognition of abuse is highly individualized, and where any individual may be observed refusing to admit to themselves abuse of themselves, as the State Department report above notes. This is a reminder that practices for making violence visible are creatively (and inescapably) engaged with modes of power; the difficulty is not simply one of uncovering hidden truths or representing the formerly left out, but also consists of a struggle, often with great frustration, to participate in the production of those truths.

Through a focus on practices that constitute domestic violence *awareness* in Poland, notions of donors/recipients, individual pioneers, or "cultural" frameworks as grounds on which domestic violence intervention policies are formed or thwarted lose their descriptive or explanatory power. Likewise, such a focus may point to less explored routes of inquiry, or blur the boundaries of dichotomies of East/West, Backward/Progressive, that often frame discussions of both domestic violence and postcommunism. But in destabilizing, or at times even erasing, entrenched spatial dichotomies in the construction of intervention infrastructures to educate, record, and protect victims of violence, awareness politics raise a series of difficult questions: What new borders arrive with the politics of awareness to take the place of geographic, national, or cultural differences? Do obstacles for making domestic violence visible exist *in* Poland in a way that they do not elsewhere? Or are the techniques, practices, and strategies for crafting awareness themselves the cultural specificity at stake? And how can struggles to render domestic violence visible in Poland be pushed to find new routes for approaching the aspirations, potentials, and possible limits of awareness as a mode of producing social change, particularly in the face of unconvincing legislative support?

A sustained focus on awareness, then, provides one non-reductive route to address predicaments and possibilities of gender-based activism amid demands of intensified individualization and other constraints of neoliberal politics (Dunn 2004). In this regard, the ambiguities and difficulties of producing visibility and recognition might be viewed as a source of political potential and creativity, rather than merely another cultural obstacle to overcome. To turn silence into voice, after all, is also to defer challenges to the repetitive structuring of aversions to hear, to under-reporting in its myriad forms.

NOTES

The ethnographic fieldwork presented in this chapter was carried out in and around Warsaw thanks to the support of a Fulbright Student Award from 2000 to 2001, and also from the support of writing grants from the Harry Frank Guggenheim Foundation and the American Council for Learned Societies. For the ethnographic descriptions, I use pseudonyms for individual people with whom I worked.

1. Dz.U. z 2005 r. Nr 180, poz. 1493. USTAWA z dnia 29 lipca 2005 r. *O przeciwdziałaniu przemocy w rodzinie.* This is most often translated as "the Law to Counteract Domestic Violence" (Mrozik 2007). A more accurate translation of *"pzremoc w rodzinie"* would be "family violence." Following an unofficial transla-

tion to English of the law by Agnieszka Mrozik, though, I use the former. I do so with some hesitation. At stake is whether the law is formed to stop violence against women (*przemoc wobec kobiet*) or child abuse (*przemoc wobec dzieci*), or some combination of the two. The latter would raise serious questions about whether, and how, a coherent set of protections could pertain to both women and children. Because the Polish law is designed to counteract "*przemoc w rodzinie*," literally "family violence," it does not provide sufficient information to know what the law pertains to, and the English term is similarly vague. In contrast, in my experience with American courts, police officers, and batterers' treatment programs, the term "domestic violence" in English has in recent decades emphasized violence against women. In this regard, translating the law's title using the word "domestic," as Agnieszka Mrozik has done, may simply be a descriptive decision; but also, to my ear, it seeks to preserve the relevance of gender to the law, even as the law makes no actual reference to gender.

2. The 1997 Polish Penal Code, Act 6 Article 115 Section 11, defines next of kin as follows: "A next of kin is a spouse, ascendant, descendant, brother, or sister, relative by marriage in the same line or degree, person being an adopted relation, as well as a spouse, and also a person actually living in cohabitation."

3. Further commentary from feminist perspectives can be found here: www.stopvaw.org/Commentary_on_the_Domestic_Violence_Law.html (accessed January 25, 2010).

4. This office has changed name and form many times since 1985. The changes, discussed in detail in the groundbreaking report by Urszula Nowakowska, ed., *Polish Women in the 90s,* highlight the tensions and conflicts surrounding efforts to stop domestic violence against women in Poland and point to a "trend toward belittling women's problems" (Nowakowska 2000: 8).

5. Ongoing and updated statistics and programs are posted on the PARPA website, http://parpa.pl/.

WORKS CITED

Aulette, Judy Root. 1999. "Polish Feminists in the Transition to Democracy." In *Democratization and Women's Grassroots Movements,* ed. Jill Bystydzienski and Joti Sekhon, 217–240. Bloomington: Indiana University Press.

Breines, Wini, and Linda Gordon. 1983. "The New Scholarship on Family Violence." *Signs* 8(3): 490–531.

Brunell, Laura. 2005. "Marginality and the New Geography of Domestic Violence in Post-Communist Poland." *Gender Place and Culture* 12(3) (September): 293–316.

De Lauretis, Teresa. 1987. *Technologies of Gender: Essays on Theory, Film, and Fiction.* Bloomington: Indiana University Press.

Daniels, Cynthia, ed. 1997. *Feminists Negotiate the State: The Politics of Domestic Violence.* Lanham, Md.: University Press of America.

Dubrowska, Magdalena. 2007. "Okaleczone prawo kobiet" [The Battered Women's Law] *Gazeta Wyborcza* (November 27): 31.

Dunn, Elizabeth. 2004. *Privatizing Poland: Baby Food, Big Business, and the Remaking of Labor.* Ithaca, N.Y.: Cornell University Press.

Fábián, Katalin. 2006. "Against Domestic Violence: The Interaction of Global Networks with Local Activism in Central Europe." In *European Responses to Globalization: Resistance, Adaptation, and Alternatives*, ed. Janet Laible and Henri J. Barkey, 111–152. New York: Elsevier Press.

Family Violence Prevention Fund. 1998. "News From the Homefront." www.fvpf.org/newsletter/winter1998-99.html (accessed July 10, 2008).

Fineman, Martha, and Roxanne Mykitiuk, eds. 1994. *The Public Nature of Private Violence: The Discovery of Domestic Abuse*. New York: Routledge.

Fraser, Nancy. 1996. *Justice Interruptus: Critical Reflections on the "Postsocialist" Condition*. New York: Routledge.

Fuszara, Małgorzata. 2005. "Between Feminism and the Catholic Church: The Women's Movement in Poland." *Sociologicky Casopis/ Czech Sociological Review* 41(6): 1057–1075.

Gordon, Linda. 1988. *Heroes of Their Own Lives: The Politics and History of Family Violence*. New York: Viking.

Gruszczyńska, Beata. 2007. *Przemoc wobec kobiet w Polsce. Aspekty prawnokryminologiczne* (Violence against Women in Poland: Legal-Criminal Aspects). Warszawa: Wolters Kluwer, OFICYNA.

Hemment, Julie. 2004. "Global Civil Society and the Local Costs of Belonging: Defining 'Violence against Women' in Russia." *Signs* 29(3): 815–840.

Johnson, Janet Elise. 2007. "Domestic Violence in Post-Soviet States." *Social Politics* 14(3): 380–405.

Kluzkik-Rostkowska, Joanna. 2007. *Introductory Statement*. Committee on the Elimination of Discrimination Against Women, January 16.

Kołakowska, Agnieszka. 2000. "Brygady poprawności politycznej" (Brigades of Political Correctness). *Rzeczpospolita* January 29.

Kwiatkowska, Anna. 1998. "Gender Stereotypes and Beliefs about Family Violence in Poland." In *Multidisciplinary Perspectives on Family Violence*, ed. Renate C. A. Klein. London and New York: Routledge, 68–80.

Marcus, Isabel. 2002. "Dark Numbers: Domestic Violence in Eastern Europe." *Gender Studies* 2002(1): 124–140. Timisoara, Romania: Revista de Studii de Gen a Centruli de studii Feministe as Universitatii de Vest.

Merry, Sally. 2001. "Spatial Governmentality and the New Urban Social Order: Controlling Gender Violence through Law." *American Anthropologist* 103(1): 16–29.

Minnesota Advocates for Human Rights 2002. *Domestic Violence in Poland*. Warsaw, Poland: Minnesota Advocates For Human Rights, Women's Rights Center, Warsaw, International Women's Human Rights Clinic, Georgetown University Law Center.

Mrozik, Agnieszka. 2005. *Counteraction Violence in Close Relations Act Discussed in Polish Parliament*. July 1. www.stopvaw.org/1Jul2005.html (accessed January 25, 2010).

————. 2006. *Commentary on the Domestic Violence Law.* www.stopvaw.org/ Commentary_on_the_Domestic_Violence_Law.html (accessed November 7, 2009).

Mrozik, Agnieszka, Ewa Rutkowska, and Iwona Stefańczyk. 2007. *Kogo Chronimy Przed Przemocą? Dwa Lata Ustawy z Dnia 29 Lipca 2005 r. o Przeciwdziałaniu Przemocy w Rodzinie: Raport Krytyczny* (Who Are We Protecting From Violence? Two Years Since the Law of July 29, 2005 to Counteract Domestic Violence: A Critical Report). Warsaw, Poland: Fundacja Heinricha Bölla/ Fundacja Feminoteka.

Niebieska Linia. *Research and Statistics.* www.niebieskalinia.pl/index .php?assign=statystyki (in Polish; accessed July 10, 2008).

Nowakowska, Urszula. 1998. Ending Domestic Violence, Actions and Measures, Proceedings of the Forum. Organized by the Steering Committee for Equality between Women and Men (CDEG) of the Council of Europe in cooperation with the Romanian Ministry of Labor and Social Affairs, 26–28 November 1998.

————. 1999. "Violence Against Women: International Standards, Polish Reality." In *Gender and Identity in Central and Eastern Europe,* ed. Chris Corrin, 41–63. London: Frank Cass.

————. 2000. *Polish Women in the 90's: The Report by the Women's Rights Center.* Warsaw: Women's Rights Center.

Nowicka, Wanda, Magdalena Pocheć, and Stana Buchowska. 2007. Statement to The Committee on the Elimination of Discrimination against Women of the United Nations 37th Session, New York, N.Y. January 15–February 2.

Open Society Institute, Network Women's Program, VAW Monitoring Program. 2007. *Country Reports and Fact Sheets from Central and Eastern Europe, the Commonwealth of Independent States, and Mongolia. Violence Against Women: Does the Government Care in Poland?* Budapest and New York: The Open Society Institute.

Piotrowska, Joanna 2007. *Antypzremocowa Ustawa Nie Chroni Kobiet* (Anti-violence Law Is Not Protecting Women). November 28. http://wiadomosci.ngo.pl/x/ 319174 (in Polish; accessed November 7, 2009).

Pleck, Elizabeth. 1987. *Domestic Tyranny: The Making of Social Policy against Family Violence from Colonial Times to the Present.* New York: Oxford University Press.

Płatek, Monika. 2005. *Women, Children and the Law in Poland.* Warsaw: Institute for Social Studies, Warsaw University.

Regulska, Joanna. 1998. "The Political" and Its Meaning for Women: Transition Politics in Poland. In *Theorising Transition: The Political Economy of Post-Communist Transformations,* ed. John Pickles and Adrian Smith. London: Routledge.

Renne, Tanya, ed. 1997. *Ana's Land: Sisterhood in Eastern Europe.* Boulder, Colo.: Westview Press.

Shepard, Melanie, and Ellen Pence, eds. 1999. *Coordinating community responses to domestic violence: Lessons from the Duluth model and Beyond.* Thousand Oaks, Calif.: Sage.

Sokoloff, Natalie, and Christina Pratt, eds. 2005. *Domestic Violence at the Margins: Readings on Race, Class, Gender, and Culture.* New Brunswick, N.J.: Rutgers University Press.

Spurek, Sylwia. 2008. *Drafting Domestic Violence Laws Panel.* Regional Conference on Domestic Violence Legal Reform, February 12–14.

United Nations Development Program (UNDP). 2007. *Gender Mainstreaming: Poland 2007 Report.* Warsaw: United Nations Development Program/Poland.

U.S. Department of State. 2005. *Country Reports on Human Rights Practices: Poland* (February). Washington, D.C.: Bureau of Democracy, Human Rights, and Labor.

Walentyna, Najdus. 1994. "O prawa kobiet w zaborze austriackim (On Women's Law from Austria)." In *Kobieta i świat polityki,* ed. Anna Żarnowska, Andrzej Szwarc, 99–118. Warsaw, Poland: Instytut Historyczny Uniwersytetu Warszawskiego.

Zarnowska, Anna, and Andrzej Szwarc. 1994. *Kobieta i Świat Polityki: Polska na the povównawczym w xixi w początkach xx wieku* (Woman and the political world: Poland in comparative perspective in the nineteenth and early twentieth century). Warsaw, Poland: Instytut Historyczny Uniwersytetu Warszawskiego.

Zielinska, Eleonora. 2005. *Equal Opportunities for Women and Men: Monitoring Law and Practice in New Member States and Accession Countries of the European Union.* New York: Open Society Institute Network Women's Program.

CHAPTER 7

Domestic Violence against Women:
When Practice Creates Legislation in Slovenia

SONJA ROBNIK

"[In] our society it is still true that for a woman the most dangerous institution is her marriage, the most unsafe place her home, and the most dangerous person her partner" (Božac Deležan 1999: 14). This is the most commonly quoted statement about domestic violence against women in Slovenia.[1] Experts, professionals, and nongovernmental organizations (NGOs) use it to demonstrate why the issue of domestic violence against women is important to address, and in this way stress the need for domestic violence legislation. The above quote is also included in Slovene political debates to redirect attention from the essence of the problem (that violence against women is gender-based violence) to the alleged damage that debates about domestic violence cause to the nurturing nature of the family as a center of love, warmth, and understanding.

The Slovene political debates are especially lively when public attention is focused on questions of fertility, the increasing rate of divorce, and the decreasing rate of marriage. Since 2004, when right-wing parties won the majority in national elections and constituted a right-wing government, the debates about fertility and the family have frequently appeared on the agenda of the Slovene National Assembly.[2]

Although no clear connection between violence against women and fertility rates can be seen, fertility issues seem to be very handy for some right-wing parliamentarians trying to prevent the adoption of any measure that may be imposed on the family where violence occurs. In November 2007, when the Parliamentary Committee for Family, Labor, Social Affairs, and the Handicapped discussed and proposed the Family Violence Prevention Act, Janez Drobnič, a very conservative right-wing male parliamentarian and a former Minister of Family, Labor and Social Affairs, stated:

> What will be the message of this Act to our youth, to boys, and girls? The message to the girls is that the society is becoming more and more violent, especially that men are violent, so be aware of tyrants. On the other hand, the message to the boys is that they

are welcome as long as they beget a child. (*Seje Državnega zbora* 2007)

For Slovene right-wing political parties the decrease in the rate of marriage and the low fertility rate are important ideological issues, connected with what they call "the decrease of family values."

At the beginning of their four-year mandate, right-wing parliamentarians (both women and men) emphasized that there was no need to adopt a special law on the prevention of domestic violence. The reasons for their claim are hard to gauge. One possible reason was simply that they disagreed with the proposed Act on the Protection against Domestic Violence, prepared by the former left-wing government in early 2009. This proposal, which could be called a "left-wing government proposal," had been prepared by the Ministry of Family, Labor, and Social Affairs and by the Expert Council just before the national elections in 2004.[3] When right-wing parties won the 2004 elections, the very conservative Janez Drobnič was appointed as the Minister of Family, Labor, and Social Affairs. Instead of adding the proposal to the government's agenda, from where the National Assembly would have ultimately adopted it, the right-wing government tabled the domestic violence bill.

Another reason right-wing parliamentarians neglected the legislation in the field of domestic violence might have been to avoid public debate on the family, which they referred to as "the basic cell of the human society." However, remarkable progress has been made since 2004. The greatest credit for that can be given to Marjeta Cotman, who replaced Janez Drobnič as the new Minister of Family, Labor, and Social Affairs at the end of 2006.[4] Despite the many efforts of the Expert Council to convince the minister that Slovenia needed domestic violence legislation, the issue of domestic violence against women was one of the least important matters during Drobnič's mandate from 2004 to 2006. The Expert Council also tried to convince Minister Drobnič that Slovenia was required to fulfill its obligations emerging from the United Nations' Convention on the Elimination of all Forms of Discrimination against Women (CEDAW), along with other binding international documents (for example, the 2002/5 Council of Europe's Recommendation of the Committee of Ministers to Member States on the protection of women against violence). The recent political upheavals show what a difficult and complicated journey domestic violence legislation has taken since 1989.

Since 1989, when the first grassroots feminist NGO came into existence in the form of *Društvo SOS telefon za ženske in otroke—žrtve nasilja* (the Association SOS Help-Line for Women and Children—Victims of Violence), remarkable progress has been made in the field of domestic violence against women. Perhaps the first most remarkable change was the fact that with the amendment to the Penal Code in 1999, domestic violence against women became a political and legal issue. At that time, the criminal offence of violence (Article 299) was supplemented by the notion of "violence in the family." Since 1999, according to the Penal Code, the criminal offence of violence is committed by anyone who seriously insults another person, behaves brutally toward them, is violent toward them, or threatens their safety, and thus in public or within the family causes a threat, disgust, or fear. As no official legal statistics on domestic violence cases exist, it is impossible to provide exact data on the number of cases this measure affected. However, for the first time in Slovenia, domestic violence found a place in legislation.

There are several factors that influenced the 1999 amendment to the Penal Code. Perhaps most important was the education of politicians, professionals, and the general public through press conferences, leaflets, and posters, which was performed by NGOs, such as the Association SOS Help-Line and *Društvo za nenasilno komunikacijo* (Association against Violent Communication), and the governmental Office for Equal Opportunities.[5] The second factor in changing the 1999 Penal Code to include "violence in the family" was the previous set of proposals in newspaper articles and radio and TV broadcasts intended to change the penal legislation, which had been introduced in 1992. These proposals resulted in roundtable discussions and led to parliamentary debate in 1993. With the 1999 amendment, domestic violence appeared for the very first time in Slovene penal legislation.

In Slovenia, the issue of violence against women is closely connected to gender equality legislation. Harmonizing its legislation with European Union directives, Slovenia adopted the Act on Equal Opportunities for Women and Men in 2001. Although the Slovene Constitution grants women gender equality, reality shows a different picture, and this difference called for remedy by effective legal measures.[6] For the first time, the Act on Equal Opportunities defined violence against women as a gender equality legislative issue and identified measures and goals to combat violence against women when implementing the National Program for Equal Opportunities for Women and Men, 2005–13.

Probably the most effective tool in the implementation procedures of the Act on Equal Opportunities was the Police Act of 2003, which provided the police with more power to intervene in cases of domestic violence and sent a clear message to potential perpetrators. Since 2003, police officers may issue a restraining order prohibiting a person from approaching a specified location, area, and a particular person, including also a ban on harassment via means of communication. This 2003 police measure was strongly influenced by Austrian and German legislations where similar measures have proved to be effective in practice. The police, as well as the government's Office for Equal Opportunities, deserve credit for supporting and adopting this measure. Likewise, NGOs argued at various forums that the police should be given more power in the field of domestic violence.

NGOs confronted many obstacles when providing help and support to victims of domestic violence, such as the fact that state institutions appeared to be only partly, if at all, responsible for addressing domestic violence against women. This problem resulted in NGO demands that state institutions and NGOs begin to coordinate their responses. The Slovene government's answer to these demands was the Family Violence Prevention Act, which established multidisciplinary teams.[7] The creation of these multidisciplinary and multi-agency teams has been another successful step forward in supporting victims of domestic violence in a systematic manner, with practice dictating the need for legislation.

In contrast to practice producing new legislative measures, the development of the NGO sector in the field of domestic violence against women resulted from legislation enabling the existence of civil society. How the law on civil society came about and what it meant to the field of services for victims of domestic violence are the questions I will answer in the next section. I apply almost a decade of experience working with the Office for Equal Opportunities and more than a decade of cooperation with various NGOs that work in the field of domestic violence against women. I argue that legislation was crucial in this field and discuss how the origin of civil society in Slovenia differs from the experience of other postcommunist countries.

Legislation Enabled the Growth of Civil Society

Slovenia's path to development of NGOs after World War II distinguishes it from other postcommunist countries in a number of respects. The political and economic regime in the former Yugoslavia was not as centralized as elsewhere in the former Soviet bloc. The main distinctive characteristic was

> the introduction of self-management in the economy and in the public sphere, which led to an increasingly decentralized public administration, higher independence of enterprises and other organizations from the state, a bigger role for market forces linking the economy to that of the West, a better standard of living, and more freedom of individuals with respect to their self-organization and contacts with the outside world. Although partially controlled, civil society was in existence in the former Yugoslavia. (Kolarič et al. 1995, 78)

During communism voluntary organizations did not completely disappear (ibid., 77–78). Church organizations had to limit their activities or transfer some of their work to the informal (i.e., gray, not officially registered) sector, while the Communist Party controlled the major social organizations, even such as the Red Cross.

New national organizations emerged in the 1950s, such as *Zveza prijateljev mladine* (the Association of Friends of Youth), founded in 1953. These NGOs managed to run activities relatively independently from the Communist Party. While associations of retired and disabled people, cultural and sport clubs, and firemen's associations were numerous, there was not a single organization dealing with the issue of domestic violence or with any form of violence against women. There are perhaps three basic reasons for this major omission. First, domestic violence was considered a taboo subject and a private matter of the couple. Second, gender-based stereotypes strongly prevailed in Yugoslav society, and gender roles were traditionally defined: although women were employed, domestic work and care for children were still understood as "their" tasks. Third, the Yugoslav feminist movements, similar to those in other countries at the time, did not begin their activities with a public debate on domestic violence against women.

In contrast to other postcommunist countries, the Slovene nongovernmental sector did not experience extensive growth after 1989. One reason there was no NGO boom during the immediate postcommunist period was that Slovenia had undergone that same process fifteen years earlier, after the adoption of the Law on Societies in 1974 (Kolarič et al. 1995: 84; Kolarič et al. 2002: 108–109). This 1974 law is an important milestone in the development of the NGO sector in Slovenia. The 1974 Law on Societies devolved the legislation on associations from the federation to the republics.[8] Slovenia consequently adopted the legislation allowing the founding of private nonprofit organizations in 1974. The liberalization of the NGO sector meant that by the late 1970s the number of NGOs tripled, reaching 186 registered groups from 85 registered in the early 1970s (Kolarič et al. 1995: 93). Therefore, no further NGO boom happened after the decline of the communist regime in the 1980s.

After independence in 1991, the development of the voluntary sector in Slovenia reveals that the change of the political regime from communist to democratic also initiated important changes in the development of private sector social services. After almost five decades of Yugoslav communism with a one-party regime (the Yugoslav Communist Party), the first democratic elections took place in Slovenia in 1991. Although NGOs existed prior to these changes, the political transformations of the 1990s did prompt new forms of NGOs to develop. The change was particularly palpable among NGOs that dedicated themselves to providing services where the state and its institutions were inadequate, either because the issue in question was neglected by the state, or because state support was ineffective in providing necessary care (such as domestic violence counseling, private homes for old people, private kindergartens, and the like). The newly decentralized public administration and public social, health, and education services managed to cover the majority of people's needs. However, not all important needs received attention. The elimination of state monopolies in social services, such as state-owned and administered homes for senior citizens and for people with special needs, and centers for social work, began at the end of the 1980s and continued into the 1990s.[9] During that period, new legislation allowed for the establishment of companies with limited liability in the field of social services. In practice, this meant that the private sector gained new opportunities to offer social services, which coincided with a time when the state provided no specialized services for women and, in particular, no attention was paid to victims of domestic violence.

The situation of not providing any services for victims of domestic violence changed substantially after the late 1980s when several NGOs were founded in Ljubljana. NGOs played a crucial role in developing viable victim support systems and nonviolent communication training for perpetrators, in raising public awareness, and in training professionals and volunteers.

The Role of Civil Society in Addressing Domestic Violence Issues

Prior to the mid-1980s, domestic violence did not become a relevant issue for state-run social services such as centers for social work

(Zaviršek 2001). While state-employed social workers addressed the issues of domestic violence within the framework of dysfunctional families (families where alcoholism and/or other major social problems prevailed), they did not specifically deal with domestic violence against women. It is not surprising that NGOs dealing with this issue emerged as a consequence of and in reaction to the "empty space" and disregard for the issue by the public social care sector and services.

The first NGO dealing with the issue of domestic violence against women was *Društvo SOS telefon za ženske in otroke—žrtve nasilja* (Association SOS Help-Line for Women and Children—Victims of Violence), founded in 1989.[10] The second NGO, *Društvo Ženska svetovalnica* (Women's Counseling Service), was founded in 1994, and the third, *Društvo za nenasilno komunikacijo* (Association against Violent Communication, www.drustvo-dnk.si), emerged in 1996. They were all established in Ljubljana, the capital of Slovenia, but operated at the national level. By 2007, there were fifteen NGOs dealing with the issue of violence against women, seven of which were headquartered in Ljubljana. Some of the NGOs operating in Ljubljana work at the national level, while local NGOs do not reach out beyond their immediate vicinity. The NGOs founded by individuals usually operate with very limited resources and often on a strictly voluntary basis. Smaller NGOs usually concentrate on one issue (awareness-raising, for instance) and are almost never involved in networking, be it domestic or international. This is in contrast to the fact that the international network of organizations provides an important dimension to the women's NGO sector in Slovenia. In 2007, for example, *Ženski lobi Slovenije* (Women's Lobby for Slovenia—WLS) became a full member of the European Women's Lobby (EWL). In January 2008, of the nine organizations that made up the WLS, three worked in the field of violence against women.

Women's NGOs and female activists (academics in particular) should be given most of the credit for improving responses to violence against women. They raised awareness, developed tools and practices for intervention, and worked on an almost exclusively voluntary basis. It was largely these NGOs that established the Slovene system of victim support (Zaviršek 2004: 1). They were the first ones to offer social skills trainings to perpetrators, support groups to victims, and different models of counseling. These same NGOs are engaged in an endless struggle of raising funds from state and local communities; they routinely meet with politicians and train social workers, police officers, and health care providers. For NGO volunteers and employees, these jobs translate into long work hours.

In the past two decades, NGOs played a crucial role in many aspects of assisting victims of domestic violence. First, they intervened to shift the focus from the perpetrators to providing help to women and children. Previously, social services (such as centers for social work, the police, and the judiciary) focused on questions like "could this man really have done something like that," "what led him to do that," "did she encourage him," and "how to help him as he was a victim in his childhood" (Zaviršek 2004: 5–6), whereby all or most of the attention is given to the perpetrator who already possesses more structural power (at the economic, social, cultural, and symbolic levels). In this context, NGOs first started to provide advocacy, counseling, shelters, support groups, and self-help groups for women and children as victims of domestic violence.

Then NGOs redefined, reframed, and renamed the problem as one of domestic violence against women, in contrast to its status as a social issue marked by notions of "dysfunctional families," "family arguments," "poor partnerships," "alcoholism," or "unemployment." Prior to this, the absence of the category "domestic violence against women" in state social services meant that such cases of violence were discussed in terms of an alternate framework, such as "dysfunctional family" (ibid., 2004: 6). But now, instead of asking "Why doesn't she leave him?" and "What has she done to provoke him?" the new NGOs started to ask questions such as "Where can she find a safe place?" etc. NGOs oppose the notion that a woman is to blame for domestic violence against her and children (ibid., 2004: 6).

Third, NGOs adopted a strategy of including in their work the women who themselves experienced domestic violence. Thus, many NGOs asked women who initially arrived at an NGO as victims to work as volunteers. This interaction brought a new dimension to practice: it is often easier for a victim to trust a person with a similar experience (ibid.).

Fourth, and probably most important for the implementation of a holistic approach to the problem of domestic violence, is the fact that NGOs have experience with promoting and producing structural change (ibid.: 7). Here structural change refers to the attention paid to the issue of domestic violence within various institutions.

Let us take a closer look at the structural changes within social care institutions, police work, and the health care system. In the field of social care, the Slovene Expert Council for the problems of violence against women (founded in 2001 by the initiative of NGOs) influenced the decision to establish twelve regional coordinators who focus on domestic violence and are all employed by state centers for social work.[11]

NGOs were the first to offer training sessions to police departments on the issue of domestic violence against women. In the 1990s, the Women's Counseling Service was the most energetic NGO working with the police. Through the Women's Counseling Service, police officers received training on different forms of violence, learned about victims' responses, perpetrators' responses, and the dynamics of a violent relationship.[12] Based on the information provided by such NGO trainings, the police developed programs for "training the trainers." In addition, NGOs started to run lectures on domestic violence against women at the Faculty of Criminal Justice and Security, where future police officers are trained.

In the field of health care, two NGOs and a government office worked together to produce guidelines regarding domestic violence. In 2004, the Association SOS Help-Line, *Delovna skupina za nenasilje pri Zbornici zdravstvene in babiške nege—Zvezi društev medicinskih sester, babic in zdravstvenih tehnikov Slovenije* (Working group for non-violence operating within the Nurses' Association of Slovenia) cooperated with the Office for Equal Opportunities in the preparation of special guidelines on the actions that nurses should take when, in the course of their work, they encounter women who may be victims of domestic violence.[13] These guidelines are meant as a guidebook offering help to battered women, support their empowerment, and provide relevant information. The Working Group trains nurses to recognize whether bruises or injuries have been caused by something other than "falling down the stairs" or "bumping into the door." Health-care providers are also trained to recognize that a seemingly "loving and caring" partner who accompanies the woman may be the cause of her injuries. Health care services can now offer the woman information about safe places, where she can talk without the presence of her partner. Nurses are taught appropriate ways to ask a woman whether or not, for example, she really fell down the stairs, and to give her at least a leaflet that contains all the phone numbers of domestic violence SOS help.

The fifth important achievement of NGOs in the field of domestic violence is the growing recognition that violence may occur without visible injuries (Zaviršek et al. 2004: 7). NGOs worked to influence the definition of domestic violence that became part of the 2008 Family Violence Prevention Act. The definition of domestic violence in the Family Violence Prevention Act includes physical, sexual, psychological, and economic violence, as well as not providing due care for the family member who is in need of it due to illness, disability, old age, or developmental or any other personal circumstance. NGOs played a crucial role in having economic violence incorporated in the legal definition of domestic violence as their work laid great emphasis on different forms of violence.[14] Therefore, in the 2008 law not only visual forms of violence (physical) are recognized as punishable. From the first draft of the definition of domestic violence, prepared by the Ministry of Family, Labor, and Social Affairs, to the final version adopted in the National Assembly in 2008, NGOs proposed some minor changes: for example, the Association SOS Help-Line, the Association against Violent Communication, and the Women's Counseling Service were among the NGOs most active in negotiating with the ministry. The reason that no dramatic changes were proposed was that the ministry followed the definitions that NGOs were already using.

Despite the many cases of good practice and strong cooperation between NGOs dealing with victims of domestic violence and the state institutions listed above, the everyday practice of Slovene NGOs remains very difficult. The many obstacles and challenges that NGOs face are discussed in the next section. It is important to understand how these obstacles have influenced the development of Slovene practices to stop domestic violence against women.

Characteristics of and Challenges for NGOs Working with Victims of Domestic Violence

In December 2006, I conducted a study of nine out of the fifteen Slovene NGOs dealing with the issue of domestic violence against women.[15] Five of the largest and oldest NGOs were included in the sample. There were three main purposes for this analysis: 1) to identify the major problems in management that NGOs focusing on domestic violence were dealing with; 2) to evaluate the cooperation among NGOs, and 3) to assess the level and effectiveness of cooperation between NGOs and government institutions.

The 2006 survey highlighted the fact that the most common problem NGOs were facing was insufficient funding and, consequently, inadequate staffing levels. At the same time, cooperation among NGOs and their cooperation with state institutions did not appear problematic; NGOs were cooperating with each other and with state institutions. Before taking a closer look at the problems NGOs listed, let me offer a general review of the geographic distribution, the foci, and the activities of the NGOs participating in the survey.

The geographic distribution of NGOs in Slovenia is rather uneven as they are concentrated in the central part of the country. However, their services are not limited to the center. Eight of the nine NGOs in the survey cover the whole country, while one is regional in its focus. With the exception of one, which is a private institution, all others are associations.[16] All nine NGOs offered services to women who were victims of domestic violence. Eight of the nine offered counseling for women, two offered counseling for perpetrators, and seven provided counseling for children. Self-help groups for women were offered by eight NGOs. Four ran shelters.[17] One provided a crisis center.[18] Six offered phone counseling and eight worked in the field of awareness-raising through information campaigns and distribution of posters, leaflets, and other materials to sensitize the general public and professionals. Five of the NGOs performed preventive workshops for different target groups, such as nurses, police officers, and prosecutors. Six worked on preparing proposals for legislative changes. Four of the nine worked to call public attention to insufficient or otherwise ineffective state institutions, while some of them also published information and training materials. Some of the best-known NGO publications include *Nasilje nad ženskami—odgovornost policije* (Violence against women—police responsibility; Van der Ent et al. 2001); *Nasilje—nenasilje: Priročnik za učiteljice, učitelje, svetovalne službe in vodstva šol* (Violence—nonviolence: A handbook for teachers, school counseling services, and school managers; Aničić et al. 2002); *Nasilje proti ženskam v družini, partnerskih in sorodstvenih zvezah* (Violence against women in families, partnerships, and relationships; Plaz 2004); *Na poti iz nasilja: prakse proti nasilju nad ženskami* (On the way out of violence: work practice in the field of violence against women; Veselič 2007). NGOs also began offered counseling via email. Sometimes email counseling has the benefit of being safer for a woman. For example, when she is at home or at her workplace and cannot make a phone call, she can write an email and feel less exposed. Emails can also be cheaper because not all NGOs have a free of charge telephone help-line. Email counseling can be safer for the victim because the perpetrator may not be able to control all of her email accounts in the way he could control her phone bills, which list the calls she has made. On occasion, relatives, friends, or neighbors seek information via email on how to help the victim.

NGOs underline that funding is the major problem they face. Although the share of funds NGOs receive from state or local authorities is fairly high, these funds are not sufficient to cover all their activities. Since tax legislation in Slovenia is not donor friendly (donors can only get a maximum of 0.3 percent income tax relief), NGOs cannot rely on private sources. With a few exceptions, there is the additional problem that donors, firms in particular, often do not see any added value when donating to NGOs dealing with the issue of domestic violence against women. "Well, I do know that someone has to do the job, but to be honest, I'd rather see our logo on the TV broadcast of a sport event or on the CD of some village chorus," was the answer that a director of a successful firm gave when I asked him why his company did not donate anything to domestic violence NGOs, given that 93 percent of his company employees were women. The director's statement reflects the thinking of many managers—though they might not all be as direct in explaining why they reject NGOs' requests to support projects related to domestic violence. For these reasons, NGOs have to put much additional effort into fundraising activities. They need to sweep deep and wide to acquire funding, which includes preparing documentation for public grants, searching for donors and sponsors, and running other profitable activities such as publishing, or garnering fees for workshops provided to different target groups.

NGOs also suffer from a general lack of experts. Only one of the nine NGOs in the study did not encounter difficulties relating to the lack of expertise. The survey revealed that NGOs often did not have funds to employ paid technical staff, such as employees responsible for mail, phones, accounting, and other office work. Indeed, seven of the nine NGOs dealt with technical staffing problems on a frequent or regular basis. Five also said that they frequently or regularly faced problems just because they did not employ a manager. Six NGOs claimed they could not afford a manager due to the absence of permanently employed fundraisers. Additionally, they faced the lack of expertise and time to undertake major fundraising directed at private sources. Six NGOs claimed they suffered from a frequent or regular lack of skilled labor, and eight noted that they frequently or regularly lacked time for fundraising.

Since insufficient funds seem to be a central problem for the NGOs in the study, let us take a closer look at their finances. In Slovenia, the state plays a primary role in financing and producing public goods and services (Kolarič et al. 2002: 127). The state provides public schools, child care, health care services, and social care services—which are a legacy of the communist regime. These public services are distributed all over the country. The role of the NGO sector is limited to filling any gaps in public sector services. Since the state does not provide sufficient funds required to operate NGOs, the majority of Slovene NGOs acquire

TABLE 7.1. INCOMES OF NINE SLOVENE ANTI–DOMESTIC
VIOLENCE NGOS IN 2005

SOURCE OF NGO FUNDING FOR DOMESTIC VIOLENCE–RELATED SERVICES	SHARE (%)
Local government[1]	31.32
Ministry of Labor, Family, and Social Affairs	30.65
Foundation for Financing the Handicapped and Humanitarian Organizations in the Republic of Slovenia (FIHO)[2]	14.01
Donations and sponsorship from individuals and firms	12.48
Employment Service of Slovenia	3.50
Ministry of Education and Sport	2.45
Office for Equal Opportunities	1.76
Membership fees	1.37
Users' contributions	0.76
Other	0.55
Own income (fees for the seminars, publishing etc.)	0.53
Ministry of Health	0.40
International grants	0.00

Source: Author's survey conducted in December 2006.
Notes: 1. There are 193 local governments in Slovenia.
2. FIHO is a public foundation. The Slovene National Assembly nominates members of FIHO's board. Its funds derive from the National Lottery.

funds by selling their expertise and various professional services. However, the field of domestic violence against women is an exception to this rule (see table 7.1).

Only two of the eleven shelters in Slovenia have been established and are run by the state. Neither does the state provide advocacy for victims of domestic violence, nor organize any support groups, run training programs about forms of nonviolent communication for perpetrators, or the like. Since the 1990s, the state has been providing the majority of funds for NGOs operating in the area of domestic violence against women. This did not change even under the past right-wing government that at the beginning of its mandate in 2004 refused to pass domestic violence legislation. It is hard to say what the reasons might have been for the contradiction between providing the funding to NGOs but not supporting the relevant legislation. One of the reasons could be that compared to other budget expenses, domestic violence expenses are negligible, yet their reduction might cause the NGOs to protest.

Public funds followed by donations and sponsorship (from individuals and firms) were the two main sources of incomes for all the NGOs in the survey. However, in practice, even incomes generated via state funding were irregular and unreliable, because they could be obtained only for a specific program. As a result, competition over limited resources was fierce, particularly among small NGOs. Only one out of the nine NGOs managed to support a full-time employee to take care of fundraising.

In terms of acquiring international funds, not a single one of the Slovene NGOs studied received international funding in the previous five years. This was primarily because the NGOs did not have their own independent matching funds, which are required in order for them to apply for EU or other international funds. Such international grants often require a minimum 20 percent contribution plus VAT. Four of the nine NGOs stated that they were regularly held back because of the lack of skilled personnel to prepare the applications for international tenders, while the other five NGOs said they frequently experienced this problem. Five NGOs also lacked the knowledge of foreign languages necessary to submit applications, while four said they never or rarely faced that problem.

Unsteady funding sources were also a problem. The survey revealed that seven NGOs confronted the problem of unstable funding sources on regular or frequent basis, whereas only two said that they rarely faced that problem. Similarly, insufficient funding was a regular problem for five of the nine NGOs, while three experienced difficulties relating to insufficient funding on a frequent basis. In fact, six of the nine NGOs designated the financial crisis (of insufficient funds) as the major problem they faced in the past five years. Most NGOs solved this problem by relying on voluntary work, by adding extra hours to regular employees' schedule (instead of employing additional staff), by minimizing costs, reducing programs, and reducing salaries. While financing was one of the greatest problems NGOs faced, they had no problems cooperating among themselves and with state institutions.

A problem emerging from the lack of funds was insufficient permanent staff that NGOs could rely on. A closer look at staffing showed that although NGOs were concerned with the dearth of permanent employees, the number of volunteers and members did not appear to them as problematic. The number of permanent staff employed by the NGOs in the survey varied from 0 to 12 (on average 7 persons were employed, while two of the nine NGOs did not have any permanent staff). Although none of the NGOs in the survey employed full-time managers, there was one person in one of the NGOs who was employed on a part-time basis on a limited time contract. NGOs were most likely to have an employee in charge of fundraising. Since NGOs compete for publicly tendered funds on a yearly basis (or, for some exceptional programs, every five years), the focus on fundraising is understandable, if unfortunate. The number of members in the NGOs surveyed ranged from 13 to 140 (on average 44 members), while the number of volunteers varied from 4 to 45 (on average 24 volunteers). Members are not necessarily volunteers who are actively involved in the daily NGO work, such as phone counseling or help with awareness-raising campaigns.

Another area in the survey was cooperation among NGOs and with state institutions. Cooperation is an integral part of NGO work. All nine NGOs surveyed cooperated in some form with other NGOs, for example, at roundtables and conferences, when organizing public awareness-raising campaigns, during trainings for professionals, or when clients' problems demanded cooperation. Eight of the nine NGOs evaluated their cooperation with other NGOs as "good," while one assessed it as "not good but not bad."[19] As advantages of good cooperation among NGOs in the field of violence against women the respondents stressed information exchange, expert knowledge exchange, successful problem solving for the clients, more lobbying possibilities, and more visibility for domestic violence. All nine NGOs surveyed cooperated with various state institutions, such as the Ministry of Labor, Family, and Social Affairs, the Office for Equal Opportunities, the police, either generally or with particular police stations, centers for social work, health care services, the judiciary (prosecutors, in particular), schools, and the human rights ombudsman. The main areas of cooperation between NGOs and state institutions were public awareness-raising campaigns, roundtables or conferences, and working together to prepare legislative proposals and other strategic documents, such as the National Program for Equal Opportunities for Women and Men.

Along with collaboration among NGOs, the cooperation between NGOs and state institutions has also increased in importance and efficiency. Such collaboration began almost two decades ago and has been improving ever since. While in the late 1980s and even in the 1990s the cooperation started because of interested and aware individuals in NGOs and state institutions (police, centers for social work, the health care system, prosecutors), the process has not yet achieved the level of "self-aware cooperation." In the field of assisting victims of domestic violence, "self-aware cooperation" means a type of cooperation so deeply incorporated in the professional life of institutions that the first reaction of any professional is to contact the relevant institutions, prompting a mutually reinforcing reaction that supports the victim, improves relevant legislation, and fills any other welfare or legislative gap, for example through better and more coordinated assistance, prevention, and awareness-raising. The NGOs that participated in this survey believed that the advantages of good cooperation between state institutions and NGOs were more coordinated activities and common strategies, the development of shared understandings, more efficient flow of information, and better legislation.

It is important to note how the numerous efforts to sensitize the Slovene public to the issue of domestic violence against women have been translated into practice and how effectively policies were carried out. Let us consider, for example, an early example of effective cooperation among different organizations. In 1999, Slovenia began a campaign entitled, *"Kaj ti je, deklica?"* (What's up, girl?), for which it received financial support from the United Nations. The primary aim of the campaign was to raise the awareness of domestic violence against women, with the goal of increasing sensitivity among both the general public and professionals. The campaign marked the first time that NGOs, a government agency, and the National Assembly united in a common action, the effects of which continue to resonate almost ten years later.[20] The campaign proved to be very successful, with the exhibition of posters in the National Assembly and throughout Slovenia, moving eventually to urban and municipal councils, thus placing the issue of domestic violence against women on the respective agendas of these central political institutions. The campaign led to wide-ranging public debates and roundtables about domestic violence against women all over the country. During the campaign, Slovenia was covered with large posters depicting the face of a young woman with sadness in her eyes and bruises all over her face. The poster asked the question "What's up, girl?" and the statement below read, "Every third woman battered, every fifth raped" (see figure 8.8). The statistics alone probably provoked as many debates as the above-mentioned statement by

Božac Deležan regarding the home being the most unsafe place for a woman. "No, that is not possible," "That is just feminists' nonsense," "I don't know any battered women" were only some of the responses heard at the time when people noticed the posters. On the other hand, the campaign was an important milestone in addressing stereotypes about domestic violence and involving the media in efforts to break the silence. Almost a decade later one can still hear people saying, "Do you remember those posters? You know, the ones with a battered woman saying every third woman is battered, every fifth is raped?" Since the campaign, the taboo of not mentioning domestic violence in public has been broken, and many services exist to support victims of domestic violence in Slovenia.

Political changes in the 1990s brought definitive changes in the Slovene state-run social services and in the NGO sector as well. In the late 1980s, NGOs started and have ever since continued to offer the majority of the services in the field of domestic violence against women. Although Slovenia has legislation regarding gender equality, it was a struggle to win acknowledgement of the existence of domestic violence and create laws and services to help its victims. While *de jure* gender equality was inherited from the communist period, EU membership has further improved this situation because of the need to harmonize Slovene legislation with European Union standards. Unfortunately, in the field of domestic violence against women, the European Union has no directives or decrees. *De facto* gender equality, however, is still something to be achieved in Slovenia, just as in every other European Union country. We cannot say that society has achieved gender equality until the gender pay gap is eliminated, imbalances in the participation of women and men in political decisionmaking are corrected, difficulties involved in reconciling work and family life are dealt with, and women's higher rates of unemployment are addressed. Likewise, we cannot say that society has achieved gender equality with gender-based violence still in existence.

Both internal and external forces worked together to affect the treatment of domestic violence Slovenia. On the one hand, demands from international organizations have thoroughly influenced policy-making in the field of domestic violence in Slovenia. The most notable influences are the Council of Europe's Recommendation on Protection of Women against Violence and the adoption of international conventions, such as the UN's CEDAW and its Optional Protocol. On the other hand, NGOs and trained professionals (police officers, social workers, and nurses) have forced the state of Slovenia to deal with the issue from within. It is difficult to measure which influence has been greater. However, it is certain that without interested, enthusiastic, aware, and motivated individuals, such as NGO representatives and trained professionals, Slovenia would not have been able to demonstrate the great progress that was accomplished during the period from 1989, when the first NGO dealing with the issue of domestic violence against women was founded, until 2008 when the Family Violence Prevention Act passed the parliamentary vote.

Slovene NGOs operating in the area of violence against women emerged mostly in the late 1980s and in 1990s. Although most NGOs were established on a voluntary basis, they have become more professionalized in the past decade; they employ skilled professionals and no longer operate on a predominantly voluntary basis. Most NGOs have become providers of women's social services, offering women assistance that the state does not, all the while keeping their legal status as NGOs (Zaviršek 2004: 12). Until the state provides stable funding to these NGOs independent of each new government's political agenda, the NGOs' operations, victim support, and perpetrator-retraining programs stand on weak legs. While state-run centers for social work are relatively evenly distributed all over the country, the NGOs that provide services for victims of domestic violence are mostly concentrated in the central part of Slovenia. As a consequence of the uneven distribution of NGOs, not all parts of the country have access to such services. The gaps in services of the centers for social work that NGOs fill include such victim support efforts as social skills trainings for perpetrators, shelters, counseling, advocacy for victims, and the like.

The question of whether domestic violence against women remains an important political issue in Slovenia cannot be answered with a simple "yes" or "no." On the one hand, the National Assembly's 2008 adoption of the Family Violence Prevention Act would seem to indicate that it has remained an important political issue. On the other hand, the adoption of the Act does not in itself assure its implementation. Whether the Act has been successfully implemented will only become clear in the course of the next few years, which may provide the necessary proof that domestic violence against women is still an important political issue.

NOTES

1. Situated in Central and Eastern Europe, Slovenia became a member of the European Union (EU) in 2004, a member of the Council of Europe (CoE) in 1993, and a member of the United Nations (UN) in 1992. Slovenia was a part of the Austro-Hungarian Empire until the end of the World War I in 1918. It became a part of the Kingdom of Serbs, Croats, and Slovenians until World War II. After World War II, Slovenia formed one of the six socialist federal republics of Yugoslavia until 1991, and it became an independent state in 1991. With a population of 2 million, Slovenia is one of the smallest European countries.

2. In 2004, Slovenia had the lowest fertility rate in the EU, according to the Eurostat (Total fertility rate, http://epp.eurostat.ec.europa.eu/portal/page?_pageid= 1996,45323734&_dad=portal&_schema=PORTAL&screen=welcomeref&open=/t_ popula/t_pop/t_demo_fer&language=en&product=REF_TB_population&root=REF_ TB_population&scrollto=0, last accessed July 29, 2008). The number of divorces per 1,000 marriages is increasing, from average 252.6 (1995–1999) to average 339.8 (2000–2004) (Statistični urad Republike Slovenije 2006).

3. NGOs working on the field of domestic violence initiated the establishment of an Expert Council. They achieved this aim in 2001, when the left-wing government created this council to consider problems of violence against women within the framework of the Ministry of Labor, Family, and Social Affairs. The Expert Council served as an advisory body to the minister. Its tasks were to prepare expert groundwork and to provide guidelines for the adoption of the relevant legislation in the field of violence against women and supervise its implementation. Representatives of several NGOs, the Ministry of Labor, Family, and Social Affairs, the Ministry of the Interior, including the Police, the governmental Office for Equal Opportunities, various centers for social work, local communities, and the Office of the Human Rights Ombudsman met monthly to prepare the position papers and draft a proposal of a fundamental legal act on the prevention of family violence. In 2004, legal experts and the Expert Council prepared a proposal for the Law on the Prevention of Domestic Violence. National elections changed the political situation in the autumn of 2004, when the right-wing Janez Drobnič was appointed as Minister for Family, Labor, and Social Affairs. The bill was withdrawn and the Council was reappointed and renamed "Expert Council for Problems of Domestic Violence" in 2005.

4. The National Assembly accorded Minister Drobnič a vote of no confidence because he did not respond to the prime minister's appeal to resign. The main reason that Drobnič was requested to resign was the very negative public opinion regarding the proposal for *Strategija za dvig rodnosti* (Strategy for Increasing Fertility), which the Ministry prepared under his guidance. Among other publicly criticized ideas of the Strategy was that the constitutional right for abortion was no longer free of charge. The Strategy for Increasing Fertility is available at: www.mddsz.gov.si/file admin/mddsz.gov.si/pageuploads/dokumenti__pdf/strategija_rodnost_osnutek_ 151106.pdf.

5. The Women's Policy Office was established in 1992 as a professional service of the Slovene Government with the aim enhancing the realization of the rights of women guaranteed by the constitution, legislation, and international treaties. It focused on producing analyses of the causes and reasons for discrimination, on improving legislation in terms of gender equality, and on providing information

on women's rights. According to the governmental decision of the establishment, organization, and working areas of the Office for Equal Opportunities, this governmental entity took on the tasks of the Office for Women's Policy in 2001. The Office for Equal Opportunities is modeled on national machineries for gender equality in the European Union member states. Equal opportunities for women and men and the related attention to women, who are still in a position of inequality, remain at the forefront of the operations of the Office for Equal Opportunities (see the official website, www.uem.gov.si.en; accessed November 23, 2009).

6. When taking a closer look at statistical data we can note that women in Slovenia are in better position than the EU average in many fields—with a higher share of employed women, a lower female unemployment rate, one of the lowest gender pay gaps in the EU, and more. For detailed statistics on EU member states, see http://epp.eurostat.ec.europa.eu (accessed November 23, 2009).

7. The tasks and organization of the multidisciplinary teams will be defined in the Act on Social Security. Such multidisciplinary teams are already in existence, but only on a case-by-case basis. The teams most often include a social worker from the regionally responsible center for social work, a regional coordinator for the problems of domestic violence, the police, an expert from an NGO working with victims of domestic violence, and—if children are involved—also a person from the school counseling service. As these multidisciplinary and multi-agency teams have not been established yet as a permanent (and legally binding) form of cooperation among institutions and NGOs, they have only appeared if interested individuals from various institutions (who have supportive and aware superiors) have been able to coordinate and work together.

8. The Socialist Federative Republic of Yugoslavia consisted of six socialist republics and two autonomous provinces. The majority of the legislation was adopted on the federal level, but some issues were transferred to the republic level.

9. State-owned and -operated centers for social work address different needs of families and individuals, such as social care services, guardianship, foster families, institutional care, financial support etc. For more information see www.mddsz.gov.si/en/areas_of_work/social_affairs/social_security_services/ (last accessed January 13, 2008).

10. The idea of opening a help-line for women and children similar to European projects arose in the feminist group Lilith in Ljubljana. In 1988, the Lilith group published two separate opinion polls of different sample sizes on violence against women and children in five different Slovenian newspapers and magazines and its own booklets. The opinion polls were based on the assumption that Slovenia is not an exception as far as violence in families and relationships is concerned, and that none of the Slovene institutions deals with this problem systematically. More than three hundred responses to the polls confirmed this assumption, as well as the need to organize a new form of assistance to women and children experiencing violence. In the year 1989 the Group for the SOS Hot-line (as the informal association was called then) carried out the necessary technical arrangements, had several meetings with the representatives of the social welfare offices and police administrations, and organized the first training course for women volunteers. The help-line began operation in October 1989 with donations. In December 1990, the group was organized and registered as the Association SOS Help-Line for entire area of Slovenia (see their website, www.drustvo-sos.si; last accessed January 13, 2008).

11. There are sixty-two state-run centers for social work, geographically distributed all over Slovenia. For the first time in 2004–2005, this network of centers employed twelve regional coordinators specifically to work with the problems of domestic violence. The tasks of these twelve coordinators are to organize and provide expert support to social workers in the centers for social work. The twelve coordinators also provide support to victims of violence and they participate in the activities carried out by the multi-agency teams for the prevention of violence.

12. Even some foreign experience was presented at police trainings as Women's Counseling Service cooperated well with the Dutch police on the issue of domestic violence against women. In addition to trainings given to the Slovene police by the Dutch, in 2001 the Women's Counseling Service also translated and published (with the financial support the Office of Equal Opportunity, the Ministry of Family, Labor, and Social Affairs, the Dutch Embassy, and some private donors) the very first book in the Slovene language on domestic violence against women. The book, titled *Violence Against Women—Police Responsibility,* was distributed to institutions, NGOs, volunteers, students, and others.

13. The Working Group was established in 2000. Its members are nurses from different fields of health care. The Working Group plays an important role in identifying possible domestic violence through the nursing personnel and their appropriate response. The operation of the Working Group is focused mainly on the role and responsibilities of those employed in health care institutions with respect to reducing tolerance of violence in general and preventing and eliminating violence in the workplace. Within the framework of its activities, since 2000 the Working Group has carried out several expert trainings for the employees on sexual violence at work, participated actively in various public campaigns during each year's international days of activism against violence against women, and prepared educational materials (such as *Nasilje in spolno nadlegovanje na delovnim mestih medicinskih sester v Sloveniji* [Violence and Sexual Harassment in Nurses' Work in Slovenia]; Klemenc and Pahor 2000), leaflets, and posters on forms of violence and other topics for those employed in nursing care, patients at hospitals and other health care institutions, visitors, and other people entering the health care institutions.

14. Article 3 of the 2008 Law on the Protection from Domestic Violence defines violence in the family as any form of physical, sexual, psychological, or economic violence exerted by one family member (hereinafter: perpetrator of violence) against another (hereinafter: victim), or disregard of any family member as found in Article 2 of the Act regardless of age, sex, or any other personal circumstance of the victim or perpetrator of violence. Physical violence denotes any use of physical force that causes pain, fear, or shame to the family member, regardless of whether physical injuries occur. Sexual violence pertains to handling a person with sexual intent that is opposed by the other family member, or if the victim is forced into acting according to these sexual expectations or because at his or her stage of development the victim does not understand the meaning of these actions. Psychological violence denotes actions by which the perpetrator of violence exerts violence against a family member that induces fear, shame, a feeling of inferiority or endangerment, and other types of anguish. Economic violence is defined as undue control or restriction of any family member concerning the disposal of their income or financial assets. It can also mean undue restriction of disposal or management of common financial assets (this is in line with the concept of economic violence defined by SOS Hotline Belgrade—see

chapter 3 in this volume, Johnson and Zaynullina, for details). Disregard falls under the forms of violence in which a person does not provide due care for the family member who is in need of it due to illness, disability, old age, or developmental or any other personal circumstance.

15. In 2006, fifteen NGOs worked with victims of domestic violence in Slovenia. Nine out of the fifteen NGOs answered my questionnaire. The questionnaire consisted of five groups of questions on their demographic data, cooperation among NGOs, cooperation among NGOs and state institutions, problems and solutions, and perceptions of other NGOs' activities.

16. According to Slovene laws, NGOs can be associations, private institutions, or foundations. There are some differences in who can be the founder, whether they need a management and supervision committee, and some other details of legal and organizational structure.

17. Shelters are defined in Slovenia as exclusively for women and children who experience violence and who need exit to a safe environment. These individuals may live in a shelter from three months to a maximum of one year. Due to the fact that shelters do not have enough room and are concentrated mostly in urban areas in central Slovenia, state- and Karitas-run homes for mothers also offer some additional places (see "Shelters, homes for mothers and other domestic violence preventive programs," Ministry of Labor; available at www.mddsz.gov.si/, in Slovenian; accessed November 23, 2009). However, homes for mothers are primarily meant for pregnant women and women with babies in the immediate post-natal period who are struggling with social and/or economic problems. In these homes the maximum stay is also one year, with the possibility of extending the period to two years.

18. A crisis center is for women and their children who are victims of domestic violence and who need to immediately escape from the violent situation at their home or who are in danger because of a high potential of domestic violence. Advocacy, information, counseling, support groups, and temporary lodging (up to three months) are services that a victim can get in crisis center. The services are free of charge (see www.drustvo-zenska-svetovalnica.si; last accessed April 1, 2008).

19. The possible answers in the survey were excellent, good, not good but not bad, bad, very bad.

20. The parties who cooperated in this campaign were the Association SOS Help-Line for Women and Children—Victims of Domestic Violence; the Association against Violent Communication; FIKS—Feminist-Information-Culture Focal Point; the Office of the Government of the Republic of Slovenia for Women's Policy (renamed the Office of Equal Opportunity in 2001), and the Commission of the National Assembly for Equal Opportunity.

WORKS CITED

Aničić, Klavdija, Doroteja Lešnik Mugnaioni, Maja Plaz, Nataša Vanček, Tatjana Dobnikar Verbnik, Špela Veselič, and Katja Zabukovec Kerin. 2002. *Nasilje— nenasilje. Priročnik za učiteljice, učitelje, svetovalne službe in vodstva šol.* [Violence—nonviolence. A handbook for teachers, school counseling services, and school managers]. Ljubljana: Založba i2.

Božac Deležan, Lorena. 1999. "Ko je najnevarnejša institucija zakon, najnevarnejši prostor dom, najnevarnejša oseba partner." [When the most dangerous institution is marriage, the most unsafe place is the home, and the most dangerous person is the partner] In *Dosje: Nasilje nad ženskami* [File: Violence against women], ed. Vera Kozmik and Mojca Dobnikar. Ljubljana: Urad Vlade Republike Slovenije za žensko politiko, Društvo SOS telefon, F-iks, Društvo za nenasilno komunikacijo.

Klemenc, Darinka, and Majda Pahor, eds. 2000. *Nasilje in spolno nadlegovanje na delovnih mestih medicinskih sester v Sloveniji* [Violence and sexual harassment in the workplace of nurses in Slovenia]. Ljubljana: Društvo medicinskih sester in zdravstvenih tehnikov.

Kolarič, Zinka, Andreja Črnak-Meglič, and Ivan Svetlik. 1995. "Slovenia." In *Družboslovne razprave* [Sociological debates] XI (19–20): 77–94.

Kolarič, Zinka, Andreja Črnak-Meglič, and Maja Vojnovič. 2002. *Zasebne neprofitno-volonterske organizacije v mednarodni perspektivi* [Private nonprofit-voluntary organizations in international perspective]. Ljubljana: Založba FDV.

Plaz, Maja. 2004. "Nasilje proti ženskam v družini, partnerskih in sorodstvenih zvezah" [Violence against women in the families, partnerships and relationships]. In *Psihosocialna pomoč ženskam in otrokom, ki preživljajo nasilje* [Psychosocial help for women and children who have survived violence], ed. Dalida Horvat, Doroteja Lešnik Mugnaioni, and Maja Plaz. Ljubljana: Društvo SOS telefon za ženske in otroke—žrtve nasilja.

Robnik, Sonja. 2007. "Nasilje nad ženskami kot ovira pri doseganju enakosti spolov [Violence against women as an obstacle to gender equality]." *Socialni izziv* [Social challenge] 13(26). Ljubljana: Socialna zbornica.

Robnik, Sonja, Tanja Skornšek-Pleš, and Špela Veselič. 2003. *Nasilje nad ženskami v družini. Analiza stanja* [Domestic violence against women]. Unpublished material. Ljubljana: Ministry for Labor, Family, and Social Affairs. Protection of Women against Violence—Recommendation Rec(2002)5 of the Committee of Ministers to Member States on the protection of women against violence, adopted on April 30, 2002. www.coe.int/t/e/human_rights/equality/05._violence_against_women/003_Rec(2002)05.asp (accessed November 23, 2009).

Seje Državnega zbora [Sessions of the National Assembly]. 2007. www.dz-rs.si/index.php?id=97&cs=1&o=10&unid=MDZ|0763A632B294D764C12573B1002E1382&showdoc=1 (accessed November 9, 2009).

Statistični urad Republike Slovenije [Slovene Statistical Office]. 2006. "Chapter 4.25: Crude marriage rate, crude divorce rate and number of divorces per 1000 marriages." *Statistical yearbook of the Republic of Slovenia 2006.* www.stat.si/letopis/2006/04_06/04-25-06.htm?jezik=en (accessed November 9, 2009).

Van der Ent, D. W., Th. D. Evers, and K. Komduur. 2001. *Nasilje nad ženskami—odgovornost policije* [Violence against women—police responsibility]. Ljubljana: Društvo Ženska svetovalnica.

Veselič, Špela, ed. 2007. *Na poti iz nasilja: prakse proti nasilju nad ženskami* [On the way out of violence: Practice of work in the field of violence against women]. Ljubljana: Društvo SOS telefon za ženske in otroke—žrtve nasilja.

Zaviršek, Darja. 1994. *Ženske in duševno zdravje. O novih kulturah skrbi* [Women and mental health: About new cultures of care]. Ljubljana: Visoka šola za socialno delo.

———. 2001. "Doktrina socialnega dela na področju nasilja nad ženskami" [The Doctrine of the social work in the field of violence against women]. *Socialni izziv* [Social challenge] 7(14). Ljubljana: Socialna zbornica.

———. 2004. "Od aktivizma do profesionalizacije: Refleksija delovanja ženskih nevladnih organizacij na področju nasilja nad ženskmi in otroki v Sloveniji" (From activism to professionalism: Reflection of the work of women's non-governmental organizations in the field of domestic violence against women and children In Slovenia). In *Psihosocialna pomoč ženskam in otrokom, ki preživljajo nasilje* (Psychosocial help for women and children who survived violence), ed. Dalida Horvat, Doroteja Lešnik Mugnaioni, and Maja Plaz. Ljubljana: Društvo SOS telefon za ženske in otroke—žrtve nasilja.

International Organizations and Domestic Violence Policy in Postcommunist States

PART 2

International
Organizations
and Domestic
Violence Policy in
Postcommunist
States

Reframing Domestic Violence: Global Networks and Local Activism in Postcommunist Central and Eastern Europe

KATALIN FÁBIÁN

In postcommunist Central and Eastern Europe, the process of acknowledging domestic violence has been, and continues to be, complex and challenging. The difficulties lie partially in the region's very recent integration into many global trends, such as democratization and respect for human rights. Poland, the Czech Republic, Slovakia, Hungary, and Slovenia not only lie in close geographic proximity to one another in Central and Eastern Europe but also have a shared history of decades of communism. Even if their respective communist systems differed considerably, the discussion of domestic violence was taboo in all of these countries—it had no name, thus its very existence went unrecognized and unacknowledged.

How then did domestic violence become a central topic of debate among Central and Eastern European general publics, governments, international organizations, and nongovernmental organizations (NGOs) from the early 1990s onward? The notable emergence of international networking about domestic violence among women's groups was not palpably evident until the beginning years of the twenty-first century. NGOs helping victims of rape and domestic violence have started to emerge in Central and Eastern Europe, partly in response to domestic needs and partly because they have found Western feminist concepts applicable to their environments and Western governments' and intergovernmental organizations' (IGOs) funding appealing.

First and most importantly, all these policy-relevant debates on the extent of globalization, democratization, gender equality, and the supremacy of the rule of law reflect how Central and Eastern Europe incorporates its most recent political past into contemporary relations— in this context, the activities of women's groups and their allies in both domestic and international politics. Second, these exchanges on domestic violence inform us about the nature of Central and Eastern European relations with powerful allies such as the European Union, the UN, the

Council of Europe, and states both far away and geographically nearby, such as the United States, Finland, Austria, and Sweden. Third, on a similarly abstract level that also affects pragmatic considerations of NGOs, the debates on domestic violence show how fundamental value orientations develop toward participation in a liberal democracy, such as individual political empowerment and respect for human rights.

Who were these global actors that exerted the most influence on Hungary and its Central and Eastern European neighbors, and how did they accomplish this task? I argue that both tangible actors such as the UN's CEDAW Committee and intangible norms such as democratization and human rights brought the frame (i.e, a particular set of conceptualizations) of domestic violence to postcommunist Central and Eastern Europe. Local NGOs adjusted—"reframed"—this concept to fit their local realities. Although all the Central and Eastern European governments and publics had a perception that they were expected to officially recognize domestic violence, their responses to this perceived external pressure have been unusually diverse. Although Hungary is the only country in the region that remains resistant to passing a separate domestic violence bill, both there and in Poland the gender-neutral interpretation of domestic violence has gained ground (see also chapter 6 in the present volume). With the notable exception of Slovenia, the conceptualization of, and especially intervention in, domestic violence remain highly contested and unstable in the region.

The response to the question of what and who are the main actors influencing the conceptualization of domestic violence can be found in the four main parts of this chapter. After the introduction of the main actors and trends, the second section locates, contextually defines, and connects to Central and Eastern Europe the concept of globalization as it relates to domestic violence. The third part describes the emerging norms affecting how domestic violence is framed internationally and regionally. Fourth, I investigate some of the unintended consequences of globalization in Central and Eastern European NGOs that have performed services and engaged with lobbying with respect to domestic violence. While the power of the many international actors and norms over Central and Eastern Europe is undoubtedly formidable, exchange between these locations is not entirely unidirectional. This section shows that while seemingly universal in their message and method, international human rights norms and policy recommendations regarding domestic violence have been partially adapted to local conditions by taking a more gender-neutral and increasingly less political approach.

Noting the emerging international interconnectedness of this special segment of NGOs, in the summer of 2003 I conducted a field study of activist networks in Poland, the Czech Republic, Slovakia, and Hungary. In the fall of 2004, I returned to these sites and also visited Slovenia. In addition, I participated in the October 14–17 international gathering of the Women Against Violence Europe (WAVE) network. WAVE consists of European NGOs providing services to victims of domestic violence, and it serves as the headquarters of coordination for the European Info Centre Against Violence (see http://www.wave-network.org).[1] Further enhancing the internationalization of NGOs, the Minnesota Advocates for Human Rights (MAHR) conducted a series of individual country reports and legal advocacy, and then in February 2008 organized a regional workshop to enhance legal reforms against domestic violence for fellow NGOs and government representatives from the postcommunist world.[2] During the next four summers I regularly visited Central and Eastern European NGOs and periodically interviewed NGO activists, government officials, and EU politicians either in person, by phone, or by email. I transcribed and analyzed the interviews for common themes, such as activists' accounts of pursuing legal change related to domestic violence in their countries, their cooperation with fellow NGOs in common applications for EU-funded projects, and the debates between activists, national politicians, and government officials on the meaning and the most appropriate measures for eliminating domestic violence. I also follow developments via related media reports. These contacts, media reports, governmental and EU official documents, CEDAW, and Open Society Institute country reports, as well as the scholarly literature, are the basis of the data on policy changes presented in appendix 1.

What Has Changed? Actors and Events Changing the Definition of Domestic Violence in Central and Eastern Europe

There are many notable changes in the empirical landscape of domestic violence policies in Poland, the Czech Republic, Slovakia, Hungary, and Slovenia. The Central and Eastern European cases show that the full denial of and widespread skepticism toward domestic violence has been at least partially transformed over the last decade. Starting from such small-scale and NGO-sponsored "wildcat" campaigns, such as the Hungarian NaNE's sticker campaign about the availability of their domestic abuse hotline in the mid-1990s in Budapest, all five Central and Eastern European countries participated in large-scale national campaigns to raise awareness of domestic violence. However, note that 2003 was the first such attempt in Hungary and the fourth in Poland.[3]

Slovenia amended the Criminal Procedure Act in 1998 and the Penal Code in 1999 and enacted a comprehensive law that includes economic violence in 2008, as described in chapter 7 of this volume. Poland and Hungary have been making incremental legal changes, often reversing the direction of movement when new governments are swept into office (Regulska 2003). In contrast to this decade of seesawing policies, Poland passed specific legislation against domestic violence in 2005, while the 2003 Hungarian National Strategy has not yet produced such legal change.

Until the early years of the twenty-first century, Central and Eastern European governments "raced to the middle" between rejecting and satisfying the demands of domestic NGOs and international NGOs/IGOs in a nearly uniform manner by performing a few, usually symbolic changes. Central and Eastern European governments, the media, and a broad spectrum of politicians and publics have remained expressively doubtful that domestic violence is a pandemic that needs special attention and a significant amount of investment, although there is emerging evidence to support this feminist claim.[4] By 2005, however, extensive modifications in domestic violence policy appeared in all Central and Eastern European countries, even if these changes did not amount to the systematic and interlocking overhaul of the legal system and social services that feminists argue is necessary for establishing meaningful support for victims of domestic violence.

It took a decade for Poland, the Czech Republic, Slovakia, Hungary, and Slovenia to develop the first activist networks capable of pressuring their respective governments into addressing the long-neglected issue of domestic violence. In each of these countries, local women's NGOs initiated and maintained the campaign to recognize domestic violence and to develop public policies that could deal with this problem. Although in Yugoslavia freer interchange of travel and information with the rest of Europe produced a viable independent women's movement in the 1970s that managed to survive through, and often vocally protested against, the Balkan wars, even its strong women's networks could not create sustained progress regarding the recognition of domestic violence (Jalušić 2002).[5] Only impending membership in the European Union brought the strategic possibility of the NGOs working with domestic violence victims to pressure their respective governments to deal substantively with this issue in the name of democracy and human rights.

Despite numerous difficulties in legitimizing their focus, many NGOs in Central and Eastern Europe devised strategies to bring attention to domestic violence, create a public discourse, establish services for victims, and start to bring about legislative action. Applying Western European and US models, the Central and Eastern European NGOs dealing with domestic violence developed a culturally and politically more fitting, complex set of arguments to reflect the lessons learned from the gender politics of the communist past and the trends in international human rights and feminist discourse. With political processes increasingly globally interdependent, these Central and Eastern European NGOs combined the processes of domestic and international politics, and applied national citizenship together with the universal language of human rights as powerful political tools in the fight against women's subordination (Lister 1998; Smith et al. 1997).

It is noteworthy that the ferment of public debates and consequent legal changes took place in the course of a decade (beginning in 1995). How could a previous taboo gain attention to this degree? As the Hungarian example of activism shows, increasing global interactions and regional integration may answer this puzzle.

Making the Term and the Policy: The Continuing Battles of Interpretation and Implementation in Postcommunist Hungary

In contrast to earlier waves of women's activism in Hungary, the movement to criminalize domestic violence represents the first and main avenue whereby the activists explicitly connected domestic and international norms and received concrete long-term assistance from abroad (Acsády 2004; Fábián 2007a; Pető 1998). At the same time, Hungarian activism concerning domestic violence also demonstrates the double-sided nature of globalization. On one hand, using a typical boomerang pattern (Keck and Sikkink 1998), globalization allowed women's groups in Central and Eastern Europe to refer to and use the leverage of various international organizations to advance their aims at home.[6] On the other hand, domestic violence was not the agenda that Hungarian or other postcommunist women's groups developed themselves. During the economically difficult years of the transition, if women organized at all, their focus was on jobs and welfare rights (Fábián 2009).

If one had surveyed Hungarians (or any other postcommunist Europeans) in the 1980s and early 1990s about domestic violence, the response would have been confusion and unease. The general public and relevant professions—the police, welfare case workers, lawyers, judges—resisted acknowledging the existence of violence in the family, most often accusing women of committing violence against children and fabricating false charges against husbands and partners. One activist described the miserable conditions of the past as follows:

Domestic violence was considered to be a family matter, even if a woman was smashed against the glass at a state-owned maternity ward. We consider rape as an aggressive power statement, not a sexual act. These topics were taboo here. The authorities dealt with them differently. Nobody took domestic violence seriously, not the police, not the judges, and the doctors blamed the victims for the events. (Interview, March 1995, NaNE)

This scenario of denial and the reversal of victimhood (making men the vulnerable party) were at least partially deconstructed by the actions of a few Hungarian NGOs focusing on domestic violence from a feminist point of view. Replicating international trends, in Hungary it was the feminist and human rights organizations that began to provide services for women and children who suffered the effects of domestic violence. *NaNE* has been one of three main Hungarian NGOs, in addition to a human rights advocacy group, *Habeas Corpus Munkacsoport/HCM* (Habeas Corpus Working Group/HCWG), and Krisztina Morvai's *Női és Gyermekjogi Kutatási és Képzőközpont* (Women's and Children's Rights Research and Training Centre) to advocate recognition of domestic violence and the provision of services to battered women and children.

NaNE, established in 1994, was the first organization in Hungary to raise awareness of the problem in public campaigns, by participating unusually energetically in the media. NaNE created the first national domestic abuse hotline, and it also immediately engaged in advocacy to establish laws against the perpetrators (Szász 2001). Due to its activism, a remarkable shift took place in the understanding and handling of domestic violence in Hungary. Members of NaNE placed stickers with the telephone number of their domestic abuse hotline on most public transportation vehicles (which the authorities scrupulously removed but NaNE members diligently and repeatedly reattached), and eventually NaNE's telephone number made its way into the general information section of the telephone books. After an initially fruitful cooperation with *Magyar Rendőrnők Szervezete* (the Hungarian Policewomen's Association), the police started to train some of its members on how to recognize and deal with domestic violence. In 2004, 240 police officers, followed by a further 80 in 2005, were trained to recognize domestic violence, but the police found that it was very difficult to find funding for the training (Amnesty International 2007: note 43). The pinnacle of the collaboration between NaNE and the police was the 2003 Budapest police directives that established directives compelling the police to intervene in all cases of domestic violence (Országos Rendőrfőkapitány/ ORFK 2003).

One major practice allowing a small NGO such as NaNE to achieve such influence with the police was that they referred to and extensively used human rights references and arguments as well as "best practices" learned from their Western counterparts. NaNE managed to establish a lively connection to a network of Western European and North American feminist women's advocates who use human rights instruments, such as the UN's CEDAW, to combat violence against women. Using connections with the West, such as becoming an affiliate of WAVE and attending trainings of the Austrian Women's Shelter Network, Central and Eastern European NGOs assisting victims of domestic violence also managed to find each other. Personal face-to-face meetings were infrequent among women activists, but an international communication network operated effectively, mostly via the Internet. These connections have started to develop an epistemic community where language and knowledge were created and information was intensely exchanged. As Walsh (2001) argues, in these communities, common discursive practices express the dominant views of the group and also serve the construction of individual and collective identities, among them gendered identities. With gender inequalities being the core issue in domestic violence, feminists' questioning male dominance in Central and Eastern European societies has generated a conflict with the prevailing, possibly even increasingly popular, hegemonic patriarchic discursive practices. The many conflicts NaNE had in making its claim heard in Hungary illustrate the rocky and unfinished path that they traveled.

NaNE has tried to establish legal services for battered women with the support of the New York– and Budapest-headquartered Open Society Fund (OSI). Although NaNE operated the hotline for temporary financial support from various (mostly foreign) foundations, the 2001 OSI funding meant it could afford regular and longer-term paid employees, rather than relying exclusively on volunteers, for more extensive hotline availability and legal advocacy. The professionalization of the organization resulted in more reliable and efficient services. While engaged in anti-violence activism, NaNE also reached out to the New York–based East-West Women's Network, which helped NaNE become part of an international comparative legal project focusing on women's rights. When this project expanded to the point where NaNE could no longer handle it alone, the organization started looking for external funding and cooperation, eventually handing the project over to the Central European University (CEU), where it became part of an academic endeavor. As a result of this international cooperation, support, and funding, Krisztina Morvai (who was later elected to serve as a CEDAW representative between 2002 and

2007) authored the first major study on domestic violence in Hungary, based on her experience as a legal scholar in residence of this branch at the CEU (Morvai 1998). Although this specific legal project closed down within a few years, NaNE's involvement in international activism and funding helped it find long-term allies in a broader advocacy movement both internationally and domestically. On the basis of learning, translating, and applying Western European and North American feminist activism, policy recommendations, and legal practices, the Hungarian movement to address and at least partially remedy domestic violence eventually managed to emerge and then slowly blossom.

In the process of increasing civil and professional alertness about the seriousness of domestic violence, other Hungarian human rights organizations such as the Women's and Children's Rights Centre and Habeas Corpus Working Group (HCWG) joined NaNE, providing legal assistance to victims as well as raising awareness to change public attitudes and laws about domestic violence. The alliance of these three NGOs serendipitously developed a successful campaign in three phases: naming domestic violence, counting its occurrences (Morvai 1998; Tóth 1998), and presenting demands to force the Hungarian Parliament to develop a definition and a process of adjudication for domestic violence (Sáfrány 2003).

Two tragic family violence cases in September 2002 created a sudden and unexpected political opportunity for the three NGOs to promote their framework and arguments. One case involved Tomi Balogh, an eight-year-old boy who was killed by his father. Another case was that of fourteen-year-old Kitti Simek, who shot her abusive father. Krisztina Morvai's spontaneous emotional appeal on television to Hungarians to demand that their parliamentary representatives pass legislation to eliminate domestic violence was followed by an unexpectedly high volume of letters and calls to her organization. The three NGOs started to gather signatures with Tomi's picture and his story prominently displayed in the center of the petition. They also wrote an open letter to the Hungarian Parliament, the prime minister, the president, the appropriate ministries, the chief justice, the chief public prosecutor, and the chief police superintendent demanding the immediate creation of legislation "aimed at the prevention and elimination of domestic violence, which would meet international standards laid down by the UN, the Council of Europe, and the European Union" (Felhívás [Petition] 2002).

The actions of the three NGOs, supported by around fifty thousand people who signed their petition, culminated in concentrated actions and thus a greater force in presenting their arguments in the media and before politicians. The three feminist organizations successfully used Hungary's then pending EU admission to consider action against domestic violence as part of the country becoming "European." Second, activists emphasized the newly acquired opportunity of democratic citizenship to urge and implore the Hungarian public to be active and demand governmental action and parliamentary legislation. However, these two frameworks might not have been sufficient without making a major compromise—namely, accepting the framing of domestic violence as child abuse. Replacing the feminist interpretation with the "family dynamics approach" de-gendered and consequently significantly toned down their political message (as shown in table 1.1 in the introduction to this volume). NaNE's subsequent poster depicting a boy states that he "would never hit a woman. And I wish it were also true for Dad." The poster focused entirely on the effects children suffer from witnessing domestic violence: "At least one million children bear witness to the father raping and beating their mother. This gravely endangers the children's physical, intellectual, and moral development! The Law on Child protection and the Penal Code promise protection. Let us use them in the best interest of children." The beaten woman/mother fell out of the focus (see figure 8.1).

Through public forums and media hype, the alliance of NaNE, the Women's and Children's Rights Centre, and HCWG convinced two members of the Hungarian Parliament to draft a comprehensive proposal for state action to handle domestic violence. The bill was presented to the Parliament in a revised form in March 2003 under number H/2483. The fact that the Hungarian Socialist Party's female representative who submitted the bill insisted during its formulation that men were equally victims of domestic violence and should therefore be protected (interview, June 2002) showed the power of dominant gender hierarchies that the alliance of feminist NGOs could not dismantle. Between March 5 and April 16, 2003, the Parliament discussed and eventually passed "Decision on the formulation of a national strategy for preventing and efficiently responding to violence in the family" (H/2483/23), which obliged the legislative body to formulate a law on domestic violence within a year. The governing coalition of the Hungarian Socialist Party and the Alliance of Free Democrats (altogether 203 representatives) voted in favor of the decision, whereas the conservatives (160 representatives) abstained.

Due to the campaign of the three NGOs referring to international human rights norms and the expectations of the EU and the UN, the parliamentary representatives were aware that they could not entirely

Figure 8.1. "*Én ugyan sosem.*" *NaNE*'s poster depicted a boy stating, "I would never hit a woman. I wish it were also true for Dad." On the website of NaNE, Budapest, Hungary. At www.nane.hu/images/kisfiu_A2.jpg. Courtesy of *NaNE*, Budapest, Hungary.

refuse to deal with the issue without conflicting with the basic premise of democracy, the implied expectations of EU accession, and the recognition of UN-backed international human rights such as those put forth in CEDAW, signed by Hungary in 1980, and the CEDAW Optional Protocol, ratified in 2000. The political opportunity to gain the attention of politicians that opened up to the three feminist NGOs was a product of a nearly universal desire in Central and Eastern Europe to fit in with the community of democratic nations, and of their lingering insecurity about their appropriate international image. The desire to be accepted was so pervasive and the peer pressure so strong among EU applicant countries that even a reference to the EU expectations was enough to create the impression of international norms. By 2003, two members of the alliance, the HCWG and the Women's and Children's Rights Centre, moved on to other related issues, such as mobilizing against legalized prostitution. Soon both of these NGOs faced many internal issues that debilitated cooperation, and by 2007 they were defunct.

The collapse of the three NGOs' strong coalition had serious long-term consequences for recognizing and dealing with domestic violence in Hungary. Lacking both a viable network of NGOs and the perception of pressure from international organizations, Hungary remained the only country in Central and Eastern Europe that neither changed the penal code nor established specific legislation on domestic violence. The most immediate consequence of the demobilization of the coalition of the three NGOs was an entirely hollow 2006 introduction of the distancing ordinance. Even the police considered this distancing ordinance useless except in the most serious cases of domestic violence, when they could intervene using other means (Országos Rendőrfőkapitány/ORFK 2007).

Despite how feeble the Hungarian distancing ordinance is, its 2006 introduction demonstrates the changing domestic and international conditions for social movement activism. Using the example of the Austrian Women's Shelter Network and the 1997 Austrian law as a successful template that was also implemented in Slovakia and Slovenia and widely used as a recommendation in WAVE manuals, NaNE and its allies had worked persistently for many years with legislators and government officials to introduce distancing as an immediately available protection that a judge or the police could order for victims of domestic violence (Farkas 2006; interviews with NaNE and HCWM summer 2006). In contrast, the 2006 ordinance made distancing conditional on a pending lawsuit and limited it to thirty days while not, however, mandating the judge to respond to a petition within any set period of time. Before HCWG became mired in infighting on personal and financial issues and ruptured over the acceptance of EU-funding for retraining services offered to perpetrators, they and NaNE published a press release signaling how enormously dissatisfied they were with the 2006 distancing ordinance (NaNE and HCWG 2006). Further protests regarding the uselessness of the new distancing ordinance, such as open letters to the Minister of Justice, followed in 2008, but Hungarian officialdom remained unresponsive (NaNE Egyesület and Patent 2008). While in 2003 the Hungarian political elite was acutely sensitive to perceptions from abroad due to its impending accession to the European Union, this pressure largely dissipated within a few years.

The 2006 distancing ordinance sidestepped the grievances of victims of domestic violence, and in this disregard the new legal measure has joined a long-established practice of hollow, for-show-only legislation regarding gender-specific and gender-sensitive matters in Hungary. On the one hand, these types of laws invoke the memory of the communist regime. On the other hand, the postcommunist period has produced plenty of similar laws that superficially respond to international expectations but lack even the pretence of implementing EU gender equality directives or the UN's CEDAW (see also chapter 11 in the present volume). The list of actions of merely minimal compliance with external expectations regarding gender equality in Hungary includes the 1997 law against rape in marriage, the gender-specific applications of anti-discrimination in employment advertising, and the December 2006 modification of the law on harassment (Fekete 2008).

The disappearance of a serious and effective alliance among the three NGOs reflects the contentious and precarious state of civil society in Hungary. While NaNE found a new, dynamic, and internationally recognized partner in Amnesty International (AI), their common campaign in late 2006 could not push the Hungarian legislature any further. By widely publicizing the unheard cries of Hungarian women who do not enjoy even rudimentary protection from rape and sexual violence in the home (Amnesty International 2007), the cooperation with NaNE became part of AI's worldwide effort to draw attention to violence against women. Inspired by the US Silent Witness National Initiative to Stop Domestic Violence campaign, which began in 1991 (www.silentwitness.net), NaNe was the first organization outside the United States to reproduce the red cutout images, but modified them by putting data about Hungarian victims on the cutouts' large identifier tags. Starting out with fourteen handmade figurines in 1998, NaNE has used these images of violence on the streets to demand attention to

Figure 8.2. A demonstration in Budapest, *"Néma tanúk"* (Silent Witnesses) project, Hungary. Courtesy of *NaNE*, Budapest, Hungary.

domestic violence in every year since then (see http://16akcionap.org and figure 8.2).

In addition to AI, the Minnesota Advocates for Human Rights (MAHR, www.mnadvocates.org) joined to exert pressure on the Hungarian government and many of its neighbors. MAHR invited fellow NGOs and government representatives to a February 2008 regional workshop to enhance legal reforms against domestic violence (correspondence with Cheryl Thomas, director of MAHR, January 2008). The notable involvements of AI and MAHR in Hungary signal the broadening spectrum of global actors and their increasing impact in holding governments liable for providing legal protection and shelter for victims of domestic violence.

The Nature of Global Influences Affecting the Definition of and Policies Regarding the Elimination of Domestic Violence in Postcommunist Central and Eastern Europe

The changes in defining and dealing with domestic violence in Central and Eastern Europe developed due to the persistent efforts of an internationally engaged set of activists. The relationship between NGOs, international organizations, and national governments is increasingly taking place on a global level. The actual phenomenon of exchanges between countries of people, ideas, and technology is certainly not novel. The term "globalization" appeared in the popular vocabulary in the early 1970s, and globalization debates in the popular press and in academic discourse have been growing steadily ever since (Mittelman 2002; Scholte 2005). Indeed, one would be hard pressed to find anyone who denies that recent decades have witnessed at least some increased interconnectedness and "greater interdependence and mutual awareness (reflexivity) among economic, political, and social units in the world, and among actors in general" (Guillén 2001: 236). Analysts consider the global economy, politics, and culture when studying what have traditionally been considered domestic affairs (Evans 1997; True and Mintrom 2001).

This section investigates to what extent globalization is driving the processes and decisions regarding domestic violence, and to what extent these decisions and actions are affecting the processes of globalization in Hungary in particular and in Central and Eastern Europe in general. To answer this question, we need to learn what kinds of global forces have affected the debates on defining and trying to eliminate violence in intimate relationships in the Central and Eastern European countries of Poland, the Czech Republic, Slovakia, Hungary, and Slovenia. The manner in which international governmental organizations (such as the European Union, the UN, and the Council of Europe), international non-governmental organizations (INGOs, such as Amnesty International), international law (for example, the UN's CEDAW Convention and EU directives), and emerging international norms (i.e., democratization and respect for human rights) impact deliberations on domestic violence are of special concern in this region, which has become more open and vulnerable to global forces during its many transformations in the past decade.

The increasing and interwoven processes of political, economic, and cultural integration are part of the many, and often contradictory, effects of globalization (Pieterse 2004). Globalization, seemingly unstoppable, is spilling further over into many fields both abstractly, for example via the dispersion of human rights norms, and more concretely, via personal travel and increased trade of goods and services, to previously less affected geographic areas, such as Central and Eastern Europe (Risse et al. 1999; Soysal 1994). Central and Eastern Europe's dramatic and rapid shift from the relatively self-contained "second" or Communist Bloc to active membership in Western alliances demonstrates the increasingly wide reach of globalization (Fábián 2007b).

The collapse of Soviet-style communism in Europe also signaled the end of the last ideologically, materially, and militarily formidable bastion outside of capitalist and globalizing trends. The effects of globalization are especially intense in this recently reintegrated part of the world. But whether globalization is "civilizing, destructive or feeble," as Mauro Guillén (2001) asks, remains a hotly debated question. Depending on one's political value orientation, globalization is welcome, and its effect of bringing up human rights norms defined in universal terms may appear liberating. On the other hand, globalization can also be seen as an intrusive force that twists, distorts, colonizes, or otherwise unfavorably changes previous cultural and political norms. This latter sentiment is one major reason why NGOs working for the criminalization of domestic violence in Central and Eastern Europe often refrain from openly identifying foreign funders as their financial or ideological supporters. For example, NaNE, Hungary's most well-known domestic abuse hotline, was very reluctant to acknowledge in an open listserve of woman activists that 95 percent of their funding has come from abroad since the organization's founding in 1994. They saw this otherwise public data as potentially compromising their effectiveness in lobbying the broader public and the circles of political decisionmaking (e-mail correspondence with NaNE activist 2007).

Globalization has profoundly affected how we recognize and deal with domestic violence. While the women's movement has, since its inception, focused on discrimination against women in its many guises, only relatively recently have activists paid attention to domestic violence and successfully campaigned against bodily harm (Keck and Sikkink 1998). The debate over the nature of domestic violence and the solutions to eliminate it in Central and Eastern Europe show not only how the borders of states became more permeable (as internationalization would suggest) but also how the characteristics of the state and many of the policy actors have fundamentally changed their features due to the multiple levels of interactions between citizens, social movements, and their many organizations of both state and nonstate origin, amounting to a deeper transnational transformation—globalization. The circulation of people, goods, norms, and social movements, with their especially powerful US-influenced rights discourses and cultural influence (see Grewal 2004), has created supraterritorial subjects that are increasingly dynamic, producing and transforming politics, economics, and culture both within and beyond national boundaries.

It is perplexing why and how women's NGOs managed to engage with various international organizations (such as the UN and EU), while national institutions have often remained closed to the politically marginal groups for whom the women's groups advocate. What does the shift from national government to global governance signify, and what are the ramifications of this shift to political participation among Hungarian women's groups? The emergence of domestic violence as a transnationally resonant theme for women's mobilization represents a departure from globalization working in favor of privacy rights, tending to make governments less transparent at the expense of the broader public interest (Sassen 2006).

The increasingly globally interconnected nature of actors who engage with domestic violence policy underlines the interpretation of globalization as supraterritorialization. This school of thought does not negate the influence of states and their local agencies; rather it highlights how the modus operandi has altered, and it adds multicentricity to the previously almost exclusively state-centered international perspective (Ferguson and Rosenau 2003). Today, this "polymorphous world" (Mittelman 2004: 221) incorporates nonstate actors, such as women's groups and their allies, and it conditions what kind of norms can travel across borders.

While globalization certainly helped to create many of the favorable political conditions that brought about the emergence of democratization and the development of civil society in the postcommunist world, it also produced many of the destabilizing economic conditions that the countries in the region continue to struggle with. The next segments will describe the effects of these global influences in more detail, with special emphasis on the symbolic order of international norms, such as democratization and human rights. Globalization is no longer exclusively about the interconnectedness of markets; it also, if partially and situationally, embraces the globalization of human rights. The long third wave of democratization (Huntington 1991) after World War II made these rights and norms more accessible throughout the world (see, for example, Langley 1991; Lockwood and Ferguson 1998).

The Production of Norms in Central and Eastern Europe: Democratization, Human Rights, and Women's Rights

The emerging global norms of engagement include democratization and respect for human rights. These norm/expectations have lifted the conceptual filter of ignoring domestic violence in Central and Eastern Europe. Norms are shared behaviors and broadly accepted beliefs that may or may not be codified. They often amount to an ethical (normative) claim about what actors should or should not do; as a result they are frequently contested in the public sphere, and they increasingly emerge as themes of national and international debate. Some of these norms become internationalized and, in the place of armies and economic might, have become the leverage of global power politics.

How do norms emerge and what are their effects? The central problem with norms is how to explain change (Finnemore and Sikkink 1998: 894). While struggling with definitional problems of normative change and an abundance of case studies, Risse and Sikkink (1999) have developed a five-step model entailing the following stages: 1) state repression, 2) denial, 3) tactical concessions, 4) prescriptive status, and 5) rule-consistent behavior. Domestic violence policies in Central and Eastern Europe have moved from the first steps to occasional denial and a vacillation between steps 3 and 4, where the governments may offer some tactical concessions and the NGOs make regular prescriptive references to international norms as valid for Central and Eastern Europe. At least in part because of high internal pressure and external expectations, Slovenia moved to step 5 by introducing specific legislation against domestic violence in 2008 and further enhanced the definition of this step by including economic violence (see chapter 7 in this volume).

Despite the significant international diversity of definitions of and policies regarding domestic violence, a set of guidelines has emerged which, after decades of practice, can be considered as an emerging set of international norms. The set of international norms related to domestic violence includes several aspects (with considerable flexibility built in for differences in legal systems and customs), such as specific domestic violence laws, separate and quickly available domestic violence courts, distancing ordinances against perpetrators, reliable funding for independent women's shelters and hotlines, and training of judges, police, social workers, and health care providers to recognize and treat domestic violence victims without further traumatizing them.

Some of the emerging rules of state behavior regarding victims of domestic violence have been codified in international treaties, such as the UN's CEDAW and the 1995 Beijing Platform for Action, national law (as in Austria, Sweden, and the United States), and they are listed in best practices handbooks (e.g., WAVE), training manuals (e.g., the EU's Daphne-financed publications). In addition, scholars also refer to these aspects of policies when assessing the reach and impact of national policies on violence against women (e.g., Bunch 1995; Buzawa and Buzawa

2002; Clarke 1997; Deanham and Gillespie 1999; Dobash and Dobash 1992; Elman 1996a; Hanmer and Itzin 2000; Weldon 2002).

Recognizing Domestic Violence as a Measure of the Quality of Democracy

In addition to the more traditional explanations citing internal economic collapse and external military pressure as the main causes of the collapse of the communist system in Central and Eastern Europe (Kotkin 2001; Roskin 2002), other explanations pointing to the effect of emerging international norms of democracy and human rights have been steadily gaining attention (Thomas 2001). Standards and norms of behavior, most notably democratization and respect for human rights, are expected to shape and legitimate states as social actors in the international arena (Meyer et al. 1997). These norms, in their many permutations, became some of the strongest influences on laws on and attitudes toward domestic violence in Central and Eastern Europe. Central and Eastern European women's groups routinely implied in their appeals to local authorities that the degree to which postcommunist countries were willing to respond to domestic violence can be used to measure their desire to honor their integration into the community of democratic nations.

In addition to referring to democratic norms, women's NGOs actively used the avenues provided by the new and more open political framework to bring their arguments to decisionmakers and the general public. NGOs devised broad public awareness campaigns complete with billboards placed at major intersections. Large-sized posters became the public image of many NGOs' campaigns that creatively combined street-shock techniques rooted in their home environments and borrowed arguments from abroad.[7] These NGOs tried to shake their environment of what they perceive as social complacency toward a widespread and devastating kind of crime: domestic violence. These posters carried the argument and an often shocking image that domestic violence crime undermines women's capability to participate as equal members of society and the state is obliged to assist them to escape such a predicament.

One of the main funding agencies of the regional public awareness-raising campaigns was the Women's Program of the New York– and Budapest-based Open Society Institute (OSI). OSI supported the movements against domestic violence in Poland, the Czech Republic, and Hungary (see figures 8.3 and 8.4).

Figure 8.3. *"Dom to nie ring"* ("The home should never be a boxing ring"). *Centrum Praw Kobiet*'s poster, Polish part of regional public awareness-raising campaign against domestic violence supported by the Women's Network Program of the New York– and Budapest-based Soros Foundation's Open Society Institute. *Zero tolerancji dla PRZEMOCY wobec kobiet.* At www.cpk.org.pl/pl.php5/on/home (accessed August 7, 2008). Courtesy of *Centrum Praw Kobiet*, Warsaw, Poland.

Figure 8.4. . . . *ta žehlička me popálila úpln ě náhodou celkem 5X* (. . . the iron burned me completely accidentally all of five times. She was afraid to speak the truth. You must not be. Stop domestic violence!) ROSA's poster. ROSA was the coordinator of ten Czech NGOs in the 2003 Campaign against Domestic Violence against Women, organized with the support of the Open Society Foundation. See www.stopnasili.cz/. Courtesy of *ROSA*, Prague, Czech Republic (www.rosa-os.cz/english-resume/about-us).

These images still reverberate in everyday conversations and political discourse. Particularly controversial and durable in its effect was the anti–domestic violence campaign in Poland (see figure 8.5 and chapter 6 in this volume).

Similarly, UNIFEM supported the publication costs of another *Centrum Praw Kobiet*'s poster against domestic violence that put a man "behind bars" for hitting his partner, while other Central and Eastern NGOs, such as the Hungarian NaNE, were successful gaining the US State Department's funding to pay for their poster. NaNE's poster depicted the statistics that every fifth women becomes victim of domestic violence in her lifetime (figure 8.6).

Other NGOs, for example in Slovenia, plastered the stairs of busy intersections with posters proclaiming the usual excuses of "falling down the stairs," reminding people not to close their eyes to such obvious lies aimed at covering up physical abuse in the home (figure 8.7).

The Slovene public awareness-raising campaign brilliantly juxtaposed lyrics from popular folk song (*"Kaj ti je, deklica?"* [What's up, girl?] with the beaten image of a woman (see figure 8.8). The NGOs connected the well-known song with the new message that "Every Fifth Woman" becomes victim of domestic violence in her lifetime, thus providing a name for the campaign.

Mobilizations by letter writing and occasional popular protests propelled NGOs working on domestic violence to challenge the sacrosanct image of the nuclear family and reverse some of the neoliberal trends of noninterference in the private sphere. The NGOs achieved this feat by not relying exclusively on foreign funding but also, and most importantly, by creating resonant outreach ideas. These NGOs constantly invited the media to their activities, used the testimony of domestic violence survivors in town meetings, held trainings for jurors, the police, welfare workers, and health professionals, organized conferences, wrote many open letters to national and local legislators and bureaucrats, and frequently and repeatedly cited the statistics of callers to their hotlines (because no other victim statistics were available). Due to the relentless activities of NGOs, the problem of domestic violence has shed its cloak of anonymity and has become an issue for public debate.

Despite the intention of many NGOs to establish a feminist-inspired, women-specific focus for discussion, terminology, and policy, they could not fully transform the media and policy focus on the abuse of children, even if most data implied that women are the most frequent victims of domestic abuse. Owing to internal resistance to feminist interpretations and the perception of EU expectations, the bills and police directives

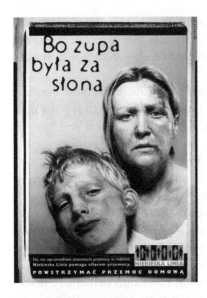

Figure 8.5. *"Bo zupa była za słona"* ("Because the soup was too salty"), *"Bo wyglądała zbyt atrakcyjnie"* ("Because she was too attractive"), *"Bo musiał jakoś odreagować"* ("Because he had to express himself"). Polish posters against domestic violence. Courtesy of *Państwowa Agencja Rozwiązywania Problemów Alkoholowych* /PARPA (State Agency for the Prevention of Alcohol-Related Problems), a specialized government agency subordinated to the Polish Minister of Health.

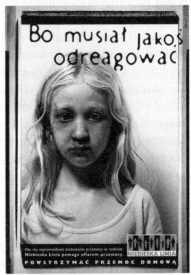

were increasingly drafted in a gender-blind manner. Membership in the European Union (in 2004) automatically made the new Central and Eastern European countries signatories to the 1997 Amsterdam Treaty, which seeks greater emphasis on citizenship and participatory democracy, and it introduced gender mainstreaming (Pollack and Hafner-Burton 2000). Curiously, and perhaps counterintuitively, these EU directives also added to the pressure to promote gender-neutrality in policy if the NGOs wanted to be successful in the legislative arena.

Figure 8.6. *Minden ötödik nőt rendszeresen ver a férje vagy élettársa* (Every fifth woman is regularly beaten by her husband or partner). NaNE's poster in Hungary. At www.nane.hu/images/mindenotodik.jpg (accessed August 7, 2008). Courtesy of *NaNE*, Budapest, Hungary.

The numerous and heated conflicts over the naming of domestic violence (see the introduction and chapter 6 in this volume) and the pursuant debates on policy reveal that domestic violence touches on a raw nerve of unsettled gender issues and belongs to the list of long-neglected social problems affecting a large segment of the population. In theory, democracy should not leave such large groups voiceless.

Figure 8.7. *"Vsaka 5. ženska, 'pada po stopnicah'"* ("Every fifth woman 'fell down the stairs'"). *Društvo Ženska svetovalnica* (Women's Counseling Service), Ljubljana, Slovenia. At www.drustvo-zenska-svetovalnica.si/a_nasilje.php (accessed November 7, 2009). Courtesy of *Društvo Ženska svetovalnica.*

However, one may agree with Arundhati Roy's viewpoint: "We know of course there's really no such thing as the 'voiceless.' There are only the deliberately silenced, or the preferably unheard" (Roy 2004).

It was the international women's movement that first pointed out the devastation and injustice created by violence in the home, and they observed that this violence disproportionately targets women and girls. Even if "preferably unheard," the women's movement worldwide has rather successfully argued that women and the issues affecting them need to be incorporated into decisionmaking. Under the all-encompassing ideal of democracy, where it is difficult to deny that women's rights are also human rights, this argument harmonizes well.

Figure 8.8. *"Kaj ti je, deklica?"* ("What's up, girl?") *"Vsaka Peta"* ("Every fifth woman") *Društvo SOS telefon za ženske in otroke—žrtve nasilja* (Association SOS Help-Line for Women and Children—Victims of Violence), Ljubljana, Slovenia. At www.drustvo-sos.si (accessed November 7, 2009). Courtesy of *Društvo SOS telefon za ženske in otroke—žrtve nasilja.*

Women's Rights as Human Rights

The diffusion of human rights norms both geographically and abstractly has emerged as a consequence of the global waves of democratization. How did the women's movement manage to frame domestic violence as part of the human rights agenda?

Since the 1970s, the international women's movement has increasingly created public forums to denounce violations of women's human rights. This activism has produced broad changes in various laws and policies, such as welfare, employment, and even immigration (Kerr and Sweetman 2003; Lockwood and Ferguson 1998). In the Beijing 1995 UN conference, defining human rights as women's rights bridged the gaps between various national agendas. The linking of women's rights to the human rights agenda has inspired and dramatically strengthened the international women's movement. From orderly UN conferences to dramatic invasions of women wearing pink slips into the 2004 US Republican National Convention in New York City, activists forced delegates to recognize violence against women as a human rights violation (Friedman 1995; Kaplan 2001; Mertus and Goldberg 1994).

The notion of human rights has become a pervasive element of contemporary international relations. The Universal Declaration of Human Rights of 1948, the European Convention on Human Rights of 1950, and the International Covenant on Civil and Political Rights of 1966, which were eventually incorporated into the laws of many countries (including those of Central and Eastern Europe), started to contest the exclusive model of politics and rights anchored in national sovereignty. Invocation of human rights established and advanced universal claims as it legitimated claims for rights both within and outside of national borders. However, these pieces of international law had no real power or influence until the end of the Cold War. After the collapse of the Soviet system, the notion of human rights strengthened and expanded. Human rights are evoked today with increased frequency and in an ever-widening circle of domestic and international issues, including the right to a clean environment, the right to marry, and the right to protection from domestic violence. The new, "third generation" of human rights can connect the "first generation" liberal agenda of political and civil liberties with the "second generation" economic rights that used to be the claim and domain of the Communist Bloc (Orend 2002), stating that the lack of physical safety prevents victims of domestic violence from fully participating in political deliberations.

Until the 1990s, human rights centered on torture, genocide, and similar extreme forms of abuse where the perpetrators are most often identifiable political organizations. Since the mid-1990s, however, the international women's movement, along with other human rights organizations such as Amnesty International, has broadened the meaning of human rights not only to include the most extreme and brutal, and often state-sponsored, atrocities, but also to reveal and prosecute human rights violations that were hidden in the private sphere, including various violations of specifically women's human rights.

Due to contact with the postcolonial and the postcommunist regions, the Western-inspired, liberal, and by 1989 dominant framework of human rights and activism was not in outright opposition to broadening the definition of domestic violence to include economic violence (see chapter 3 in this volume for details). However, this broadening is tenuous at best, because these conceptualizations, at least partly, contradict. Empirically, this conflict first emerged as many postcommunist women's groups struggled to include job- and welfare-related matters on their agenda when they applied for funding from abroad.

The Western-inspired human rights concept frames social change as a problem of individual responsibility and rights. Its proposed solution is to teach recognition of the illegitimacy of intimate violence, to learn about the dreadful consequences, especially for women, for the workplace, for children who witness it, etc., as well as the importance of understanding the existing legal provisions (calling the police, reporting to a social worker). These steps are potentially empowering, though this liberal framework presumes and naturalizes the concept of the individual. Consequently, the liberal framework of domestic violence does not critique the conditions that produce violence. For instance, within this framework, it does not make sense to question the lack of public housing or challenge any other sort of structural inequality that is reproduced in private spaces. Cultural institutions that maintain violence as normal also fall outside of the purview of the individual-centered liberal framework. Thus being a victim or a witness of violence equals to moving to the margins, and these situations are experienced as shameful. Without a functioning system that questions the political, economic, and cultural foundations of violence, attempting to leave an abusive situation can be deadly or a dead-end.

Notwithstanding these important limitations, framing women's deprivations as a violation of human rights is not merely a shift in rhetoric; it is a fundamental, legally oriented trend in social movement activism that has been taking place worldwide, possibly due to the global effect of US legal traditions that moved most social movement activities into the legal arena (see, for example, on abortion, Hull et al. 2004; on animal rights, Trägårdh 2004; on hate crimes, Jenness 2001; on and the peace movement Dewar et al. 1986). Groups providing assistance for victims of domestic violence extended the meaning of human rights to relations in the private sphere. The NGOs pointed to the connection between a victim's survival and gender-sensitive state institutions, such as state-sponsored crisis intervention centers, domestic violence courts, and specially trained police officers who investigate rape and abuse charges. Without such provisions, they claim, the state is in flagrant violation of its duty to protect its citizens from abuse.

Unintended Consequences of Global Interactions: Limited NGO Autonomy and Professionalization

In becoming part of an international trend, domestic violence has become an issue with an identifiable extent and character throughout postcommunist Central and Eastern Europe. Even more importantly, the sustained presence of the issue in public discourse has facilitated political discussions resulting in legislative and policy changes that aim to prevent and prosecute cases of domestic violence. At the time of writing in 2009, every postcommunist Central and Eastern European country, with the notable exception of Hungary, has passed legislation specifically addressing domestic violence.

Raising the profile of this issue has been the self-assigned task of maverick women's groups and human rights social movement organizations that saw an opportunity in applying feminist arguments to their own environments. Responding to a narrowing reception of their claims after the early democratic transition period, these women's groups increasingly adapted themes of activism that had Western philosophical and policy background as well as potential sources of foreign funding. Acting in unison with global social movement trends, activists in Central and Eastern Europe chose to steer their organizations in a single-issue–oriented direction, for example by targeting domestic violence, in contrast to pursuing broad welfare themes such as retirement age or maternity leave.

The success (albeit limited) of social movement activism related to domestic violence demonstrates the significant impact of the increasing interconnectedness of Central and Eastern European women's activism with global actors and trends. The NGOs in Central and Eastern Europe developed later than and differently from their predecessors in the West, and they ended up rather dependent on their foreign donors and the state. Such unintended consequences will likely influence their activities and, in the long term, the quality of the resulting democracy.

The NGOs working with victims of domestic violence adjusted to both the global and the domestic environment, but this triggered at least two types of accidental consequences: limited autonomy and professionalization. Facing a stalemate regarding the feminist and gender-neutral interpretations driving domestic violence policy, some NGOs moved into service provision by becoming professionalized and thus often co-opted by the state, while others responded by trying to strengthen their international connections and mounting the occasional open protest to draw attention to their claim. While the NGOs invoked feminist reasoning to draw attention to the gendered nature of domestic violence, supported their claims by citing international treaties (such as the UN's CEDAW) signed by each of these countries, and extensively referred to the norms of human rights and democratization, many groups were willing to work with gender-neutral terminology and a more traditional and child-centered image of the family if that would bring more allies and government cooperation as a result.

These consequences are interrelated because they both emerge from the weaknesses of civil society in Central and Eastern Europe and a consequent dependence on state or foreign funding. Some scholar-activists claim that "where feminists cannot create options beyond those three sites [of state, market, and family], women's welfare, safety, and equality are profoundly compromised" (Brush 2002: 169). But civil society, and within it the women's groups assisting victims of domestic violence, did not start out, and has not become, autonomous. The weakness of civil society traditions in Central and Eastern Europe pressed the emerging NGOs dealing with domestic violence victims to rely on state and/or international donors for survival.

The NGOs in the Central European postcommunist countries, and especially the associations working with domestic violence victims, emerged rather differently from the trajectory of the similarly aimed Western European and North American groups. In Western Europe and North America these groups originally organized largely on a volunteer basis, more strictly following nongovernmental and non-familial logic to shelter women battered by husbands and boyfriends. While the Western European and North American shelter NGOs emerged as an unaffiliated sphere between state, market, and family to protect women and only later, and even then only partially, accepted state funding, the Central and Eastern European NGOs became immediately dependent on state funding and/or international donors. In the case of Russian shelter groups, this support reached a level of near full reliance on one major foreign financial supporter, the Ford Foundation (see Hemment 2004; Henderson 2000).

International support for NGOs in Central and Eastern Europe has undoubtedly been crucial in promoting democracy, but dependence on foreign funding calls into question the quality and type of the resulting democracy (Diamond 1999: 252–255). In the fight for institutional survival, especially when international donors move on to other parts of the world, NGOs often turn to local and national governments for funding and become (partial) replacements for state social service providers.

Shelter NGOs all over the world have a rather contradictory relationship with the state. Just like its many Western counterparts, the Central and Eastern European movement argues that the state has to take responsibility for the basic welfare of domestic violence victims. In addition to the theoretical and normative arguments of referring to basic human rights and democratic citizenship, NGOs observe on the everyday practical level that battered persons need a wide array of public provisions. This frequent contact also pushes the NGOs to establish a close connection with state representatives and service providers.

However, over-reliance on state funding can easily compromise the hard-won autonomy of women's groups. Also, upon contracting the state or local government for supplying services for battered persons, NGOs offer an avenue to "offload public provisions" (Banaszak et al. 2003: 7). By outsourcing services, states do not need to give an assurance that these services will be continued long-term if the targeted population grows or when conditions of austerity strike. These are gendered ramifications of neoliberal "dumping" of responsibility on individuals, many of them women (Fraser 1989).

The lack of autonomy also makes NGOs susceptible to changing their agenda. Central and Eastern European NGOs' foci came to reflect external funding expectations. To avoid competing against one another for funds, the main groups often informally divided up the roles of taking care of domestic violence victims by focusing exclusively on, for example, psychological services, or providing an information hotline or perpetrator programs, as happened between the three main provider organizations in Hungary and Slovenia (interviews, NaNE, HCWG in Budapest, Hungary, and the Association against Violent Communication, Ljubljana, October 2004 and May 2006; see also chapter 7 of this volume). To fit the funder's expectations, many NGOs also streamlined their operations and became more (single-) issue–oriented and often professionalized.

The second major accidental consequence of globalization is professionalization. Instead of relying on volunteers, the survival method among Central and Eastern European associations was to register as an NGO and to become quickly institutionalized and professionalized. Because they could not rely on their own resources and constituencies, the NGOs immediately turned to outside funding sources, which also forced them to employ professional staff, first for grant writing and, upon its success, to contract social workers to lead or to replace volunteers. In the process of professionalization, NGOs may lose their connection to social movements. Shelters may become like state social service agencies, effectively excluding most women from participation (Morgan 1981).[8]

Professionalization, and the transparency and accountability required of social movement organizations in postcommunist Europe by state and foreign funding sources, also shifted the focus of women's organizations from broad demands for more ephemeral goals, such as justice and gender equality, to much more narrowly defined themes. As women's organizations began to institutionalize in the form of NGOs, the ones that managed to survive and become successful most often became single-issue–focused and professionalized. In contrast, the beginnings of the Western European and North American shelter organizations were both organizationally and politically very different. The early shelter movement prided itself on not requiring official documentation from the women seeking a place to stay and emphasized awareness-raising and community building as political education. In the West, many former victims became shelter workers, but this step was largely omitted in Central and Eastern Europe because financial sponsors gave preference to professionally accredited service organizations whom they considered more trustworthy (and potentially less controversial). Consequently, many Central and Eastern European NGOs shunned and isolated those victims who wanted to become part of their activities. Integrating these women into NGOs could have provided sorely needed permanent legitimacy in the domestic environments by their personal testimonials that the abstract international human rights norms alone could not provide. Missing out rather persistently on this link to domestic violence survivors in Central and Eastern Europe highlights the constraining conditions of NGOs filled with the short-term anxieties of funding and truncated feminist political mandates.

Postcommunist Central and Eastern Europe has been balancing between two contested positions regarding domestic violence. On the one hand, most governments and NGOs do not wish to challenge the traditional gender roles. By focusing on children, they could avoid slipping into the contested (gender) territories. On the other hand, some Central and Eastern European NGOs and the international shelter movement have found that this accommodation unacceptably reinforces women's traditional roles (Geske and Bourque 2001: 259; Itzin 2000). Non-accommodationists point to the UN's CEDAW, according to which neutrality should have no legitimacy (Landsberg-Lewis 1998: 3).

Anti–domestic violence movements across Central and Eastern Europe have been interconnected both regionally and internationally, reinforcing, borrowing, and cross-fertilizing in aims and methods. The most active Central and Eastern European NGOs have been fundamentally influenced by feminist interpretations of democracy and the international human rights agenda. These NGOs skillfully maneuvered around their own national state apparatus to find a leverage point by raising at least the image of international expectations, thereby applying a threat of a boomerang effect. These NGOs' efforts affected a broad segment of the population and opened public space by making visible the previously hidden/invisible phenomenon of domestic violence.

The emerging network of communication and coordination among the activists dealing with domestic violence testifies how culture, power, and public space are increasingly interconnected and becoming transnational in the process (Guidry, Kennedy, and Zald 2000). Without the globalization of human rights issues, the spread of corresponding legal concepts, and increasing personal connections and information networks, the mobilization of activists on domestic violence could not have happened so soon after the 1989 revolutions in Central and Eastern Europe (see also Colás 2002).

The new, traveling nature of human rights reflects a different logic and praxis of the international system. Rights previously defined as national (in Western liberal frameworks) are becoming entitlements, globally legitimized on the basis of personhood. The normative framework for, and the legitimacy of, this model derives from transnational discourse and structures that choose to raise human rights as a world-level organizing principle. The expansion of political discourse beyond national closure establishes a "supraterritorialized" (Scholte 2005) or "post-national" (Soysal 1994) polity. The global system shapes the parameters of membership: aspects that have been crucial to Central and Eastern Europe's integration into regional (EU), transatlantic (NATO), and global (UN, etc.) political, cultural, and economic currents through at least nominal democratization and the incorporation of human rights.

The tedious contestations of how to define, prevent, and deal with domestic violence prove that the political discourse only partially, and only under duress, demonstrates a readiness for integrating voices that challenge the status quo of existing gender hierarchies. From the viewpoints of activists and victims of domestic violence, the political aim of EU accession and the image of returning to the community of democratic nations have been proven at least partially helpful because they enabled social movement activists to challenge dominant discourses more successfully.

The contested nature of dealing with domestic violence in Central and Eastern Europe, and especially the fact that shelter NGOs have all encountered major opposition in their plight, demonstrate how "low-intensity" is the current state of democracy, particularly regarding women's issues and gender equality. The general requirements of this "hollow" democracy can be qualified as establishing regular electoral competition, which makes it exceedingly difficult to nudge publics and political representatives beyond this threshold. Social movements, most often in the institutional form of NGOs (domestic and international), counter this "low-intensity" democracy to forge democracy from below. The social movements have implicitly developed, via various NGOs, a "high-intensity" version of democracy that provides a much broader alternative to the minimalist form by inviting people to a more intense exchange of views and actions. The conflict and the contestation between these interpretations of democracy, especially regarding domestic violence, remain relevant and strong in contemporary Central and Eastern Europe.

NOTES

1. To learn more about WAVE's notable effect, see chapter 9 of this volume.

2. See the extensive data on country-specific laws and background materials available on the website dedicated to the 2008 Regional Conference on Domestic Violence Legal Reformworkshop: www.stopvaw.org/Regional_Conference_on_Domestic_Violence_Legal_Reform.html (accessed January 20, 2010).

3. With the exception of Slovenia, the 2003 Central and Eastern European campaigns were funded by the Women's Program of the New York– and Budapest-based Soros Foundation's Open Society Institute (OSI). Funded by financier George Soros in 1993, OSI is a private grantmaking institution to support his foundations in Central and Eastern Europe and the former Soviet Union. These foundations were established starting in 1984 to help countries make the transition from communism. OSI has expanded the activities of the Soros foundations network to encompass the United States and more than sixty countries in Europe, Asia, Africa, and Latin America. To achieve its "mission to build vibrant and tolerant democracies whose governments are accountable to their citizens," OSI seeks "to shape public policies that assure greater fairness in political, legal, and economic systems and safeguard fundamental rights." www.soros.org (accessed November 7, 2009).

4. While there are relatively few empirical studies on the prevalence of domestic violence in postcommunist Europe, a preponderance of evidence, from the ledger of hotline calls to domestic violence NGOs to scholarly data and police reports, supports the pandemic label. For example, Olga Tóth found in her 1999 and 2002 studies that over one-third of Hungarians were raised in a threatening environment, and approximately 20 percent witnessed their father beat their mother. Similarly, Serbanescu and Goodwin note stunningly high proportions of domestic violence in various postcommunist countries, ranging from 5 percent in Georgia to 29 percent in Romania for reported lifetime experience of spousal physical abuse (2005).

5. The Slovene exception to the Central and Eastern European pattern may have two important explanations that provide hope for both the future development of democratization and, for our purposes here, the development of better services for

victims of domestic violence. First, Slovenia's earlier and more complete implementation of domestic violence laws and services may arise from passage of the 1974 Law on Societies. This law allowed the formation of NGOs and let civil society begin to take root fifteen years earlier than in the other Central and Eastern European countries that allowed NGOs to form (Fink-Hafner 1993). Second, Slovenia also took an earlier and stronger part in global and European regional integration than the other then-communist countries. Building on the more open nature of travel and exchange of goods and information, Slovenia integrated to global and European trends decades earlier than other parts of the region (Bandelj 2004; Mrak et al. 2004). It escaped the Third Balkan Wars (1991–2001) relatively unscathed and, as a sign of a robust economy, managed to adopt the euro in January 2007, first among the 2004 Central and Eastern European EU entrants. In addition to recognition of its achievements in economic integration, Slovenia gained further political and symbolical approval by acting as the first postcommunist president of the Council of the European Union (EU) during the first half of 2008. The two factors of a viable civil society and global/regional integration have produced a 2008 Slovene domestic violence legislation that stands out in the region as comprehensive in recognizing and supporting victims of domestic violence, even though many problems remain regarding financing of these operations (see chapter 7 in this volume for more details). Both of these factors (civil society in the form of local NGOs, and integration into global/European trends) play a formidable role in explaining how domestic violence is constructed and dealt with in the Central and Eastern European postcommunist contexts.

6. Keck and Sikkink (1998) demonstrate that local activist networks can exert pressure on their own governments via their international connections. Local NGOs, when blocked by authoritarian rule or other obstacles from reaching their own governments, contact their counterparts abroad, who in return enter into dialogue with their government. This foreign government can then exert direct leverage on the original country's leadership, thereby finishing the return of the "boomerang."

7. Central and Eastern European NGOs have often produced signature-gathering campaigns to push for legislation recognizing domestic violence as a distinct type of crime. Some NGOs have also set up public testimonials or mock trials, where witnesses of domestic violence could tell their stories. The public testimonial was a novel type of communication that they learned from each other and adapted from Western Europe and the United States to raise attention to their plight.

8. Similar tensions emerged between the broad issue-based grassroots organizations and NGOs in Latin America, where NGOs' international engagement has exacerbated the gap between those with skills in international diplomacy and the average activist population (see Geske and Bourque 2001).

WORKS CITED

Acsády, Judit. 2004. *Emancipáció és identitás* (Emancipation and identity). Ph.D. diss., Budapest: ELTE Sociology Department.

Amnesty International. 2007. *Magyarország: Meg nem hallott segélykiáltások—A nők nem kapnak megfelelő védelmet a családon belüli szexális erőszak ellen.* (Hungary: Cries unheard—The failure to protect women from rape). www.amnesty.org/en/library/info/EUR27/002/2007 (accessed November 8, 2009).

Avdeyeva, Olga. 2006. "The Beijing Platform for Action, Domestic Violence, and a Symbolic Policy Response: Policies Against Domestic Violence in Post-communist Countries." Paper delivered at the APSA Annual Meeting, Philadelphia, Pa., August 31–September 3, www.allacademic.com/meta/p152156_index.html (accessed November 8, 2009).

Banaszak, Lee, Karen Beckwith, and Dieter Rucht, eds. 2003. "When Power Relocates: Interactive Changes in Women's Movements and States." *Women's Movements Facing the Reconfigured State*, 1–29. Cambridge: Cambridge University Press.

Bandelj, Nina. 2004. "Negotiating Global, Regional, and National Forces: Foreign Investment in Slovenia." *East European Politics and Societies* 18(3): 455–480.

Brush, Lisa. 2002. "Changing the Subject: Gender and Welfare Regime Studies." *Social Politics* 9 (Summer): 161–186.

Bunch, Charlotte. 1995. "On Globalizing Gender Justice: Women of the World Unite." *The Nation* 261(7): 230–235.

Buzawa, Eve, and Carl Buzawa. 2002. *Domestic Violence: The Criminal Justice Response*. Thousand Oaks, Calif.: Sage.

Clarke, Roberta. 1997. "Combating Violence Against Women in the Caribbean." In *Women against Violence: Breaking the Silence*, ed. Ana Maria Brasiliero. Reflecting on Experience in Latin America and the Caribbean. New York: UNIFEM.

Colás, Alejandro. 2002. *International Civil Society*. Malden, Mass.: Polity Press.

Deanham, Dinna, and Joan Gillespie. 1999. *Two Steps Forward . . . One Step Back*. Health Canada: Family Violence Prevention Unit.

Dewar, John, Abdul Paliwala, Sol Picciotto, and Matthias Ruete, eds. 1986. *Nuclear Weapons, the Peace Movement and the Law*. Houndmills, UK: Macmillan.

Diamond, Larry, ed. 1999. *Developing Democracy: Toward Consolidation*. Baltimore, Md.: Johns Hopkins University Press.

Dobash, Emerson, and Russell Dobash. 1992. *Women, Violence and Social Change*. New York: Routledge.

Elman, Amy. 1996. *Sexual Subordination and State Intervention: Comparing Sweden and the United States*. Providence, R.I.: Beghahn.

Evans, Mary. 1997. *Introducing Contemporary Feminist Thought*. Cambridge;UK: Polity Press.

Fábián, Katalin. 2007a. Making an Appearance: The Formation of Women's Groups in Hungary. Vol. 1, No. 1, *Aspasia: International Yearbook for Women's and Gender History of Central, Eastern, and South Eastern Europe*, ed. Maria Bucur-Deckard, Francisca de Haan, and Krassimira Daskalova, 103–127. New York and Oxford: Berghahn Books.

———. 2009. *Contemporary Women's Movements in Hungary: Globalization, Democracy, and Gender Equality*. Washington, D.C.: Woodrow Wilson Center Press and Johns Hopkins University Press.

Fábián, Katalin, ed. 2007b. *Globalization: Perspectives from Central and Eastern Europe*. Oxford, UK: Elsevier Publishing.

Farkas, Tímea. 2006. "Csak, ha vér folyik?" (Only if blood is spilt?) *Népszabadság*, March 11. www.nol.hu/cikk/396981 (accessed November 8, 2009).

Fekete, Attila. 2008. "Bűncselekmény lett a zaklatás: Útmutatók híján a rendőrség nem tudja, mit tegyen" (Harassment has become a crime: Without clear orders, the police do not know what to do) *Népszabadság*, January 10, www.nol.hu/cikk/477156/ (November 8, 2009).

Felhívás (Petition) 2002. September 20. www.nane.hu/egyesulet/mediafigyelem/csalber_tv.html.

Ferguson, Yale, and James Rosenau. 2003. "Superpowerdom before and after September 11, 2001: A Postinternational Perspective." Paper presented at the annual meeting of the International Studies Association, Portland, Ore.

Fink-Hafner, Danica. 1993. "Slovenia in a Process of Transition to Political Democracy." In *The Legacy of the Democratic Opposition*, ed. Adolf Bibic and Gigi Graziano, 137–151. Ljubljana, Slovenia: SPSA.

Finnemore, Martha, and Kathryn Sikkink. 1998. "International Norms and Political Change." *International Organization* (Autumn): 887–917.

Fraser, Nancy. 1989. *Unruly Practices: Power, Discourse, and Gender in Contemporary Social Theory*. Minneapolis: University of Minnesota Press.

Friedman, Elisabeth. 1995. "Women's Human Rights: The Emergence of a Movement." In *Women's Rights Human Rights: International Feminist Perspectives*, ed. Julie Peters and Andrea Wolper, 8–35. New York: Routledge.

Geske, Mary, and Susan Bourque. 2001. "Grassroots Organizations and Women's Human Rights: Meeting the Challenge of the Local-global Link." In *Women, Gender, and Human Rights: A Global Perspective*, ed. Marjorie Agosín, 240–264. New Brunswick, N.J.: Rutgers University Press.

Grewal, Inderpal. 2004. *Transnational America: Feminisms, Diasporas, Neoliberalisms*. Chapel Hill, N.C.: Duke University Press.

Guidry, John, Michael Kennedy, and Meyer Zald, eds. 2000. *Globalizations and Social Movements: Culture, Power, and Transnational Public Sphere*. Ann Arbor: University of Michigan Press.

Guillén, Mauro. 2001. "Is Globalization Civilizing, Destructive, or Feeble? A Critique of Five Key Debates in the Social Science Literature." *Annual Review of Sociology* 27: 235–260.

Hanmer, Jalna, and Catherine Itzin, eds. 2000. *Home Truths about Domestic Violence: Feminist Influences on Policy and Practice*. New York: Routledge.

Hemment, Julie. 2004. "Global Civil Society and the Local Costs of Belonging: Defining Violence against Women in Russia." *Signs* 29(3): 815–840.

Henderson, Sarah. 2000. "Importing Civil Society." *Demokratizatsia* 8(1): 65–82.

Hughes, Donna, Lepa Mladjenovic, and Zorica Mrsevic. 1995. "Feminist Resistance in Serbia." *European Journal of Women's Studies* 2(4): 509–532.

Hull, Neh, William Hoffer, and Peter Hoffer, eds. 2004. *The Abortion Rights Controversy in America: A Legal Reader.* Chapel Hill: University of North Carolina Press.

Huntington, Samuel. 1991. *The Third Wave: Democratization in the Late Twentieth Century.* Norman: University of Oklahoma Press.

Jalušić, Vlasta. 2002. *Kako smo hodile v feministično gimnazijo.* (How we attended feminist high school). Ljubljana: Mirovni Inštitut (Peace Institute).

Jenness, Valerie, and Ryken Grattet. 2001. *Making Hate a Crime: From Social Movement to Law Enforcement.* New York: Russell Sage.

Kaplan, Temma. 2001. "Women's Rights as Human Rights: Women as Agents of Social Change." In *Women, Gender, and Human Rights: A Global Perspective,* ed. Marjorie Agosín, 191–204. New Brunswick, N.J.: Rutgers University Press.

Keck, Margaret, and Kathryn Sikkink. 1998. *Activists Beyond Borders: Transnational Activist Networks in International Politics.* Ithaca, N.Y.: Cornell University Press.

Kerr, Joanna, and Caroline Sweetman, eds. 2003. *Women Reinventing Globalisation.* Oxford: Oxfam.

Khan, Mehr. 2000. Editorial: Domestic Violence against Women and Girls. *Innocenti Digest* 6 (June). Florence, Italy: UNICEF. www.unicef-icdc.org/publications/pdf/digest6e.pdf (accessed November 8, 2009).

Kotkin, Stephen. 2001. *Armageddon Averted: The Soviet Collapse 1970–2000.* Oxford: Oxford University Press.

Landsberg-Lewis, Ilana, ed. 1998. Introduction. *Bringing Equality Home: Implementing the Convention on the Elimination of All Forms of Discrimination against Women,* 1–12. New York, NY: UNIFEM. www.unifem.org/attachments/products/BringingEqualityHome_eng.pdf (accessed November 8, 2009).

Langley, Winston, ed. 1991. *Women's Rights in International Documents: A Sourcebook with Commentary.* Jefferson, N.C.: McFarland.

Lister, Ruth. 1998. *Citizenship: Feminist Perspectives.* New York: New York University Press.

Lockwood, Carol, and Adelaide Ferguson, eds. 1998. *The International Human Rights of Women: Instruments of Change.* Washington, D.C.: American Bar Association, Section of International Law and Practice.

Mertus, Julie, and Pamela Goldberg. 1994. "A Perspective on Women and International Human Rights after the Vienna Declaration: The Inside/Outside Construct." *New York University Journal of International Law and Politics* 26(78): 201–230.

Meyer, John, John Boli, George Thomas, and Francisco Ramirez. 1997. "World Society and the Nation-state." *American Journal of Sociology* 103(1): 144–181.

Mittelman, James. 2004. "What Is Critical Globalization Studies?" *International Studies Perspectives* 5(3): 219–230.

Morgan, Patricia. 1981. "From Battered Wife to Program Client: The State's Shaping of Social Problems." *Kapitalistate* 9: 17–39.

Morvai, Krisztina. 1998. *Terror a családban: A feleségbántalmazás és a jog* (Terror in the family: Wife-battering and the law). Budapest: Kossuth Kiadó.

Mrak, Mojmir, Matija Rojec, and Carlos Silva-Jáuregui, eds. 2004. *Slovenia: From Yugoslavia to the European Union.* World Bank Publications.

NaNE Egyesület (NaNE Association) and Patent Egyesület (PATENT Association [People Against Patriarchy Association]). 2008. *Nyílt levél Draskovics Tibor Miniszter Úrnak* (Open letter to Tibor Draskovics, Minister of Justice and the Police). June 30. www.nane.hu/tavoltartas_2008_nane_patent.pdf (accessed July 29, 2008).

NaNE and HCWG. 2006. *Sajtóközlemény a 2006. Július elsején hatályba lépő távoltartásról szóló törvényi rendelkezésről* (Press release on the distancing ordinance to enter Hungarian law as of July 1, 2006). http://nane.hu/egyesulet/mediafigyelem/Tavoltartas_sajto_20060701_NANE_HCM.pdf (accessed November 8, 2009).

Open Society Institute. 2002. *Bending the Bow: Targeting Women's Human Rights and Opportunities.* New York: Network Women's Program, Open Society Institute. www.soros.org/initiatives/women/articles_publications/publications/bending bow_20020801/bending_the_bow.pdf.

————. 2006a. Violence against Women: Does the Government Care in the Czech Republic? *Fact Sheet 2006.* www.stopvaw.org/sites/3f6d15f4-c12d-4515-8544-26b7a3a5a41e/uploads/CZECHREPUBLIC_VAW_FACT_SHEET_2006_3.pdf (accessed November 8, 2009).

————. 2006b. Violence against Women: Does the Government Care in Hungary? *Fact Sheet 2006.* www.stopvaw.org/sites/3f6d15f4-c12d-4515-8544-26b7a3a5a41e/uploads/HUNGARY_VAW_FACT_SHEET_2006_FINAL_3.pdf (accessed November 8, 2009).

————. 2006c. Violence against Women: Does the Government Care in Poland? *Fact Sheet 2006.* www.stopvaw.org/sites/3f6d15f4-c12d-4515-8544-26b7a3a5a41e/uploads/POLAND_VAW_FACT_SHEET_2006_3.pdf (accessed November 8, 2009).

————. 2006d. Violence against Women: Does the Government Care in Slovakia? *Fact Sheet 2006.* www.stopvaw.org/sites/3f6d15f4-c12d-4515-8544-26b7a3a5a41e/uploads/SLOVAKIA_VAW_FACT_SHEET_2006_3.pdf (accessed November 8, 2009).

Orend, Brian. 2002. *Human Rights: Concept and Context.* Petersburg, Ontario: Broadview Press.

Országos Rendőrfőkapitány/ORFK. 2007. *Jelentés a családon belüli erőszak rendőri kezelésének 2006. évi tapasztalatairól: A távoltartás szabályozása és bevezetésének első tapasztalatai.* (Report on the actions of the police regarding domestic violence: First results of introducing the distancing ordinance). March 28. Budapest: Országos Rendőrfőkapitány. www.kriminologiaitdk.hu/tdk/download/je12006.doc (accessed November 8, 2009).

Országos Rendőrfőkapitány/ORFK. 2003. ORFK Intézkedése a családon belüli erőszak kezelésével és a kiskorúak védelmével kapcsolatos rendőri feladatok végrehajtására 13/2003 (Order No. 2003-13 of the Hungarian National Police Headquarters on police duties regarding domestic violence and the protection of children). March 27. Budapest: Országos Rendőrfőkapitány. www.nane.hu/eroszak/index.html (accessed June 8, 2009).

Pető, Andrea. 1998. *Nőhistóriák: A politizáló magyar nők története (1945–1951)* (Women's Stories: History of Hungarian Women in Politics (1945–1951). Budapest: Seneca. Published in English as *Women in Hungarian Politics, 1945–1951*. New York, NY: 2003.

Pieterse, Jan Nederveen. 2004. *Globalization and Culture.* Boulder, Colo.: Rowman and Littlefield.

Pollack, Mark, and Emilie Hafner-Burton. 2000. "Mainstreaming Gender in the European Union." *Journal of European Public Policy* 7(1) (September): 432–456.

Regulska, Joanna. 2003. "Constructing Supranational Political Spaces: Women's Agency in an Enlarged Europe." Paper presented at the 2003 annual convention of the American Association for the Advancement for Slavic Studies (AAASS). Toronto, Canada.

Risse, Thomas, Stephen Ropp, and Kathryn Sikkink, eds. 1999. *The Power of Human Rights: International Norms and Domestic Change.* New York: Cambridge University Press.

Roskin, Michael. 2002. *The Rebirth of East Europe.* Upper Saddle River, N.J.: Prentice Hall.

Roy, Arundhati. 2004. *Peace and the New Corporate Liberation Theology.* (The 2004 Sydney Peace Prize Lecture), November 4. www.usyd.edu.au/news/84.html?newsstoryid=279 (accessed November 8, 2009).

Sáfrány, Réka. 2003. *Public and Political Discourse on Domestic Violence in Hungary: The Prospects and Limits of Feminist Strategies.* MA thesis. Budapest: Central European University.

Sassen, Saskia. 2006. *Territory, Authority, Rights: From Medieval to Global Assemblages.* Princeton, N.J.: Princeton University Press.

Scholte, Jan Aart. 2005. *Globalization: A Critical Introduction.* 2nd rev. ed. New York: Palgrave Macmillian.

Serbanescu, Florina, and Mary Goodwin. 2005. "Domestic Violence in Eastern Europe: Levels, Risk Factors, and Selected Reproductive Health Consequences." Paper delivered at the European Conference on Interpersonal Violence, 26 September. Paris, France.

Smith, Jackie, Charles Chatfield, and Ron Pagnucco, eds. 1997. *Transnational Social Movements and Global Politics.* Syracuse, N.Y.: Syracuse University Press.

Soysal, Yasemin. 1994. *Limits of Citizenship: Migrants and Post-National Membership in Europe.* Chicago: University of Chicago.

Szász, Anna. 2001. A bántalmazott nők életét, érdekeit védelmező szervezetek. (Organizations that protect battered women). *Esély—Journal of Social Policy* 3.

Thomas, Daniel. 2001. *The Helsinki Effect: International Norms, Human Rights, and the Demise of Communism.* Princeton, N.J.: Princeton University Press.

Tóth, Olga. 1998. Erőszak a családban (Violence in the family). In *Vegyesváltó* (Mixed relay), ed. Katalin Lévai et al. Budapest: Egyenlő Esélyek Alapítvány.

Trägårdh, Lars, ed. 2004. *After National Democracy: Rights, Law and Power in America and the New Europe.* Oxford, UK: Hart Publishing.

True, Jacqui, and Michael Mintrom. 2001. "Transnational Networks and Policy Diffusion: The Case of Gender Mainstreaming." *International Studies Quarterly* 45(1): 27–57.

VAW Monitoring Program (UNIFEM, MAHR, Open Society Institute Network Women's Program, and ROSA). 2006. *Czech Republic. Stop Violence Against Women: A project by the advocates for human rights.* www.stopvaw.org/Czech_ Republic2.html (accessed November 8, 2009).

VAW Monitoring Program (UNIFEM, MAHR, Open Society Institute Network Women's Program, and NaNE). 2006. *Hungary. Stop Violence Against Women: A project by the advocates for human rights.* www.stopvaw.org/Hungary.html (accessed November 8, 2009).

VAW Monitoring Program (UNIFEM, MAHR, Open Society Institute Network Women's Program, and East-West Women's Network) 2006. *Poland. Stop Violence Against Women: A project by the advocates for human rights.* www.stopvaw.org/ Poland2.html (accessed November 8, 2009).

VAW Monitoring Program (UNIFEM, MAHR, Open Society Institute Network Women's Program, and ZZZ Fenestra) 2007. *Violence against Women: Does the Government Care in Slovakia? Country Monitoring Report.* www.stopvaw.org/ sites/3f6d15f4-c12d-4515-8544-26b7a3a5a41e/uploads/Slovakia_2.pdf (accessed November 8, 2009).

Walsh, Clare. 2001. *Gender and Discourse: Language and Power in Politics, the Church, and Organisations.* Harlow: Pearson Education.

Weldon, Laurel. 2002. *Protest, Policy, and the Problem of Violence against Women: A Cross-National Comparison.* Pittsburgh: University of Pittsburgh Press.

———. 2006. "Inclusion, Solidarity, and Social Movements: The Global Movement against Gender Violence." *Perspectives and Politics* 4(1): 55–74.

World Health Organization (WHO). 2002. *World Report on Violence and Health.* www .who.int/violence_injury_prevention/publications/violence/album/en/index .html (accessed November 8, 2009).

CHAPTER 9

The New WAVE: How Transnational Feminist Networks Promote Domestic Violence Reform in Postcommunist Europe

LAURA BRUNELL AND JANET ELISE JOHNSON

The concept "domestic violence"—referring to violence against women occurring in the private sphere that is construed as an act of injustice, a violation of human rights, and a criminal act—is new to postcommunist societies.[1] Over the course of the 1990s several terms for such violence emerged, varying somewhat from country to country. In some countries the most common term is "violence in the family," for example, *przemoc w rodzinnie* in Polish and *nasilie v sem'e* in Russian. In other cases, such as among some feminist-identified crisis centers in Russia and in Bulgaria, a more direct cognate to the term "domestic violence" is used (*domashnee nasilie* and *domashno nasilie,* respectively). Finally, Katalin Fábián finds that across Central Europe "domestic violence has been given a name and it is becoming part of the everyday vocabulary" (Fábián 2006: 127).

How is such change occurring? What are the mechanisms for allowing such notions to be articulated and transmitted to would-be activists, policymakers, law enforcement officers, and citizens in postcommunist Europe? And, perhaps most importantly, what are the effects of this new conceptualization of violence against women? Has domestic violence moved from the stages of naming and consciousness-raising to eliciting new and meaningful state responses to it?

We hypothesize that the mechanism through which definitions of and remedies for domestic violence against women are being developed, appropriated, and transmitted to postcommunist Europe is the transnational feminist network against gendered violence. The history of "global feminism" is contentious, with many women activists from the developing world balking at the assertion that there is a single, universal women's condition or experience (Basu 1995: 3). Our purpose is not to suggest that women's experiences with domestic violence in the postcommunist world are identical to those of women in the West or elsewhere in the world. Yet we are fascinated with the process of the dissemination of ideas about violence against women, which has occurred rapidly and subtly but unevenly, incompletely, and sometimes, unjustly.

We became aware of the need for a new term to describe feminist anti-violence activism in the course of seeking to understand the role of nongovernmental organizations (NGOs) active in this policy area in postcommunist European and Eurasian countries. Through several years of fieldwork, it became increasingly clear that important connections had developed between feminists in Western and Eastern Europe, connections that could not be dismissed as mere patronage or colonization of East European civil societies on the part of Western political entrepreneurs. For example, in a 1997 interview, Stanislawa Walczewska, founder of *eFKa* (the Women's Foundation) in Krakow, mentioned that her group had been visiting and exchanging information with the East-West Women's Network for several years, since the mid- to late 1980s, in fact. Similarly, several women activists we interviewed in Poland and Russia during the mid-1990s spoke about the importance of connections made through the NGO forum at the 1995 United Nations (UN) Conference on Women in Beijing. Other scholars of the region, such as Katalin Fábián (2006: 139), also found regional and international networks to be important in facilitating communication and coordination, and fostering similar aims and methods.

Whereas many observers have been critical of the influence that West European and North American funders have wielded over the agendas and activities of NGOs in postcommunist societies (see Henderson 2002: 139–167; Wedel 1998), the kinds of connections among activists in the East and West that interest us are more than monetary. Rather, we note the emergence of a set of shared understandings of the phenomenon of gender-based violence and gender justice, of human rights and male dominance, of a vocabulary and a set of expectations of state government and transnational organizations that have informed East European attempts to reform domestic violence policy.

In other work (Johnson and Brunell 2006), we created a typology of domestic violence reform in postcommunist Europe and then compared case studies to tease out the multiple factors—domestic and transnational, grassroots and state-initiated—involved in this reform process. This study raised questions for us about the role of transnational feminist networks, mentioned by activists in many of our cases, and so we focus on this phenomenon here. As part of this book's attempt to understand reform of domestic violence policies in postcommunist Europe, we seek to illuminate the role of transnational feminist networking. In the language of Fábián (in the preceding chapter in this volume), is feminist networking an effective mechanism of norm diffusion, value change, and legal-institutional changes?

We begin by describing the global changes that fostered the emergence of transnational feminist networking. We see the rise of transnational feminist networking as a significant cause of the shift in domestic violence policymaking. It is one answer to the question raised by Fábián in chapter 8: What has changed in the domestic and international environment to allow domestic violence to emerge as an area of political contest?

In the bulk of the chapter, we use bi-variate regressions to assess the impact of such networks on domestic violence policies in eleven postcommunist countries. We also explore other possible influences on domestic violence policies proposed by mainstream social science (foreign funding, political and economic reform, culture, and geographic diffusion). We find few statistically significant relationships other than our measures of transnational feminist networks and state responsiveness to domestic violence. These findings suggest that, at least through the middle of the first decade of the new millennium, links between NGOs in the postcommunist countries and the West, cultivated in part by funding from the European Union, have provided a mechanism for the diffusion of anti–domestic violence policies. They may also suggest that the process of norm diffusion, fostered by transnational networks, may be at work in other areas of postcommunist policy reform.[2]

Our analysis is grounded in long-term fieldwork in the region. Between us, we have lived in or traveled to Russia and Poland for more than a decade, interviewing activists and policymakers and observing the local activism. More recently, we added other countries in the region—such as the Czech Republic and Armenia—and some of the transnational spaces we write about—such as the postcommunist women's caucus at the United Nations' 2005 Commission on the Status of Women in New York, a 2005 Nordic gender violence conference,[3] and a 2006 European Union conference.[4] Reflecting the global changes, our research has become the political science equivalent of "deterritorialized ethnography" (Merry 2006). This approach allows us to develop a narrative that can account for the statistical relationship we uncover between transnational feminist networks (TFNs) and new state responses to domestic violence policy in postcommunist Europe. For the quantitative part of our argument, we counted the number of domestic violence policy reforms that have occurred in eleven postcommunist countries by drawing upon our existing research, by corresponding with others conducting research in the specific countries, and through research from secondary sources and activists. Our sample of postcommunist countries comprises Albania, Armenia, Bulgaria, the Czech Republic, Hungary, Moldova, Poland, Romania, Russia, The Slovak Republic, and Ukraine. We chose these countries for several reasons. These countries' histories of communism and their attempts to adopt some form of "market democracy" during the 1990s allow us to treat them as "most similar systems." Yet, based on our previous research, we also knew that the sample included those that were likely to be totally unreformed in the area of domestic violence policies as well as others that had already attempted or enacted several types of state responses to domestic violence.

In the next section, we will discuss how globalization has created the conditions allowing the growth of TFNs and creating opportunities for the diffusion of policy norms related to domestic violence.

Globalization and Women's Rights

A new understanding of domestic violence and rights and new types of transnational feminist organizing have emerged under the conditions presented by globalization. One of the most important political aspects of globalization has been that it transforms the sovereignty of the state and creates incentives to transfer governance and cooperation to other levels, such as those of subnational units, transnational regions, and the global scale. International governmental organizations (IGOs), such as the United Nations and the European Union, have become important venues for the development of international agreements as well as the development and diffusion of legal norms across national boundaries. We agree with Sidney Tarrow's conceptualization of international institutions as "coral reefs in the oceans of global anarchy"[5] (Tarrow 2002: 242), creating focal points for collective action and knowledge exchange. Although not unmarked by the global inequalities that the critics of neoliberalism highlight and the economic aspects of globalization, these global "coral reefs" seem to be the most consensual, transnational opportunity for activists to deliberate over standards to which states should be held accountable to (Merry 2006, 226–227). In the language of cultural anthropology, these are the spaces of "transnational consensus building" (ibid., 19).

Over the last two decades, these international governmental institutions have become important arenas for creating a transnational consensus on the meaning and content of women's rights globally. The UN, as the oldest and most broadly based such international governmental organization, has accomplished these tasks primarily through the following three main means:

1. Establishing international human rights standards, such as the Universal Declaration of Human Rights (United Nations 1948) and the Convention on Consent to Marriage, Minimum Age for Marriage, and Registration for Marriages (UN 1962)

2. Articulating woman-specific human rights standards, such as the Convention on the Political Rights of Women (UN 1952)

3. Bringing attention to issues that disproportionately affect women or where women tend to be consistently discriminated against, as through the Convention for the Suppression of the Traffic in Persons and of the Exploitation of the Prostitution of Others (UN 1949), the International Labor Organization Convention on Equal Remuneration (UN 1951), the Convention against Discrimination in Education (UNESCO 1960), the Convention on the Elimination of All Forms of Discrimination against Women (CEDAW; UN 1979) with its subsequent recommendations, and the Declaration on the Elimination of Violence against Women (UN 1993).

These changes have made it possible for scholars, activists, and politicians to consider the role of gender politics in shaping global governance (Prügl and Meyer 1999). Moreover, attention to the issues by bodies such as the UN creates the opportunity for dialogue between women's NGOs and their national governments. For example, while CEDAW has not had the legally binding power to establish state laws, Sally Merry found that mandatory periodic reports on each signatory country's compliance with CEDAW goals has "generate(d) consultation between NGOs and governments" (2006: 175). All of the postcommunist states examined here have ratified CEDAW, either while under communism or shortly thereafter, and all have submitted at least one of the mandatory reports for examination by the CEDAW committee.[6] This acceptance of CEDAW oversight suggests the potential for this CEDAW process helping to diffuse new ideas about violence against women into postcommunist countries' public spheres.

Although international governmental organizations were initially quite resistant to participation from NGOs, women's rights activists have successfully "found or carved out niches for themselves and their interests as women" in a variety of international governmental organizations (Prügl and Meyer 1999: 4). These new institutional spaces allow women's rights activists from varied national backgrounds to meet face to face with each other, to talk about their common concerns, to share information on their status in their home states, to learn about the plight of women in other parts of the world, to gain knowledge about successful means of enhancing women's status, and to call for specific action toward established policy goals. The most globally inclusive of these meetings have been the nongovernmental forums at the UN's World Conferences on the Status of Women (1975, Mexico City; 1980, Copenhagen; 1985, Nairobi; 1995, Beijing; 2000, Beijing+5 in New York). The NGO forums at these meetings have provided a global forum for dialogue among women's rights activists (Johnson 2007; Merry 2006). They allowed the evolution of a common language to talk about women's rights and status, the emergence of more broadly shared conceptions of women's problems and of the legal norms and policies that may be useful in addressing them. For example, at the 2005 CSW (Commission on the Status of Women)—the Beijing+10 meeting—there were not only spaces at the parallel NGO forum for global activists to get together, but also almost daily caucuses for postcommunist activists at the UN, right outside the meeting areas for the official representatives. Chaired by various women throughout the session, the daily discussions involved representatives from the different regions raising particular issues, collective strategizing about how to reaffirm the Beijing Platform (in the face of US resistance), and "visits" by representatives of other countries or organizations, such as the European Women's Lobby.

We think it is important to note that these forums are not free from hierarchies that skew the nature and content of the discussions among IGO/INGO actors. Indeed, it would be naïve to assert that women from all parts of the world and economic classes enjoy equal voice in developing a common language to describe women's lives, and the norms and policies that seek to improve them. The first two UN-organized world conferences, in 1975 and 1980, were particularly troubled by North–South hierarchies as the activists from the North, perhaps unwittingly, sought to impose their vision of "global sisterhood" on activists from the South. We recognize the tendency to engage in Western-influenced rights-based discourse and to rely on legalistic and aid-based remedies that allow for neither alternative conceptualizations of women's problems nor the full range of their possible solutions. While acknowledging this critique of the way domestic violence has become framed globally, we understand this convergence around framing domestic violence as a human rights issue to be a product of the processes of globalization, rather than simply the result of the hegemonic influence of Western (or Northern) concepts and norms (Fábián 2006). A common framing for domestic violence policy and relationships among women's NGO activists have proliferated as a result of the information/communication revolution of the late twentieth and early twenty-first centuries. The rapid increase in access to computers, email, and the Internet throughout postcommunist Europe during the 1990s enabled low-cost, ongoing communication with activists in the West, as well as nearly free access to a host of legal documents, discussions of best practices, invitations to conferences and trainings, and so forth.

We are persuaded by Laurel Weldon's (2006) finding that much of the success of the transnational movement against gender violence stems from its remarkable commitment to norms of inclusivity—that is, allowing women from the developing world and non-Western contexts to speak for themselves. She argues that it was precisely this approach that allowed a consensus of concern around violence to materialize, spawning a global gender violence movement. Further, these global feminist agreements and declarations represent the best global collective wisdom we have, deriving as it does from a transnational and relatively consensual process of deliberation and remaining open to negotiation by activists (Merry 2006: 227).

Europe's Transnational Feminist Networks Working against Domestic Violence

For over a decade now, scholars have developed an extensive literature that names and describes these new transnational forms of collective action with terms such as transnational social movements (Kriesberg 1997; McCarthy 1997) and transnational advocacy networks (Keck and Sikkink 1998). Building on the transnational advocacy literature but looking specifically at transnational feminist organizing, Valentine Moghadam (2005) coined the term "transnational feminist networks" (TFNs). She defines TFNs as

> structures organized above the national level that unite women from three or more countries around a common agenda, such as women's human rights, reproductive health and rights, violence against women, peace and anti-militarism, or feminist economics. They are part of the family of political change organizations operating above and across national borders that have been variously described as global civil society organizations, transnational

advocacy networks, and transnational social movement organizations—and which, along with international nongovernmental organizations, constitute the making of a transnational public sphere (2005: 4).

Our fieldwork uncovered a number of organizing structures active in postcommunist Europe and Eurasia around the issue of domestic violence that resembled this definition of TFN: the European Union's Daphne Program,[7] the Open Society Institute's Internet Project (OSI-IP),[8] the Women's Project of the Minnesota Advocates for Human Rights (MAHR),[9] the Network of Crisis Centers in the Barents Region (NCRB; Saarinen, Liapounova, and Drachova 2003), Women Against Violence in Europe Network (WAVE Network),[10] and hundreds of NGOs in the West and the East offering services to victims of domestic violence, lobbying their governments for policy change and other actions, and who often have informal ties to each other.

For example, OSI-IP laid the groundwork for transnational feminist organizing around domestic violence, sponsoring the participation of women from Central and Eastern Europe in the Regional Women's Connectivity Program. Through it, women from Russia, Ukraine, Slovenia, Hungary, the Czech Republic, and the former Yugoslavia participated in the Beijing UN World Conference on Women, where they learned about the Internet. After their return, they engaged in outreach work to other women's NGOs requiring connectivity and training. In 1996, OSI continued to sponsor Eastern European women (from the former Yugoslavia, Romania, Hungary, Ukraine), who had taken part in the Connectivity Program, to ensure that they received training and connectivity to the Internet. OSI also funded the participation of two women representing Eastern and Central European women at a global conference on "net" initiatives. In 1998, OSI-IP sponsored a sweeping project coordinated by the OSI Network Women's Program to provide access, training, and content development services to women's NGOs throughout the region supported specifically by foundation programs. In 1999, additional funding was provided to integrate Roma women's participation in the project. More recently, OSI was the co-sponsor of the postcommunist women's caucus at the Beijing+10 meeting.

The creation of the Daphne Program illustrates that violence against women has found a place on the political agenda of the European Union (see chapter 10 in this volume). The Daphne Program aims to establish or reinforce "networks at [the] European level to promote and coordinate information and actions on measures aimed at protecting, and preventing violence toward, children, young people and women, including the promotion of cooperation between NGOs and voluntary organizations and authorities involved in these areas" (see www.daphne-toolkit.org/). With a budget of €20 million for its readoption (2000–2003; Kantola 2006: 150), the Daphne Program has been one of the WAVE Network's major funders.

Another European network is the NCRB. Built upon an already existing network among Nordic feminists, Femina Borealis, the NCRB was founded in 1999 to link together women's crisis centers in Finland, Sweden, Norway, and northwest Russia (Saarinen, Liapounova, and Drachova 2003). The network's leadership purposefully crossed the old East-West divide—directed by a Finn and a Russian—to foster a model of horizontal sharing of knowledge and experience across the region. At the same time, the network recognized the economic inequalities within the region, giving financial resources to help support and found women's crisis centers in northwest Russia.[11]

The experience of MAHR illustrates that North American organizations also sought to influence the development of domestic violence policy in Eastern European countries. In 1993, this Minnesota-based organization established a Women's Program that "works to improve the lives of women by using international human rights standards to advocate for women's rights in the United States and around the world."[12] Using conventional human rights tactics, conducting field research working with local women's organizations, MAHR published a series of reports documenting state failures to respond to domestic violence, mostly in postcommunist Europe and Eurasia. In 2000, based on this experience, MAHR joined up with the UN's Development Fund for Women (UNIFEM) and the OSI's Women's Program to establish a Stop Violence Against Women campaign centered around a website in English and Russian.[13]

Of all these, the best example of a TFN for our study is WAVE. Based in Vienna, WAVE was founded after the 1994 UN-organized Vienna conference on human rights and in preparation for the 1995 World Conference on Women in Beijing (Kaselitz 2006). More grassroots than the EU's European Women's Lobby (Kantola 2006: 145), WAVE has fostered a network of NGOs and other entities, such as ministries of health, women, and family; local governments; and psychologists active in the fight against domestic violence, in all eleven of the countries in our sample.[14] WAVE's mission is to gather information in relation to male violence against women and children; to exchange information on women's organizations, research, applicable laws, and prevention strategies; to influence national and European/international policies on violence; to take common action and further feminist analysis; to promote feminist analyses of violence against women; to develop and promote criteria and guidelines at the European level in relation to legislation, services, and prevention strategies; to offer mutual aid (financial, training, resources) to members of the WAVE network and others seeking to develop expertise in addressing domestic violence; to enhance awareness and create a deeper understanding of male violence against women; to strengthen the links among the regions in Europe; and to strengthen the rights of marginalized women (see www.wave-network.org).

WAVE's activities expanded dramatically after 1997, the first year in which it obtained money from the European Commission.[15] In January 1998 WAVE held its first conference, with fifty-seven participants from twenty-three European countries. Since 2000 it has offered Train-the-Trainer Seminars to train women working in European countries with "little or no experience in training professions" to go on to offer such training in their home countries. One of WAVE's recent projects includes Bridging Gaps workshops, which are documenting models of cooperation between women's NGOs and the state authorities to prevent violence against women and children (funded by an EU Daphne II Program grant). The other major WAVE project is the Coordination Action on Human Rights Violations, a research project bringing together academic institutions, policy networks, and individual researchers to identify and profile victimization, to analyze the roots of interpersonal violence, and to intervene in gender-based human rights violations. All this networking, both actual and virtual through its website, creates a discursive space for information exchange among professionals and activists. WAVE has developed a library and an archive, a database of anti-violence NGOs' addresses, as well as a resource for women in various languages who are victims of domestic violence to find help within specific countries.

All these TFN organizations constitute a web of relationships among NGO activists, bureaucrats, and elected officials from various levels of government across Europe. They comprise Europe's transnational feminist network against violence against women, henceforth referred to as Europe's anti-violence TFN. We use the concept of TFNs because these organizations, along with other transnational advocacy networks, are not traditional social movements characterized by the mobilization of masses and by their confrontational tactics (Sperling et al. 2001:

1157). Rather, these networks "mobilize smaller numbers of individual activists who use more specialized resources of expertise and access to elites."[16] They often aid NGOs in organizing by providing web-based resources, and they organize gatherings to exchange information and ideas rather than hosting mass demonstrations or dramatic confrontations with authorities. Because WAVE is the best example of this larger phenomenon, we use the WAVE database to develop measures of the density of the TFN in each of our countries and to test whether this network was succeeding in attaining new state responses to domestic violence policy. We elaborate the ways of measuring the WAVE-affiliated network in a later section, but first we turn our attention to detailing our dependent variable, namely state responses to domestic violence.

State Responses to Domestic Violence

Transnational feminist networks can have many positive effects—including fostering increased networking among activists or simply providing many of them with jobs—but for most, the stated goal is to influence public policy. We use the term "state responses to domestic violence" to refer to systematic concrete actions of governments, such as changes in laws and public policy initiatives. These systematic actions differ from the ad hoc "bureaucratic responsiveness" to specific complaints or requests that are so often the subject of public policy research (Weldon 2002: 7). State response to domestic violence is also not to be confused with effectiveness (ibid.: 7)—as we do not attempt the still almost impossible task of measuring how effective the emerging laws or programs have been in reducing the incidence of domestic violence or in helping women escape abusive relationships. Rather, we are noting whether the state has adopted a range of policies related to the problem of domestic violence. We relied on our decade of field research experience in postcommunist Europe and Eurasia to draw up our list of the state responses most commonly advocated by domestic violence specialists and activists, but these types of reforms are also used by other comparative scholars of domestic violence (e.g., Merry 2006; Weldon 2002). It includes

1) Recognizing domestic violence as a specific crime in the state's criminal code

2) Allowing victims to obtain court orders of protection from perpetrators of violence

3) Recognizing marital rape as a crime

4) Enacting legislation specifically addressing domestic violence

5) Sponsoring publicly funded information campaigns about domestic violence

6) Training the police to intervene in domestic violence incidents

7) Keeping separate statistics on these interventions.[17]

These policies together signify an understanding of domestic violence as a specific type of criminal phenomenon separate from other kinds of assault.

In systems where domestic violence has not historically been recognized as a distinct problem, treating domestic violence separately in criminal codes or statutes—Measure 1—shows that the state endorses the notion of domestic violence promoted by feminist anti-violence advocates: that it is a serious crime. It also allows police and policymakers to estimate the incidence of domestic violence crimes for the first time. Measure 2 creates a new legal mechanism for protection, often to temporarily exclude an abuser from the shared home or from contacting the victim and is usually available more quickly and with less evidence than criminal prosecution. Measure 3 recognizes that criminal sexual violence does indeed occur within marriage. This means that the law stipulates punishment regardless of the relationship between the rapist and victim, but in practice, marital rape is virtually never prosecuted (in the cases coded "no," a husband cannot be charged with raping his wife). Measure 4 indicates that the problem of domestic violence has achieved enough currency to prompt more comprehensive national legislation. Measure 5 also indicates that awareness of the problem among political elites has reached the point where they feel educating the public about the problem is warranted. Measure 6 indicates that policymakers recognize domestic violence incidents as a specific kind of crime requiring specialized training on the part of police. Measure 7 allows police and policymakers to track rates of domestic violence over time.

The results for the eleven cases appear in table 9.1.

The last column of table 9.1 lists the total number of state responses occurring in each country. The cases are listed in the table in descending order by total number of state responses. The two most common types of responses across our cases classify marital rape as crime and have some form of parliamentary action, each undertaken by seven of our cases. It seems logical that criminalizing marital rape would be among the less controversial reforms, requiring only the nullification of previous statues that may have excepted husbands from criminality or defined rape as occurring between nonmarried persons. Parliamentary action means that the parliaments of our countries have enacted some form of legislation pertaining to domestic violence. That seven of our countries have done so is evidence that changing ideas about domestic violence have percolated up to the level of political elites. Such actions could result from pressure to conform with the norms of the European Union as well as pressure from women's NGOs in the respective countries. Nearly as many of our countries (six of them) have undertaken training the police to better intervene in domestic violence cases or are for the first time keeping track of the number of domestic violence interventions. These two reforms are commonly called for among domestic violence activists. Fewer countries have gone so far as to enact separate criminal statutes for domestic violence; only two, the Czech Republic and Romania, have done so in ways that address the gendered dynamics of violence, while Poland, the Slovak Republic, and Moldova have gender-neutral statutes framed in, mostly in terms of violence within the family, especially against children. It is worth noting that only four of the countries have made orders of protection available to victims (Poland, Hungary, the Slovak Republic, and Bulgaria) and only three (Poland, Hungary, and Russia) have had publicly funded public information campaigns against domestic violence.

In the next sections, we will attempt to discover why some postcommunist countries have adopted more reforms than others considering the impact of transnational feminist networks as well as other variables widely discussed in the literature on other kinds of postcommunist political and economic reforms.

Identifying the Causes of State Responses to Domestic Violence

To assess the effect of transnational feminist networks on the reform of state responses to domestic violence, we examine this hypothesis in comparison to the other most common hypotheses for reform in order to consider a variety of possible influences on state policies, including both the international and national conditions. In brief, these internal and external conditions are the amount of foreign funding each state receives from other states and international agencies (not exclusively for domestic violence, but in toto); ratings of each country's political and economic stability and reform, as operationalized by Fish (1998); indices of levels of development according to standard measures published by the United Nations; gender empowerment as measured by the UN's Gender Empowerment Index; the degree of women's participation

TABLE 9.1. STATE REFORMS THROUGH 2005

	SEPARATE DOMESTIC VIOLENCE STATUTES	ORDERS OF PROTECTION	MARITAL RAPE IS A CRIME	PARLIA-MENTARY ACTION
Poland[1]	.5[2]	1[3]	1	1[4]
Czech Republic[5]	1[6]	0	1[7]	1
Hungary	0	1[9]	1[10]	1[11]
Slovak Republic[13]	.5[14]	1	0	1[15]
Russia	0	0	1	0[16]
Ukraine[17]	0	0	1	1
Moldova	.5[19]	0	1	0
Romania[20]	1[21]	0	0	1[22]
Bulgaria	0	1[23]	0	1[24]
Armenia	0	0	1	0
Albania	0	0	0	0

Notes: 1. Council of Europe, 2001: 91–99.

2. The Polish Penal code, passed June 6, 1997, enumerates penalties for violence against a member of one's family (Council of Europe 2001: 83).

3. The Counteraction of Violence in Close Relations Bill, enacted in November 2005, allows for pre-trial police supervision of perpetrators of domestic violence. Courts may also require perpetrators to stay away from victims as part of a suspended sentence. Minnesota Advocates for Human Rights (hereafter MAHR), "Poland, Country Pages," www.stopvaw.org/Poland2.html (accessed September 22, 2006).

4. The Counteraction of Violence in Close Relations Bill, Poland, enacted in November 2005.

5. Council of Europe 2001: 129–141.

6. An amendment to the Czech Criminal Code making domestic violence a crime was signed into law on February 13, 2004. MAHR, "Czech Republic, Country Pages," www.stopvaw.org/Czech_Republic2.html (accessed September 22, 2006).

7. Council of Europe 2001: 88.

8. MAHR, "Czech Republic, Country Pages," www.stopvaw.org/Czech_Republic2 .html (accessed September 22, 2006).

9. Legislation providing for protection orders for victims of family violence was proposed but not passed in 2004. As of July 2006, "Any person can apply for a restrictive order who needs protections during the course of a criminal procedure" (NANE Women's Rights Association and Habeas Corpus Munkacsoport, Közhasznú Jogvédő Egyesület Press Release, July 1, 2006, www.nane.hu). The women's rights group NANE's press release criticized the form of the law for not linking women's need for such orders to the phenomenon of domestic violence or to the particular kinds of protection it requires.

DV PUBLIC INFO CAMPAIGN	DV POLICE TRAINING/ RECORD KEEPING	TOTAL NUMBER OF STATE RESPONSES
1	1	5.5
0	1[8]	4
1	0[12]	4
0	1	3.5
1	1	3
0	1[18]	3
0	1	2.5
0	0	2
0	0	2
0	0	1
0	0	0

10. Council of Europe 2001: 207–220.

11. The Hungarian Parliament did pass a national strategy for preventing and responding to family violence on April 26, 2003, but this was not legislation (Vanya 2006, 164).

12. In 2003, the chief of the National Police Headquarters issued a directive stating that the police were obliged to intervene in cases of domestic violence but required or offered no training for the police in this area. MAHR, "Hungary: National Plan of Action," www.stopvaw.org/Nationa_Plan_of_Action11.html (accessed September 22, 2006, URL no longer active).

13. Council of Europe, 2001: 135–152.

14. Section 215 of the Slovak Penal Code does not enumerate violence against women or violence among intimate partners per se; rather it discusses the penalties for assault, abuse, etc., to a "close person," i.e., spouse, relative, or a ward under one's care (Council of Europe 2001: 135).

15. The Act on Social Assistance included provisions to reduce the incidence of domestic violence and aimed to assist victims (Council of Europe 2001: 140–41).

16. Legislation was considered in 1993–1997 but was tabled. According to the Russian Ministry of Labor and Social Development, there were also 23 governmental women's crisis centers in 2004, but this was not the result of legislation. Russian Ministry of Health and Social Development, "Informational material on social policy on the family, women, and children," www.mzsrrf.ru/inf_soc_pol_wom_cild/64.htm (accessed March 22, 2006, URL no longer active).

17. Council of Europe, 2001: 171–174; MAHR, "Ukraine, Country Page," www .stopvaw.org/Ukraine.html (accessed September 22, 2006).

18. Banwell et al. 2000: 22).

continued on following page

in politics; cultural influences as measured by the predominant religion practiced in each state; and geographic proximity to the West. We compare these alternative explanations to the influence of WAVE, measured by the density of each country's NGOs' connections to the European domestic violence TFN. More on why we chose these variables and how we operationalized them follows below. We use bivariate regression analysis to establish whether there is a causal relationship between each independent variable and our dependent variable, the number of state responses enacted in the field of domestic violence policy.[18]

Foreign Funding

Several East European scholars highlighted that foreign organizations and foreign governments have been vital to the development of

---

19. Article 151, paragraph 2 of the new criminal code added violence against a spouse or close relative as an aggravating factor in assault (Council of Europe, 2001: 61).

20. "Romania." Council of Europe, 2001: 109–116.

21. In November 2002, the Romanian Parliament adopted a new criminal provision, stipulating harsher punishment for bodily injuries when the victim is a member of the family from 1 to 3 months (or a fine) in the case of non-related victims to 6 months to a year (or a fine) for family victims. The imprisonment may be increased up to 2 years in cases of serious physical injuries. However, whereas criminal proceedings initiate in situations of violence not involving a family member regardless of whether the victim files a complaint, in the case of family violence, prosecution begins only upon complaint by the injured party and is negated upon reconciliation between the parties. UNIFEM, "Stop Violence Against Women: Romania Country Report," UNIFEM, www.stopvaw.org/Romania2.html (accessed July 9, 2007).

22. The law targeting the prevention and the punishment of domestic violence was adopted in Romania in May 2003. The law defined domestic violence as physical or verbal action deliberately perpetrated by a family member against another family member, resulting in physical, mental, or sexual suffering or material loss (Article 2[1]), as well as encroachments on his/her fundamental rights and freedom. The law enumerates the role of social workers, prevention measures, mediation, shelters, protection measures, and sanctions (Council of Europe, 2003: 140–141).

23. The Bulgarian Parliament enacted legislation enabling victims of domestic violence to be granted orders of protection against their abusers in March 2005. MAHR, "Bulgaria, 2006," www.stopvaw.org/Bulgaria2.html (accessed November 27, 2006).

24. The 2005 Bulgarian law defined domestic violence as "any act of physical, mental or sexual violence, and any attempted such violence, as well as the forcible restriction of individual freedom and of privacy, carried out against individuals who have or have had family or kinship ties or cohabit or dwell in the same home." MAHR, "Bulgaria, 2006," www.stopvaw.org/Bulgaria2.html (accessed November 27, 2006). The law also requires the state to implement prevention and protection programs as well as to provide assistance to victims.

postcommunist civil societies, especially to the organization and maintenance of NGOs. Henderson (2002), Sperling (1999), and Wedel (1998) each argue that postcommunist societies are distinguished by the fact that most of the financial resources available for the third sector come from foreign assistance. Thus we hypothesized that the amount of foreign funding for democratic initiatives might impact state responsiveness, especially spending by the EU and USAID. We tested the following variables:

1. Funding from the EU's PHARE program (1990–1998) or TACIS program (1991–1998)[19]

2. USAID spending on democracy building through the Support for East European Democracy (SEED) program in Central and Eastern Europe (1990–1996) and the Former Soviet Union (1992–1997)[20]

3. Economic aid as estimated in the CIA World Factbook (2006).

Results of the regression analysis: the only statistically significant relationship is that between economic aid and state response (signif. or t = .007). Thus, while spending by the European Union and the United States specifically aimed at economic and political reform is not a strong predictor of state responses to domestic violence, overall economic aid is. This may be because the overall level of economic aid is more important than aid only from EU and US sources. It also suggests that economic reform may be a good predictor of state responses to domestic violence, something we test in the following section.

Political Context and Economic Reform

Next we considered whether other aspects of each country's political context and economic reform influenced state responses to domestic violence. We tested a variety of institutional and structural variables' ability to predict state responsiveness. We drew upon the literature on postcommunist democratization and reform (Fish 1998: 31–78; Kopstein and Reilly 1999: 613–624; Przeworski 1991; Wedel 1998), as well as the feminist policy literature (Baldez 2003; Mazur 1999: 483–506; Moghadam 2005; Stetson and Mazur 1995; Weldon 2002) in order to generate a list of independent variables to test.

First, based on the literature on postcommunist democratization (e.g., Fish), we hypothesized that the countries that exhibit the highest levels of political stability and reform would be most responsive to domestic violence. The measures of political and economic reform we examined are measures of political stability, government effectiveness, and the rule of law.[21] The assertion is that states that have achieved a measure of stability and reform are more likely and able to pursue progressive policies, including addressing domestic violence.

Second, drawing on the mainstream political science literature on postcommunism, we hypothesized that countries with the greatest degree of political rights and civil liberties would be most responsive to domestic violence. Political rights include such prerogatives as the right to vote and to stand for office, while civil liberties include freedom of speech, freedom of assembly, and the like. We used Freedom House's (2000) annual assessment of the state of freedom in countries around the world.

Third, drawing upon many recent studies suggesting the importance of women legislators on public policy (see Weldon 2002, ch. 4, for a summary of this literature), we also hypothesized that those countries with a greater number of women in politics would be most responsive to domestic violence. There is a substantial literature finding that women legislators are more likely to introduce legislation pertaining to women and children and to transform the political agendas of their political parties and the committees and bodies in which they serve (Dahlerup 1987; Dobson 1991; Kathlene 1994; Norris and Lovenduski 1989; Powley 2006; *Impact of Women in Public Office: Findings at a Glance* 1991). We used the typical comparative measure, the percent of women in the lower house of parliament. We used this data listed by the Interparliamentary Union (http://www.ipu.org/wmn-e/world.htm).

Fourth, we tested what seemed a reasonable assumption, that countries that elected reform-minded governments in their initial postcommunist elections—the earliest reformers—would be more responsive to domestic violence. Such reform-minded governments would seem more likely to pursue a wide range of reforms, including reforms on the issue of domestic violence. We used an index developed by Fish (1998), rating the outcomes of the initial (first freely contested) postcommunist era elections in each country.[22] This follows Fish's logic that political reform will lead to economic reform; we are interested in seeing whether political reform creates opportunities for domestic violence policy change as well.

In addition to these political variables, we also pursued economic hypotheses. Milton Friedman's theory that economic reform fosters political reform has become a mantra of many political scientists and policymakers around the world, a justification for the neoliberalism that dominates. In what is seen as a key study in the process of democratic consolidation, Linz and Stepan (1996) find the importance of minimal economic performance distributed broadly. Weldon (2002: 51–55) also finds that several scholars of gender violence policy suggest the importance of increasing economic development within one country and in neighboring countries. Based on these two approaches, we test whether countries that are better economically developed or have economies that are growing more quickly are in a better position to respond to issues like domestic violence. The logic is that economically more affluent people are in a better position in a democratic society to devote their time and energy to participation in social movements, while more prosperous states can have more resources to devote to public policy. Because it is women activists who most often devote their resources to domestic violence policy reform, we have also included one gender-specific development index: the gender empowerment index. Thus, the economic development measures we considered are:

1) Measures of economic reform developed by Fish (1998), such as
   a) degree of economic liberalization
   b) percent of GDP generated by the private sector
   c) an economic reform index computed by combining the two above measures
   d) World Bank Group lending 1990–1995 as a percentage of GDP
   e) foreign direct investment 1989–95 as a percentage of GDP

2) The United Nations Development Program's human development index (HDI)

3) The UNDP's gender empowerment index (GEM).[23]

The results of the regression analysis show that of the political variables, only the ratings for civil liberties 1991–1992 and political rights' rating for 1999–2000 were statistically significant (significant at the .04 and .022 level, respectively).

Geographical Diffusion

Next, we considered the hypothesis that state response is a result of the geographic diffusion of norms, ideas, and institutions. Kopstein and Reilly (1999) suggest geographic proximity to the West allows for the diffusion of Western ideas and institutions related to democratization and capitalist economic reform. Kopstein and Reilly speculate that diffusion occurs when political and economic elites from the West travel east to instruct their Eastern cohorts in professional norms, institution building, and so forth. Likewise, Easterners may visit the West to observe the functioning of Western political and economic institutions in their home context or to receive specialized training. Finally, mass media spills over borders and spreads knowledge of "how they do things" in the West, especially in bordering countries.

We sought to test the influence of geographical proximity to the West on state responses to domestic violence. In this section we tested the following variables, following Kopstein and Reilly:

1) The distance from a country's capital and Berlin or to Vienna (we used whichever was shorter). We also computed the average of these two distances.

2) A variable that broke our cases into three groups: 1001–1500 miles from the West[24] = 2; 501–1000 miles from the West = 1; >500 miles from the West = 0.

The result of the regression analysis was: none of these variables were statistically significant. This implies that physical distance may be a poor predictor of the diffusion of ideas about domestic violence from one region or country to another. It does not mean, however, that diffusion is not happening according to some other mechanism or logic. We wondered whether transnational NGO networks were an important mechanism for transfusion of Western ideas, norms, and legal standards about domestic violence. Thus we tested whether transnational feminist networks could be the mechanism through which this diffusion was taking place.

Transnational Feminist Networks

Based on the growing evidence that women's movement activity has influenced public policy in many states (Araujo et al. 2000; Mazur 1999; Weldon 2002) and a growing literature on transnational feminist networks (Keck and Sikkink 1998; Moghadam 2005), we hypothesized that the countries with the densest transnational feminist network would be most responsive and most likely to enact laws specifically related to criminalizing domestic violence. We used the number and geographical distribution of a variety of women's and anti–domestic violence NGOs listed in the WAVE database (on October 6, 2006) to measure the density of this network in each country in our sample.

Specifically, we employed the following measures (see table 9.2):

1) The number of listings with WAVE for each country

2) The number of NGOs listed with WAVE

3) The number of government entities listed in WAVE's database for each country

4) The number of NGOs listed with WAVE that list male/domestic violence as their main field of activity

5) The number of shelters for victims of domestic violence—an indication of more extensive services, since many NGOs simply provide counseling either by phone or in person but leave the victim at home with the abuser—listed in the WAVE database.[25]

While the raw number of organizations, shelters, or government links in each of these categories are three measures of the degree to which NGOs are linked to Europe's antiviolence TFN, geographical spread within the country is also essential. It shows that activism on the issue of domestic violence has spread beyond the capital city of each country and has achieved a wider degree of outreach. We use the number of cities with NGO links to WAVE as a measure of the density of the network against violence. Thus, we also included additional variables, measuring:

6) The number of cities with shelter services with one or more NGO links listed in the WAVE database

7) The number of cities with one or more entity providing shelter listed in the WAVE database. We include this measure to test for the spread in availability of shelters, based on the rationale given above that shelters constitute a more extensive range of services.

The regression analysis showed that several of the TFN measures were significant, including: the number of cities with at least one WAVE listing (.009); the number of listings for shelter (.006); and the number of cities with shelters listed (.003). This evidence suggests that not only does WAVE matter in terms of creating new state responses to domestic violence, but so does the density of this TFN.

Discussion of Findings: WAVE Matters

In sum, our key measures of TFN strength—the number of shelters and the geographical reach of WAVE—show transnational organized feminism made a difference in postcommunist policies regarding domestic violence at least up through the mid-2000s. Our findings suggest that WAVE is a key part of the informal and ideational networks that Fábián (2006) found to be essential in spreading ideas about domestic violence in Poland, the Czech and Slovak Republics, Hungary, and

TABLE 9.2. ESTIMATE OF THE ANTI-VIOLENCE TRANSNATIONAL FEMINIST NETWORK IN SELECTED POSTCOMMUNIST COUNTRIES (OCTOBER 2006)

	TOTAL NO. OF LINKS TO WAVE	NO. OF NGO LINKS TO WAVE	NO. OF GOV'T LINKS TO WAVE	NO. OF CITIES WITH WAVE LINKS	NO. MALE/ DOMESTIC VIOLENCE AS MAIN FIELD LISTED WITH WAVE	NO. PRO- VIDING SHELTER LISTED WITH WAVE	NO. OF CITIES WITH SHELTER SERVICE LISTED WITH WAVE
Poland	50	50	0	28	21	12	8
Slovak Republic	39	38	1	6	16	8	6
Hungary	19	18	1	3	3	10	3
Romania	18	16	2	7	12	2	2
Ukraine	17	16	1	9	12	2	2
Bulgaria	15	14	1	1	10	2	2
Russia	14	14	0	9	12	2	2
Albania	13	12	0	1	1	1	1
Czech Republic	7	7	0	1	4	3	1
Moldova	2	2	0	1	2	1	1
Armenia	1	1	0	1	2	1	1

Source: WAVE Database, Address Section, accessed October 6, 2006.

Slovenia. This confirms Keck's and Sikkink's (1998) and Moghadam's (2005) arguments about the power of transnational feminist networks in other contexts. It suggests that such networks can be an agent of the geographical diffusion Kopstein and Reilly theorized by suggesting that, especially in close proximity, transnational policy networks are a particularly robust mechanism for transmission of ideas, legal norms, and technical expertise. As WAVE was only one of the anti–gender violence TFNs active in the region, TFNs may play an even bigger role than we found by just looking at the density of connections to just such a network: WAVE.

This quantitative finding makes sense considering what we know about the eleven cases taken as a whole. For example, Poland, one of the most economically reformed postcommunist case study countries, was an early reformer in domestic violence as well, achieving its three reforms by 1997. One of the driving forces lobbying for reform in Poland has been the Women's Rights Center (*Centrum Praw Kobiet*) in Warsaw. The Center's director, Urszula Nowakowska, is a founding member of the WAVE network. She was instrumental in promulgating contemporary feminist understandings of domestic violence in Poland, and as early as the mid-1990s she lobbied Polish members of Parliament for new legal codes and penalties (although these were not ultimately enacted into law by the Sejm). Nowakowska worked closely with other NGO activists (who had many links of their own to other NGOs and professional associations in Western Europe) to establish and secure public funding for Poland's national hotline for victims of domestic violence as early as 1995 and to train police to better intervene in domestic violence interventions in 1997 (Brunell interviews, with Nowakowska July 2000; Jacek Lelonkiewicz, Director of the Hostel for Women and Children Protecting them Against Violence, Lodz, spring 1997; and Stanisława Walczewska, *Fundacja Kobiet, eFKa,* Krakow, spring 1997).

Russia, on the other hand, is generally not singled out as among the more politically or economically reformed countries in the postcommunist world. However, Russia ranks in the middle of the pack of postcommunist domestic violence policy reformers. This is the result of the relatively strong degree of Western technical assistance, information sharing, and funding extended to Russian activists. For example, one of Russia's strongest anti-violence NGOs is the Moscow-based crisis center ANNA. Begun in 1993 as a one-person hotline, ANNA has become a national advocate, training telephone consultants and social advocates for crisis centers around Russia, coordinating several national campaigns, lobbying parliament, collaborating with the social service ministry, conducting trainings for police, and creating its own network of 170 organizations (Ponarina and Matvienko 2005). According to ANNA's founder and director, Marina Pisklakova, after several years of informal connections with WAVE, a meeting with WAVE director Rosa Lugar in 2000 led ANNA to invite WAVE to partner with them in an EU-funded project. This led to further collaboration:

> Rosa and others came to do training in Russia. They also have had a chance to meet with a lot of women from our network from different regions. Since that [*sic*] WAVE have done a number of training[s] for us on networking, principles of training for professionals on violence against women, [and] women's human rights. [W]e have translated and adapted materials they developed for

Europe. The affiliation did help with developing our ANNA
Network in Russia through training, and contacts that we provide
for regional centers with other members of WAVE (Johnson correspondence, November 17, 2005).

According to Pisklakova, ANNA's and WAVE's formal relationship was
a result of shared understandings of violence against women, but of
course there are also benefits for each group, especially furthering their
credibility as feminist networks. This alliance came about just as ANNA
was transforming itself from a local women's crisis center to a national
leader of the Russian movement. The connection between WAVE and
ANNA has grown despite initial resistance among Central and Eastern
European activists to the inclusion of Russians.[26] WAVE was also connected through the Nordic TFN—the NCRB (Network of Crisis Centers
in the Barents Region) to Northwestern Russian crisis centers, including
one center whose leader had a falling out with the ANNA leadership.[27]
The newly flourishing links further strengthened with the 2004 EU
expansion (which excluded Russia), even though Putin has consolidated a semi-authoritarian regime that has threatened to cut off energy
supplies to Europe. In the new millennium, anti–gender violence affinities have outweighed nationalism for these activists (even helping to
ameliorate some personality conflicts).

Finally, our two least responsive cases to changing DV legislation,
Albania and Armenia, have a much more tenuous connection with
WAVE, Western donor organizations, and the EU. While Albania has
many more links than Armenia, in both countries all NGO links to WAVE
and shelters are in one city, the capital. Many of the NGOs in Albania are
therapeutic in nature and/or related to sex trafficking and the genocidal
sexual violence perpetrated against women in Kosovo, rather than to violence against intimate partners. In these cases, the absence of a broader
network of transnational feminist ties, coupled with strong nationalistic
pressures, negates gender-based claims for justice, and this has fore-
stalled meaningful reforms in both Armenia and Albania (Ishkanian
2004: 281; Johnson and Brunell 2006: 586).

Taken together with the statistical analysis, the various pieces of
our field research create a rich description of how domestic violence
reform became possible in the postcommunist world. First, the reas-
sertion of civil and political rights following communism's collapse, or
at least the demise of communist coercion, created a political context
where feminist organizing and consciousness-raising became possible.
Second, the region's proximity to Western Europe, and the Western

world's interest in creating a stable and democratic order in Eastern Europe, created strong incentives to fund, mentor, and in some cases establish NGOs during the 1990s. The mentoring, relationship building, and sharing of information fostered by the TFN have led to tangible changes in the way these newly democratic regimes are responding to domestic violence.

Conclusion: The Role of Transnational Feminist Networking in Domestic Violence Reform in Postcommunist Europe

To assert that there have been some notable reforms is not to say that the lives of women living under the severe conditions of domestic violence have necessarily improved greatly as a result. Even in the most reformed domestic violence contexts in postcommunist Europe and Eurasia, shelters and prosecution for domestic violence are rare. In short, we know of no countries that have thoroughly and successfully responded to domestic violence. The decline in women's labor market position and their overall living standards since communism's collapse has left most women with fewer solutions for economic survival (Varbanova 2006). Lower rates of young women's workforce participation across the region suggests that this crucial segment of women are even more economically dependent on their intimate partners than the generations before. Although there is no credible comparable data, a variety of studies suggest that levels of domestic violence are higher than during communism and than in established democracies.[28] Further, as domestic violence–specific policies are adopted, unless there are agencies specifically charged with addressing gender equality, domestic violence issues generally fall within the jurisdiction of mainstream policymakers, who distort the domestic violence policies away from their original, feminist intent. For example, a recent study comparing domestic violence policies in the Netherlands, Hungary, and the EU as a whole found that policymakers have de-radicalized and de-gendered the issue (Krizsán, Paantjens, and van Lamoen 2005: 63–92).

Yet, as progress toward more domestic violence responsiveness was facilitated by WAVE, our study suggests that the most fruitful way to create a climate hospitable to further reforms across postcommunist Europe and Eurasia is to foster linkages among activists. Most importantly, these linkages should be fostered in a larger number of places rather than with multiple organizations in the same city. Despite the concrete policy impact of WAVE as documented in this chapter, the WAVE network has long struggled to secure funding, especially in support for its day-to-day activities. More recently, WAVE had difficulty finding even the project funding that had enabled its survival over its first ten years. According to the former coordinator of WAVE, Verena Kaselitz (2006), the problem is rooted in the failure of the international system to accommodate such transnational networks. Even within the EU, there are no legal procedures to allow NGOs to register transnationally (e.g., at the EU level), forcing them to locate in one state (or many different states with one state as headquarters). As a TFN's work spreads transnationally, the national government is unlikely to provide permanent funding since the organization works transnationally. The only TFN that has received sustained EU funding for day-to-day activities is the European Women's Lobby. Kaselitz argues that the lack of a transnational legal charter also facilitates the centralization of TFN activities, eroding feminist attempts to establish less hierarchical organizations and driving away potential affiliates as they cannot legally be equal partners. Of course, there are significant differences in power and resources between the wealthier mostly Western societies and most of the postcommunist societies, but the legal requirements only reinforce these inequalities. When WAVE was forced to downsize due to limited resources, the network was forced to focus its resources on its headquarters in Vienna. Despite these problems, we found the region's activists to be embracing networking.[29]

Transnational feminist networks such as WAVE have proven to be crucial facilitators of domestic violence reform in postcommunist European and Eurasian countries. Our analysis suggests that the concerted efforts of an internationally connected feminist network has much potential to diminish domestic violence. Those concerned with women's rights should encourage states and supranational organizations to provide more support, including long-term funding for day-to-day activities, and to create new mechanisms for transnational networking among activists and policymakers.

In conclusion, our discussion has mapped the institutions of domestic violence policymaking in Europe showing how changes in the international political opportunity structure created by globalization and European integration have facilitated transnational feminist organizing, which has in turn led to domestic violence policy reform.

NOTES

The data for this article were also analyzed, for a different purpose, in Janet Johnson and Laura Brunell, "The Emergence of Contrasting Domestic Violence Regimes in Postcommunist Europe," *Policy & Politics* 24(4) (October 2006): 575–595.

1. Czech feminist and Prague Center for Gender Studies founder Jirina Siklova (2007) notes that "violence against women in the family" is sometimes seen as a problem only arising in democracies, but in reality it was a problem that Czechs had been unable to talk about.

2. While our measures of policy impact detect the influence of Western-derived legal norms and policies as well as public information strategies spreading to the East, our work does not address some of the questions raised by Fábián in chapter 8 of this volume regarding the impact of Central and Eastern European conceptions of the problem of domestic violence on NGO activists based in the West or globally.

3. The Nordic conference was "Gender and Violence," Gothenburg, Sweden, June 2005.

4. The EU conference was the "Together for the Future" European Union forum on Russian civil society, Lahti, Finland, November 2006. The conference was preceded by a meeting of activist-scholars from the postcommunist region (including the former director of WAVE) discussing gender violence work, and the second day included a panel on the topic.

5. We understand Tarrow to use this metaphor to describe the physical geography of this new organizational terrain rather than to indicate that they are ecologically threatened in the same way that coral reefs are today.

6. Available at www.un.org/womenwatch/daw/cedaw/states.htm and www.un.org/womenwatch/daw/cedaw/reports.htm.

7. Available at http://europa.eu.int/comm/justice_home/funding/daphne/funding_daphne_en.htm.

8. Available at www.soros.org/initiatives/women

9. See Minnesota Advocates for Human Rights, "Women's Program," www.mnadvocates.org/Women_s_Program.html (accessed June 28, 2006).

10. Available at www.wave-network.org.

11. In total, this project (up to 2002) was supported through fifteen grants, from various Nordic and EU sources, totaling €363,078 (Saarinen, Liapounova, and Drachova 2003).

12. Minnesota Advocates for Human Rights, "Women's Program," www.mnadvocates.org/Women_s_Program.html [accessed June 28, 2006].

13. The English-language website is www.stopvaw.org and the Russian www.russian.stopvaw.org.

14. WAVE Database on women's organizations and experts working in the field of domestic violence, as well as the relevant public authorities and information on the fields they work in and the services they offer, includes entries for every country in Europe and was expanded in 2007 to include information on the US, Canada, and other countries, as well as international governmental organizations such as the World Bank (see www.wave-network.org/start.asp?b=3).

15. The Commission, which serves as the main executive body for the European Union, funded WAVE as part of its new Daphne Initiative in 1997.

16. Note that, in and of itself, WAVE meets the criteria for being a TFN: it is organized above the national level, unites women from three or more countries around a common agenda, and consists of political change organizations operating above and across national borders.

17. Our data were collected through 2006, so there may be some differences between the way our cases were coded and the way they are described in the more

recent research reported by Fábián in chapter 8 of this volume. She discusses some, though not all, of the state responses we consider here, such as public information campaigns and new legislation. Also, because we are engaging in a more quantitative analysis of the range of state responses across a number of cases, we have made distinctions among state responses that are very specific but that may all have been part of, for example, discussions in parliament and the process of drafting legislations that she describes.

18. Because we have only eleven cases and we are interested in revealing the influence of TFNs alone, we do not conduct multivariate analysis that could measure more complex relationships such as the combined effects of several of our variables working together.

19. European Union, PHARE 1998 Annual Report, http://europa.eu.int/comm/enlargement/pas/phare/ar98/index_ar98.htm, and Tables Summarizing the Allocation of TACIS Resources, 1991–1999, http://europa.eu.int/comm/external_relations/ceeca/tacis/figures.pdf

20. Wedel (1998) gives these figures for Poland, Hungary, the Czech Republic, the Slovak Republic, and "Other CEE Countries" (Albania, Bulgaria, Romania) for 1990–1996. We summed the populations of these three countries, divided the other CEE figures by the population size of each—Albania, Bulgaria, and Romania—and then divided the CEE totals for 1995 by this percentage to arrive at an estimated spending for the individual countries. We repeated this procedure to estimate the spending in Armenia and Moldova as Wedel gives figures for Russia, Ukraine and "Other FSU" 1992–1997.

21. Percentile rank indicates the percentage of countries worldwide that rate below the selected country (subject to margin of error) for year 2000–2001. The governance indicators of reform reported in these maps reflect the statistical compilation of citizens' perceptions of the quality of governance of a large number of survey respondents in industrial and developing countries, as well as in their nongovernmental organizations, commercial risk rating agencies, and think-tanks during 1997 and 1998, and during 2000 and (up to mid-) 2001. For complete explanation or to view data, see http://info.worldbank.org/governance/kkz/.

22. Fish scored the countries as follows for three questions: 1) Who won the initial elections? (2=clear victory by reformers/non-communists; 1=equivocal outcome; 0=clear victory by communists/custodians of the old regime); 2) Were the results of the elections quickly annulled by illegitimate means (force)? (no=1; yes=0); 3) Were the elections freely contested, meaning did they involve elections for all important offices on the national level or for only a portion of them? (complete=1; partial=0).

23. GDI combines factors such as life expectancy at birth, adult literacy, education, estimated earned income, female economic activity as percent of male economic activity, ratio of estimated female to male earned income, and the percent of unemployed who are women. These are indicators of what kind of educational, health, and financial resources women can receive in each country.

24. Measured as the distance from the country's capital to Berlin or Vienna, whichever was closer.

25. Included in our counts were only WAVE database links that listed shelter for women. The database does not stipulate whether the shelters are for women only or only for women with dependent children.

26. Central and Eastern European feminists, following the communist collapse, quickly chose English as their lingua franca even though almost all spoke Russian. For example, when Johnson first spoke with Czech activists in 1999, they would not communicate in Russian. But in 2001 she conducted several interviews with Czech activists in Russian. When other activists overheard one Russian conversation, they were curious and then excited to try out their long-unused Russian. Earlier, they had seemed to equate the Russian language with the Soviet Russian colonization of the Eastern bloc. When the Prague Center for Gender Studies founded the KARAT Coalition of women's NGOs in the region, they explicitly excluded Russia. See Jirina Siklova "Women's Issues in the Czech Republic since EU Accession: An Update," paper presented at the New York University Gender and Transition Workshop, June 2, 2007.

27. The personal links between the northwestern Russian crisis centers and WAVE were evident at the 2005 Nordic and the 2006 EU conferences on gender violence. Russian and WAVE activists not only served together on panels organized by NCRB leaders, but they also befriended each other socially.

28. See surveys reported in the various reports of the Minnesota Advocates for Human Rights on domestic violence in the region; also UNICEF's document "Domestic Violence against Women and Girls," Florence, Italy, Innocenti Research Centre, 2000.

29. Czech feminist Siklova (2007), for example, takes pride in the founding of the postcommunist feminist network the KARAT coalition by the Prague Center for Gender Studies, as well as its membership in other TFNs headed in Western Europe or the United States, such as the European Women's Lobby and the Coalition Against Trafficking. For Siklova, this support extends to the EU as a whole. She has seen a "positive influence of the European Union," pushing the Czech authorities to consider issues that the local leaders would not have considered. There has been no official financial support either for the Prague Center for Gender Studies or for organizing against domestic violence. On the other hand, while she praises "North American and Western European feminism [as] positive" in its impact on Czech feminism, she agrees that Western feminism gave priority to "violence against women" to the detriment of other issues.

WORKS CITED

Araujo, Kathy, Virginia Guzman, and Amalia Mauro. 2000. "How Domestic Violence Came to Be Viewed as a Public Issue and Policy Object." *CEPAL Review* 70 (April): 137–150.

Baldez, Lisa. 2003. "Women's Movements and Democratic Transition in Brazil, Chile, East Germany and Poland." *Comparative Politics* 35(3): 253–272.

Banwell, Suzanna, Erin Barclay, Elisabeth Dubay, and Robin Philips. 2000. *Domestic Violence in Ukraine.* Minneapolis: Minnesota Advocates for Human Rights.

Basu, Amrita. 1995. *The Challenge of Local Feminisms: Women's Movements in Global Perspective.* Boulder, Colo.: Westview Press.

Central Intelligence Agency (US CIA). 2002. "2001 World Factbook." Available at www.odci.gov/cia/publications/factbook/index.html.

————. 2006. "2006 World Factbook." Available at www.cia.gov/cia/publications/factbook/index.html.

Council of Europe. 2001. "Legislation in the Member States of the Council of Europe in the Field of Domestic Violence." January 2001, EG (2001) vols. I and II. Strasbourg: Council of Europe.

Dahlerup, Drude. 1987. *New Women's Movement: Feminism and Political Power in Europe and the USA*. London: Sage.

Dobson, James. 1991. *Straight Talk: What Men Need to Know and What Women Should Understand*. Nashville: W Publishing Group.

European Union. 1991. Tables Summarizing the Allocation of TACIS Resources, 1991.

————. 1998. PHARE 1998 Annual Report.

Fábián, Katalin. 2006. "Against Domestic Violence: The Interaction of Global Networks With Local Activism in Central Europe." In *European Responses to Globalization: Resistance, Adaptation, and Alternatives*, ed. Janet Laible and Henri J. Barkey. New York: Elsevier Press.

Fish, M. Steven. 1998. "The Determinants of Economic Reform in the Postcommunist World." *East European Politics and Societies* 12: 31–78.

Freedom House. 2000. "Freedom House Country Ratings." Available at www.freedomhouse.org.

Henderson, Sarah. 2002. "Selling Civil Society: Western Aid and the Nongovernmental Organization Sector in Russia." *Comparative Political Studies* 35 (March): 139–167.

Impact of Women in Public Office: Findings at a Glance. 2002. Fairfax, Va.: League of Women Voters of the Fairfax Area Education Fund.

Ishkanian, Armine. 2004. "Working at the Local-Global Intersection: The Challenges Facing Women in Armenia's Nongovernmental Sector." In *Post-Soviet Women Encountering Transition: Nation-Building, Economic Survival, and Civic Activism*, ed. Kathleen Kuenhast, and Carol Nechemias, 262–278. Washington, D.C.: Woodrow Wilson Center Press/Johns Hopkins University Press.

Johnson, Janet Elise. 2007. "Can Intervention Help Women? The Global Campaign against Gender Violence in the New Russia." Unpublished manuscript.

Johnson, Janet Elise, and Laura Brunell. 2006. "The Emergence of Contrasting Domestic Violence Regimes in Postcommunist Europe." *Policy & Politics* 34(4): 578–598.

Kantola, Johanna. 2006. *Feminists Theorize the State*. New York: Palgrave Macmillan.

Kaselitz, Verena. 2006. "The Networking of European Women's Organizations and Women's Researchers as Transnational Action against Human Rights Violations: Benefits and Obstacles." Paper given at seminar Gendered Domains: Politics and Democracy in Russia Today, Aleskanteri Institute, Helsinki, Finland, November 16.

Keck, Margaret E., and Kathryn Sikkink. 1998. *Activists Beyond Borders: Advocacy Networks in International Politics*. Ithaca: Cornell University Press.

Kopstein, Jeffrey, and David Reilly. 1999. "Explaining the Why of the Why: A Comment on Fish's 'Determinants of Economic Reform in the Postcommunist World.'" *East European Politics and Societies* 13 (Fall): 613–624.

Kriesberg, Louis. 1997. "Social Movements and Global Transformation." In *Transnational Social Movements and Global Politics: Solidarity Beyond the State,* ed. Jackie Smith, Charles Chatfield, and Ron Pagnucco. Syracuse, N.Y.: Syracuse University Press.

Krizsán, Andrea, Marjolein Paantjens, and Else van Lamoen. 2005. "Domestic Violence: Who's [sic] Problem." *The Greek Review of Social Research* 117 (B).

Linz, Juan J., and Alfred Stepan. 1996. "Toward Consolidated Democracies." *Journal of Democracy* 7(2): 14–33.

Mazur, Amy. 1999. "Feminist Comparative Policy: A New Field of Study." *European Journal of Political Research* 35: 483–506.

McCarthy, John D. 1997. "The Globalization of Social Movement Theory." In *Transnational Social Movements and Global Politics: Solidarity Beyond the State,* ed. Jackie Smith, Charles Chatfield, and Ron Pagnucco. Syracuse, N.Y.: Syracuse University Press.

Merry, Sally Engle. 2006. *Human Rights and Gender Violence: Translating International Law into Local Justice.* Chicago: University of Chicago Press.

Moghadam, Valentine M. 2005. *Globalizing Women: Transnational Feminist Networks.* Baltimore: Johns Hopkins University Press.

Ponarina, L. V., and I. V. Matvienko. 2005. "Protivodeistvie domashnemu nasiliiu: Ot idei k effektifivnoi praktike" (Opposition to domestic violence: From idea to effective practice). In *Razorvat' krug molchaniia: O nasilii v otnoshenii zhen-shchin* (To break the circle of silence: On violence against women), ed. N. M. Rimasheevskaia. Moscow.

Prügl, Elisabeth, and Mary K. Meyer. 1999. "Gender Politics in Global Governance." In *Gender Politics in Global Governance,* ed. Mary Meyer and Elisabeth Prügl. Lanham, Md.: Rowman and Littlefield.

Przeworski, Adam. 1991. *Democracy and the Market.* New York: Cambridge University Press.

Saarinen, Aino, Olga Liapounova, and Irina Drachova, eds. 2003. "NCRB: A Network for Crisis Centres for Women in the Barents Region (Report of the Nordic-Russian Development Project, 1999–2002)." In *Gender Research: Methodology and Practice,* ed. E. V. Kudriashova, R. I. Danilova, M. R. Kalinina, N. N. Koukarenko, O. E. Liapounova, I. R. Lugovskaia, and L. S. Malik. 1–248. Arkhangelsk, Russia: M. V. Lomonosov Pomor State University.

Sperling, Valerie. 1999. *Organizing Women in Contemporary Russia: Engendering Transition.* Cambridge: Cambridge University Press.

Sperling, Valerie, Myra Marx Ferree, and Barbara Risman. 2001. "Constructing Global Feminism: Transnational Advocacy Networks and Russian Women's Activism." *Signs: Journal of Women in Culture and Society* 26(4): 1155–1186.

Stetson, Dorothy McBride, and Amy Mazur. 1995. *Comparative State Feminism.* Thousand Oaks: Sage.

Tarrow, Sidney. 2002. "From Lumping to Splitting: Specifying Globalization and Resistance." In *Globalization and Resistance: Transnational Dimensions of Social Movements,* ed. Jackie Smith and Hank Johnston. Boston: Rowman and Littlefield.

United Nations General Assembly. 1948. *Universal Declaration on Human Rights,* UN General Assembly Resolution 217A(III). Geneva: UN General Assembly.

————. 1962. *Convention on Marriage, Minimum Age for Marriage, and Registration of Marriages,* UN General Assembly Resolution 1763A(XVII). Geneva: UN General Assembly.

Vanya, Magdalena. 2006. "Making Domestic Violence: Gender, Collective Action, and Emerging Civil Society in Postcommunist Hungary and Slovakia." Ph.D. dissertation. University of California, Davis.

Varbanova, Asya. 2006. *The Story Behind the Numbers: Women and Employment in Central and Eastern Europe and the Western Commonwealth of Independent States.* Bratislava: UNIFEM.

Wedel, Janine. 1998. *Collision and Collusion: The Strange Case of Western Aid to Eastern Europe.* New York: St. Martin's Press.

Weldon, S. Laurel. 2002. *Protest, Policy, and the Problem of Violence Against Women: A Cross-National Comparison.* Pittsburgh: University of Pittsburgh Press.

————. 2006. "Inclusion, Solidarity, and Social Movements: The Global Movement against Gender Violence." *Perspectives on Politics* 4(1): 55–74.

CHAPTER 10

The European Union, Transnational Advocacy, and Violence against Women in Postcommunist States

CELESTE MONTOYA

Although the origins of the European Union (EU) revolved largely around economic issues, its expansion into social policy has included issues related to women's rights. Gender equality has been a unique social issue within the EU. Article 141 of the Treaty of Rome, the founding document of what is now the EU, required that member state ensure equal pay for equal work, a measure that received very little attention until feminist organizations in the 1970s pressured the EU to enforce this requirement. A series of rulings and directives by the European Court of Justice and the European Commission, respectively, started a precedent for EU involvement in gender equality issues in the workplace.[1] Since then, the EU has become an important alternative policy venue for feminists in their campaign for gender equality more broadly.

The institutions within the EU that have been more involved in issues of gender equality are the European Commission and the European Parliament. Whereas the European Council represents the governments of member states, the European Parliament represents the people, and the European Commission represents the EU itself. Within these EU institutions, women are more strongly represented than in many of the member state national governments. As of the 2004 elections, women hold approximately 30 percent of the seats in the European Parliament, a percentage higher than that found in a majority of national legislatures. Approximately one-third of the current European Commissioners are women. In addition, there are a number of committees and units designed specifically to address issues related to gender equality. The European Parliament has a Committee on Women's Rights and Gender Equality. In the European Commission, under the Employment, Social Affairs, and Equal Opportunities Directorate, there are two units that deal with gender equality issues: the Equal Opportunities for Women and Men: Strategy and Program Unit and the Equality of Treatment between Women and Men: Legal Questions Unit. Other committees pertaining to gender equality include the Fundamental Rights Committee; the

Anti-discrimination and Equal Opportunity Group (of Commissioners); the High Level Group on Gender Mainstreaming; the Advisory Committee on Equal Opportunities for Women and Men; the Inter-service Group on Gender Equality; and the Group of Experts on Gender, Social Inclusion, and Employment.

An important institution for the advocacy of gender equality in the EU is the European Women's Lobby (EWL). The EWL was created with the support of the European Commission. Its mission is to "work together to achieve equality between women and men, to eliminate all forms of discrimination against women, to ensure that women's human rights are respected, to eradicate violence against women, and to make sure that gender equality is taken into consideration in all European Union policies."[2] It is the largest umbrella organization of women's associations in Europe and provides an important link between nongovernmental organizations (NGOs) and the EU institutions. It has actively advocated on behalf of a number of gender equality issues, including violence against women. In 1997, the EWL created the European Observatory on Violence against Women, an expert group made up of representatives from each member state, each with extensive expertise on the issue of gender violence.[3]

In recent years the EU institutions and the European Women's Lobby have all been involved in addressing issues of gender equality that go beyond the workplace, including violence against women. These institutions have been a part of the effort to advocate for better domestic policies aimed at improving women's human rights. However, despite the support and effort of these institutional actors, many issues related to gender equality are treated less seriously. As stated by members of the United Development Fund for Women (UNIFEM) in a consultative meeting held in April of 2006, "The strong focus of EU directives related predominantly to gender equality on labor market issues leaves other areas that are fundamental to achieving gender equality insufficiently addressed and uncovered by legally binding instruments" (UNIFEM 2006: 2). Whereas equal treatment and equal employment fall within the scope of hard law policy (policy that is legally binding and enforceable), efforts to address issues such as violence against women have come primarily in the form of soft law policy—nonbinding resolutions and recommendations. Despite limitations, soft law measures are still means of raising public awareness, legitimizing issues, and placing them on the political agenda.

The EU and the Rhetorical Advocacy of Combating Violence against Women

In the past ten years, the EU has issued and adopted numerous communications, reports, recommendations, and resolutions addressing violence against women in its many forms (see appendix 1). After Vienna hosted the United Nations Conference on Human Rights in 1993, and in the subsequent Fourth UN World Conference on Women held in Beijing in 1995, the EU responded to their agenda items, starting with increased attention to sexual trafficking. In 1996, the European Commission issued a Communication on Trafficking in Women stating the objectives of increasing cooperation and coordination among the member states and providing greater protection for victims. Two years later, in 1998, the Commission's Second Communication on Further Actions in the Fight Against Trafficking in Women reinforced the stated commitment to the issue and their intent for better cooperation, but went a step further by including new objectives focusing on prevention, research, law-enforcement, sanctions for traffickers, and support to victims.

In 1998, the Council of the European Union held the first meeting of experts addressing violence against women, resulting in the creation and adoption of the Measures to Combat Male (Domestic) Violence against Women Standards and Recommendations. Included in the document were fifty-two explicit norms and recommendations, particularly for police organizations and criminal proceedings. It also emphasized the need for cooperation between state institutions and women's organizations. In March and November of 1999, two follow-up meetings were held that resulted in ten additional recommendations. Added provisions emphasized the need for member states to establish explicit legal regulations pertaining to domestic violence, to improve and closely monitor implementation, and to increase state provisions of extensive services for battered women (for example, providing shelters, hotlines, crisis centers, legal aid, housing, training, and employment). In addition, the new recommendations included a focus on the importance of expanding transnational networks and the need for training those who come into contact with victims (social workers, health providers, police, etc.).

During this time period, the European Commission launched the Campaign for Zero Tolerance of Violence against Women. The Commission allocated €4 million to the campaign, whose primary objectives were to raise public awareness about domestic violence and to work towards better prevention. A number of slogans and messages were disseminated through posters, brochures, and Internet sites in order to raise awareness of the issue and work toward better prevention. The campaign closed in May 2000 at the International Conference in Lisbon with the president of the European Council Presidency, Jaime Gama of Portugal, calling on the Council, the Commission, and member states to "make the solemn commitment to combat all forms of violence against women, through the adoption of legal, administrative and other provisions, to ensure a study of violence and its prevention and the protection, assistance and compensation of the victims" (Gama 2000: 23).

The European Union has continued to speak about the issue of violence against women and to urge member states to take more definitive measures. More recently, in February 2006, the European Parliament passed a Recommendation on Combating Violence against Women, which thoroughly discussed the different forms of violence and is explicit in its encouragement to take action. In addition, the EU has dedicated €50 million to the creation of a Gender Institute in Vilnius, Lithuania, focused on gender equality, and has designed a roadmap for five years with six priority areas of action, one of which is the eradication of violence against women.[4]

Although the EU has been vocal about the issue of violence against women and despite undertaking a number of initiatives, it is important to reiterate that none of these actions has committed member states to changing their policies and practices. There are no legally binding treaty provisions or directions that specifically address violence against women. The European Commission confirmed this stance in its 2004 *Report on Equality between Men and Women,* stating that "the prevention of and fight against domestic violence fall mainly under local and national competences of member states." Because of this failure to take a more definitive stance, the EU has elicited much criticism from women's NGOs. There remains considerable skepticism that the EU efforts have amounted to more then mere rhetoric. That skepticism has carried over into the assessment of the accession process.

EU Accession and the Conditionality of Membership

The conditionality of EU membership has been a major impetus for policy change in many postcommunist countries. In order to become members of the EU, candidate countries are required to meet a number of criteria. These criteria were laid out by the European Council in 1993, and have been referred to as the Copenhagen Conditions or the

Copenhagen Criteria. In addition to economic criteria, membership has required that candidate countries guarantee democracy, the rule of law, human rights, and respect for and protection of minorities. In addition, candidates are required to adopt the *acquis communautaire*, the entire accumulated body of EU law, including treaties, regulations, directives, and judgments made by European institutions. The *acquis communautaire* is considered to be "hard law," legally binding and enforceable. However, the European Commission has argued that social dialogue is also to be considered a part of the *acquis* for applicants (Grabbe 2002: 253). This includes soft-law measures (nonbinding resolutions and recommendations). Applicants are required to adopt and meet the conditions of these measures, meaning that applicant states are, at least theoretically, held to a significantly higher standard than member states in regard to a number of issues.

Although violence against women has by no means been a prioritized condition for membership, successive reforms in acceding countries' domestic legislation can be observed beginning during the negotiation process. Though it is unlikely that the EU was the only impetus behind these policy reforms, the timing and nature of the changes strongly suggest that the EU played a role in changing the legal situation for women in its new member states.[5]

Timing of the Change in Legislation Addressing Violence against Women

For EU members before 2004, there are two waves of policy reform pertaining to violence against women. The first wave occurs in the early 1990s concurrently with the rise in international activism on behalf of violence against women, as seen at the Vienna and Beijing conferences. This wave includes such countries as Denmark, France, Sweden, and the UK. The second wave occurs in the late 1990s and early 2000s after the EU starts promoting policy change. This wave includes countries with governments that had previously been more reluctant to address violence against women, such as Germany and Italy. The third wave contains the postcommunist member and candidate states. It starts building in the late 1990s, but reaches its peak right around the time of the 2004 accession. Looking at the timing of the reforms made within individual countries (shown in appendix 1), there is also a distinction to be made between those countries that joined the EU in 2004 (the Czech Republic, Estonia, Hungary, Latvia, Lithuania, Poland, Slovakia, and Slovenia), and those scheduled for accession later (Bulgaria, Croatia,

Romania, and the Former Yugoslav Republic of Macedonia). Countries scheduled to join the EU in 2004 start making their reforms in the late 1990s, the remaining postcommunist countries after 2000.

While this evidence does not determine a direct causality between the EU efforts and domestic policy reforms, the timing is suggestive that there is some relationship. This by no means downplays the role of advocacy groups at the local level or efforts by other international institutions in support of violence against women. However, it does provide evidence of a pattern that merits further exploration. The aggregate pattern should be compared with national level studies. The subsequent section takes a closer look at the type of reforms made.

Nature of the Change

This section provides a comparative overview of the legislative reforms made in the postcommunist member and candidate states (see appendix 1). Below I discuss the legislative reforms in relation to the type of violence they address. I distinguish between laws dealing with rape, domestic violence, trafficking, and sexual harassment.

In the history of policies addressing violence against women, statutes dealing with rape often constitute the first type of law to appear on the books for many countries. However, the legal definition of rape has often been very narrowly construed, referring to a visibly violent act (as produced by a severe battering) and perpetrated by a stranger. These early policies did not account for acquaintance or spousal rape. Punishments were rare and light, and in some cases perpetrators could go free if they married their victims. Postcommunist countries with older legislation against rape include the Czech Republic, Hungary, and Romania. EU recommendations reflect the international feminist movements and call for broader legal definitions of rape and harsher penalties. Such reforms have started to appear in a few postcommunist countries. Countries amending or adding legislation include the Czech Republic, Hungary, Latvia, and the Former Republic of Macedonia. Among the policies addressing violence against women, rape is the type of violence that has received the least amount of legislative attention.

Although women's mobilization on the issue of domestic violence is not new, it has taken much longer for states to address the issue. Patriarchal constructions of family have allowed for, even prescribed, violence against children and women by the male head of the household. The public/private divide has been used as a justification for maintaining policy silence on the issue. Of the policies discussed in this chapter, this is the type of violence that has seen the greatest amount of legislative reform in the postcommunist member and candidate states, and in a short amount of time. In 1996, when preparations were first beginning for the EU accession of the new member states, none of these countries, with the exception of Slovenia, had any laws regarding domestic violence. However, by 2005, five of the eight new member states had introduced legislation prohibiting violence within the family (including the Czech Republic, Hungary, Lithuania, Poland, and Slovakia) and Slovenia had amended its policy. Today, Estonia and Latvia remain two of the only EU member states without an explicit domestic violence policy (see appendix 1).[6]

Sexual harassment has been an issue receiving much attention by the European Union, particularly sexual harassment within the workplace, an area where the EU has established legal competency. None of the new member states had laws prohibiting sexual harassment prior to initiating the integration process. However, by 2005, five of the countries had amended their labor codes to contain wording specifically banning sexual harassment, including the Czech Republic, Estonia, Lithuania, Poland, and Slovenia. Slovakia enacted an anti-discrimination law in 2004 that defined and prohibited "degrading" or "intimidating" harassment in the workplace. Hungary, Latvia, and the Former Republic of Macedonia remain without an explicit law on sexual harassment, allowing prosecution of sexual harassment under gender discrimination laws.

Within the past decade, sexual trafficking has become a more predominant issue on the international agenda. Though many of the postcommunist countries provided legislation punishing "forced illegal immigration," it was not until the incentive of EU accession was presented that many of these countries began specifically outlawing trafficking in humans for the purpose of sexual exploitation. Five new member states adopted new legislation during or after the year 1997, including Hungary, Lithuania, Poland, Latvia, and Slovenia. Since then, all of the postcommunist countries except for Estonia have adopted and/or reformed trafficking legislation.

Despite these legislative reforms, there is still much work to be done by all of these countries in addressing violence against women. The EU's failure in assuming a more authoritative role with respect to violence against women has resulted in uneven and inconsistent policy reforms. The gender equality laws of new member states suffer from serious flaws and inadequacies. A lack of specific and distinct laws prohibiting the various types of violence against women (for example, a separate law addressing spousal rape rather than allowing for prosecution under general rape laws, or a law specifically prohibiting sexual harassment rather than using general anti-discrimination laws to prosecute such cases) frequently allows perpetrators to avoid receiving punishment commensurate with their crime. In addition, the gender neutrality in the language of many of the laws and lack of gender disaggregated statistics and data tend to hinder improving the situation of women at a significant rate. Most important, however, are the issues regarding lack of enforcement and inadequate victim assistance, both of which are severe in most of the postcommunist countries.

The adoption of new laws addressing violence against women in the new EU member and applicant postcommunist countries has not necessarily reflected a commitment to combating violence against women. More often than not, many of these changes in the law were merely part of the signaling game played between applicant states and the EU in the accession process, or between these countries and the international community more broadly. The postcommunist countries have a lot of work to complete before they actually improve the de facto situation of women in their respective states. However, the introduction of new laws addressing violence against women has been an important step forward. Although a policy is only as good as its implementation, having a policy there in the first place is a significant accomplishment. Formal legislation is one means of legitimizing an issue within the society. It also provides a point of mobilization around which groups can join to push for implementation. The next section addresses EU measures aimed at building NGO capacity in member states. NGO capacity is another important part of improving measures to combat violence against women, as it is likely that implementation will require an organized societal effort to work with and place continual pressure on state institutions.

EU Initiatives to Build Domestic Capacity for Combating Violence against Women

In addition to urging member and candidate states to improve policy measures combating violence against women, the EU has demonstrated its advocacy by providing resources for domestic and transnational organizations. The European Commission has started several programs to oversee efforts aimed at domestic capacity building. For example, in 1996, the EU initiated the STOP, an incentive and exchange program for persons responsible for combating trade in human beings and the sexual exploitation of children. The Commission helps fund the EWL's Observatory on Violence and the EU Gender Institute.[7] One of the EU's most important endeavors for addressing the issue of violence against women has been the development of a program called Daphne. The European Commission created Daphne in 1997 with the purpose of developing a coordinated and comprehensive approach to dealing with the issue of domestic violence in European society by supporting and promoting cooperation with and among NGOs, increasing and improving the research on violence in order to provide more accurate information on domestic violence, developing preventative measures, and strengthening the protection of victims. Daphne has funded numerous projects dealing with domestic violence broadly, some of which focus primarily on children, others on women or women and children. Because this chapter is concerned with violence against women, I will include in my subsequent analysis only efforts that address violence against women.[8] Daphne has also supported a wide array of projects addressing violence against women that go beyond domestic violence, including projects dealing with sexual assault, sexual harassment, sexual trafficking, forced prostitution, and other forms of violence against women. Some of the supported projects address violence against women more broadly, while others focus on certain groups: young women, old women, disabled women, women from different ethnic diasporas, trafficked women, immigrants, etc. The goals and activities of these projects are also varied, with projects focused on public awareness campaigns, development and improvement of victim services, conferences, and research.

Since its founding in 1997, the Daphne Program has contributed to the advocacy of combating domestic violence by serving as a significant source of resources to domestic organizations. Daphne has run in three phases: the Daphne Initiative (1997–1999); the Daphne Program (2000–2003); and Daphne II (2004–2008).[9] The Daphne Initiative was run by the European Commission with a starting budget of €3 million per year, which was increased to €5 million in 1999.[10] The Initiative was open to all member states (which at that time included Austria, Belgium, Denmark, Finland, France, Germany, Great Britain, Greece, Ireland, Italy, Luxembourg, the Netherlands, Portugal, Spain, and Sweden), although candidate states could be included in the proposed projects as associate organizations. The second phase, the Daphne Program, expanded the focus on NGOs to include local public institutions. With a renewed budget of €20 million, extending for four years, it was able to start funding multi-annual projects, whereas before it was necessary to restrict project funding to twelve months. In the third phase of Daphne, the budget was increased to €50 million extending over five years (€10 million per year as opposed to the €5 million per year in Daphne I).[11] This increase was necessary as a response not only to the high number of proposals but to the completed accession of the new member states. The third phase has also allowed for a wider array of activities aimed at addressing violence against women. The next phase of Daphne, Daphne III, was approved in May 2007, with a budget of €138 million.

In order to receive funding from Daphne, organizations must undergo a rigorous proposal process that is highly competitive.[12] The increasing demand for funding has resulted in a steady increase of the budget provided by the EU, but the acceptance rate is still relatively low. Some countries' organizations have been more successful at securing funding themselves or have been more likely to be asked to participate as associate partners. From the first phase, the Daphne Initiative, postcommunist countries have been included in Daphne projects; however, only member states have been able to serve as the lead organizations for projects.[13] It was not until 2004 that any of the postcommunist countries were able to direct and lead a Daphne sponsored program.

In order to analyze the participation of organizations from postcommunist countries in Daphne, I have put together a database of all Daphne projects related to violence against women by using the Daphne Toolkit, a website keeping a public record of the projects.[14] The website includes a summary of all projects as well as relevant reports and documents. From these reports, I was able to gather data on project participants, goals, and activities. My database includes projects from 1997 to 2004.[15]

Relatively few projects include the organizations from postcommunist states prior to the EU accession. Out of the 97 projects funded in the first phase, organizations from the postcommunist countries participated in only 9 projects. The Czech Republic, Estonia, Lithuania, and Slovakia each have organizations participating in one program. Only Poland, and surprisingly Romania, have organizations participating in more than one program. In the second phase, the Daphne Program, there is only a slight increase in participation. Out of 95 projects, the postcommunist countries participate in only 12 projects. Estonia, Latvia, and Slovenia each have organizations participating in one project. Lithuania and Romania have organizations participating in three projects, Hungary and Poland in four, and Bulgaria in five. It is not until the third phase of Daphne, after these postcommunist countries' membership is official, that there was a significant increase in participation. In 2004, all of the new postcommunist member states participated in at least four projects. Hungarian organizations participate in 10 projects, falling behind only Belgium and Italy. In addition to increased participation, some of the postcommunist organizations even take on leadership positions, with organizations from the Czech Republic, Hungary, Latvia, and Lithuania all serving on projects where they are the lead organizations. As of 2004, of the then candidate countries, only Bulgaria and Romania had organizations that participated in Daphne programs, whereas Croatia and Macedonia had not.

Another way to examine postcommunist countries' participation in Daphne is by looking at their placement within the Daphne network. In addition to examining the number of projects that organizations from postcommunist countries participated in, I employed social network analysis. Social network analysis (SNA) is a visual and mathematical analysis of relationships among entities. SNA maps out the location of actors within the network; it illustrates which actors are most central to the network and which operate more on the periphery. Used cross-temporally, social network analysis can show the changes or developments in a network. Nodes and links are two concepts central to social network analysis. Nodes are the individual actors within a network (people, groups, organizations, etc.). The links, or ties, between the nodes denote the relationships between actors. In applying SNA to Daphne, the nodes represent organizations aggregated by domestic origin.[16] The links represent the cooperation between groups on projects funded by Daphne.[17] After counting the linkages between countries, project by project, from 1997 to 2004, I constructed a binary matrix that identified partnerships between countries.[18] The data were then transformed into a graphic visualization of the 1997–2004 Daphne network, as can be seen in the figure 10.1.[19]

Figure 10.1 illustrates the placement of countries within the larger Daphne network. Countries with a higher number of and diversity of partnerships are placed more centrally in the figure. Those with a lesser number of partnerships and with a more limited range of partners are placed in the periphery. The postcommunist countries are primarily located in the periphery. In fact, Slovenia is the only country taking a more central position in the network. Slovenia is not the country with the most projects; however, its more central position illustrates that on the projects it did participate in, there were more partners, meaning it had more transnational interaction.

Daphne has provided many resources to organizations and has helped to facilitate transnational cooperation. However, its impact on the newer postcommunist member and candidates states, in comparison to other member states, has been less impressive. The postcommunist states have participated in fewer projects and are still on the periphery of the Daphne transnational network. On the other hand, it is important to note that the data included in this analysis derive primarily from the period before accession. The increased participation of the postcommunist countries in 2004 shows promising improvement. As grassroots organizations in the postcommunist countries continue forward they should be better situated to take advantage of resources, such as those provided by Daphne. In fact, their participation as conference attendees and associated partners should better prepare them to initiate their own projects and take on a more active leadership role within the Daphne networks, as well as other international and transnational advocacy networks.

In addition, the above network analysis focuses on participation in project planning and not on the participation in individual projects, thus potentially underestimating Daphne's facilitation of transnational cooperation. For example, Daphne has also funded numerous conferences that may be run by only a handful of organizations, but are attended by hundreds of participants representing numerous organizations from all of the member and candidate states. In addition, Daphne has funded a number of efforts that promote transnational cooperation. For instance, Daphne funded Women against Violence in Europe (WAVE), the most extensive violence network in Europe. Founded in 1994, WAVE was only able to get its work underway after receiving sizeable funding from the Daphne Initiative in 1997.[20] WAVE has since become a network of approximately 2,500 European women's NGOs working to combat violence against women (including women's shelters, counseling centers, hotlines, and the like).

Despite its failure to take a more definitive stance on violence against women, the EU has still served as an important advocate for combating violence against women in at least three key ways. First, the EU has helped to further legitimize the issue. It has placed violence against women on the European political agenda by issuing recommendations, resolutions and reports; by holding various conferences and expert meetings to address the issue; and through public awareness campaigns such as the Zero Tolerance Campaign. Second, the EU has encouraged policy change in member and candidate states. The timeline of legislative reforms regarding violence against women in postcommunist states suggests a correlation between the process of EU accession and new laws addressing violence against women. Particularly compelling have been the two waves of reform in the postcommunist member and candidate states, one beginning in the late 1990s for states that entered the EU in 2004, and the second beginning in 2000 as Macedonia, Romania, Bulgaria, and Croatia worked towards their accession. Although these reforms may not yet have improved the situation for women in the postcommunist states, local NGOs can now point to these new laws when demanding state support. Finally, the EU has provided resources for local organizations and simultaneously helped to facilitate transnational cooperation among them. In particular, the creation and expansion of Daphne has been the EU's most impressive effort to address violence against women so far.

However, there is still more work to be done. Until the EU takes a more definitive stance on violence against women, reform in many member states may continue to lag. Until then, more research is necessary for understanding the variations between countries. Why were more extensive legislative reforms made in some countries than in others? Why are some countries more likely to be within the center of the transnational networks? I believe these answers can be found in future research that more closely addresses the role of NGOS in the larger transnational networks. While this paper has focused primarily on EU actions, additional work needs to be done examining the EU linkages with local organizations.

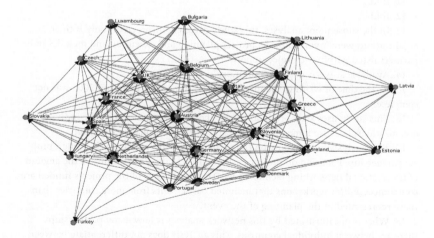

Figure 10.1. Social network analysis of Daphne participants, 1997–2004.

NOTES

1. For a more complete account of the European Union and gender equality in employment policy, see Cichowski 2002; Ellina 2003; Elman 1996; Hoskyns 1995; Kilpatrick 2001; Mazey 1998.

2. This mission statement and more information about the European Women's Lobby (EWL) can be found on their website at www.womenlobby.org.

3. The Observatory's mission is to work towards improving the monitoring and implementation of national policy regarding violence against women. Its goal is to accomplish this by helping to set up national observatories in every member state. As of 2007, observatories have been set up in only five countries: Denmark, France, Finland, Greece, and Ireland.

4. Communication from the Commission to the Council, the European Parliament, the European Economic and Social Committee, and the Committee of the Regions: A Roadmap for Equality between Women and Men 2006–2010.

5. As discussed in other chapters in this book, the United Nations and local groups must also be recognized for their advocacy efforts to combat violence against women.

6. It is important to note that although domestic violence is considered one of the important women's rights issues, it is not always treated as such. In some countries, there has been greater responsiveness towards prioritizing the issue of child abuse than wife battering. Thus, as with other legislative reform, how and whether the policy is implemented remains to be seen.

7. These organizations were discussed in previous sections. More information on the Observatory can be found on the European Women's Lobby's website www .womenlobby.org. The European Institute of Gender Equality will be operational in 2008. More information can be found on the EU's webpage, including the original proposal, available at http://europa.eu/scadplus/leg/en/cha/c10938.htm.

8. I have excluded projects that focus on child abuse in a gender-neutral fashion.

9. See European Commission (2005), *The Daphne Experience: 1997–2003.*

10. Ibid.

11. Ibid.

12. Ibid.

13. In the subsequent analyses, this study gives countries credit only if their organizations were involved in the project planning and execution and includes only partners listed within the project reports.

14. Available at www.daphne-toolkit.org.

15. At the time of writing, the information on projects in 2005 and 2006 was not complete.

16. This study uses state origin as the level of analysis rather than the individual organizations, because it measures the degree of transnational cooperation.

17. This analysis focuses only on the networking that has occurred through project partnership. Focusing on project partnership actually underestimates the amount of transnational networking facilitated by Daphne, as some of the projects funded are conferences and/or workshops that included participants from more countries than those represented in the planning of the event.

18. What is not illustrated by this network analysis is how many partnerships there are between individual countries. This analysis does not differentiate between

lead organizations and other associated organizations; such issues are outside the scope of this study but will be addressed in future research.

19. Figure 10.1 was created with the program NetDraw.

20. For more information on the activities and history of WAVE, see their website: http://wave-network.org.

WORKS CITED

Cichowski, Rachel. 2002. "No Discrimination Whatsoever: Women's Transnational Activism and the Evolution of EU Sex Equality Policy." In *Women's Activism and Globalization: Linking Local Struggles and Transnational Politics,* ed. Nancy A. Naples and Manisha Desai 220–238. New York: Routledge.

Commission of the European Communities. 2006. Communication from the Commission to the Council, the European Parliament, the European Economic and Social Committee, and the Committee of the Regions: A Roadmap for Equality between Women and Men 2006–2010.

Ellina, Chrystalla. 2003. *Promoting Women's Rights: The Politics of Gender in the European Union.* New York: Routledge.

Elman, Amy. 1996. "Introduction: The EU from Feminist Perspectives." In *Sexual Politics and the European Union,* ed. Amy Elman. Providence: Berghahn Books.

European Commission. 2005. *The Daphne Experience: 1997–2003.*

———. 2004. *Report on Equality between Women and Men, 2004.*

Gama, Jaime. 2000. Statement by the Presidency: Closing of the Zero Tolerance Campaign. May 6. Lisbon: European Union.

Grabbe, Heather. 2002. "European Union Conditionality and the *Acquis Communautaire.*" *International political Science Review* 23(3): 249–268.

Hoskyns, Catherine. 1999. "Gender and Transnational Democracy: The Case of the European Union." In *Gender Politics in Global Governance,* ed. Mary K. Meyer and Elisabeth Prügl. Lanham, Md.: Rowman and Littlefield.

———. 1995. "The European Union and the Women Within: An Overview of Women's Rights Policy." In *Sexual Politics and the European Union,* ed. Amy Elman. Providence: Berghahn Books.

Kilpatrick, Claire. 2001. "Gender Equality: A Fundamental Dialogue." In *Labour Law in the Courts: National Judges and the European Court of Justice,* ed. Silvana Sciarra. Portland: Hart Publishing.

Mazey, Sonia. 1998. "The European Union and Women's Rights." In *Beyond the Market: The EU and National Social Policy,* ed. David Hine and Hussein Kassim. London: Routledge.

UNIFEM CEE. 2006. Statement on Gender Equality in the EU. UNIFEM.

CHAPTER 11

The Promise and Perils of International Treaties

OLGA AVDEYEVA

This chapter investigates the impact of international treaties about women's rights (the CEDAW and the Beijing Platform for Action) on government action concerning violence against women in fifteen post-Soviet countries. In recent years, scholars of international relations noted a remarkable diffusion of similar policies, including policies promoting women's rights, across widely differing nation-states (Bunch 1995; Goodman and Jinks 2004; True and Mintrom 2001). A formal ratification of international human rights treaties, however, does not always generate changes in states' policy practices. Analysis of government action concerning violence against women in fifteen post-Soviet states reveals that despite the fact that all these states are parties to the CEDAW and the Beijing Platform for Action, the governments of these countries continue to violate international policy recommendations.

In this chapter, I explore a gap between the states' proclivity to join international human rights agreements and their readiness to improve their domestic policy practices. Two questions drive my analysis: 1) Why do governments ratify international treaties and not comply with them? 2) What explains the improvement of states' practices in some areas of policy on gender violence in several countries (Lithuania, Belarus, Estonia, Ukraine, Russia, Azerbaijan, Latvia, and Kazakhstan)?

By 1997, governments of all analyzed countries ratified the CEDAW and the Beijing Platform for Action, which recommend that states combat violence against women through a systematic policy program. In these documents, the term "violence against women" means "any act of gender-based violence that results in, or is likely to result in, physical, sexual or psychological harm or suffering to women, including threats of such acts, coercion or arbitrary deprivation of liberty, whether occurring in public or private life" (Commission on the Status of Women 1995). Accordingly, the term covers violent actions against women occurring in the family, in the community in general, and perpetrated by the state. Violence against women encompasses wife-battering, sexual abuse of female children in the household, dowry-related violence, marital rape, female genital mutilation and other traditional practices harmful to women, and non-spousal violence.

The international treaties recommend that governments pursue an integrated approach to eliminating and preventing violence against women including provisions for assisting victims and potential victims (Commission on the Status of Women 1995). Among specific measures, governments are recommended to create institutions to oversee this problem, develop training, preventive, and rehabilitation programs, provide well-funded shelters and relief support for victims of violence, and raise public awareness about the scope of the social problem and also about services available to victims. In my analysis I employ these policy recommendations for developing the criteria for assessment of government action. Government action, the dependent variable in this study, is evaluated along three parameters:

1) Adoption of a separate law on violence against women

2) Establishment of government offices on violence against women

3) Implementation of several policy components (police training, judiciary training, government-sponsored shelters, government-sponsored awareness-raising campaigns, and cooperation with nongovernmental organizations [NGOs]).

Among my cases, no government pursues systematic enforcement of the policy; some governments, however, took some steps to conform to international recommendations. For example, Kyrgyzstan and Ukraine adopted a separate law on domestic violence; Ukraine, Russia, Kazakhstan, and Belarus provided some financial support to shelters; Ukrainian, Estonian, Lithuanian, and Latvian governments conducted some training programs for police. Eight governments did not take any steps to comply with international agreements. What explains the fact that all governments ratified these international treaties? Why did several governments initiate some implementation of these policies?

Theoretically, I propose to consider these questions from the sociological perspective, which argues that states are social actors who respond to imagined or real social pressures to formally assimilate with other states in a global community. In recent years many states ratified international human rights treaties (Goodman and Jinks 2003, 2004; Hafner-Burton and Tsutsui 2005). The growing number of parties to these treaties reinforced the legitimacy of human rights agreements in the international arena. The reinforced legitimacy of international agreements created an additional incentive for states to join them, because ratification of human rights treaties became an act of appropriate behavior. The act of ratification demonstrates the state's commitment to human rights. Ratification of human rights treaties, however, does not always generate government compliance with these international treaties, because the enforcement mechanism of international human rights treaties is very weak: states do not face any substantial punishments, for instance fines, exclusion from international organizations, or direct intervention in their domestic affairs by international observers if they continue their violating practices (Goodman and Jinks 2004). Thus, we find that many governments can get away with taking no steps to change their domestic practice and enforce new policies.

Why do some states start to enforce at least some policy recommendations in cases when no coercive measures were taken by the international organizations? Analysis of seven countries where governments attempted to reconcile their policy commitments and policy practice demonstrates that policy enforcement is facilitated by several factors: 1) involvement of international organizations, including the United Nations Development Program (UNDP), the United Nations Children's Fund (UNICEF), and the Organization for Security and Cooperation in Europe (OSCE), who took the initiative in designing and funding collaborative programs to combat violence against women; these international organizations are actively involved in developing anti-violence programs across the region, but in Ukraine they pushed governments to develop sustained (lasting over time) program commitments. 2) The existence of a broad network of domestic NGOs improved policy compliance in Russia and Kazakhstan: governments in these states grant financial support to women's NGOs on a competitive basis. 3) Intergovernmental programs between several states, usually Western and Eastern states, create avenues for government action in the Baltic states: in Lithuania, Latvia, and Estonia governments initiated training seminars for police in cooperation with governments of Denmark and Norway during the Daphne collaborative project.

The chapter builds on case studies on Ukraine by Hrycak and on Russia by Johnson and Zaynullina in this volume (chapters 2 and 3). It places these cases in a larger comparative picture of government compliance across the former post-Soviet republics. The analysis of arguments and data are presented in the following order. First I will discuss theoretical arguments of sociological neoinstitutionalism, which views states as social actors. Then I will provide a brief overview of the UN's efforts to promote and enforce policies on violence against women in national legislations around the world. After presenting the research framework of this project, I will analyze the data on the implementation of policies regarding violence against women and explore possible reasons for policy failure and success.

States as Social Actors

In recent decades scholars of international relations have paid increasing attention to norms of behavior, intersubjective understanding, identity, and culture. The theoretical perspective called sociological neoinstitutionalism offers "a particularly powerful set of arguments about the role of norms and culture" in international relations (Finnemore 1996: 325). Developed from organizational theory, sociological neoinstitutionalism was originally concerned with the effects of a wider social environment on the goals and composition of organizations (Meyer and Rowan 1977). Noting an increasing isomorphism or structural similarity across organizations, scholars of this approach argue that organizations routinely copy taken-for-granted models deemed legitimate in the environment where they function (Meyer and Scott 1992). Legitimacy, therefore, becomes a key mechanism for increasing convergence of organizational structures.

Applied to the study of international political processes, sociological neoinstitutionalism views states as social actors shaped and legitimated by internationally accepted standards and norms of behavior (Meyer et al. 1997). As many governments accept and institutionalize shared models and standards of behavior, they reinforce the legitimacy of these standards in the global arena, which encourages other states to restructure and reorganize their national policies around these international models.

At the core of this sociological argument is the idea that states as social actors are driven to form associational ties with other states. This drive is cognitive; it is understood through sociopsychological self-perception of the state and the way the state is perceived by other states in a group. Sociopsychological perceptions generate pressure on the state to conform to group norms of behavior. The pressure takes the form of various sociopsychological costs (cognitive dissonance, discomfort, and exclusion) and benefits (social inclusion, social approval, comfort, membership, and high social status) associated with conformity (Goodman and Jinks 2004). To avoid sociopsychological discomfort and to gain social recognition and acceptance by others in a group, the states formally accept the group actions and beliefs as legitimate, a ubiquitous strategy to signal to others that the state is not a deviant actor (Hafner-Burton and Tsutsui 2005). The sociological perspective sheds light on why many states choose to ratify international human rights treaties that a group of other states views as legitimate. Non-ratifying actors look like deviant members of the international community. To save their reputation, governments choose to ratify international agreements, often without the intention or capability to change their domestic practices and implement recommended provisions (Hafner-Burton and Tsutsui 2005).

The sociological perspective recognizes the likelihood of a decoupling, or gap, between the states' formal commitment to international treaties and their domestic practices, highlighting a complex dynamics of states' compliance (Meyer and Rowan 1977; Meyer et al. 1997). Weak enforcement capacities of international human rights treaties cannot coerce states to change their domestic practices. Governments of noncomplying states are aware of this flaw and, if implementation implies high costs and goes against domestic interests, governments put little effort toward changing their behavior and practices in line with prescribed norms. This consideration explains why noncompliant governments adopt international human rights treaties and continue their violating practices.

To fully evaluate the decoupling between states' ratification of international treaties on women's rights, it is important to consider the strategies of enforcement that the UN uses to encourage compliance with the CEDAW and the Beijing Platform for Action. As the next section will demonstrate, the main UN strategies rely on voluntary participation and voluntary compliance by the states-parties to these treaties. The UN does not employ coercive mechanisms to foster compliance and punish violators, which leaves a lot of room for noncompliant behavior.

The UN Efforts to Promote Policies on Violence against Women

The Platform for Action of the Fourth World Conference on Women (Beijing, 1995) contains a comprehensive set of measures to combat violence against women on the local, national, and international levels. It establishes three strategic objectives to enforce this problem globally: 1) "take integrated measures to eliminate violence against women"; 2) "study the causes and the consequences of violence against women and the effectiveness of preventive measures"; and 3) "eliminate trafficking in women and assist victims of violence due to prostitution and trafficking" (Commission on the Status of Women 1995).

According to this 1995 document, governments assume the primary responsibility for developing and implementing national policy against domestic violence. A broad set of recommended measures refers to the strengthening and expanding of domestic legislation, including penal, civil, labor, and administrative codes, in order to punish the perpetrators and redress the wrongs done to women. The final document recommends addressing cases of violence against women in a separate penal code, or national law. The Platform for Action recommends that governments create, develop, and fund training programs on violence against women for judicial, legal, police, medical, and immigration services personnel, which will introduce the objectives of the Platform for Action to these public servants. It also states that these public servants must be trained in how to avoid the abuse of power that leads to violence. A set of legislative measures must be introduced to punish police, security forces, and other agents of the state who engage in acts of violence against women (Commission on the Status of Women 1995).

The Platform recommends that governments ensure that the work of all units is coordinated by the state office on combating violence against women or by the state office on women's policy. Ideally, these offices collaborate with a broad range of other institutional actors, such as legislative bodies, academic and research institutions, international NGOs, and local women's NGOs. Governments are advised to cooperate with the Special Rapporteur of the Commission on Human Rights on violence against women and furnish all information requested by her. Since these recommended measures constitute the criteria for analysis of government action in this study, I will introduce the operationalization of these concepts in detail in a following section. At this point, I would like to address the question about the main strategies the UN relies on to enforce these recommendations.

It is well established in the literature that the efforts of the United Nations to protect the rights of individuals and groups can take the form of direct or indirect action (Barnett and Finnemore 2004). Direct action involves activities within states in order to protect the rights of individuals through preventive or protective measures, for instance, a humanitarian intervention (Ofuatey-Kodjoe 2004). Direct actions are quite rare; there have been no cases of the UN directly intervening in order to protect women's rights. UN direct actions to combat gender violence are possible only in those situations when it acts in territories that are under the UN protectorate, such as Kosovo (Coomaraswamy 2003; Minnesota Advocates for Human Rights 2006). In Kosovo, the

UN Mission established three government offices in collaboration with regional authorities for preventing violence against women and assisting victims of violence. In other cases, UN actions take the form of indirect influence; that is, the UN depends on the states to honor their obligations incurred under several standard-setting treaties, such as the CEDAW and the Beijing Platform for Action.

Indirect influence by the UN mainly involves interaction between multiple governmental and nongovernmental actors who engage in various strategies of exchanging information about women's rights and women's issues, including debates, seminars, conferences, and collaborative projects. One of the strategies employed to encourage such interactions is to organize international conferences and meetings. The UN International Women's Decade 1975–1985 started a new era in international women's activism: the four UN women's conferences hosted thousands of participants in Mexico City (1975), Copenhagen (1980), and Nairobi (1985). The UN-led dialogue on women's rights continued in Beijing in 1995. The Beijing Conference was the largest ever event devoted to women's rights, hosting 4,995 official delegates from 189 countries and 4,035 representatives from 2,602 nongovernmental organizations (Freeman 1996; UNIFEM, 1995). These conferences invited governmental officials and activists from national, regional, and international nongovernmental organizations to participate in a dialogue on women's rights and discrimination against women.

As a result of the UN-initiated discussions, representatives of national governments were invited to sign and ensure the implementation of the Platform for Action in their home countries. As an enforcement strategy to foster compliance, the UN officials require that within one year governments-signatories of this document develop and ratify National Plans of Action as the first step in implementing the UN Platform for Action and report this ratification to the Commission on the Status of Women (the CSW). The CSW assumes the main responsibility for monitoring the implementation of national plans of action by various means: analyzing national reports, sending out questionnaires to governments, collecting extensive empirical data, and analyzing changes in domestic legislations (Division for the Advancement of Women 1998). National reporting is the main tool the CSW employs in their assessment of policy enforcement on the national level. Monitoring by UN experts occurs in rare cases; and even when UN experts prepare the report, they rely heavily on national reports (Horowitz and Schnabel 2004). Thus, due to lack of independent monitoring, the monitoring process has the potential for obscuring the assessment of actual policies on the national level.

To facilitate national reporting, in October 1998 the CSW sent out the *Questionnaire to the Governments on Implementation of the Beijing Platform for Action*. The questionnaire addresses the issue of violence against women under the section Critical Areas of Concern. Included questions are broad and inadequate in capturing the complexity of the objectives set by the Platform for Action: 1) "Examples of successful policies, programmes and projects to implement the critical areas of concern of the Beijing Platform for Action (Indicate any targets and strategies set and related achievements)"; 2) "Examples of obstacles/lessons learned"; 3) "Commitment to further action/new initiatives" (Division for the Advancement of Women 1998: 5). The questionnaire downplays the importance of violence against women as an area of policy concern. This is reflected in national action plans across the region: no government has developed a comprehensive policy action in the National Action Plan submitted to the UN except for Estonia and Lithuania, which developed their plans much later, in 2002 and 2006 respectively (Kaljurand 2002; Minnesota Advocates for Human Rights 2006). Moreover, the UN recommends that all areas of concern discussed in the Platform for Action are mentioned in national action plans. However, governments are free to choose which critical areas they will focus on when designing national action plans. Due to this option, in three countries—Latvia, Georgia, and Turkmenistan—the national action plans did not develop policy programs on violence against women as an area of concern.

Government compliance is also impeded by weak enforcement capacities of the CSW: no conditional requirements, fines, or other plausible punishments are imposed on states to enforce compliance. Rather, governments are expected to comply and implement the UN provisions on a voluntary basis. It is no wonder that the analysis of policies on violence against women in post-Soviet countries demonstrates that most governments were not successful in bringing their legislation and policies in line with the UN recommendations. Only eight countries of the fifteen analyzed here have attempted to change their domestic policies and practices during the ten years since the Beijing Conference. The next section will develop study variables of the project, and then I will present and investigate the empirical data.

Conceptualization of Government Action and Study Methods

To assess to what degree national governments in fifteen post-Soviet countries have implemented the provisions of the CEDAW and the Beijing Platform for Action on violence against women, I conceptualize government action as constituted by three parameters. These parameters are developed from the CEDAW and the Beijing Platform for Action recommendations to national governments in the area of violence against women. These documents, therefore, provide the foundation for the assessment of government action on violence against women in the fifteen countries of my analysis. First, I consider *legislative change,* or the adoption of a comprehensive set of laws to prevent violence against women and create avenues for legal redress for victims of violence. I develop the following categories of government response: adopted bill on violence against women; drafted bill on VAW; changes to existing penal code; no legislative change.

The second parameter refers to the UN recommendation to establish a *government institution* that oversees the implementation of policy on gender violence. This involves the establishment of an office within national and regional governmental structures that enjoys various functions, such as legislative (drafting national bills on violence against women and supervising changes in legislation on regional level); advisory and coordination (advising various branches of the government on how to coordinate policy enforcement); enforcement and monitoring (suggesting or drafting specific administrative orders for ensuring policy implementation); and it may include legal redress (assisting victims in court hearings).

The third parameter, implementation of several other policy components—police training, judicial training, public officer training, government-sponsored awareness-raising campaigns against domestic violence or gender violence in the broader sense, and support to NGOs—is assessed along the following criteria:

No provisions (no): no action has been taken by governments;

Minimal: one-time narrow-scope action by the government, no systematic action. For instance, the government in Moldova opened one shelter for victims of gender violence; but it soon transferred it to the responsibility of NGOs and stopped the financial support of this shelter.

Some: several actions, may include sporadic government program; no systematic action. For instance, governments in Lithuania and Estonia organized several seminars and training sessions for police; police officers from two capital cities and several other towns participated in the training. But these sessions did not comprehensively cover all regions in these countries and did not become a systematic event (annual or semi-annual trainings);

Adequate: systematic long-term cross-country action.

These individual elements measuring each of the three analytical concepts are compared across the fifteen post-Soviet states. The analysis takes into consideration only government actions aimed at strengthening national policies against violence. Efforts of local, national, and international nongovernmental organizations to help victims of violence, raise public awareness, and train police, public officers, and judges are excluded from this research project.

The study uses several data sources. Data on institutional and legislative changes are adopted from the Minnesota Advocates for Human Rights (online database 2006) and the International Helsinki Federation Report *Women 2000* (2000). Information on the implementation of policies on violence against women uses data collected from the *Report of the Special Rapporteur on Violence against Women, Its Causes and Consequences* (Coomaraswamy 2003), national reports, and responses of national governments to the UN *Questionnaire on the Implementation of the Beijing Platform for Action.*

Analysis: What Actions Do the Governments Take?

In this section, I analyze how governments in the fifteen post-Soviet states changed their legislation and practices. For clarity, the analysis is presented in three subsections—legislative changes, institutional supervision, and the implementation of policy components—followed by a brief summary of findings at the end.

Legislative Changes

Since 1995, two of the fifteen post-Soviet countries of Eastern Europe and Central Asia have adopted laws against domestic violence: Ukraine (2001) and Kyrgyzstan (2003). Two other countries have drafted such laws: Kazakhstan and Russia. Four countries adopted some changes to national penal codes: Azerbaijan, Georgia, Estonia, and Belarus. Seven countries did not take any action to change their national legislation in accordance with the UN recommendations to provide a definition of gender violence in national law, establish avenues for legal redress, and change legal procedures to introduce a victim-centered approach in cases of violence. The victim-centered approach includes changing humiliating procedures involved in investigating cases of rape, including marital rape; providing rehabilitation services, including counseling and medical assistance, to victims of violence; and shifting the burden of proof from victim to perpetrator. I evaluate changes in national legislation using the UN criteria for policy assessment.

The governments of Ukraine and Kyrgyzstan adopted comprehensive laws on domestic violence. In November 2001, the Parliament of Ukraine adopted a law titled On the Prevention of Domestic Violence, which defined legal and institutional grounds for preventing domestic violence and implementing the law. This law outlines the legal and organizational aspects of policy aimed at preventing domestic violence; it also defines institutions and bodies that are responsible for taking the law into action: the Ministry of Interior is charged with the responsibility of enforcing it. The law adopts a wide definition of violence, including physical, sexual, psychological, and economic violence in the family. Violence in the family is defined as "all deliberate acts of a physical, sexual, psychological and economic nature by one family member toward another family member, if such acts violate constitutional rights and freedoms of the family member and cause moral damage, or damage to physical or psychological health" (cited in Coomaraswamy 2003: 388). Although the law provides a legal basis for restraining orders, due to lack of housing and shelters in the country it does not allow expelling perpetrators from their residences. This law establishes criminal responsibility for domestic violence and sexual abuse; overall, the new law extends the terms of imprisonment for sexual abuse and rape compared to the previous Criminal Code stipulations (for additional information on the Ukrainian case, see chapter 2 in this volume).

Article 1 of the Kyrgyz law "On Social and Legal Protection against Domestic Violence," adopted in 2003, provides definitions for domestic violence, physical domestic violence, psychological abuse, and sexual domestic violence. The definition also applies to family members and relatives who reside with, and experience physical, psychological, or other harm from, abusive family members (Article 5). In addition, Articles 23 and 24 address temporary restraining orders, and Article 25 and 27 provide for protective court orders (Law "On Social and Legal Protection Against Domestic Violence" 2003). In addition to definitions and clarification of punishment procedures, this law specifies the role and responsibilities of social workers, police, and medical personnel in preventing cases of domestic violence. Social workers, police, and medical doctors can start cases on violence against women for victims of violence on the grounds of suspicion that their clients are subject to violence. Overall, the UN experts positively assessed legal changes in Kyrgyzstan and Ukraine, recognizing the comprehensiveness of legal redress and legal provisions but noting poor enforcement capacities allocated by the government (Coomaraswamy 2003).

Russia and Kazakhstan drafted laws on violence against women, but these laws were never adopted by national parliaments: over forty drafts of the law were rejected by the State Duma in Russia. It is important to note that since early 2000 issues of violence against women, as well as other human rights aspects, have not surfaced high on the policymaking agenda of Russian parliamentarians and the government (Amnesty International 2006). Moreover, by eliminating the State Commission on Equal Rights of Women and Men in April 2004, the government demonstrated its lack of commitment to securing the rights of women in Russia. The UN experts note that the existing penal code of the Russian Federation did not change to include recommended provisions on violence against women (Coomaraswamy 2003).

Several countries did not adopt separate legislation on domestic violence but instead amended their national penal codes to provide legal redress for violence against women. It is important to note that adopted laws and legislative changes concerned domestic violence, meaning violence in the private sphere: families, friends, and intimate partners. In general, the amendments increased the punishment for rape and severe cruelty (Azerbaijan, Georgia, Estonia) and addressed marital rape (Georgia) and violence against children (Azerbaijan) and dependent family members (Georgia). Several countries initiated national action plans on violence against women. The Estonian government adopted the Government Action Plan for Mitigation and Prevention of Violence against Women in 2003. Among other issues, this document seeks to raise awareness about violence against women in Estonia, improve domestic legislation to combat this problem, introduce a victim-centered approach to the judicial and prosecution process, and increase inter-agency cooperation on this policy issue (Kaljurand 2002). The Georgian government, in cooperation with the UNDP and the World Bank, developed the State Policy for the Advancement of Women and the Action Plan on Combating Violence against Women. These documents became the grounds for the Presidential Decree on Violence against Women and Order #64 "On Approval of the Action Plan on Combating Violence against Women (2000–2002)." The experts note that this action plan has not been updated since 2002 and no comprehensive action has been taken by the government to enforce this program (Minnesota Advocates for Human Rights 2006). Armenia and Belarus developed government programs on combating violence against women with the help of the UNDP and other international organizations (Minnesota Advocates for Human Rights 2006). The Russian Action Plan of 1997 only marginally addressed violence against women: out of thirty-seven sections of the Plan, only three were devoted to violence against women. These sections provided legal definitions of violence but did not develop a clear action plan for the enforcement of the policy.

To conclude the analysis of legal changes in the fifteen post-Soviet states, I note a marginal government action in the area of legal redress of violence against women across the region overall. Two countries provide a remarkable exception—Kyrgyzstan and Ukraine, where governments pursued comprehensive legal changes and adopted separate bills on domestic violence, leaving some hope that other states will follow suit in the future. But even these laws did not address violence against women in the public sphere, e.g. prisons, hospitals, the army, courts, and other public settings. This finding demonstrates that governments in post-Soviet countries adopted a narrow view on the CEDAW provisions against gender violence.

Institutional Supervision

No government of post-Soviet countries established a state office to coordinate the implementation of policy on violence against women between various institutional actors, including police, social workers, doctors, and judicial bodies. Such offices could be established within the relevant institutional structures, e.g. the ministry of the interior, the ombudsman's office, or the ministry of social affairs. In a few other post-communist countries of Eastern and Central Europe such state offices were opened, although with controversial agendas: namely Poland, Romania, and the Czech Republic. For instance, in Poland the policy on violence against women is enforced by the State Agency on Fighting Alcoholism, which clearly demonstrates the agenda of this office and links violence against women to problems with alcoholism.

Almost all governments of the post-Soviet countries, except for Moldova and Uzbekistan, opened offices on women's affairs (they may have various official titles), which are meant to coordinate government policy on women's issues and gender equality. But these offices did not assume the responsibility of enforcing policies on violence against women, although some of them may work on issues of violence in collaborative projects with women's nongovernmental organizations and international organizations. These offices, however, do not have legislative, monitoring, and enforcement capacities to oversee the implementation of policies on violence against women, which allows me to conclude that no post-Soviet government complies with UN recommendations to establish viable government institutions to oversee the implementation of this policy.

Policy Enforcement

Only a few governments in the region attempted to follow some of the UN recommendations on violence against women, and there is no government that systematically complies with all aspects of the policy: support to shelters, training of police, judges, and social workers, and organizing public awareness campaigns. The UN experts note marginal government actions in seven countries of analysis (Lithuania, Russia, Belarus, Ukraine, Estonia, Kazakhstan, Latvia, and Azerbaijan) and express concern about the state of policy enforcement in the seven other countries included in this analysis.

The governments of four countries provide some modest support to shelters and crises centers for victims of violence that are usually run by NGOs: these are Russia, Ukraine, Belarus, and Kazakhstan. In Russia, about fifty-five shelters for battered women across the country qualify for governmental grants that are distributed by the Public Chamber of the Russian Federation. Financial support is provided on a competitive basis, through competition open to all Russian-based NGOs (Public Chamber of the Russian Federation, official website, 2007). The decisionmaking on grant distribution, however, is very arbitrary, and grants often go to insider organizations. Thus there is no guarantee that all NGOs concerned with violence against women will get financial support when they apply.

The government in Belarus supports several centers for battered women; most of them are located in big cities, such as Minsk, Mogilev, Vitebsk, and Gomel. A program of financial support to NGO-run centers falls under the government program on combating violence against women adopted by the government in response to the UN recommendations. The Ukrainian government has established several shelters for battered women and prevention centers in cooperation with the UNDP and UNICEF. The plan of a cooperative program between the State Committee for Family and Youth Affairs and UNICEF was to open five centers/shelters every year in the period of 2002–2005, which are to be funded partially by UNICEF and partially by local governments (Coomaraswamy 2003). This program has been only partially implemented, because the Ukrainian government did not find resources to match the expenses. The Kazakhstani government supported one shelter in Almaty, but since early 2005 they were able to increase the support to women's NGOs through the Public Chamber of Kazakhstan, which is comparable to the Russian government grant-giving institution designed to support the nongovernmental sector (interview, Nurtazina, 2007). In Moldova, the government organized one shelter sponsored from governmental funds. However, this center was transferred to the supervision of NGOs and the governmental funding was shut down (Coomaraswamy 2003).

Some governments attempted to improve the preparedness of police forces to address issues of violence against women although, overall, governmental action in this area of policy enforcement is minimal across the countries. In accordance with the Government Action Plan for Mitigation and Prevention of Violence against Women (2003), the Estonian government initiated a program on training the police and social workers to cooperate in preventing domestic violence. The Lithuanian government introduced seminars on violence prevention in the State Police Academy (Coomaraswamy 2003). In 2004, Estonia, Lithuania, and Latvia participated in the Daphne Project on violence against women. Together with governmental and nongovernmental organizations from Norway and Denmark, governments in these countries administered several police trainings across the countries to increase the effectiveness of response to domestic violence (Daphne Project REF: 2004-1144-WC).

Governments of several countries initiated campaigns on raising public awareness about violence against women, domestic violence, and trafficking in people. The Azeri and Ukrainian governments, in collaboration with the UNDP and the OECD, conducted a campaign titled *Sixteen-Day Activity against Violence against Women in the Caucasus* (see chapters 4 and 8 on parallel activism in postcommunist countries). The Russian Ministry of the Interior conducted a nationwide campaign against domestic violence in the spring of 2006. The Belarusian and Ukrainian governments have sponsored several public awareness-raising campaigns with the help of the UNDP and UNICEF since 2001. The Kazakhstani government introduced violence against women as a policy issue in the school program (see chapter 4 in this volume). In other countries, public awareness campaigns were largely supported and funded by NGOs.

To conclude, the analysis of the implementation of critical policy components reveals low compliance with the CEDAW and the Beijing Platform for Action. Several governments addressed two or three areas of policy implementation; these are the governments of Ukraine, Belarus, Estonia, Kazakhstan, Lithuania, and Russia. Less developed countries of the region such as Armenia, Georgia, Kyrgyzstan, Tajikistan, Turkmenistan, and Uzbekistan, as well as Latvia, score the lowest in the assessment of government implementation of critical policy components. There are no examples of adequate policy enforcement in the post-Soviet region.

Overall, the empirical findings for three analyzed parameters of government action suggest that governments of the post-Soviet countries made very modest attempts to comply with the UN recommendations on violence against women. Government compliance varies by category of analyzed action: only two countries adopted laws on domestic violence (Kyrgyzstan and Ukraine); several others pursued some enforcement of recommended policies (Lithuania, Ukraine, Belarus, Russia, and Kazakhstan). The pattern of policy enforcement, however, is not uniform: rural women do not have any access to governmental provisions and assistance against violence. Such minimal governmental provisions as public campaigns and police training are concentrated in large cities and virtually absent in rural areas. This uneven rural-urban distribution is explained by several factors: a lack of resources on the part of local governments in rural areas; a smaller number of domestic NGOs in villages and small towns; and lower levels of IGO and INGO programs for rural areas.

A troubling finding of the analysis reveals that governments of four countries did not take steps to pursue any policy changes: Tajikistan, Uzbekistan, Turkmenistan, and Armenia. Governments of three other countries made minimal changes to their legislation but did not take any action to enforce it: Georgia, Moldova, and Latvia (until 2004). This suggests that governments in the region do not prioritize women's concerns, which raises concerns about the viability of international treaties on human rights to challenge domestic practices.

Are International Treaties Capable of Ensuring Policy Change?

Low levels of government compliance with the UN treaties and agreements raise important questions about the capacity of international treaties to influence state behavior, and about the motivations of violating states to sign and ratify international human rights treaties. Drawing on scholarship and the evidence from the cases, I will provide some tentative answers to three questions, which will drive the discussion in the next section.

Why Do Post-Soviet States Not Comply with International Treaties?

Extensive scholarship on international relations and comparative politics regarding states' compliance with international law notes that the weak enforcement capacities and poor incentive structures of human rights treaties allow violating states continue their discriminating practices after ratification of human rights treaties (Goodman and Jinks 2004; Hafner-Burton and Tsutsui 2005). Therefore, lack of coercive measures—for instance, fines or economic sanctions—as well as lack of material or political incentives for states to enforce human rights practices in national contexts explain low levels of state compliance with human rights treaties. The enforcement and incentive structure of the UN treaties on violence against women is not different from any other international human rights treaties: it relies on voluntary compliance by states and offers no material rewards for changing domestic practices. Moreover, as I have already reviewed, the CSW monitoring procedures rely heavily on governmental self-reporting, which gives governments a lot of leverage about the way they present their information, on one hand, and gives violating states the impression that no one is watching them, on the other hand. Thus, violators can get away with not changing their practices.

A weak incentive structure for compliance, in my opinion, is an even more serious drawback of international treaties: if the cost of changing discriminatory practices is higher than the rewards for compliance, why would violating states pursue these changes? The difference in incentive structure between international trade treaties and international human rights treaties explains the differing levels of state compliance with these treaties. International trade treaties establish rules for economic exchange that can be favorable for state-participants of these agreements, which often leads to increased cooperation (Keohane 1984). Human rights treaties do not offer a state-participant an incentive to cooperate with other states in order to secure its own interests, as many economic treaties do. For instance, there is no clear material loss to neighboring states from a state engaging in human rights violations. Therefore, there is no incentive for neighboring states to impose any sanctions on violators or interfere with others' internal practices. Moreover, the cost of interference in the national affairs of other states in order to improve their human rights practices can easily overshadow any potential material gains that these changes might bring. Thus, all traditional explanations in international relations (realist and neoliberal) suggest that low government compliance with international human rights treaties is not surprising. Our cases in general support these theoretical expectations, but these explanations do not answer the question about the states' motivations to join international human rights agreements, which takes us to the next question of the discussion.

Why Did Post-Soviet States Ratify the UN Treaties on Violence against Women?

Governments are aware of the weak enforcement capacities of international human rights treaties and unclear non-existent material benefits that their participation in these treaties will bring. Given this awareness, why would these states bother to sign and ratify international treaties if they are purely rational actors? This question brings us to the explanations advanced by the sociological neoinstitutionalists, who view states not only as rational actors, but as social actors driven by the desire for membership in a large group of states that they deem to be legitimate. This drive for association creates pressures on states to assimilate with other actors and conform to rules shared by the group, especially if it does not involve any substantial costs. This is exactly what the UN treaties provide: membership in a large group of states and no obligation to comply.

The data suggest that sociological explanations are especially pertinent to the newly independent post-Soviet states. The difficult transition of the 1990s in these states should not be underestimated: the post-Soviet states were not only going through a tremendous change in their political, economic, and social structures, but also they were engaged in the difficult task of state-building as newly independent members of the international community. The countries of the former Soviet Union acquired international recognition and standing as independent states, and thus had to act according to the rules of the international community. Their political and economic vulnerability, as well as uncertainty about their new status, made the post-Soviet states especially susceptible to the pressures of the international community, on one hand, and propelled their desire to be welcome and proper members of this community, on the other hand.

In the context of state-building, the act of ratification of the human rights treaties for post-Soviet countries served several important social functions. First, it was an act that demonstrated of their independence and sovereignty: they became parties of international treaties independently from a larger state of which they were part before. Second, a formal acceptance of international treaties on human rights served as an act for demonstrating both their commitment to human rights and their desire to be accepted as "civilized" members of the international community. It is important to note that at the time of their emergence as independent countries many of the post-Soviet states wanted to dissociate themselves from the communist past and legacy and tried to create strong ties with Western democracies. (Of course, the degree of such intents and actions was very different from one country to another, but most states sought the connections with the West.) Since human rights is essentially a Western idea promoted by "Western-based" international organizations, such as the UN, the Organization for Security and Cooperation in Europe, and the Council of Europe, to name a few, the act of ratification of human rights treaties was an important step to demonstrate to the Western democracies that these countries shared their commitment to human rights. Finally, for some post-Soviet states the act of ratification of international treaties was a mirroring behavior: the CEDAW had been ratified by the Soviet Union, and the newly independent states signed it again when they became sovereign (Ukraine ratified CEDAW while part of the Soviet Union; it had a seat in the UN during the Soviet era). Other treaties were signed because other states in the region did it: the emulation effect is well noted in the literature, and this logic makes a lot of sense for understanding the behavior of states in a situation of uncertainty and novelty (Meyer and Scott 1992; Meyer et al. 1997). Thus, ratification of international human rights treaties served an important socializing function for newly independent post-Soviet states. This takes us to the last question that we have to answer:

Which Factors Impeded and Which Facilitated the Enforcement of Some Policy Components by Post-Soviet Governments in the Area of Violence against Women?

In other words, why did governments in Estonia, Lithuania, Russia, Belarus, Ukraine, Kazakhstan, Latvia, and Azerbaijan try to enforce some of the UN recommendations, although partially and non-systematically, whereas seven other countries, namely Moldova, Armenia, Georgia, Kyrgyzstan, Uzbekistan, Tajikistan, and Turkmenistan, did not make any effort to comply with their commitments to international treaties? The literature on comparative politics offers several compelling explanations to these questions, drawing on scholarship on modernization, economic development, and political regimes, which could affect government action on policies on violence against women. I will consider these arguments in a brief analysis below.

In the literature on comparative politics, it is well established that economic development can produce an effect on the ability of governments to allocate budget monies to human rights policies and change their violating practices (Inglehart 1997; Mitchell and McCormick 1988; Sen 1999). Moreover, Inglehart argues that economic development, modernization, and cultural development, including a shift to human rights values, go hand in hand (1997). Thus, we can expect that post-Soviet states which fared better in terms of their economic development would score higher on the scale of enforcement of human rights policies, including policies against gender violence. Table 11.1 demonstrates that these expectations are true: levels of economic development at least partially explain the difference in levels of government compliance with international human rights treaties in the area of gender violence.

Table 11.1 presents data on GDP per capita in 2003 by levels of government implementation of policy components. The findings clearly demonstrate that in countries with higher levels of GDP per capita, governments attempted at least partial enforcement of policies on violence against women. To conclude with this portion of the analysis, I argue that the level of economic development is at least partially correlated with government action in the area of gender violence.

The second argument of comparative politics that I would like to consider here refers to the levels of brutality of political regimes and their impact on the enforcement of human rights. It is a logical expectation that abusive nontransparent authoritative regimes impede the enforcement of international human rights laws, including policies against gender violence. Political regimes in four countries of analysis are considered abusive and nontransparent by international human rights experts: Belarus, Uzbekistan, Turkmenistan, and Tajikistan (US Department of State 2004). It is not surprising that three of these countries score the lowest in the chart of policy enforcement in the area of violence against women. Thus, the brutality of a country's political regime also affects the degree of its human rights enforcement.

The third explanation refers to the literature on transnational networks, which argues that international governmental and nongovernmental organizations facilitate change in human rights practices (Keck and Sikkink 1997; Risse and Sikkink 1999; True and Mintrom 2001). This argument is supported by evidence from the post-Soviet countries.

TABLE 11.1. GROSS DOMESTIC PRODUCT PER CAPITA IN PPP, USD BY ENFORCEMENT OF POLICY COMPONENTS

GDP PER CAPITA, PPP USD	YEAR	GDP PER CAPITA, PPP USD
Lithuania	2003	11,036
Estonia	2003	12,190
Russian Federation	2003	9,001
Belarus	2003	6,432
Ukraine	2003	5,312
Kazakhstan	2003	6,583
Azerbaijan	2003	3,491
Latvia	2003	9,683
Georgia	2003	2,384
Kyrgyzstan	2003	1,741
Armenia	2003	2,663
Republic of Moldova	2003	1,906
Tajikistan	2003	996
Turkmenistan	2003	5,836
Uzbekistan	2003	1,645

Source: UNICEF. 2005, *Trends in Europe and North America: The Statistical Yearbook of the Economic Commission for Europe 2005*, at www.unece.org/stats/trends2005/economy.htm (accessed May 15, 2007).

In most countries, governments cooperated with the UNDP, UNICEF, or the OECD. The Belarusian and Ukrainian projects on shelters and crises centers are run in cooperation with the UNDP and UNICEF. The project on shelters in Ukraine is by 50 percent supported by UNICEF (chapter 2 in this volume; Minnesota Advocates for Human Rights 2006). Public awareness campaigns in Azerbaijan and Ukraine were organized and supported by the UNDP and the OECD. It is clear that international governmental organizations reached agreements with national governments to implement these programs together; they pushed government action, designed programs, trained personnel to implement these programs, designed and coordinated the implementation; and finally, they provided financial support for the realization of these projects (chapter 9 in this volume). Thus, the role of international governmental organizations in pushing governments to enforce at least some policy aspects and programs is very important. We also find that in countries where the operations of international governmental organizations are restricted, there is no government action at all. For instance, a non-complying Uzbekistan prohibited OECD operations on its territory; in Belarus and Turkmenistan the work of international organizations is restricted as well.

Governments of other states can also facilitate the enforcement of policies on gender violence in newly democratized states, as Anne-Marie Slaughter (2004) argues. For instance, so called twinning projects, or collaborative projects between governments of Western and Eastern European states, became one of the EU strategies to socialize new EU members into best policy practices. Governments of the East and West are encouraged to organize collaborative projects on introducing best policy practices to colleagues from the East. Among the noteworthy collaborative projects on violence against women is the Notes Project: Combating Violence against Women in Five Baltic and Nordic States, supported by the EU Daphne Program. Launched in 2004, this project aims to stimulate government response to violence against women in the three Baltic countries. The goal of the Notes Project is to introduce the gender equality approach in prevention and combating violence against women. During a year of common activities, several organizations called National Task Groups (NTGs), which included governmental institutions and NGOs from five countries, formed a multidisciplinary network. The NTGs worked both at national and local levels to inform, train, and exchange information on how to prevent domestic violence and respond to and assist victims of violence. The project had a very large teaching component. For instance, police training supervised by the experts from Denmark and Norway was a significant part of the project (for more information, see Daphne 2004).

This collaborative intergovernmental program had a positive effect on the development of policies on violence against women in three Baltic states. For instance, one result in Lithuania was that the Ministry of Social Security and Labor drafted the National Strategy for Reduction of Domestic Violence Against Women for 2007–2009 in 2006. The Notes Project initiated government action in the area of violence against women in Latvia. It is important to note here that the Latvian government was a laggard in developing and implementing any policy in the area of gender violence, nor was Latvia in a hurry to adopt the EU gender equality directives required for the accession to the European

Union. In 2002, the European Commission noted that if the Latvian government did not speed reform of its national legislation in accordance with EU equality requirements, the EC would halt accession negotiations with this country (European Commission 2002). The Latvian government demonstrated a lack of commitment to the development of gender policies on several occasions, but a twinning intergovernmental program with two Nordic states propelled some policy change in this country.

I would also like to highlight the role of domestic nongovernmental actors in stimulating government action in the area of gender violence. The Russian case provides an interesting example for analyzing how the existence of a large domestic nongovernmental sector created incentives for governments to initiate financial support of these organizations. The Russian government partially conforms to the CEDAW requirements: it supports fifty-five shelters for battered women across the country, and in 2006 the Ministry of the Interior launched a nationwide awareness campaign against domestic violence (Johnson 2006). These actions are motivated by two factors: the demands of local, national, and international NGOs (INGOs) that the government address rampant violence against women, on the one hand, and a concerted effort by the government to reduce the influence of INGOs on the Russian social and political environment, on the other. Under pressure from international and national women's organizations, the government began to recognize its responsibility for the lives of many women victims of violence and supported a 2006 awareness campaign across the country (chapter 3 in this volume). According to UNICEF, in 1999 alone 14,000 women were murdered in cases of domestic violence in Russia (UNICEF 2000).

But international observers and political experts in the country note that the increase in government financial support to the Russian-based nongovernmental sector is explained by another factor: the government's desire to control the agenda of these organizations (Amnesty International Report 2006). In this effort, the government took several measures to reduce the number of INGOs operating in Russia through establishing complex registration procedures for foreign-based NGOs. To diminish financial dependency of Russian-based NGOs on foreign sponsors, the government created a federal agency, the Public Chamber, for distributing financial support to domestic NGOs. Several programs run by the agency focus on grassroots service-provider organizations, including shelters for battered women; thus enabling these organizations to compete for governmental grants. To a certain degree, in Russia government actions on anti-violence programs are driven by the intention to decrease the presence of INGOs and reduce the visibility of government and their actions to international observers. Recent measures to reduce the presence of international organizations in Russia have made external monitoring difficult and have limited the influence of the international community on the Russian domestic politics. The Russian case, then, can be considered a case of negative conformity with international recommendations on violence against women.

The Belarusian case is another example of negative conformity with international treaties. With the expulsion of INGOs and a crackdown on many domestic NGOs, the government assumed total control over political and social activities in the country. The state assault against the nongovernmental sector mainly targeted those organizations that expressed some political ambition to oppose the authoritative rule of President Alexandr Lukashenka. In this situation of political repression, the issue of domestic violence and violence against women gained some legitimacy in the eyes of the authoritarian state, because it did not pose a substantial threat to the regime of Lukashenka. Moreover, the repressive regime supported some OECD and UNDP programs on violence against women (shelters and media campaigns), developed a National Plan of Action in the area of domestic violence, and channeled some state monies to local NGOs working in the area of gender violence. Thus, the state perception of violence against women as a politically nonthreatening issue generated negative conformity with international requirements in Belarus.

The final explanation is offered by international relations literature and refers to the idea of increasing Westernization of those post-Soviet states that seek recognition and membership in Western organizations such as the EU and NATO. The Westernization argument explains government compliance with some international provisions in Ukraine and the Baltic states, countries that expressed their desire to be associated with the West and live up to the Western legal norms. This argument is especially interesting in the case of the Ukraine (which did not have the same EU support as the three Baltic countries), where despite the economic difficulties of last fifteen years and political instability, the government sought resources to support several programs on violence against women and adopted a comprehensive law on domestic violence.

To conclude, although the capacities of international human rights treaties are weak and do not stimulate government compliance with treaty recommendations, we still notice that there are some modest attempts by governments to bring domestic practices in line with international expectations. Governments on their own, however, are not very eager to enforce new policies, even if they have formally adopted and ratified international human rights treaties. Case study analysis reveals that governments are more likely to start the enforcement of new policies when they are pushed to do so by other actors: either international organizations, like the OECD, UNICEF, and the UNDP; or by nongovernmental organizations; or by governments of other states who act as collaborators in twinning projects. Another finding of this study suggests that economic difficulties, the authoritarian nature of the political regime, and political instability in the country significantly impede the realization of human rights treaties by national governments. Although not surprising, this finding confirms that states' voluntary participation in the enforcement of human rights treaties is very problematic in repressive states and states torn by economic difficulties.

Participation in international human rights treaties can serve as a socializing strategy for newly independent states wanting to demonstrate to others in the international community that they share the principles and norms embedded in international treaties. But for many governments the ratification of international treaties often means formal acceptance of human rights principles rather than actual change of domestic practices. Weak enforcement capacities of international human rights treaties, which largely rely on states' voluntary observance of these laws, reinforce the decoupling between states' formal ratification and their actual compliance with these treaties. The evidence on government compliance with the CEDAW and the Beijing Platform for Action on violence against women from the fifteen post-Soviet states confirms a decoupling between the rates of states' ratification of these documents and their enforcement of the UN policy recommendations. As the data demonstrate, government action in three categories of analysis (legislative change, institutional change, and policy enforcement) is very low across the region. However, we note that governments in eight countries made some modest steps to comply with international recommendations. Does this imply that international human rights treaties have a potential to change states' practices? It certainly does, especially under certain circumstances that create favorable conditions for changing government action. Several lessons can be learned from the analysis of cases in the fifteen post-Soviet states.

1. International human rights law can be viewed as a symbolic
   instrument that does not have real power to enforce its recommendations on sovereign states. But in spite of its low
   enforcement capacities, the influence of human rights treaties
   should not be underestimated: states start slowly changing
   their practices when other actors create favorable conditions
   for compliance.

2. Voluntary participation of states in the implementation of
   human rights treaties is therefore not the only strategy that
   international human rights treaties depend on. Compliance
   is also stimulated by actors within and outside the states and
   the state governments, who create opportunities for governments to engage in observance of these treaties.

3. Findings from my case studies demonstrate that active engagement of international governmental organizations (IGO), such
   as the OECD, the UNDP, UNICEF, and others, can significantly
   improve levels of government compliance with international
   human rights requirements. To boost government response,
   often these organizations serve not only as "teachers" (those
   who initiate dialogue on human rights, raise public awareness about the issue, and "teach" governments new norms
   of behavior). Often the effectiveness of IGOs also depends
   on how much money they are willing or able to invest in the
   implementation of these policies. This fact is especially important in the poorer countries of Eastern Europe. For instance,
   in Ukraine, the government supported the UNICEF program
   on shelters only when UNICEF agreed to cover 50 percent of
   expenses. Overall, the findings demonstrate that the involvement of IGOs improved governments' performance on policies
   concerning violence against women.

4. Intergovernmental programs can also strengthen the government response to violence against women, as the case of the
   Notes Project demonstrates. Many governments engage in
   supporting the implementation of policies on violence against
   women or assisting grassroots nongovernmental organizations
   that assist victims of violence (for example, the governments
   of Canada, Holland, and Denmark support many programs
   on gender violence across Eastern Europe). Twinning projects led by the EU Daphne Program are particularly effective,
   and not only because of the innovative idea of collaboration
   between Western and Eastern EU members, which stimulates
   learning and socialization. They are also effective because of
   the implied conditional requirement: if you are a member of

the EU, you should do it. The UN and the Council of Europe, whose programs on violence against women overlap and reinforce each other, could probably incorporate the EU's experience of twinning programs (promoting best policy practices through collaborative projects between member states) in their strategies.

5. The existence of a large network of nongovernmental organizations strengthens government compliance with international treaties even in such controversial cases as Russia. Thus, UN attention and support to these organizations is an important strategy to ensure policy change in the future.

WORKS CITED

Amnesty International. 2006. Amnesty International Report. POL 10/001/2006. May 22. www.amnesty.org/en/library/info/POL10/001/2006 (accessed November 10, 2009).

Barnett, Michael, and Martha Finnemore. 2004. *Rules for the World: International Organizations in Global Politics.* Ithaca, N.Y.: Cornell University Press.

Bunch, Charlotte. 1995. "On Globalizing Gender Justice: Women of the World Unite." *The Nation* (September 11): 230–235.

Clarke, Roberta. 1997. "Combating Violence in the Caribbean." In *Women against Violence: Breaking the Silence: Reflecting on Experience in Latin America and the Caribbean,* ed. Anna Maria Brasiliero. New York: UNIFEM.

Commission on the Status of Women (CSW). 1995. The Fourth World Conference on Women Platform for Action. New York: CSW.

Coomaraswamy, Radhika. 2003. Report of the Special Rapporteur on Violence against Women, Its Causes and Consequences. *Integration of the Human Rights of Women and the Gender Perspective: Violence against Women.* New York: United Nations, Economic and Social Council.

Daphne. 2004. "Combating violence against women in 5 Baltic and Nordic countries—Good Practices" Daphne Project REF: 2004-1144-WC ec.europa.eu/justice_home/daphnetoolkit/html/projects/dpt_2004_1_144_wc_en.html (accessed November 8, 2009).

Division for the Advancement of Women (DAW). 1998. *Questionnaire to Governments on Implementation of the Beijing Platform for Action.* New York: DAW.

Elman, R. Amy. 1996. *Sexual Subordination and State Intervention: Comparing Sweden and the United States.* Providence: Beghahn.

European Commission. 2002. *Annual Report on Equal Opportunities for Women and Men in the European Union in 2001.* Brussels: European Commission.

Finnemore, Martha. 1996. *National Interests in International Society.* Ithaca, N.Y.: Cornell University Press.

Freeman, Jo. 1996. "The Real Story of Beijing." *Off our Backs* 26(3): 1, 8–11, 22–27.

Goodman, Ryan, and Derek Jinks. 2003. "Measuring the Effects of Human Rights Treaties." *European Journal of International Law* 14(1): 171–183.

————. 2004. "How to Influence States: Socialization and International Human Rights Law." *The Duke Law Journal* 54: 621.

Hafner-Burton, Emilie, and Kiyoteru Tsutsui. 2005. "Human Rights in a Globalizing World: The Paradox of Empty Promises." *American Journal of Sociology* 110(5): 1373–1411.

Horowitz, Shale, and Albrecht Schnabel, eds. 2004. *Human Rights and Societies in Transition: Causes, Consequences, Responses.* New York: United Nations University Press.

Inglehart, Ronald. 1997. *Modernization and Postmodernization: Cultural, Economic, and Political Change in 43 Societies.* Princeton, N.J.: Princeton University Press.

Johnson, Janet Elise. 2006. "How Global Feminism Almost Succeeded: The Campaign against Gender Violence in the New Russia." Paper presented at the 2006 Annual Meeting of the American Political Science Association, August 30–September 3, 2006. Philadelphia, Pa.

Kaljurand, Marina. 2002. "Consideration of the Report of the Republic of Estonia submitted under Article 18 of the Convention on the Elimination of All Forms of Discrimination against Women." Introductory Statement of the Deputy Under-Secretary, Ministry of Foreign Affairs, Republic of Estonia.

Keohane, Robertr. 1984. *After Hegemony.* Princeton, N.J.: Princeton University Press.

Keck, Margaret E., and Kathryn Sikkink. 1998. *Activist beyond Borders: Advocacy Networks in International Politics.* Ithaca, N.Y.: Cornell University Press.

Law on Social and Legal Protection Against Domestic Violence. Kyrgyz Republic. Bishkek: January 2003.

Meyer, John W., John Boli, George M. Thomas, and Francisco O. Ramirez. 1997. "World Society and the Nation-State." *American Journal of Sociology* 103: 144–181.

Meyer, John W., and Brian Rowan. 1977. "Institutionalized Organizations: Formal Structure as Myth and Ceremony." *American Journal of Sociology* 83: 340–363.

Meyer, John W., and W. Richard Scott. 1992. *Organizational Environments: Ritual and Rationality.* 2nd ed. Beverly Hills, Calif.: Sage.

Mitchell, Neil J., and James M. McCormick. 1988. "Economic and Political Explanations of Human Rights Violations." *World Politics* 40(4) (July): 476–498.

Minnesota Advocates for Human Rights (MAHR). 2006. *Stop Violence Against Women: VAW Monitor.* www.stopvaw.org/The_VAW_Monitor.html (accessed November 8, 2009).

Nurtazina, Roza A. 2007. Professor and Chair, Eurasian University, Astana, Kazakhstan. Personal interview by Olga Avdeyeva. Louisville, Ky.

Ofuatey-Kodjoe, W. 2004. "The United Nations and Human Rights." *Human Rights and Societies in Transition: Causes, Consequences, Responses,* ed. Shale Horowitz and Albrecht Schnabel. New York: United Nations University Press.

Organization for Security and Cooperation in Europe (OSCE). 2007. "Kazakhstan Focused on 2009 OSCE Chairmanship, on Course with Democratic Reforms, Says Foreign Minister." Press release. Vienna, 30 April 2007.

Risse, Thomas, and Kathryn Sikkink. 1999. "The Socialization of International Human Rights Norms into Domestic Practices: Introduction." In *The Power of Human Rights*, ed. Thomas Risse, Stephen C. Rop, and Kathryn Sikkink. Cambridge: Cambridge University Press

Sen, Amartya. 1999. "Human Rights and Economic Achievements." In *The East Asian Challenge to Human Rights*, ed. Joanne R. Bauer and Daniel A. Bell, 88–102. Cambridge: Cambridge University Press.

Slaughter, Anne-Marie. 2004. *A New World Order*. Princeton, N.J.: Princeton University Press.

The International Helsinki Federation for Human Rights. 2000. *Women 2000: An Investigation into the Status of Women's Rights in Central and South-Eastern Europe and the Newly Independent States*. Vienna: The IHF-HR.

US Department of State. 2004. *Country Reports on Human Rights Practices—2003: Kyrgyz Republic*. Washington, D.C.: Bureau of Democracy, Human Rights, and Labor. February 24, 2004. www.state.gov/g/drl/rls/hrrpt/2003/27846.html (accessed November 8, 2009).

True, Jacqui, and Michael Mintrom. 2001. "Transnational Networks and Policy Diffusion: The Case of Gender Mainstreaming." *International Studies Quarterly* 45: 27–57.

Tsutsui, Kiyoteru, and Christine Min Wotipka. 2004. "Global Civil Society and the International Human Rights Movement: Citizen Participation in Human Rights International Nongovernmental Organizations." *Social Forces* 83(2): 587–620.

United Nations Children's Fund (UNICEF). 2000. *Women in Transition: Regional Monitoring Reports*. No. 6. Florence: UNICEF International Child Development Center. www.unicef-irc.org/cgi-bin/unicef/Lunga.sql?ProductID=36 (accessed November 8, 2009).

United Nations Development Fund for Women (UNIFEM). 1995. *Putting Gender on the Agenda: A Guide to Participating in UN World Conferences*. New York: UNIFEM.

United Nations Development Fund for Women (UNIFEM) and the Minnesota Advocates for Human Rights. Stop Violence against Women. www.stopvaw.org/ (accessed October 2006).

Weldon, S. Laurel. 2002. *Protest, Policy, and the Problem of Violence against Women: A Cross-National Comparison*. Pittsburgh: University of Pittsburgh Press.

APPENDIX 1

POLICY CHANGES IN THE FIELD OF DOMESTIC VIOLENCE (DV)

	DV FIRST ACKNOWLEDGED IN A POLICY DOCUMENT	DV RECOGNIZED AS A SPECIFIC CRIME IN THE CRIMINAL CODE	SPECIFIC LEGISLATION AGAINST DV ADOPTED	NATIONAL STRATEGY ADOPTED	DISTANCING ORDINANCE LEGISLATION*	LEGISLATION AGAINST OTHER FORMS OF VAW
Bulgaria	1996: National Action Plan implementing the Beijing Platform for Action.	Not recognized yet. Considered to be a private issue.	1997: Law on the Ministry of Interior. 2005: The Act on Protection against DV.	2005: Act on Protection against DV. 2006: Program for Prevention and Protection against DV.	Type 3, depth 2. Year: 2005	2002: Law on Countering Trafficking in Human Beings. 2002: Amendment to Penal Code: Trafficking. 2004: Amendment to Penal Code: Trafficking. 2004: Anti-Discrimination Law: Sexual Harassment.

	DV FIRST ACKNOWLEDGED IN A POLICY DOCUMENT	DV RECOGNIZED AS A SPECIFIC CRIME IN THE CRIMINAL CODE	SPECIFIC LEGISLATION AGAINST DV ADOPTED	NATIONAL STRATEGY ADOPTED	DISTANCING ORDINANCE LEGISLATION*	LEGISLATION AGAINST OTHER FORMS OF VAW
Croatia	1997: National Policy for the Promotion of Equality (National Action Plan for the Beijing Platform for Action).	DV is recognized by the 1998 Criminal Code.	1998: Family Law, which prohibits violent behavior of the spouse or any other full age family member. 2000: Specific Penal Code provision for DV. 2001: Law on Misdemeanors, under which the Court may order the detention of a perpetrator of DV. 2000: Amendment to Law on Misdemeanors, which provides additional protection to victims. 2003: Law on Protection from DV.	2005–2007: National Strategy for the Protection against Violence in the Family.	Type 3, depth 2. Year: 2005	2003: Amendment to Labor Law: Sexual Harassment. 2004: Amendment to Criminal Law: Trafficking.

	DV FIRST ACKNOWLEDGED IN A POLICY DOCUMENT	DV RECOGNIZED AS A SPECIFIC CRIME IN THE CRIMINAL CODE	SPECIFIC LEGISLATION AGAINST DV ADOPTED	NATIONAL STRATEGY ADOPTED	DISTANCING ORDINANCE LEGISLATION*	LEGISLATION AGAINST OTHER FORMS OF VAW
Czech Republic	1998: Priorities and Procedure of the Government in Promoting Gender Equality.	DV is defined by the 2004 amendment of Act No.140/1961 of the Criminal Code.	2004: Law related to domestic violence crimes enacted. 2007: Expulsion of Perpetrator act.	2004: National Action Plan focused on the Beijing Platform for Action.	Type 3, depth 2. Year: 2007	1961: Criminal Code, Section 241: Rape. 1962: Czech Penal Code, Article 246: Trafficking. 2000: Amendment to Czech Employment Act: Sexual Harassment. 2001: Criminal Code, Section 241 Amendment: Rape. 2004: Amendment to Labor Code: Sexual Harassment.
Estonia	1999: Initiative of the Baltic–Nordic working group for gender equality cooperation.	DV not recognized yet.	No legislation yet.	2004: Professional Police against DV. The National Plan of Action for Combating DV is in preparation.	Type 2. Year: 2001	2004: Gender Equality Act: Sexual Harassment.

	DV FIRST ACKNOWLEDGED IN A POLICY DOCUMENT	DV RECOGNIZED AS A SPECIFIC CRIME IN THE CRIMINAL CODE	SPECIFIC LEGISLATION AGAINST DV ADOPTED	NATIONAL STRATEGY ADOPTED	DISTANCING ORDINANCE LEGISLATION*	LEGISLATION AGAINST OTHER FORMS OF VAW
Hungary	**1997:** National Action Plan implementing the Beijing Platform for action.	DV not recognized yet. Spousal rape has been considered a crime since 1997.	**1997:** Amendment to Penal Code: assault against decency in marriage constitutes a criminal offense. **2003:** Comprehensive Resolution on the Creation of a National Strategy to Effectively Combat and Prevent DV—not executed. **2005:** Amendment to the Criminal Code. **2006:** Act XIX on the Criminal Process.	**2003:** National Strategy on Crime Prevention.	Type 3, depth 2. Year: 2006, amended in 2009.	**1978:** Article 197 of the Penal Code: Rape. **1997:** Amendment to Penal Code: Rape. **1999:** Resolution No. 1074/1999: Rape.
Latvia	**1995:** National Action Plan implementing the Beijing Platform for Action.	DV not recognized yet.	No legislation yet.	No national strategy adopted.	Type 2. Year: n/a	**1999:** Criminal Code: Rape. **2000:** Revision to Criminal Code: Trafficking.

	DV FIRST ACKNOWLEDGED IN A POLICY DOCUMENT	DV RECOGNIZED AS A SPECIFIC CRIME IN THE CRIMINAL CODE	SPECIFIC LEGISLATION AGAINST DV ADOPTED	NATIONAL STRATEGY ADOPTED	DISTANCING ORDINANCE LEGISLATION*	LEGISLATION AGAINST OTHER FORMS OF VAW
Lithuania	**1996:** Lithuanian Women's Advancement Program.	DV not recognized yet.	**2004:** Amendment to Criminal Code (Crimes against Family and Children Act Section XXIII): removal of the perpetrator in DV cases.	**2003:** Strategy for the Reduction of Domestic Violence against Women (not implemented until 2007).	Type 3, depth 1. Year: 2004	**1998:** Law on Equal Opportunities: Sexual Harassment. **1998:** Article 131 of Penal Code Amended: Trafficking. **2003:** Amendment to Penal Code: Sexual Harassment. **2003:** Amendment to Criminal Code: Trafficking. **2005:** Amendment to Criminal Code: Trafficking.

	DV FIRST ACKNOWLEDGED IN A POLICY DOCUMENT	DV RECOGNIZED AS A SPECIFIC CRIME IN THE CRIMINAL CODE	SPECIFIC LEGISLATION AGAINST DV ADOPTED	NATIONAL STRATEGY ADOPTED	DISTANCING ORDINANCE LEGISLATION*	LEGISLATION AGAINST OTHER FORMS OF VAW
Macedonia	**2004:** Amendments to the Criminal and Family Codes.	DV is recognized by the Criminal Code.	**2004:** Amendment to the Criminal Code; DV is addressed with a maximum sentence of life imprisonment; Amendment to the Family Code. **2006:** Amendment to Law on the Family.	**2000:** National Action Plan for Gender Equality—regulations against VAW. **2002:** National Program for Combating. Trafficking in Human Beings and Illegal Migration.	Type 3, depth 2. Year: 2004	**2002:** Amendment to Criminal Code: Trafficking.

	DV FIRST ACKNOWLEDGED IN A POLICY DOCUMENT	DV RECOGNIZED AS A SPECIFIC CRIME IN THE CRIMINAL CODE	SPECIFIC LEGISLATION AGAINST DV ADOPTED	NATIONAL STRATEGY ADOPTED	DISTANCING ORDINANCE LEGISLATION*	LEGISLATION AGAINST OTHER FORMS OF VAW
Montenegro	**2002:** Amendment of the Criminal Code.	DV is recognized as a crime punishable by a fine or imprisonment.	**2002:** Amendment of the Criminal Code. **2006:** Bill on Protection against DV.	**2003–2006:** National Program on Preventing Violence.	Type 1	**2003:** Criminal Code punishes sexual offenses: sexual intercourse with a juvenile, sexual intercourse through coercion, other punishable sexual acts, and the procurement and permitting of such sexual abuse. Spousal rape is also an offense under the Criminal Code. **2003:** Criminal Code punishes trafficking in persons.
Poland	**1992:** Safety in the Family program, preventing violence in families with alcohol problems 1992–2002.	DV is recognized legally in 1997.	**1997:** New Penal Code and Code of Criminal Procedure. **2005:** Polish Law on DV; Counteraction of Violence in Close Relations Bill.	**1997–2005:** National Action Plan for Women; not implemented successfully.	Type 3, depth 2. Year: 2005	**2004:** Article 18 of Polish Labor Code: Sexual Harassment.

	DV FIRST ACKNOWLEDGED IN A POLICY DOCUMENT	DV RECOGNIZED AS A SPECIFIC CRIME IN THE CRIMINAL CODE	SPECIFIC LEGISLATION AGAINST DV ADOPTED	NATIONAL STRATEGY ADOPTED	DISTANCING ORDINANCE LEGISLATION*	LEGISLATION AGAINST OTHER FORMS OF VAW
Romania	**1996:** Government Pilot Center for Assisting and Protecting the Victims of Violence in the Family.	**2000:** Romanian legislation addresses VAW by focusing on family violence, recognizing family as society's primary unit.	**2003:** Law on Preventing and Combating Family Violence. **2004:** Law no. 211 on Protection of Victims.	**2001:** "16 Days of Activism against Gender Violence."	Type 1	Article 197 of the Romanian Criminal Code: Rape. **2001:** Amendment to Criminal Code: Trafficking. **2002:** The Act on Equality for both Men and Women: Sexual Harassment.

	DV FIRST ACKNOWLEDGED IN A POLICY DOCUMENT	DV RECOGNIZED AS A SPECIFIC CRIME IN THE CRIMINAL CODE	SPECIFIC LEGISLATION AGAINST DV ADOPTED	NATIONAL STRATEGY ADOPTED	DISTANCING ORDINANCE LEGISLATION*	LEGISLATION AGAINST OTHER FORMS OF VAW
Slovakia	1997: National Action Plan for Women in the Slovak Republic.	1997: Penal Code punishes the mental or physical mistreatment of a person close to or dependent on the perpetrator; spousal rape is a crime. No specific law against domestic violence.	2002: Amendment to the Penal Code. 2003: VAW laws strengthened, expanding definition and increasing penalties.	2001: Gender violence awareness campaign by Fifth Woman. 2003: NGOs and the police organized campaigns to raise awareness of DV. 2004: National Strategy for Prevention and Elimination of VAW and in Families. 2005–2008: National Action Plan for Prevention and Elimination of VAW.	Type 1	1961: Act No. 140 of the Penal Code: Trafficking. 2002: Amendment to Penal Code, Section 246: Trafficking.

	DV FIRST ACKNOWLEDGED IN A POLICY DOCUMENT	DV RECOGNIZED AS A SPECIFIC CRIME IN THE CRIMINAL CODE	SPECIFIC LEGISLATION AGAINST DV ADOPTED	NATIONAL STRATEGY ADOPTED	DISTANCING ORDINANCE LEGISLATION*	LEGISLATION AGAINST OTHER FORMS OF VAW
Slovenia	**1992–1993:** Proposal to amend criminal legislation for the adoption of some protection measures against VAW. **2001:** First glossary concerning VAW.	DV is prosecuted by the Penal Code.	**1999:** Penal Code change, including criminal act of bullying within the family. **2002–2005:** Penal Code and Civil Code strengthened, expanding the definition of DV and increasing penalties. **2008:** Specific law against DV, including economic violence.	**1999:** Joint campaign "What's up, girl?" of Women's Policy Office, NGOs and National Assembly Equal Opportunities Commission on VAW. **2005:** National Program for Equal Opportunities of women and Men (2005–2013) adopted. **2009:** National Program for DV prevention (2009–2014) adopted.	Type 3	**2003:** Employment Relations Act: Sexual Harassment. **2004:** Amendment to Penal Code: Trafficking.

VAW: Violence Against Women

* Distancing ordinance is also called restraining order.
Countries were classified into three different types:

1) No distancing order or restraining order in the legislation.

2) Distancing orders exist in the legislation, but they are not specifically directed to domestic violence. In some cases they can be used to protect victims of domestic violence.

3) There are specific distancing orders in the legislation for cases of domestic violence.

For category 3, there are some differences between countries regarding the depth of the legislation. In this table, case 3 countries were classified into two different types:

1) When the perpetrator can be expelled from the home.

2) When the perpetrator is both expelled from the home and forbidden to approach the victim.

CONTRIBUTORS

OLGA AVDEYEVA is Assistant Professor of Political Science at Loyola University Chicago. Her research and teaching interests are in comparative social policy, gender politics, comparative politics and institutions, and EU enlargement. She has published articles in *International Studies Quarterly; PS: Political Science and Politics; International Journal of Social Welfare;* and other journals.

LAURA BRUNELL is Associate Professor of Political Science at Gonzaga University. In addition to domestic violence policies and movements, her research and teaching interests are women's status and gender politics in comparative perspective, and European politics, especially the politics of immigration and diversity. She is currently working on the book *Global Gender Regimes: Women's Status in Comparative Perspective,* which presents case studies of women's status in five countries: the United States, Sweden, India, China, and Rwanda.

THOMAS CHIVENS teaches at the University of Michigan in the Department of Anthropology and the Center for Russian and East European Studies. His work addresses the anthropology of violence, gender, and security in the United States and Poland. He conducted fieldwork that spanned the southeast United States (1997) and Warsaw, Poland (2000–2001), following the circulation of model domestic violence intervention programs. He is currently teaching and writing on the politics and poetics of security, postcommunist state integration, and the boundaries of Europe.

KATALIN FÁBIÁN is Associate Professor of Government and Law at Lafayette College. She has published extensively on gender equality and women's political activism in Central and Eastern Europe. She is editor of *Globalization: Perspectives from Central and Eastern Europe* and of a special issue of *Canadian-American Slavic Studies* that focused on the changing international relations of Central and Eastern Europe. Her book *Contemporary Women's Movements in Hungary: Globalization, Democracy, and Gender Equality* was published in 2009.

ALEXANDRA HRYCAK is Associate Professor in the Department of Sociology at Reed College. Her work focuses on the role of women in post-Soviet democratization. It has appeared in a range of journals, including *Women's Studies Quarterly, Advances in Gender Research, Journal of Communist Studies and Transition Politics,* and *East European Politics and Societies,* and also in edited volumes.

JANET ELISE JOHNSON is Associate Professor of Political Science and Women's Studies at Brooklyn College, City University of New York. Her research examines gender politics, especially women's organizing, and gender violence policy. She is author of *Gender Violence in Russia: The Politics of Feminist Intervention* (Indiana University Press, 2009) and co-editor of *Living Gender after Communism* (Indiana University Press, 2007).

CELESTE MONTOYA is Assistant Professor of Women and Gender Studies at the University of Colorado at Boulder. Her research addresses the ways in which marginalized groups mobilize to improve human rights conditions. In addition to her work on European translational efforts to address violence against women, she has also written on Latino/a immigrants and domestic violence for women of color. She has published in *International Organizational Politics and Gender* and *Urban Affairs Review.*

SONJA ROBNIK is Senior Advisor in the Office of the Republic of Slovenia for Equal Opportunities. She has written about equal opportunities, sexual harassment, domestic violence against women, and workplace bullying. Recently she published "Workplace Bullying: The Results of the Slovenian Banking Union Research." Her most recent book is *Saying No—Misunderstood: Sexual and Gender Based Harassment in the Workplace.*

MUBORAK SHARIPOVA has been a researcher at the National Research Centre for the Working Environment in Denmark and a consultant for Human Rights Watch, Radio Free Europe/Radio Liberty, the United Nations, and other international organizations in Tajikistan and Denmark. She participated in developing the Tajik National Policy on Women's Empowerment and prepared a draft of the Tajik National Program for Reducing Violence against Women in 2000. She has written about the integration of immigrants in the Danish labor market and on workplace violence and harassment.

EDWARD SNAJDR is Associate Professor of Anthropology at John Jay College, City University of New York. His research interests include violence, ethnicity, gender, environmentalism, and applying anthropological perspectives in the fields of development, legal reform, and criminology. He has conducted fieldwork throughout postcommunist Eurasia (Slovakia, Kazakhstan, Bosnia, Bulgaria, Romania, Russia, and the Czech Republic) and in the United States (Florida and New York City). He is author of *Nature Protests: The End of Ecology in Slovakia* and other publications.

GULNARA ZAYNULLINA, who was born in Tashkent, Uzbekistan, is an independent scholar and human rights researcher, previously with Human Rights Watch. She currently works within the Russian-speaking community in New York City.

INDEX

Page locators in italics refer to figures and tables.

Printed and bound by CPI Group (UK) Ltd, Croydon, CR0 4YY

13/04/2025

14656552-0003